HOME FIRES BURNING

HOME FIRES BURNING

FOOD, POLITICS, AND EVERYDAY LIFE IN WORLD WAR I BERLIN

Belinda J. Davis

The University of North Carolina Press   *Chapel Hill & London*

© 2000 The University of North Carolina Press
All rights reserved
Manufactured in the United States of America
Set in Monotype Garamond and Eagle types
The paper in this book meets the guidelines for permanence
and durability of the Committee on Production Guidelines for
Book Longevity of the Council on Library Resources.
Library of Congress Cataloging-in-Publication Data
Davis, Belinda
Home fires burning : food, politics, and everyday life in World War I
Berlin / Belinda Davis.
    p.   cm.
Includes bibliographical references and index.
ISBN 978-0-8078-2526-6 (alk. paper).—ISBN 978-0-8078-4837-1 (pbk. : alk. paper)
1. World War, 1914–1918—Germany—Berlin. 2. Berlin (Germany)—
History—1918–1945. 3. Women—Germany—History—20th century.
4. World War, 1914–1918—Women—Germany. 5. World War,
1914–1918—Food supply—Germany. I. Title.
D538.5.B47D38   2000
943'.155084—dc21   99-32578

cloth   04 03 02 01 00   5 4 3 2 1
paper   12 11 10 09   5 4 3

FRONTISPIECE:

Queuing for meat, 1916/17. (IMLGA/ZPA 38259)

THIS BOOK WAS DIGITALLY PRINTED.

FOR ALLAN DAVIS

CONTENTS

ILLUSTRATIONS

MAPS & FIGURES

ACKNOWLEDGMENTS

It has not been lost on me that even as I read and wrote day after day about people operating under conditions of extreme discomfort and distress, my own experience in writing this book has been joyful, due largely to the many people who have offered kind support over several years. This book began as a dissertation under the guidance of Geoff Eley, Bill Sewell, Bill Rosenberg, and Sherry Ortner, whose influence still deeply marks the project. Geoff Eley remains a wonderful mentor. I deeply thank my extraordinary colleagues at Rutgers University, among whom I can only name a few here, including Michael Adas, Omer Bartov, Mia Bay, Rudy Bell, Paul Clemens, Ziva Galili, Dee Garrison, John Gillis, Jennifer Jones, Donald Kelley, Alice Kessler-Harris, Jim Livingston, Phyllis Mack, Matt Matsuda, David Oshinsky, and Bonnie Smith. I am thankful for fellowships at the Rutgers Center for Historical Analysis, under directors Victoria de Grazia and John Chambers; at the Georgetown Center for German and European Studies, under Samuel Barnes and Roger Chickering; and at the Max-Planck-Institut für Geschichte, directed by Hartmut Lehmann. I am grateful for the uniformly kind help of staff members at the archives in which I worked, including particularly Dr. Beck, Dr. Lippert, and Frau Bühring of the Brandenburgische Landeshauptarchiv; Herr Zarwell at the Bundesarchiv Lichterfelde; and Jürgen Wetzel of the Landesarchiv Berlin. Many thanks also to Lewis Bateman, Paula Wald, and Stephanie Wenzel at the University of North Carolina Press. Rutgers University provided a grant to support this book.

I am extremely grateful to the friends and colleagues who saw this project through with me. Bonnie Smith, Peter Appelbaum, Marion Kaplan, and Nancy Reagin commented on the entire manuscript and helped in myriad other ways; I thank them, as well as two very helpful anonymous press readers, deeply. Members of the German Women's History Study Group, including Bonnie Anderson, Delores Augustine, Maria Baader, Rebecca Boehling, Renate Bridenthal, Jane Caplan, Atina Grossmann, Amy Hackett, Deborah Hertz, Maria Hoehn, Young Sun Hong, Marion Kaplan, Jan Lambertz, Molly Nolan, Molly O'Donnell, and Nancy Reagin, provided insightful comments on several chapters along with much moral support. In

Germany, Alf Lüdtke has had enormous influence on this work, though the result reflects that influence too little. He and Julia Brüggemann, Andreas Daum, Karl Christian Führer, Thomas Lindenberger, Elisabeth Meyer-Renschhausen, Adelheid von Saldern, and Anne-Charlott Trepp have demonstrated unceasing generosity. I also thank Ute Daniel, Christiane Eifert, Ute Frevert, Martin Geyer, Karen Hagemann, Karin Hausen, John Horne, Carola Lipp, Tony McElligott, Avner Offer, Susanne Rouette, Till von Rahden, Eve Rosenhaft, and Bernd Weisbrod in Europe. Doris Bergen, Thierry Bonzon, David Crew, Barbara Engel, Heide Fehrenbach, Peter Fritzsche, Stephen Herschkorn, Jan Lambertz, Daniel Mattern, Jean Quataert, Andy Rabinbach, Jim Retallack, Eve Rosenhaft, Robert Scholz, and Jay Winter have been friends and *Gesprächspartner*. Thanks, too, to Mickey Davis, Lara Davis, and Margaret Tenenbaum.

My greatest debt is to my family, Peter Appelbaum, Noah Appelbaum, and Sophia Appelbaum. They make every day a joy. The next book is for them. My father, Allan Davis, spends his life giving to other people. This book I give to him.

HOME FIRES BURNING

INTRODUCTION

In typically understated fashion, Berlin police commissioner Traugott von Jagow warned authorities in February 1915 that the "economic war," as Germans dubbed the British wartime blockade of goods to Central Europe, increasingly overshadowed Germany's military successes in the minds of the capital city public. "Unpleasant scenes," he explained, "are taking place more than ever in front of butcher shops." He counseled, "To intervene in the price of meat lies very much in the state's interest."[1] These scenes, of crowds gathering for food, captivated public attention even when no protest took place. As Officer Paul Rhein of the Berlin political police described one such incident in Berlin in February 1915, "Thousands of women and children had gathered at the municipal market hall in Andreas Street to get a few pounds of potatoes. As the sale commenced, everyone stormed the market stands. The police . . . were powerless against the onslaught. A life-threatening press ensued at the stands. . . . Women who got away from the crowds with some ten pounds of potatoes were bathed in sweat and dropped to their knees involuntarily before they could continue home."[2]

By October 1915 — still long before the devastating "turnip winter" of 1916–17 — such scenes frequently culminated in riots, protests against merchants, rural producers, and the government. "It should certainly come as no surprise," Officer Ludwig commented in late 1915, "if enormous butter riots arise [again] very soon. . . . The bad humor among the people, especially the proletariat and also the *Mittelstand*, grows from day to day. The view is frequently voiced that the war will not be decided on the front but, rather, through Germany's economic defeat."[3]

This sentiment was widespread. The most conservative press took a public stand demanding government satisfaction of the needs of poor urban consumers, even declaring its identification with this population. The Evangelical *Reichsbote* chastised the imperial government for its reckless inattention to the "food question," commenting, "Unfortunately we people cannot yet live entirely on air alone."[4] The conservative *Deutsche Kurier* concurred: "One is asking for . . . an insured daily bread. . . . To care for our infantrymen and young officers is to do only half the work. . . . What use is it to us to defeat the outer enemy, when our people at home fall to the inner one?"[5]

The press, the police, and others drew state and public attention to those they characterized as "those of lesser means" and especially "women of lesser means" (*minderbemittelte Frauen*): the poorer consumers who waited in food queues and who protested in the streets of Germany's cities, above all Berlin. Officer Gustav Gerhardt reported, "It is impossible for the population of lesser means to continue for any length of time only approximately nourishing themselves. The populace maintains the most heartfelt desire that the ongoing manipulation of prices soon be ended once and for all, and that the government take energetic steps against it."[6] This population seemed to offer specific suggestions to address the food question.

Caught up in their own concerns regarding civilian and soldier morale, international prestige, and ambitious military plans, Prussian and imperial authorities moved rapidly to respond to the demands of poor consumers, as translated through public media and inside reports. This was a marked contrast to the prewar habit of forcefully repressing protesters. Government measures to combat the effects of economic war won widespread popular approval for the state over and over again during the course of World War I. This apparent responsiveness helps explain why the German revolution did not take place earlier than November 1918.[7] But because these measures were consistently piecemeal, reactive, and confusing, they were never adequate to subduing the food crisis for any length of time. In the end, officials' actions were far more effective in legitimating popular demands than in defending the state's right to rule. Berliners and other urban Germans came to interpret state actions as deferring leadership on the central domestic issue of food management to these poor women in the streets.

Even before the turnip winter, food scarcity and inflation affected a broadening population of Germans, especially those living in cities. Berliners' support for the war plummeted by early 1916, in no small part because of rising popular concern that, despite official efforts on behalf of consumers' interests, the state was helpless against a new set of "inner enemies." Berliners and other urban Germans now styled these enemies as deceptive merchants of foodstuffs and exploitative rural producers. Berliners believed merchants and farmers profited through the war, by their actions fighting against their "fellow Germans," on the wrong side of the economic war. Such beliefs reinforced particular social divisions, as the broad public grappled with issues of patriotism, "Germanness," and a German community. At the same time, this characterization helped paper over deep class rifts among Berliners, bringing about a fragile unity, a kind of "civil peace," as the kaiser had asked for. But this civil peace, which centered on women of lesser means, operated ultimately not with but against the state.

These wartime dynamics spelled a new vision of the German nation, not only located in the people rather than in the state or monarchy, but also centered in cities, drawing in the working class. This metamorphosis also speaks to Germany's democratic potential that emerged with unprecedented strength in the course of the war, along with the seeds of other possible political futures. It provided the basis for a new view of "social politics" and welfare.[8] Still, beneath a surface of widely perceived overall consensus on these issues lay deep, unresolved conflicts and contradictions concerning the terms of mutual obligation between individuals and the state, and regarding who or what represented the nation.

Gender plays a central role in this account of the war. It both divided and unified segments of society. Urban Germans cast the woman of lesser means in the role of representative of the nation; both German women and men identified with this figure. At the same time they most often figured the inner enemy as male. Gender helps shape this story of how politics worked in World War I Germany. Conversely, this account of the war tells us something about women's integration into nineteenth- and twentieth-century political systems, raising questions about women's political identities, perceived natural versus civic rights, the role of suffrage, and state protections of women. How did women participate in politics before being granted citizenship? How do we constitute such a view of politics? Are politics distinct here from personal interests or from economic needs? Contemporary accounts reveal the links between women's (often contradictory) identification, by themselves and by others, as consumers, producers, reproducers, and political agents, and how this identification translated into particular acts. The following is the story of poorer, primarily working-class women in Germany's capital city in World War I. But it is also the story of the image of such women and how various segments of the population deployed this image, with significant political ends.

This account challenges still-dominant assumptions regarding the nature of politics itself as representing a narrow terrain of activity, largely separated from the rest of everyday life, practiced only at particular moments and often by limited segments of society.[9] Contemporary documents suggest that officials interpreted bread riots in the street—and even the simple act of queuing in long lines for bread—as political by implication. Officials' treatment of this activity as political set the pace for the public interpretation of the economic war and its unwilling victims.[10] The broader public, too—including the disenfranchised—played a role in defining politics. Women of lesser means came to assert a new view of the state and its responsibilities and obligations to the German people. Their words and deeds, and those of journalists, social reformers, and others who invoked these women, illuminate the relationship between imagination and political action, as well as between the most fundamental personal needs and questions of political philosophy. This perspective informs a study that focuses as much or more on the first years of the war as on the last, as the wartime transformations that informed the ultimate fall of the regime and revolution developed cumulatively in the course of the entire war.

Our collective knowledge of the war in Germany is enormous. German scholars' attention to the war burgeoned in the 1960s, as historians began to look at the First World War relative to the horrors of the Second, tracing continuities between the two wars.[11] The late 1960s also saw considerable discussion in Germany of the revolution and of the Weimar Republic.[12] Both sets of interpretations are consistent with a view of the Wilhelmine state that ruled as a fundamentally top-down structure, by some lights repressing the masses until their only recourse was revolt. Both literatures intimate that Germans rebelled against the tyrannical militarism of the Third Supreme Army Command, representing the worst in the Prussian tradition of leadership. It is certainly the case that the Supreme Army commanders pursued military visions that seriously compromised the basic living conditions of many Germans, particularly those of the urban poor. However, police reports and other official sources suggest that the masses of Germans were far more powerful in their ability to extract concessions from authorities than these interpretations indicate. Moreover, this power, which developed quite early in the war, grew the longer hostilities endured. These literatures read the events of war through the lens of Germany's military defeat. In doing so, this work often ignores changes in German sociopolitical life that transpired over the course of the war.

Building on the foundational social histories of the 1960s, historians of each of the belligerent nations have in the last decade begun to focus attention on the wartime homefront.[13] This work has rewritten the history of war formerly conceived as a province uniquely of males.[14] But these studies tend overall to emphasize the effects of the war on civilians — to view civilians as historical objects — rather than to look at those on the homefront as historical actors whose beliefs and everyday acts might have changed what politicians said and did, and even how the war was fought. Thus Ute Daniel's splendid volume on working-class women in World War I Germany offers insights into the broad spectrum of her subjects' lives, touching on changes in women's roles as workers, consumers, wives, and mothers.[15] She brings us new understanding on numerous issues, from the nature of changes in the labor market during the war years to the knotty question of whether women were "better" or "worse off" societally as a result of wartime transformations. Yet, because of Daniel's focus on the big picture of German women's lives during the war, decisions and actions appear largely as monodirectional. The women she portrays are not without agency, but they appear on the whole as the target of the policy of others, her careful emphasis on the category of experience notwithstanding. Building on Daniel's achievements, the present study, as a microhistory of Berlin, examines a single locality in its complexities. It traces changes in the capital city throughout the war years and, thereby, recounts the important role that civilians—including poorer women—played in political decision making.

Police and military reports on popular morale or "mood" (*Stimmungsberichte*) provide a central source for this account. Other historians have employed these sources for studies on wartime and revolutionary Germany.[16] But street-level police reports remain underused; they are most often evoked aggregately, to supplement arguments founded on other evidence.[17] Looked at from day to day alongside contemporary press, writings of concerned associations, political pamphlets, and documents from throughout the government hierarchy, these reports offer fresh perspective, for example, on relations between police and their superiors and between police and those they observe. Police reports transmitted popular concerns and desiderata upward to the highest-level officials in many respects as effectively as representatives of the state communicated their decrees downward. Mood reports, the press, and the "street scene" (*Straßenbild*) itself influenced one another and worked collectively to pressure officials to respond to popular concerns. Read against one another, these various documents permit us to detect unofficial relations of power and to examine how these relations promoted change.

This examination gives further nuance to the now standard class interpretation of the war. It is true that antagonisms between workers and the German *Mittelstand* during the war promoted corrosive resentment, especially in the latter.[18] But the experience of the economic war in Berlin and in cities across the country fostered a temporary solidarity between these populations, on the basis of their common experience as deprived consumers. These consumers, buttressed by this sense of solidarity, expressed common demands on the state. It was the combined force of these populations that impelled authorities to attempt continually to meet these demands throughout the hostilities. This story of women of lesser means is as much about the needs and demands of those who observed and reported on them, particularly the lower middle-class political police. These police officers found their own most successful political strategies through their representation of these women.

To trace changes as they occurred through the course of the war, Chapter 1 describes Berlin and Germany on the eve of hostilities. The second chapter considers the bread shortage of fall 1914, the first civilian manifestation of the British blockade of goods. Poorer Berliners, among others, astonished authorities by protesting separation allowances as a form of war profiteering and undue privilege and demanding government subsidies for all consumers to offset rising food prices. Chapter 3 examines early 1915 potato shortages, popularly perceived as evidence of an inner economic war fought by women of lesser means against merchants and rural producers. The physical display of assemblies in the streets riveted public attention, moving a wide population of Germans to demand government control over production and distribution of foodstuffs on behalf of consumers. The fourth chapter shows how women of lesser means realized officials' worst fears, loudly protesting butter and meat fat shortages in the streets of the capital and initiating a pattern of protest and appeasement that officials could not escape. Chapter 5 traces the patterns of influence among the women of little means, the press, the police, and higher government officials in the dynamic of domestic policy decisions.

The sixth chapter looks at the midwar popular demand for and responses to a new "food dictatorship." The subsequent two chapters cover the debates over what characterized equitable food distribution under such a controlled economy, with implications beyond wartime. Though little concerned for the well-being of German civilians, military officials provided better than their civilian counterparts for the needs of at least some poorer women. But, as Chapter 9 demonstrates, even the apparently substantial efforts of the civilian and military governments left Berliners starving through the turnip winter and beyond. Poorer Berliners' last hopes for the controlled economy and the "reformability" of the imperial government were dashed by scandals providing evidence of officials' corruption and willful disregard for their own rules. By 1918, the subject of Chapter 10, they vowed to rely only on "self-help," uninterested in maintaining one-sidedly the social compact they had established with the regime early in the war. Street demonstrations and protest on the shop floor merged in a single chorus. By November 1918 the effete state collapsed largely from within, unable finally to act successfully in the role of a government as the populace now fashioned it. The popular vision of a state that responded to popular demand, respecting the rights of the people and guaranteeing their basic needs, arose out of the experience of the food crises as they played out in the streets, figured around women of lesser means. This vision contributed to the foundations of the Weimar Republic. But the disparities and contradictions in this vision, in part hidden in the flush of revolution, were to surface to create trouble throughout Weimar and contributed to the downfall of that state.

I GERMANY FROM PEACE TO WAR

Germany entered the war in 1914 a country in which rapid industrialization and urbanization had helped to produce a polarized society, often discontented and anomic, a nation that inspired both great pride and a gnawing sense of inadequacy among its subjects. Germany boasted a booming commercial sector and unequaled consumer offerings coupled with inflation, reliance on imports, new strains on small shops, and a perceived distancing between merchant and customer. In the years before the war, the young nation experienced the power of mass politics and the rise of extremist pressures on politics. In this mix, people formulated notions of what it meant to be German. Such notions made war appealing to some. In turn, the war experience drew on and transformed these notions.

WILHELMINE STATE AND SOCIETY

Throughout 1890 to 1918, Wilhelmine officials sought to rule by coalition, buttressing the leadership of the Conservative and National Liberal Parties with, variously, Center and Free Liberal Party support while attempting to stave off the growing influence of the Social Democratic Party (Sozialdemokratische Partei Deutschlands, or SPD). As historians have often characterized Wilhelmine rule, its leaders offered reforms from above to quash populist challenges and nourished popular societal divisions to create inner enemies, segments of the population whose true Germanness was cast in doubt. Yet Wilhelmine leaders were from the outset sensitive to popular desires and demands, contradictory as they were, and often conceded to them in some fashion. The state attempted to diminish its susceptibility to popular influences at the outbreak of war, a war fought in part in deference to such forces.[1] Officials invoked the Prussian Law of Siege, instituting new chains of command, intensifying restrictions in public expression and public assembly, and permitting more general militarization of civil society. Despite such measures, the Wilhelmine government grew increasingly vulnerable to the popular mood in the course of the war, in part as a consequences of its own strategies.

The structure of the German political hierarchy bred crossed jurisdictions and considerable resentment between imperial and Prussian authorities, between the executive and legislative branches, between civilian and military officials, and between state and locality. Rancorous conflicts among the parties, the Prussian ministries, and the states contributed to the discord. Powerful extragovernmental interest groups offered a chorus of opinions on government policy, including representatives of heavy industry and large-scale agriculture.[2] The conflicts of these multiple interests were intensified at the outbreak of war, as state-level and other subordinate offices were put under dual civilian and military authority. Prussian dominance was built into the governing structures. Prussian ministries overpowered imperial-level offices. The structure of the Bundesrat (federal council), the supreme imperial organ, guaranteed Prussia's dominance over imperial politics and left relatively little authority to the popularly elected Reichstag. Prussia's own franchise was the narrowest in the empire, despite ongoing prewar campaigns for reform, constituting the infamous "three-class vote," through which the will of 90 percent of the population was expressed in the lowest of the three classes.[3]

Universal manhood suffrage for Reichstag elections nonetheless made the SPD the lead vote getter in the 1912 elections, despite executive efforts to suppress the party's appeal.[4] The SPD's electoral success is traceable to numerous factors, including its rapprochement with trade union reformism and integration into the Wilhelmine system, and its record in providing a range of services and opportunities to its membership.[5] Central among these factors was the party's role in opposing Free Conservative Chancellor Theobald von Bethmann Hollweg's 1911 tariffs, new indirect taxes, and other measures that promoted the ongoing inflation.[6] Consumer interests were central in the coalition of Free Liberals and Social Democrats in the prewar battles against protective agricultural tariffs. This must also account in part for the SPD's major electoral wins in 1903 and relate to Chancellor Bernhard von Bülow's defeat in 1909. These electoral results might seem to indicate both a functioning mass politics in Germany (if at limited levels and without the formal participation of women) and the legitimacy of the Wilhelmine system, broadly speaking. Yet polarization and divisiveness marked both Wilhelmine politics and society. Bloc politics fell apart in the last decade before the war, while the state's fiscal condition weakened.

These new divisions reflected prevailing controversies over who and what was German. By the 1890s, many Germans asserted new, biologically rooted notions of nationality; increasingly, unmitigated devotion to the state was insufficient to mark one's Germanness. It was in this period that Jews joined Social Democrats in the minds of many as non-German and as potential or actual enemies of the nation.[7] Some Germans espoused the notion of a "community of the people" (*Volksgemeinschaft*) in this period, though during the war this idea solidified into a broadly compelling notion of popular sovereignty.[8] Germanness meant living the culture too, through ritual and material objects, even as that culture was transformed in this period of great social flux. Living the culture remained highly relevant in war, as Berliners and others contested issues of "eating German" and transacting business in "German" fashion.

For most Wilhelmine Germans, including most in positions of power, the nation was located in the state. As such, German subjects held few real entitlements. Turning points such as passage of the Civil Code in 1896 and the 1913 Citizenship Reform Act attended little to new rights for German citizens or expansion of citizenship within the empire.[9] Otto von Bismarck's well-known "social insurance" of the 1880s was pathbreaking in its provision of health insurance, worker's compensation, and pension benefits for (male) workers. But these programs clearly maintained traditional relations of authority; moreover, they placed the primary obligation on communal officials. Only the churches, private charities, and communal governments offered poor relief, in the form of haphazard aid that stigmatized and marginalized its recipients.[10] As consumers rather than producers, Germans received nothing from the state; it was Germans' responsibility to serve rather than to be served.

Despite interest in the idea of a community of the people, divisions among social classes and other cleavages deepened in the years before the war. The urgent questions concerning rising food prices and economic distress more generally contributed to these rifts. Working-class Berliners protested that they could ill afford wheat and meat products, part of the modern, urban diet.[11] Social Democrats in the Reichstag were unable to reverse the new fiscal policies despite their majority status in 1912. National Liberal and Conservative leaders looked increasingly to the powers of war to unify Germans and distract them from such domestic discontents.[12]

The greater German population began to accept the idea of an imminent war in the years before hostilities. For some the international conflagrations in Asia, in Morocco, and in the Balkans in the years before the war exposed the nation's need to prove itself militarily.[13] For others, war represented a cathartic cleansing of the nation and the victory of a hard, male, German culture over the soft, degenerate Western civilization into which the nation had sunk.[14] Many came to support the idea of a defensive, even preventa-tive, war fought on one's own terms, though the majority of the population seems to have experienced ambivalent and even negative feelings about a looming confrontation.[15]

The question of food supply and inflation was also relevant to any move to hostilities. From 1905 Germans heard rumors that if Britain entered the war, it planned to exercise a full economic blockade on goods into Germany. Germany depended on imports to feed its population of 67 million.[16] A key German war aim was to open new markets, over which it would have con-trol.[17] Thus, military planners wanted least of all to instigate Britain's entry into the war or to fight a long war. In 1911 imperial officials charged a spe-cial committee to organize for domestic consumer needs, coincident with the arrangements for requisite military raw materials. While the latter flour-ished at some level at least, members dissolved the former committee in 1913, laying their hopes on military strategists' plans for a brief war and de-termining to concentrate efforts instead on domestic propaganda.[18] Formal political control, military pressures, popular politics, and the availability and affordability of food remained in conflict and provided a springboard to do-mestic political crisis in the war years that followed.

POLICE AND OTHER "INTERMEDIARIES" BETWEEN STATE AND SOCIETY

Policing developed alongside the state in Europe, providing security, maintaining order, and protecting the state from danger—especially revo-lutionary danger.[19] Police had long protected the citadel of Prussian power and ensured Prussia's monopoly over power and violence throughout the nineteenth century.[20] In the course of the 1890s the police in Prussia (as elsewhere in Germany) underwent professionalization and, in principle, both demilitarization and reform of their habit of physical violence.[21] But professionalization accompanied a "policecization" of society: the growth of the police, both in numbers and in spheres of influence.[22] And, in prac-tice, the physical violence continued as officials' fear of "enemies" to the unified empire intensified in the wake of urbanization, industrialization, and the growth of the SPD.[23]

Protector of state and empire, the Berlin police commission was the largest and most politically powerful in the country. The police commis-sioner held unique direct relations with Prussian and even imperial author-

Caricature of Berlin policeman in Wilhelmine Germany. The policeman protects the state and nation from the masses. (Karl Dietz Verlag)

ities. The position was directly subordinate to the powerful Prussian interior minister. The commissioner acted simultaneously as the president of the district of Berlin, giving him considerable control over municipal politics. Thus, the Berlin police force mediated directly between the edifice of the state and the broad population of Germans. These connections were strengthened, expanded, and explicitly militarized at the outset of the war, as Kaiser Wilhelm II made the police commissioner directly subordinate to the military high commander in the marches. The Berlin police commissioner reigned over an expanding hierarchy of forces. As war commenced this included 177 officers, 460 police sergeants, and 5,559 patrolmen.[24] This hierarchy included a political police force (other large cities also boasted such forces), operating under an impressively wide definition of what constituted the political.[25] Until the outbreak of war, plainclothes political police spent much of their time at Social Democratic and other suspect political assemblies.[26]

Regular patrolmen also closely monitored activities of the German working class in capital streets and neighborhoods; Berliners fashioned jingles about policemen's irritating ubiquity. Patrolmen carried sabers and guns and, from 1898, were charged to fire warning shots at signs of unrest. Berliners responded with scorn for the self-important patrolmen, calling them "bloodhounds" and "slobs" (*Polenten*). The patrolman's spiked helmet, uniform, and sword, emulating those of the Prussian soldier, may have drawn fear, but they also drew laughter rather than respect. Berlin workers fought police in a virtual guerrilla war in the streets in the prewar years.[27] Berliners denounced police power as "arbitrary," a term that resurfaced with broad resonance during the war. Working-class Berliners also recognized the plainclothes, "secret" political police, insofar as they came through their neighborhoods before the war, and spoke of them with similar disdain.[28]

Police did not always return this animosity, despite widespread bourgeois fear of the working class. Patrolmen complained of their assignment to impose quasi-military order on the street.[29]

The police were historically representatives of the German state, and they identified with the state.[30] Low-level police, like other lower civil servants, were not well paid but, rather, marked their social distinction from the working class by the perquisites of honor and other intangible class privileges, which often indeed translated into material advantages in the prewar empire. With the onset of war, authorities proclaimed the quasi-military role of the police, acting as soldiers within, upholding order on the inner front.[31] But as the ability of policemen to provide for themselves and their families diminished, the Berlin political police began to distance themselves from the state and mark their common lot with the people they observed in the streets. Police dissatisfaction intensified as women protesting in the streets scorned policemen's lack of military status, questioning their fitness for battle and, by extension, their virility.

Other organizations and sites, too, acted as intermediates between state and society on the eve of war. The social, economic, and political growth of the capital in the new century spawned the proliferation of newspapers. By 1895 there were over 830 papers published in Greater Berlin. Many daily newspapers increased distribution to mass proportions; the *Berliner Morgenpost* led the way with 390,000 subscribers in 1913.[32] Papers competed for the working- and lower middle-class public; a large number of dailies concentrated on "bread articles" covering issues of fundamental concern for this population. Berlin was a metropolis in the news; its residents were avid consumers as well as producers of this news.[33] In the course of the war, the broad press played a vital role in publicity, in the Habermasian sense, giving voice—or at least a verisimilitude thereof—to hungering working-class women who demanded government attention to their plight.[34] The press did not conversely fulfill officials' hopes as a conduit of propaganda; popular reception of such propaganda often did not match authorities' intent.

The state communicated its interests—and learned in return of the broader public's needs and desires—through a wide variety of sources in addition to the police and the press. The participation of these groups in the web of communications existed sometimes at official behest, often in the name of sincere concern to represent the needs of the populace, and nearly always in the service of the agenda of the intervening organizations. As war began, three types of bodies acted as such a link between Prussian and imperial officials and the wider populace. The first encompassed private organizations and associations, above all, the League of German Women's

Groups (Bund Deutscher Frauenvereine, or BDF), the Evangelical Church, the Organization for Social Policy (Verein für Sozialpolitik), and the Cultural Union of German Intellectuals and Artists (Kulturbund Deutscher Gelehrten und Künstler). The second included political party and trade union apparatuses. The various communal governments constituted the third type of intermediary. High-level authorities eschewed direct relations with the broad German populace and particularly with the working class. Through the Office of Information high-ranking officials attempted to utilize existing organizational structures with access to the German masses, urban and rural, in order to establish one-way communications, particularly on the matter of appropriate service to the state.[35] There was, however, both considerable redundancy and contradiction among propaganda efforts. The Ministry of Agriculture and Forests competed with the Interior Ministry to tell the story of German food supply. The National News Service conflicted with the War Press Office, established in 1915, and both ran up against military propaganda.[36] Moreover, in spite of this apparent surfeit of official effort, authorities allotted almost no funding or personnel to domestic propaganda efforts in wartime, targeting resources for propaganda in enemy territory instead.[37]

Relying heavily on private organizations and their resources, authorities saved effort and money, maintained their customary distance, and attempted to legitimate the propaganda through its issue from unofficial sources. But this also limited official control in crucial ways. The BDF used its new role as intermediary between state and masses to promote its own campaign for creating a space for women (particularly middle-class women) within the formal political process.[38] Like the political police and the press, the BDF and its subsidiary, the National Women's Service, as well as the churches, communicated back up to state authorities the increasingly unlivable circumstances brought by the war, particularly to the poorer populations. This reversed the one-way line of communication Prussian and imperial authorities had intended to open. Leaders of these organizations communicated their sense of inadequacy in addressing the magnitude of the economic problem. They insinuated to officials that the state was responsible for contending with the needs of the wider population.

The nation's majority party, the SPD, took on a more powerful role in high-level political decision making during the war than it had in the past. High-ranking officials considered the SPD a strange ally, regardless of the loyalty the party had declared to the government and to the war effort.[39] Yet Prussian and imperial officials ended up adopting one after another policies promulgated by the SPD, above all through its leading organ, *Vorwärts*, to

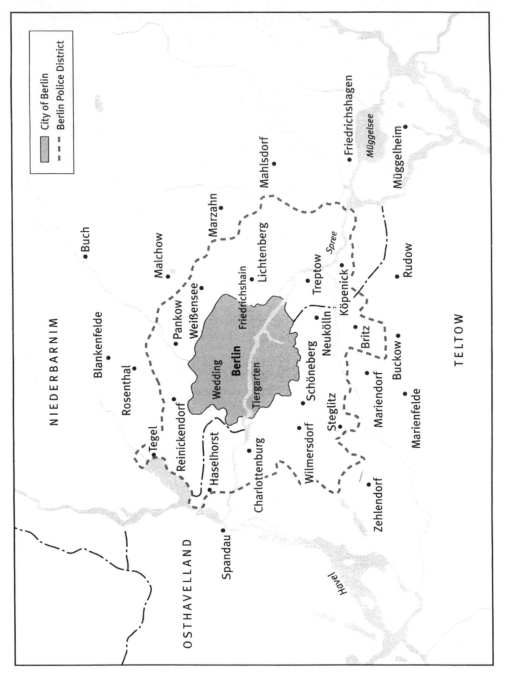

NIEDERBARNIM

OSTHAVELLAND

TELTOW

City of Berlin
Berlin Police District

Buch

Blankenfelde

Rosenthal

Marzahn

Malchow

Pankow

Weißensee

Mahlsdorf

Lichtenberg

Friedrichshain

Berlin

Wedding

Tiergarten

Friedrichshagen

Müggelsee

Müggelheim

Treptow

Köpenick

Rudow

Spree

Neukölln

Schöneberg

Britz

Buckow

Steglitz

Mariendorf

Marienfelde

Wilmersdorf

Zehlendorf

Charlottenburg

Haselhorst

Reinickendorf

Tegel

Spandau

Havel

Greater Berlin, 1914–1918

ameliorate the wartime conditions, particularly as these policies were translated through demands in the streets. Here again, communications traveled
in the wrong direction, from the government's point of view. Other party
leaders also often put themselves in the role of mouthpieces for the broader
populace, claiming that only proper government attention to popular needs
could prevent unrest and even more threatening activity.

Provincial, metropolitan, municipal, and communal governments, too,
acted as important mediums of exchange between the state and broader society, particularly through the parliament of cities (Städtetag), representing
the nation's urban strength. While provincial governments claimed to defend their inhabitants in wartime often by refusing imperial orders for food
collection and regional export, the Städtetag used its power to proclaim the
need for coordinated food policy at the highest government level. City governments may have been concerned about issues of autonomy and power,
but their public face in wartime was one of beseeching, then demanding,
imperial action, disclaiming the effectiveness of local-level aid.[40]

BERLIN: CITY OF INDUSTRY AND EMPIRE

In the decades surrounding the turn of the twentieth century, Berlin grew
from city to metropolis to world city (*Weltstadt*).[41] Berlin was the seat of the
governments of the empire, of Prussia, and of the metropolis alike. The city
expanded in area during these years, incorporating surrounding suburbs and
rural districts, culminating in the official geographical creation of "Groß
Berlin" in 1920. Berlin provides a microcosm, at least for urban Germany at
large, in light of its industrialization and population growth. But in other
ways it was clearly unique within the empire. It was the site at which state
and society interacted with the greatest physical proximity and with the
greatest traffic of words and images. It was as well the spot in Germany most
watched by the balance of the nation and by the world at large. Both these
aspects were magnified in the course of the war.[42]

Berlin housed the offices of both the empire and Prussia, acting further
as the official "residence city" of Wilhelm II. The Reichstag, Bundesrat, and
Prussian Landtag all met in Berlin, as well as the municipal magistrate, municipal assembly, and Städtetag. The assemblies of both Brandenburg and
the Potsdam district met in nearby Potsdam. The powerful Prussian ministries and imperial offices stood side by side on Wilhelm Street, in the center of the city proper, not far from predominantly working-class neighborhoods that would become key sites of wartime street protest. Berlin also

boasted the presence of the military chiefs of staff. General Headquarters, the Imperial Marine Office, the Admiralty, and the Prussian Ministry of War all sat within easy access of one another.

The interconnectedness of Germany's ruling hierarchies deeply affected the governance of Berlin. The high commander in the marches was also governor of the district of Berlin; for nearly the entire war, Gustav von Kessel held this position. Responsible only to the emperor, Kessel had tremendous power over politics and law in Greater Berlin, all the more under the state of siege declared on 31 July 1914. The putatively independent Berlin municipal assembly reported to the high commander as well as to the high president (*Oberpräsident*) of Brandenburg. The magistrate of Berlin, over which the lord mayor presided, overlapped in jurisdiction with the municipal assembly. The lord mayor, from 1912 to 1920 Adolf Wermuth, was directly responsible to the emperor as well as to the high president of Brandenburg.[43] He shared control of the city with the police commissioner of Berlin, from 1909 to 1916 Traugott von Jagow. Personal connections also closely linked governing figures. In light of these controls, communal self-rule in Berlin was highly limited.[44] The interior minister approved the city's budget. Prussian electoral statutes governed the city.[45] Berlin; the surrounding suburbs of Charlottenburg, Schöneberg, Neukölln, Lichtenberg, and Wilmersdorf; and the rural areas of Teltow and Niederbarnim participated together in the process of government at the metropolitan level, but their decisions were likewise subordinated to higher authorities. At the same time, rapidly changing metropolitan boundaries created a certain anarchy within local rule.[46] In addition to the magistrate and the municipal assembly, the task forces formed in 1912 held political and economic power over the metropolis, coordinating housing, development, and transport in the city and the surrounding areas. During the war these different bodies struggled to manage food distribution within the diverse metropolis.

Governmental capital of the empire, Berlin had also grown to be one of Germany's greatest industrial and commercial centers.[47] The Commerce and Industry Exhibition of 1896 in Berlin helped launch this development. In the next two decades Berlin came to house an enormous industrial infrastructure. The war enhanced this role, as Berlin competed only with the Ruhr as armaments and munitions capital of the country. Borsig, AEG, Siemens-Schuckert, Siemens and Halske, Knorr-Bremse, AGFA, Deutsche Waffen und Munitionsfabriken (Muna), and scores of smaller companies burgeoned in the war years. Berlin was also the finance capital of the country. Behren Street, site of several major banks as well as the Imperial Bank, intersected Wilhelm Street, a symbol of the active negotiations between the sectors of government, industry, and commerce, as well as within governmental echelons.

This industrial activity brought with it the migration of hundreds of thousands into the metropolis and the attendant growth of other urban structures. The population of Berlin grew from 827,000 in 1871 to 2,010,000 in 1910,[48] making its 63.4 square kilometers the most densely populated in the world at this time.[49] By the eve of war the population of Greater Berlin had reached nearly 4 million.[50] The new migrants were, above all, workers, who settled particularly in the suburbs and outlying districts of Neukölln, Friedrichshain, Lichtenberg, Rummelsburg, and Karlshorst, to the south and east, and in "islands" in the more central Charlottenburg and Schöneberg. This migration generated a remarkable growth in housing, especially of the large, high buildings, or "rental barracks," into which workers squeezed by the thousands.[51] Émigrés from the German countryside, particularly from East Prussia, dominated this population. Thousands of East Europeans also streamed in, eager for the employment opportunities.[52] Among these were Jews escaping religious persecution. In response to the mushrooming population, local commerce blossomed, from stands at the weekly markets to small shops that lined the streets to the emergence of the department store, realm of the bourgeoisie. Berlin's nexus of municipal buildings and services also expanded to accommodate the population rise.

Prussian and imperial authorities feared the perceived revolutionary potential of Germany's workers in their growing numbers.[53] Berlin workers especially inspired apprehension because of their independence, their proclivity to protest, and their proximity to the center of German government, industry, and press. Berlin was headquarters for the SPD and bastion of the independent-minded radical German Metalworkers Union.[54] On the eve of war, wage workers constituted 63 percent of the population of Berlin proper; two-thirds voted SPD, making Berlin the strongest Social Democratic city in Germany. Over 20,000 women in Berlin joined the party, despite the organization's "proletarian anti-feminism"; the most widely read book among workers was August Bebel's *Die Frau und die Sozialismus*, and Rosa Luxemburg was one of the most popular speakers.[55]

Authorities also feared spontaneous unrest in the streets and the image of a disorderly "street scene," above all in the capital, which drew domestic and international attention.[56] To forestall attacks on the "fortress state," at the turn of the century the city built broad avenues to cut through the working-class areas of Berlin, including Frankfurter, Landsberger, and Prenzlauer Avenues; to officials' chagrin, these were the sites of some of the most populous street demonstrations in the war years. Authorities wielded the 22,000 active troops quartered in Berlin in peacetime as a symbol of the strength of the state and its ability to hold order. The army held public parade drills on the Tempelhof field to demonstrate a strong presence in the city and a practical force known to be used against civilians.

The wartime changes in the city made Berlin both more vulnerable to protest and more visible to external scrutiny. As Germany entered hostilities, official concern to mobilize the nation and project an image of order, unity, and national commitment focused largely on Berlin. At the same time, Berlin drew ever greater numbers of workers into the city to labor in war-industry factories. As a garrison city Berlin permitted easy interaction between front-line soldiers and the civilian population, a grave security issue for authorities. As a large city it was the end of the line for many food supplies. And Germans all around the country kept their eyes on the capital, for clues to how to interpret political and military events.[57] It was no wonder that authorities simultaneously banned public reporting of unrestful activity in the streets of Berlin in 1915 and avidly sought news of such activity for themselves through police reports. Unrest in Berlin spread around the nation, even as Berliners themselves kept close track of rumored activity in the Ruhr, Leipzig, and Königsberg. Most cities showed grave food difficulties by 1916, though circumstances were highly variable. The monthly reports of the deputy commanders stationed around the country indicate consistency in urban popular response to conditions within the cities.

GERMANS, FOOD, AND ECONOMIC WAR

At the declaration of war the *Berliner Tageblatt* noted that "responding to the food question for the coming months was, next to the military and financial arming for war, naturally the weightiest and most important concern" of many German authorities.[58] Historians have long characterized the food shortages of wartime Germany, particularly during the turnip winter of 1916–17, as compromising morale on the German homefront. But even before the midwar crises, the food question ruled popular morale and played a significant role throughout the war in transforming relations between state and society.

Joseph Beuys wrote, "With food, two problems emerge immediately: what may I eat and what may I not eat, what will harm me and what will not? And this is where good and evil begins."[59] This link derives from food's role as a fundamental human need, the pleasure or danger in choosing well or poorly, and food's role in mediating human relations. Anthropological, cultural, and economic historians have in recent years given considerable scholarly attention to the subject of food. The scarcity of food, as well as perceived injustices in its distribution, has historically inspired social upheaval and even political change.[60] The recent historical interest in consumption has included discussion of food and food culture.[61] Work on the German case has focused on themes of food culture and industrialization, class patterns of consumption, subsistence crises and the end of cyclical famine, and food shortage and protest.[62] In the late nineteenth century, city dwellers, including the urban poor, became increasingly dependent on animal products as well as on imported goods. This late nineteenth-century "food revolution" transformed the relation between food and commerce as well. As it became technologically possible to stretch the distance between food producer and consumer, the number of middlemen who handled the food and profited from its distribution grew enormously. Concomitantly, practices of food adulteration spread across Europe; rumors thereof were even more abundant.[63] Many new working- and lower middle-class migrants to the cities also regretted the absence of sufficient space to grow their own foods, to ward off hunger in hard times.

Following on its prewar warnings, England introduced the concept of the economic war with the declaration of hostilities, putting pressure on civilian food supplies to lower morale as well as cutting off sources of raw materials for war production. Kinks in supply lines for civilian food affected all the belligerent nations as well as neutral countries. Food was rationed in England as it was in Germany, but in the former the process both ensured adequate nutrition and prevented perceptions of serious injustice in the distribution of food.[64] If the caloric intake of a British man remained virtually the same or even increased during the course of the war, averaging 3,400 calories, that of the average German male had fallen by the second half of the war to well under half this amount.[65] For poorer urban residents, above all women, the figures were far lower still. France did not fare as well as Britain; still, catastrophic food shortage was never an issue there. In France, as nowhere else, officials were conscious of the relation of the food question to popular unrest and to government legitimacy.[66] Coal and especially housing, both of which would also be problems for Germany, caused greater difficulties in France than food and instigated greater agitation among the working population.[67] Still, the war changed the attitudes of the French regarding the role of the state, as it did in Germany, concerning to what degree state authorities ought to intervene and plan, and regarding the right of popular organizations to participate in this planning.[68] In both Russia and Austria, as in Germany, food shortages were central to the deterioration of popular toleration of the war and faith in the existing regime.[69]

In Germany the end of famine augered by the food revolution was put to the test in the war years under the dismaying conditions of "man-made" hunger. If Germans did not starve in the war,[70] certainly the health of most poorer urban dwellers was seriously compromised as a result of the nutritional deficiencies of the war era and in combination with other conditions and deprivations. In part this had to do with Germany's prewar reliance on imports. On the eve of war, Germany imported about one-third of its overall food supply; contemporary nutritional experts reckoned this represented approximately 19 percent of needed calories, 27 percent of proteins, and 42 percent of fats.[71] This last domestic deficiency proved fateful in the course of the war. The country relied on imports of meat, milk, and butter, as well as of coffee and other colonial goods, to provide for its population's demands. Germany was strongest in supplying its own carbohydrates, via its harvests of potato and rye. However, the country lacked indigenous supplies of nitrogenous and phosphatic fertilizers necessary for the high yield of its crops, crops central not only to human nourishment but also to the feeding of German livestock. Thus, even domestic production hinged on the availability of imported fertilizers.

In light of Germany's economic dependence, the English blockade of seaborne imports to Central Europe resulted in German hardship already by late fall in 1914—in other words, by the time it became clear in Germany that the war would not be the blitzkrieg that the country's officials had promised. As the war progressed, Germany became increasingly isolated commercially. Britain and France prohibited continental neutrals from supplying dairy products and other important foods to Central Europe through the trade agreements of early 1915. One after another, anticipated supplies of grain and other basic foods from Siberia, Romania, the United States, and Ukraine failed to materialize, due to military circumstances.[72] Conversely, military tactics were increasingly influenced by the immediate need for food, such as the 1916 campaign against Romania. Likewise, Germany's submarine war campaign of 1916–17 aimed to smash the British blockade in order to make way for desperately needed food supplies, as well as to disturb shipments, including those of food bound for Britain. But the mission failed in this regard. From mid-1917 through the end of the war, Germany depended nearly entirely on its limited indigenous food supply.

Simultaneously, natural and man-made conditions wreaked havoc with domestic harvests throughout the war, making a travesty of the optimistic predictions by the Eltzbacher Food Commission, and by other expert advisers and state policy makers at the onset of the war, trying to measure the nation's productivity, imports, and exports for the first time. The mobilization of Germany for war counteracted the buffers that could have compensated for the unpropitious weather conditions. The military had siphoned off 60 percent of Germany's agricultural laborers by the end of the war.[73] The loss was scarcely made up by the intensified efforts of the remaining rural population and by the government-sponsored migration of urban laborers and POWs to the countryside, which the military administration later reversed in any case. From the first wartime harvest, even existing supplies could not be fully reaped. Draft animals, too, were confiscated in large numbers, and farmers could not work the available land. This in turn encouraged production of more livestock, which competed with humans for decreasing vegetable food supplies. Feed for these animals was also appropriated, which initially encouraged farmers to use potatoes and other human consumables as fodder, then forced the sacrifice of much of Germany's pig and cattle stock. Finally, the military requisitioned remaining nitrogen supplies and other materials requisite to farming. Scientists developed means to fix nitrogen, also necessary for munitions, but the phosphate deficiency was fatal for agriculture.

Modern transport and storage of food, linchpins breaking the cyclical famine, were also sacrificed to military priorities. Military transport tied up the rails, which translated into constant bottlenecks in the movement of food from one German state to another and from the countryside to urban centers. Fuel for domestic transport was in severely short supply, particularly after 1916. Officials directed state and municipal bodies to take responsibility for the food storage so that supplies could be kept available within city limits; spoilage and pests thereby consumed enormous quantities.[74] Facilities to dehydrate the delicate potato—central to the vanquishing of periodic famine—were also limited in the war years.[75] The knowledge (and rumor) that desperately needed foods had been available but had gone bad aggravated the misery of urban Germans. Germany's position on the eve of war, in material, cultural, social, and political terms, informed Germans' everyday experiences as they lived through the increasing hardships.

2 BREAD, CAKE, AND JUST DESERTS

The first important food to run into short supply during the war was bread. Bread remained scarce for the entirety of the war, but its absence made the sharpest impact in many respects in the fall and winter of 1914. Working-class and lower middle-class Berliners felt unduly burdened by the shortage and sought to identify who had squandered the precious grain and flour that authorities insisted existed in adequate supply. Poorer Berliners fingered a variety of culprits they determined to be responsible for their misfortunes. These Berliners cast the imagined transgressors, all female consumers, as unfairly privileged. Drawing on officials' characterization of the British blockade as an economic war, a broad population of Berliners arrayed themselves against these new perceived inner enemies in the battle for bread.

Poorer Berliners sought to establish the injustice of their lack of access to bread and demanded protection of their right to this important food, against their traitorous fellow German consumers. By the end of 1914 the bread scarcity and government propaganda together engendered broad public debate on state intervention on the food question, debate that transcended attacks on the unjust privilege of certain female populations. Disadvantaged consumers in the streets, as interpreted by police reporters and the press, urged authorities to provide a generalized system of benefits and subsidies that would aid anyone whose living conditions had been compromised by the war. The broad public lent unexpected support to these demands for a variety of reasons. The strength of public pressure on the vulnerable wartime state led Prussian and imperial authorities to respond positively, despite competing pressures, to the call for intervention.

RESTRAINT AND WAR BREAD

On the first day of war Berliners bought up massive food supplies, and prices temporarily doubled. The first few months of the war passed in general with relatively little disruption of the food market. By October 1914,

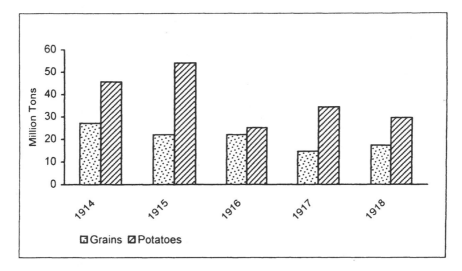

Figure 2.1. Grain and Potato Harvests, 1914–1918
Source: Burchardt, "Auswirkung der Kriegswirtschaft," 68.

however, while bright red, black, and white imperial flags waved from Berliners' windows, first bread, then potatoes became scarce in the capital, and prices for these foods rose sharply. Circumstances combined to decree this fate. German soil was not favorable for growing wheat; Germany customarily relied on imports for over one-third of its wheat supplies, sources largely cut off to Germany in 1914.[1] Conversely, Germany was an exporter of rye, which thrived in poorer soils; although war was imminent in July 1914, producers made good on their promises of rye to Russia just before hostilities began. The scarcity of grain haunted German officials for the entirety of the war. The 1915 harvest was poor; that of 1916 fared no better. Harvests of the second half of the war were worse still, a consequence of factors comprising total war. Potatoes also remained in extremely short supply throughout, especially after the disastrous harvest of 1916, a product of unseasonably cold and wet weather.

As a consequence of the blockade, moreover, farmers lost access to Russian barley for animal feed and fatty oilcake fodder from England. In response, rural producers foddered much of their grain and potato harvest. As a result, Germans had entirely depleted the 1914–15 stock of bread grains by December 1914.[2] Increased public demand for potatoes to compensate for the deficiency of flour and bread, along with foddering, quickly drove potato prices up. In turn, potatoes became scarce by early 1915. Agitated Berliners discussed the unavailability of bread and potatoes on street corners and in private homes for months following the initial scare in October 1914.

The high cost and dearth of both bread and potatoes generated widespread outrage and fear. These foods constituted at once staples of the German diet and the main food sources of the working classes. The figurative use of bread in contemporary German language telegraphs this centrality. The "bread of life" represented "that which one can least do without."[3] "The daily bread" cast this food as both a central element in one's nourishment and a symbol for all sustenance. By the end of 1914, *Vorwärts* ran a regular column titled "The Daily Bread," which covered news on all foods for the duration of the war. "The daily bread" denoted the customary way of life; the loss of bread was a painful symbol of the upheaval of war.

For the working class this was no mere symbol alone. Bread was the main constituent of workers' meals, in the form of the rolls (*Schrippen, Semmeln*) Berliners ate for breakfast and the convenient sandwich (*Stulle*) for supper that one brought to work. Breakfast and supper were the "bread meals." One labored virtually to "earn one's bread"[4] — though one's wages were "scarcely enough for dry bread," as a contemporary song lamented.[5] Under the conditions of soaring unemployment that characterized the first months of the war,[6] hundreds of thousands stood "without bread," that is, without employment. It was no wonder that "bread was the first food [officials] thought of in caring for Berlin's needs in the war."[7] The importance of bread for all Germans inspired demonstrations of public sympathy across Berlin for the population hardest hit by the absence of this staple. This widespread sympathy and empathy for working-class privations on the basis of a common sense of loss exercised considerable influence on Prussian and imperial officials.

These circumstances were not entirely surprising to officials who had, after all, declined to plan for domestic food shortages, but they were very worrisome. Even as the kaiser announced the national "civil peace" (*Burgfrieden*) to fight this new "struggle for existence," State Secretary of the Interior Clemens von Delbrück connected that struggle to the food question.[8] Authorities, particularly Kessel, the military high commander, attempted to address the scarcity by stepping up propaganda, appealing primarily to consumers. This propaganda insisted that adequate grain supplies existed, certainly for a war still expected to end long before the next harvest.[9] Officials suggested that any deficiencies of grain supply could be traced to civilians' lack of reason and restraint. Building on the Britons' idea of an economic war, this literature suggested that such civilian foibles threatened to sabotage the military war effort generally, rendering successful the enemy's blockade. The National News Service spread the word that "those who stuff themselves full, those who push out their paunches in all directions, are traitors to the fatherland."[10] Bread and cake consumption was unusually high in the first months of war, particularly among those who could afford the rising prices. Many hoarded what they could; some claimed that they were attempting to demonstrate to the enemy that the war to "starve Germans out" was ineffective. Others admitted that it was comforting in a time of upheaval to eat more and to cling to the pleasurable experiences of more normal times.[11]

Such official castigations deliberately exploited the anxieties of the Berlin population and of urban Germans more generally. Propaganda attempted to goad civilians into "contributing to the war effort" in various ways, warning that civilians served as ballast on the national effort, hindering the achievement of German war aims and even potentially lengthening the war. Working-class Berliners appropriated this notion indeed to taunt the police in their neighborhoods. Officer Theophil Klonicki of the Berlin political police noted grimly that "it has been remarked that many able-bodied men have not yet been conscripted. . . . For example, . . . the Berlin police could be called up."[12] But civilians all felt the sting of this official rhetoric. To demonstrate their own patriotic commitment, private associations contributing to the deluge of literature and news releases reinforced these themes. Both public and private propaganda suggested explicitly that tightening one's belt and doing without represented a direct defense against England's economic war, and that these sacrifices were minimal. The *Brandenburger Zeitung* published a letter from the front in October 1914 (courtesy of authorities) in which a soldier claimed all he was eating was dry bread; he noted, too, that he was "sleeping in a hole with Fritz R." Apologizing that his birthday greetings came late because "things were tied up for the moment," he sent money also, noting there was nothing for him to buy with it.[13]

Going one step further, some official propaganda intimated that the war was good for Germans, ridding them of their nasty habits of overconsumption, which threatened national culture. In this regard the literature admonished particularly urban populations, which, the writings claimed, had "grown used to the luxury of overeating" and had lost the hardness and thriftiness with which the German people were associated.[14] Officials spread the word that "the civilized person" (associated particularly with French culture) "is almost without exception a waster of food, a glutton, a gourmand."[15] Wartime might provide an opportunity for redemption.

This propaganda reflected a cluster of prevailing tensions and anxieties surrounding modernism, urbanization, and mass consumption, part of the national debate over the degeneration of the national culture, which put Germany's majority urban population on the defensive. It recalled gendered notions of seduction by feminine and effeminizing foreign luxury items. The propaganda also invoked related class divisions, such as the concerns of lower middle-class town and village dwellers that the urban proletariat ate better than they did. Conflicts over who characterized and controlled German culture and who represented Germany overlaid the wartime debates over food.

From late fall of 1914, civil servants and private volunteers hung posters on kiosks in Berlin and other German cities urging probity in food consumption. These signs were only a source of irritation to poorer Berliners, who by this time most often could not obtain bread at all. Imperial and Prussian officials were extremely reluctant to engage in legislating domestic food policy on behalf of these consumers, because of close ties with big agriculture and because of deeply held convictions concerning property rights.[16] But by the end of October, disaffected shoppers venting their frustrations in the streets as they hurried from one bakery to another bespoke the ineffectiveness of propaganda alone to mitigate food shortages and to quell prevailing concerns. Working-class Berliners demanded that authorities themselves address the shortages. In a striking departure from convention, the press across the political spectrum echoed popular demand in the streets in urging some form of government intervention in food distribution. The liberal *Berliner Tageblatt* observed, "But it seems to us that the situation of war makes even interventions into the free market unavoidable—if only for a limited, short time, of course."[17] In November 1914 the German Consumers League called a meeting in Berlin to address the rising prices; the result was formation of the War Committee for Consumers' Interests (Kriegsausschuß für Konsumenteninteressen, or KAKI). KAKI brought together representatives from some seventy organizations and interests groups, including the League of German Women's Groups (BDF) and the League of Fixed Income-earners (Bund der Festbesoldeten), who provided an ongoing wartime symbol of widespread German interests across class and other divisions, working and lobbying in the interests of the consumer.[18]

Anxious to fend off evidence on the streets and in the press of domestic food woes that exposed the success of the blockade, on 28 October 1914 the imperial Bundesrat moved to compensate for the absence of bread cereals by mandating the use of 5 percent potato in the production of rye bread and "gray" bread (mixed rye and wheat). Officials called this bread *K-Brot,* an intentionally ambiguous abbreviation of potato bread (*Kartoffelbrot*) and war bread (*Kriegsbrot*), suggesting both that the product was particularly healthy and that it accreted patriotism to those who ate it. Officials intimated that civilian sacrifice and urban rejection of refined imported wheat in bread symbolized true Germanness. This refuted the virtues of the late nineteenth-century revolution of the German diet. Wheat's whiteness was, among other qualities, a symbol for its purity, refinement, and superiority; its perishability in bread compared with that made with rye confirmed this. Workers normally consumed gray bread, containing at least some wheat; bakers mixed the morning roll, which all Berliners ate, entirely from wheat flour.

Wheat was especially scarce in Germany under the blockade. Conversely, the potato was, along with rye, an indigenous crop. Besides encouraging reliance on available products, officials also offered a nod to the Prussian Junkers through this new policy. Further exhibiting the class-based influences of the policy, the directive requiring potato additives did not apply to all-wheat bread. In a crassly political statement, the Imperial Health Office maintained that wares normally baked with wheat flour only would lose all associated characteristics if adulterated by potato.[19] Those with the means still bought all-wheat bread — and cake.

Thus war bread caused disgruntlement particularly in the German working class, on aesthetic, cultural, and political grounds. Loaves baked with potato additives lacked the "crunchy crisp of a crust" and were deficient in other characteristics associated with good bread.[20] Here the pleasure of good taste and flavor, or what was constituted as such, was tightly imbricated with notions of sharing in Germanness, which consumers viewed in this context as modern, urban, and luxurious, across class lines.[21] It quickly became clear that only those who could afford no better ate the distasteful war bread. Social Democratic Party (SPD) leaders across the country countered the official rhetoric on its salutary qualities, "but we just can't approve of [war bread], since it would damage the health and well-being of the people."[22] Poorer Berliners found propaganda stating that "the kaiser eats war bread: follow his example"[23] a bitter contrast to what they observed around them.

The Bundesrat's plan for war bread soon showed itself to be ill conceived for other reasons. The percentage of potato additives increased as cereals grew ever scarcer, so that by the end of November 1914 the council ordered that *K-Brot* contain at least 10 percent potato; by January 1915, *KK-Brot,* for the especially poor (and, presumably, especially patriotic), contained over 20 percent. But in the face of concomitant potato shortages, neither bakers nor consumers could adhere to the official ordinances. Whether anxious to comply with imperial regulations or to demonstrate their dissatisfaction with these invasive rules, bakers often ceased bread production altogether when the necessary quantities of "bread-stretching" potato were not available.[24] The Berlin city council actively attempted to control wheat and rye supplies,

Bread line, 1915. (Rütten & Loening Verlag)

building up the city's own stocks and setting price ceilings inside the city limits.[25] But local measures were meaningless against producers outside the city, who could take their goods elsewhere. The city's ability to control trade of even local retailers was limited until the Bundesrat provided municipalities with such powers through the decree of 25 January 1915.[26] By spring of 1915 — and for much of the war from then on — it was impossible to get any war bread at all.[27]

Although it appears officials attempted to divide urban consumers through such measures, pleasing wealthier Germans at the expense of the less wealthy, the effort to isolate working-class discontent was unsuccessful. The surprisingly widespread protest against bread shortages in Berlin emerged from an incipient common identity as urban consumers. Even before the war, while the "urban consumer" was an amorphous entity, Berliners and residents of Germany's other rapidly growing cities shared concerns across socioeconomic divisions, for example, about the growing number of middlemen.[28] As they stood in long lines for bread, working-class consumers cynically pointed up the discrepancy between the concept of the civil peace, which was to bind all Germans together, and the reality of war bread, which only exacerbated the unequal burden of food scarcity on the poor. Paradoxically, many wealthier Berliners affirmed this unity, at least among urban consumers, as they expressed public concern for this inequity. The broad press continued its surprising stance, crossing class lines to support the protesters' case, and raising the stakes by calling directly on Delbrück and other high-level officials to "take truly energetic measures" to contend with the bread problem.[29]

Fearful of this urban pressure, and despite counterpressure from farmers and big landowners, in November 1914 the Bundesrat decreed the establishment of the Imperial Grain Authority. The authority, headed by Georg Michaelis, was initially charged only to purchase wheat from abroad. But in a move of dramatic intervention and compromise of the heretofore inviolable principle of personal property, on 25 January 1915 the government began to confiscate limited stores of grain from German farms to prevent its use as fodder. This was the first act ever of the imperial government to regulate the production and use of foodstuffs for civilian use across the country. The state cast its acquiescence to public demand in terms of the place of bread as "the most important food of all."[30] Officials pointed to earlier experiences of periodic famine as well as the tradition of providing both "sugar bread and whip" (*Zuckerbrot und Peitsche*) to control unruly subjects. Of course, the whip seemed to be absent here. The grain authority moved to institute ration cards, allotting 2,000 grams (about 4.5 pounds) of bread per person per week. This measure was as remarkable as confiscation for its attempt to equalize distribution, at least for this basic food. In this way authorities tried to check the behavior of both producers and wealthier consumers.

Although the state attempted to equalize the consumption of bread, the new policies too, as they were practiced, tended to reinforce class distinctions, incensing working-class Berliners. Bakers were, for example, permitted to fill customers' rations with flour rather than bread and did so, particularly for working-class patrons. This represented an assault on urban tradition. Baking one's own bread was a sign of meanness; for working-class families it represented a further diminution of their right to maintain customary food habits. Baking bread also placed a terrific imposition on poorer women, who had to add this time-consuming task to their other new responsibilities, such as waiting in long lines, first for ration coupons, then for meager flour allotments. Women responded with exasperation to propaganda and advice literature, noting that foods that could be prepared more quickly, such as dumplings, did not serve the same purpose as bread, which was the mainstay of the two cold meals—not to mention that dumplings were normally made with coarsely ground meal.

The new measures also marked officials' own class biases. Authorities suggested that eating day-old bread and even two-day-old bread was, like eating war bread, a health measure as well as an act of patriotism. Bundesrat councillor Eschbach defended the new policies: "It is now well known that fresh-baked bread is being consumed in completely immoderate amounts to satisfy the necessary physiological feeling of satisfaction. . . . Indeed," he added counterproductively, "it is enjoyed while all too fresh, above all in the worker families and families with many children, which up till now bought fresh bread every single day. But a diminished ration of this bread will [in addition to conserving grain] also represent no small savings of money for them."[31] Hammering home civilians' potential treachery through consumption, Eschbach continued ominously that "the demand only for good taste . . . is in present times a crime against our people and our brothers who are struggling out there."[32]

Thus the grain authority policies designed to limit consumption most negatively affected those urban residents for whom bread was most important. Officials prohibited night baking from 5 January 1915 so that the lack of fresh bread in the mornings would discourage overeating. But, as officials knew, it was above all the "little person"—who could no longer afford to overeat—for whom "the customary breakfast roll, which stood, fresh and crisp, next to the coffee on the table," was important.[33] The roll might actually stand next to the flask, but the roll was most significant. In the late nineteenth century Berliner Adolf Glassbrenner wrote, in "Breakfast,"

> I have the best life
> I can't complain
> Even if the wind whistles through my sleeve
> I can deal with it.
> In the morning when I'm hungry
> I eat a buttered roll
> Along with it the schnapps tastes good
> Out of my full bottle.[34]

One might add that the roll stood ungraced by meat or cheese, for this population. Poor Berliners found the dried-out bread still more unbearable in light of the diminishing availability of butter and lard to spread on it and the lack of coffee to dunk it in. The loss of the fresh rolls also intensified the impact of absent husbands and fathers, as usually the male head of the household procured the morning *Reisebrot* or *Hasenbrot,* as Berliners called it.

WOMEN VERSUS WORKERS

Thus working-class Germans felt uniquely hard hit by the absence of bread and believed they had been unfairly singled out to bear the burden of the economic war. Yet government propaganda indicated that adequate supplies of both grain and potatoes existed. Who or what, then, if not the blockade, was responsible for the deficiency? In the last months of 1914 the working class found an immediate answer, as they perceived it, through a combination of government policy and propaganda. Poor consumers who queued for bread identified the "soldier's wife" as an important economic adversary, along with the "mother of many children" and the "munitions worker's wife." High-level officials were taken aback by the popular attacks on the soldier's wife as the source of the widespread hardship. They had anticipated that this persona would elicit universal sympathy and admiration. But prevailing circumstances transformed these sentiments.

Officials deferred to the wives and families of active soldiers in the first months of war. The "wife of the active soldier" was an already existing entity in Prussia who, however, had had no physical incarnation since the rapid and successful Wars of Unification between 1864 and 1870. Perceiving this identity to bear popular legitimacy, which carried with it specific state obligations, officials reinstituted and broadened support of the wives of active soldiers across the nation immediately upon the outset of hostilities. The identity of the soldier's wife emerged initially under specific historical conditions; perception of soldiers' wives early in the war did not match the positive image anticipated by the state.

The state's own propaganda was, in part, to blame, because it returned to the civilian population the responsibility for forestalling shortages. Although women did not necessarily consume the greater part of the family's food products (often the obverse was true), women customarily controlled the major part of the purchase, preparation, and consumption of food in a German household at this time.[35] Women's control over household consumption was magnified by men's departure to the battle front; so, too, was the proportion of the family's food eaten by adult women. Certainly bourgeois standards presumed a female procurer of food; thus propaganda addressed itself to women, as in the "ten wartime missions of the housewife."[36] Weaving together the threads of the various strategies of appeal, Prussian interior minister Friedrich Wilhelm von Loebell instructed doctors in Berlin and greater Prussia to "teach housewives about the 'food question,' to implore them to use available supplies propitiously, and to warn them to curb their consumption," in other words, to "run a healthy and thrifty household—and thereby forestall unnecessary unrest."[37] So, officials concluded, "with goodwill and appropriate handling, there will be enough for everyone. Housewives will grow through these new tasks."[38] Housewives were responsible for securing adequate, but only adequate, food supplies.

Directed particularly to women, such literature often reflected and effectively deployed dominant negative images of women. Civilian officials anticipated food shortages and soaring prices in the event of war, certainly in the event of a prolonged war. With the memory of the 1912 food riots still fresh in their minds, authorities feared reprisals particularly among women. Officials responded with a preemptive strike, emphasizing the need for women to overcome their irrationality when purchasing goods and intimating that women specifically were the point of vulnerability for the otherwise invincible German nation. Propaganda drew on images of women's softness and sexual penetrability and their susceptibility to seduction. This rhetoric metonymically related femaleness to the uncontrollable consumption of luxury items, unreasonable hoarding, and potential sabotage of the war effort by civilians. Women's groups anxious to display their patriotism actively played themselves on such images.[39]

Propaganda challenged women to disprove these notions by acting collectively as a "voluntary homefront army, which supports the soldiers by fighting the battle of the economy."[40] It averred that "every German, above all every German woman, is a soldier in this economic war. Just as our soldiers are dead tired but courageous before the enemy, so at home you must be thrifty and do without." Only in this fashion would women overcome their "lack of consciousness" and attention only to their immediate world, to demonstrate their "willingness to sacrifice" and to fulfill their "patriotic obligation."[41] Deployed to deflect government responsibility for food management, such sharp admonitions to women were, initially, partially effective in redirecting blame. Berliners and other Germans envisioned this potentially traitorous woman specifically as the soldier's wife. By December 1914, struggling Berliners identified the soldier's wife as a primary internal opponent in the economic war, due to her perceived unjustified privilege. How was the soldier's wife implicated in this way?

Authorities first observed the shift in public opinion immediately following the Battle of the Marne, in the second week of September 1914, when it became clear that the war would not be over by Christmas. Property owners expressed resentment of the special position of soldiers' wives. Landlords claimed soldiers' wives withheld rent that they were capable of paying, capitalizing on their status as "willing to sacrifice." Some soldiers' wives asserted they were exempt from paying their rent, certainly an inspired strategy on their part.[42] Still believing that the special status of soldiers' wives was important to the greater population, in October 1914 imperial officials quickly responded, authorizing special rent allowances in the city of Berlin paid on the dependents' behalf directly to landlords.[43]

But the soldier's wife grew increasingly unpopular with other segments of society as well, who resented her privileged status. Police claiming to represent the widespread, indignant response, asserted, "These malicious sol-

diers' wives . . . in fact live now much better than they did before the war. . . .
They receive separation and rent allowances and still pay the landlord no
rent."[44] Commissioner Jagow noted, "The claim is made that subvention
often flows too richly, and that, above all, soldiers' wives are spending their
money in other than the prescribed fashion."[45] To those already financially
squeezed, the new rent supplement added insult to injury. In the face of expensive bread and other economic hardships, the working poor saw only
that the soldier's wife, often from the working class herself, suddenly held
an exclusive position of privilege vis-à-vis her prewar class cohorts and
even "superiors": workers and, increasingly, the lower *Mittelstand.* Indeed,
the attacks in this period that identified soldiers' wives as a culprit in inadequate food supplies used the term as a shorthand for "soldiers' wives from
the working class." Police Sergeant Bernhard Schwarz reported in December 1914, "It must be a painful fact that, among the poorer population, dependents of soldiers are often considerably better off than those even temporarily unemployed. The wives of active soldiers are well taken care of: the
city covers the rent. . . . The others, the city lets drop." This, he claimed, explained the "reigning bitter despair at home."[46] Sergeant Schwarz moved in
his report from a description of "dependents of soldiers" to "wives of active soldiers" to "workers' wives."

By the end of 1914 these protests had spread. Members of Berlin's old and
especially new lower middle class joined in these accusations, announcing
their own rising difficulty in obtaining bread and claiming, moreover, that
the state had disturbed the natural order of class.[47] Police spies poignantly
recorded this sentiment, clearly feeling increasingly slighted themselves. Policemen used their reports to intimate that, as civil servants who defended
the state, they deserved special status at least as much as did soldiers' wives.
Police added that wealthier consumers continued to lend sympathy to such
protests, likely in order to deflect their own responsibility for the run on
bread grains.

To be sure, opinion was far from uniform on the issue of the soldier's
wife. City dwellers noted with pity the tension as war dependents fought for
a look at casualty lists displayed in major squares around the city, especially
at the weekly list posted each Monday; they observed the rise in incidence
of mourning clothing.[48] The Berlin press had little to say about the soldier's
wife as a rule, though *Vorwärts* frequently ran stories praising her brave and
stalwart nature, perhaps as a way to establish Social Democrats' own patriotism, and perhaps in part to overcome an image tarnished in November 1914,
when a prominent Social Democratic legislator evicted his tenant, a soldier's wife. *Vorwärts* often emphasized the victimized position of soldiers'

wives, realigning them with working people and poor consumers.[49] This did not diminish the impact of the popular protests against this figure; rather, officials were simply more confused about how to respond to reinstate public calm. Soldiers' wives themselves made demands on the state. Officials worried considerably about morale on the front and were for this reason little inclined to react to popular indignation by withdrawing dependents' benefits.

The vast number of workers left unemployed by the war joined family members in the streets to voice their sharp resentment of aid offered only to soldiers' wives and families. These protesters made it known that "in contrast to soldiers' families, the unemployed and their families [were] in pretty bad shape."[50] All those affected grumbled about how the rich could still afford anything they wanted, and how wealthy women hoarded shamelessly. But for "precisely the soldier's wife" to get essential foods when others could not defined "unfair" in this period. In this way, working-class and lower middle-class Berliners united in their protest, effectively defending the prewar class system. At the same time, those who protested separation allowances seemed to suggest that the prewar ideal of a woman's primary role as wife no longer held the same merit. Police reports intimate that women ought not to benefit from the sacrifice their husbands made to the war effort; likewise, protesters belittled the notion that these wives made their own unusual sacrifices by living without their husbands.

Protesters aired this resentment above all around the issue of bread and flour goods. By late fall 1914, members of the lower *Mittelstand* could not afford their afternoon cake—an important symbol of their status and of their distinction from the working class. A growing percentage of them, like the majority of workers in Berlin, no longer regularly obtained bread. It is no wonder, then, that Berlin police reported "jealous utterances . . . in many circles," condemning soldiers' wives, when it was rumored that the latter now regularly spent the afternoons "consuming quantities of cake and whipped cream with their children."[51] The ironic image on the streets embittered the populace: "Also, the number of women dressed in somber clothing, claiming to be robbed of their breadwinner or other close family member, is increasing, creating a sobering image; but one must on the other hand note that the women are untouched by either neediness or despair." Officer Hinrich Diercks added cynically, "One can see for oneself that it is exactly the poorer women who daily occupy the cafes of department stores, sampling delicacies that certainly don't number among the most necessary foods."[52] It is unclear what the individuals who made these claims were doing in department store cafés themselves, or how with certainty they would have recognized women eating cake as soldiers' wives from the working class, other than, perhaps, by their somber clothes. But Berliners insisted that the scarcity of wheat flour must be related to its unreasonable and profligate use by these privileged consumers, who had the means for such luxuries. Here, as throughout the war, the attitude toward particular foods reflected, informed, and transformed popular perceptions, and recast social identities and alliances. The image of cake-eaters versus bread-eaters defined for this moment the adversaries in the economic war.[53] For officials, this resonated ominously with historical precedents of revolutionary unrest.

Who was this soldier's wife who raised such ire? She was a composite, a persona characterized by her position of unfair privilege in the economic and social transformations of wartime. Police Officer Hermann Schulz made transparent the primacy of gender in the characterization, asserting in an April 1915 report, in shorthand fashion, that "only the women" had protested the recent popular prohibition on the production of cakes, though he referred specifically to war dependents.[54] Now all war dependents, including children, siblings, and elderly parents of soldiers, could qualify for separation allowances, and this fact did not go unnoted by the greater public. Berliners protested primarily against the figure of the soldier's wife, however. The reality that she was, indeed, in not so exclusive a category makes the fact that she was singled out in this fashion still more notable.

Moreover, the perception that the soldier's wife fared economically better than she had before the war may have been more fantasy than fact. Legislation of 4 August 1914, following from the law of 1888, spelled out a monthly support in the amount of 9 to 12 marks, plus 6 marks for each child through the age of fourteen, and full supplements for other adult dependents living in the same household.[55] The average working man earned about 25 marks a week on the eve of war (about twice that of a woman), though wages in war industries had already begun to rise.[56] Thus it is possible that soldiers' wives could have exceeded their prewar household income, particularly if they also claimed more than two children. Germans expected this income to remain secure, while many already experienced unemployment or feared it was not long in coming. After October the Berlin municipal authorities paid out rent allowances on behalf of the state. Many thriving war-industry factories also provided small allowances to women whose husbands had been affiliated with these concerns; political parties, private organizations, and the church offered support to soldiers' wives. Considering that soldiers' wives no longer bore the daily expenses of their husbands (whose actual contributions to the family were, moreover, highly variable), in the fall and winter of 1914 in principle they perhaps could have fared better than other class cohorts (and particularly the unemployed). On the whole, however, it is difficult to ascertain how much these women and families actually received in Berlin. Ute Daniel and Birthe Kundrus agree that, above all in the larger cities, soldiers' wives had no particular economic advantage in the end. In Berlin the Social Democratic *Mitteilungsblatt* reported that official support "has been received very unevenly"—possibly in part a function of this popular opposition.[57]

So, in this early period, a group distinguished by an ambiguous class identity—beleaguered consumers—was, in effect, pitted against another group defined by gender. Working- and lower middle-class Berliners intimated that the soldier's wife held a position of exclusive privilege, one that breached prewar norms. The position of the soldier's wife seemed to be inscribed by inviolable legal characteristics: one was either the wife of a man in active service, or one was not. Many capital residents perceived this exclusivity to be unjust, for it allowed certain individuals to escape the constraints of other aspects of their identity in order to ameliorate their situation. That is, working-class wives of soldiers could apparently transcend their class identity merely by virtue of a role that only women could fill.

The conflict may also have been related to age and other factors. Working-class and lower middle-class women over twenty-five may have resented the young married woman, perhaps without children, who now seemed to have income for leisure without the responsibilities of matrimony, a situation all the more galling if she also brought in her own wages while others were unemployed. Or perhaps she was the young mother of a small child with whom she could stroll through the streets toward cafés, while her counterparts without husbands on the front worked at home cramped together with children (and in danger of losing even that space) or had to leave them at home alone while they worked in a factory or office. But other Berliners distinguished this figure in terms of gender.

Thus, as the daily battle for food became ever more central in the life of the average Berliner, the emphasis on struggles over the means of production turned to a primacy of conflicts over the means of consumption. Police reports, the press, and ultimately, legislation marked this shift. Observers described those most affected by the scarcity and high cost of bread and potatoes as "workers and some of the *Mittelstand*," then increasingly as "the poorer population," and finally, as the "population of lesser means" or "of little means" (*die Minderbemittelte*). Thus, new social identities coalesced on both sides of the axis of privilege, transforming prewar relations of power in the struggle to defend them.

The furor of capital city residents over the deficiency of bread grain and the differentiation in access to the scarce food instigated two discrete but related trends. The first was the popular establishment of a feminized societal enemy who appeared to have used her new status to subvert the prewar economic and class arrangement. Working- and lower middle-class Germans rejected the participation of soldiers' wives in protests over the cost of bread. Police recorded the sentiment that "soldiers' wives ought not to make so much racket so they won't have to stuff their muzzles so much."[58] The second trend was the emergence of a new social protagonist, the population of lesser means, constituted in opposition to the soldier's wife and defined loosely by a common deficiency of means and concomitant deprivation as consumers.

Why did gender figure with such primacy in the image of this inner enemy? First, because of the place of gender and specific gender roles in dictating privileged status.[59] Poorer Berliners held in contempt other categories, such as the mother of many children (*kinderreiche Mutter,* literally, the child-rich mother, most often still a member of the working class and often also a soldier's wife) as well as the now better-compensated munitions worker's wife, for they appeared to have shed their class identities merely through their attachment to men. The primacy of gender related to more than just this position of privilege, however. A soldier's son and dependent father also received state aid. It was the male munitions worker, not his wife, who received proportionally higher wages at this point. It is easy enough to see this as a straightforward class issue. These feminized categories, all told, actually comprised a large portion of working-class women, along with their families. Conversely, the police who narrated this social tragedy through their reports were civil servants suffering from status anxiety and loss of purchasing power. The class element stands out in police reports. These commentaries consistently elide descriptions such as "the wives of active soldiers" and "workers' wives."[60] But police and other contemporaries (including women) defined these prominent personae primarily by their femaleness. Police reports consistently note that "those of little means" leveled complaints against "dependent wives," "munitions workers' wives," "these women," and "the women." Such language reinforced the negative quality of femaleness.[61]

These vilified women all acted in idealized female roles, as wives and mothers. Under the conditions of wartime scarcity, emiserated Berliners intimated that women performed no special service through these roles and should not be rewarded as such. The new public prominence of women, in part a function of food shortages, likely spurred this way of thinking, although in nineteenth-century food riots, women won sympathy precisely as wives and mothers. The transformation in the meaning of the family unit was also both cause and effect of this new conceptualization. Government propaganda on the subject of food played heavily on notions of women's purported irrationality, weakness, vulnerability, and associated lack of patriotism. The ubiquitous wartime bogey of the traitorous spy most often took the form of a woman who lacked understanding and allegiance outside her narrow world.[62] Thus, blending old and new images of the inner enemy, military officials suggested, for example, that "the wives of German Social Democrats are reportedly spying against the fatherland, frequently traveling to England for the express purpose of treachery."[63] Officials regularly called in women's rights advocates for questioning on the basis of their presumed "lack of national identity"; Minna Cauer describes the censorship authorities challenging her patriotism.[64]

The munitions worker's wife and the mother with many children also stood out, like the soldier's wife, for their special status in relation to bread. These personae began to appear in press and police reports particularly in the first months of 1915, in the wake of government policy meant to assuage the clamor for more bread. Officials had strongly encouraged large Berlin war-industry concerns to raise the pay particularly of their skilled workers and heavy laborers in order to guarantee military supplies. Individuals who were unemployed, who worked in the sagging "peace industries,"[65] or who were employed in the civil service resented this new source of privilege. They also chafed under the intimation that war-industry workers contributed more to the nation than they did.

Aggrieved Berliners expressed this resentment at the point where they saw it: when munitions workers' wives, like soldiers' wives, did their shopping. So offended Berliners complained that "precisely the munitions workers' wives often buy the most expensive things."[66] Police Officer Starost telegraphed this confounding of class by gender, noting that "only women with a head scarf, whose husbands earn high wages through arms work" can afford to buy goose; "the lower middle class and civil servants are entirely absent."[67]

Government policy also fostered the animus toward the mother of many children, a figure who raised ethnic and religious associations as well as class questions. Though working-class birthrates fell in Wilhelmine Germany, the mother of many children was more likely to be working class, especially Catholic and perhaps Polish, or an immigrant to the city from East Prussia or Silesia—all qualities that would have mitigated against the likeliness of a strong financial status before the war. In early 1915, as many munitions

workers received pay raises, the newly established Imperial Grain Authority issued its rations for bread and flour, allotting 1,000 grams, or half the
adult portion, for children ages one to eight. The authority intended this
measure, like official pressure to raise wages, precisely to quell the public
disquiet over bread shortages, prices, and distributional inequities. Many
Berliners claimed to be outraged by such allotments, however, because they
were so large for young children. Officer Paul Kurtz reported that "families
with grown children who work all day at factories, etc., cannot make do with
the prescribed amounts, while families with three or four [young] children
couldn't possibly need as much as they have."[68]

Again police reported the sentiment that it was the woman who would
benefit from such measures: the mother herself, for example, might consume the food she had purchased with her children's coupons. Lack of
good evidence that such children were doing particularly well led to assumptions that "there are mothers who send their children to school scant-
ily clothed, but who cannot give up constantly eating doughnuts."[69] Finally,
many among the populace resented the notion, spread by some private organizations, that the mother of many young children contributed more to
her country's needs and that she should therefore be rewarded for her efforts. Among some nationalist groups, support for mothers of many children was strong, in light of perceived "birth strikes" of the prewar era as
well as already predictable war-related demographic effects. The BDF targeted both soldiers' wives and women with many small children as particularly sympathetic groups to aid. In light of the insecure economic conditions, however, many regarded with bitterness any entreaty to have more
babies in the interest of the nation.[70] This bitterness reflects a significant
trend, consistent throughout the war, that women were not valued for their
child-bearing—or child-rearing—abilities in this period. The general populace scarcely accepted women's responsibilities as mothers and seems to
have deemed selfish—and suspect—women who became pregnant.

Hard-struck Berliners found it unbearable if a mother with many young
children received separation allowances in addition to large ration allotments for her children, for this woman then held both the coupons and the
money to take advantage of those coupons. Such mothers might also send
their young children to stand in numerous bread and other food lines simultaneously. Of course, trusting small children to be able to carry out the
task under complicated and tense circumstances did not guarantee success.
In principle, however, such women had the best chance of getting scarce
foods at all. Other poorer Berliners expressed concern that, in this way, too,

the advantages of child-rich women approximated those of bourgeois women, equally despised but more resignedly accepted, who sent their numerous servants to procure food.

Finally, mothers of many small children were least likely to work in factory jobs. Before the war Germans viewed this as either an economic liability or a social virtue; now it was just the opposite. These women could spend their days scouting out where and when a delivery of flour or potatoes might be coming through. This was a real advantage, as knowledge of such random and unpredictable deliveries was increasingly needed in the quest to procure scarce goods, which might be sold out by the time factory workers left their jobs. Indeed, by the end of 1915, women had quit their jobs away from home in droves, for their wages meant nothing if they could not find food to spend them on. It is ironic that a family of adults, in which all were employed, resented the advantages of the woman who was unable to bring in even a single factory wage. This resentment revealed anxiety over the perceived inversion of prewar status, over one's contribution to the war effort, and over the challenges of a transformed world, where money alone no longer guaranteed one's bread.

Berliners' attacks on these prominent images of wives and mothers suggested in part that these women poorly filled the virtuous roles that had won them their position of privilege and honor. Mothers of many young children were "bad mothers," interested not in the propagation of young Germans but in enjoying delicacies, even at the expense of their children. Adults in food queues grumbled that allowing children to stand in lines by themselves demonstrated neglect of the children, as well as exploitation of the ration system.[71] Police claimed that women pushed children to protest for them as well, goading them to break shop windows. Some officers suggested that the government intervene more deeply into the affairs of war dependents, to control them in their husbands' absence.[72] Many dubbed soldiers' wives faithless wives, flaunting their somber dress while submitting to all their appetites. The press frequently raised the specter of the adulterous escapades of the soldier's wife.[73] Sergeant Schwarz believed there were soldiers' wives with four or five children who "don't give a damn whether their husbands come back."[74] Schwarz was, however, not entirely without understanding of the situation, adding that the apparent lack of concern might reflect that "since [before the war, the husband] was unemployed [and] . . . was 'boss of the poorhouse' . . . or for whatever reason didn't take care of his family, or even often abused them"—though it was for this reason Schwarz questioned the appropriateness of the allowances. Marlene Dietrich, who lived in Berlin as a child, noted indeed that in this wartime "women's world," "the women didn't seem to suffer in a world without men, they were quite calm about it."[75]

This latter attitude may speak to a deeper, structural challenge that some Germans asserted in such attacks on these female figures. We have noted that these protests by workers and middle-class Berliners early in the war seemed to defend the prewar hierarchy, but that the very fact of common protests seemed to transform earlier socioeconomic relations. In like fashion, the populace denounced these women's proclaimed breach of prewar gender and familial relations but, at the same time, impugned the validity of those relations. So protesters intimated that munitions workers' wives themselves worked no harder than before the war; they personally had made no contribution to the war effort. Therefore, they challenged the notion that these wives should benefit from the efforts of their husbands. Thus, the story of the soldier's wife tells us about more than the historically contingent validity of particular social identities. Behind the denunciation of this identity lurked at least a temporary instability in the place of the bourgeois family and a related confrontation with how women ought to negotiate in public life.[76]

This challenge grew out of the transformations in everyday life that had come with war, shifts that shattered the illusion of upholding the ideal family and the roles of its members.[77] Before the war, working-class family life posed ongoing concerns and challenges for the middle classes as they failed to conform to the nuclear family unit.[78] One of the first government debates following the declaration of war concerned separation allowances for illegitimate children and children with whom the soldier had not shared a domicile. Working-class women rarely depended entirely on their husbands for the family income; employers had explicitly rejected the concept of a family wage before the war. Beyond the question of income, the prewar working-class husband and father sometimes played an ambiguous role in the family, creating a looser family structure than bourgeois ideals promulgated.[79]

Naturally the war brought removal of male heads of household and other family members as soldiers. As the war continued, family members that remained on the homefront often took on work (including under official duress) that prohibited a shared domicile or that required sacrifice of home or care of one's own children.[80] Life was less than ever centered among a closed circle of people within the four walls of a rented room, but was played out far more on the streets, in bread and other food lines as well as in factories.[81] By the second half of the war, relations among family members were ever more difficult and estranged, beyond the separations of home and battlefront, as adults and children competed for the same hopelessly inade-

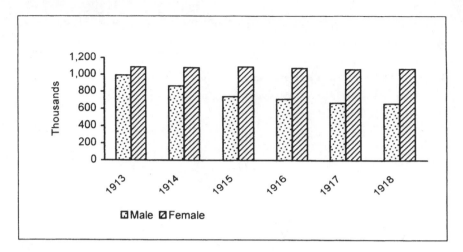

Figure 2.2. Population by Sex, City of Berlin, 1913–1918
Source: Statistik der Stadt Berlin, *190*.

quate rations, as young children represented an ever greater burden to adults, and as all human interactions grew more tense, reproducing a sense of embattlement. It is no coincidence that by early 1915, talk on the street in Berlin suggested a generalized disapprobation for female identities that were grounded in the bourgeois family structure and its particular system of interdependency. New public mores frowned on women's efforts to mediate relations with the state and greater public via the figure of their husbands. The identity of soldier's wife lost its political validity, in part by virtue of its inscription exclusively in the private sphere, both within the bourgeois family unit and within the realm of privilege. In the changing terrain of image and experience brought by the war, the public legitimated those "feminine" identities that operated primarily in the public sphere and those that were open to the public, in which gender did not operate as a closed category.

Broad societal demonization of the soldier's wife rested, therefore, on two implicit charges. First, popular parlance condemning separation allowances intimated that it was not the family unit but the soldier alone who had entered relations of reciprocal obligation with the state. Many people were dubious about the appropriateness of guaranteeing a family's living wage in wartime based on the husband's absence. Second, many Berliners discredited the notion of neediness based on loss of family head and breadwinner, as dependents appeared to be operating relatively well in public, outside the sphere that was to have enclosed their roles, and certainly relative to their potentially undependable and insufficient prewar income. The idealized, bourgeois family had lost a certain significance as an economic unit; likewise, absence of the male family head generated only intensified questioning of the role of the family as the appropriate political unit. The particular circumstances of the war thus worked to foreground alternative standards regarding the place of the family and women. One initial result was, essentially, the vilification of femaleness.

FROM SPECIAL SUBVENTION TO GENERALIZED PROTECTION

On the eve of war the state took for granted that the civilian populace would demand government care of soldiers' wives, no less than would the soldiers who had left for the front. Instead much of the population appears to have felt very differently about the soldier's wife. Police spies themselves sneered at the "lack of suffering" that these "soldiers wives from the 'simple circles'" endured.[82] Most important, Berliners who felt deprived did not subscribe to the notion that the soldier's wife had sacrificed more to the war effort than themselves and that she therefore deserved supplemental income. The greater civilian population perceived as a slight this legislated differentiation between the soldier's wife and others. Separation allowances were "arbitrary" and "unreasonable." So the populace found the "distribution of subvention [to be] unjust."[83] But it was only natural that war dependents would accept the subsidies offered to them; it was the state, which ruled the entire German people, that had acted unfairly in offering the monies to this particular population. It was the government that paid thoughtless soldiers' wives to buy the cake that robbed those of little means of their bread.

By the end of 1914 the point for many was not to strip the support of war dependents. It was, rather, to recognize both the needs and the contributions of the greater civilian population. In this atmosphere, popular demand arose for a far more generalized form of support that, like separation allowances, would not bear the stigma associated with municipal poor relief but would signal the state's obligation to its subjects. Soldiers' wives themselves reinforced the distinction through their own disdain for "charitable" contributions.[84] The "population at home" now considered it "the most urgent responsibility of the government" to care for the nutritional needs of all the people, by "distributing food equally to the entire population at prices affordable for all."[85]

In the eyes of state officials this demand clearly had to be quelled. Although the military administration supported the specialized care of the soldier's wife, fearing the effects of any change on morale at the front, civilian officials defied military authorities in light of protests at home, opting to cut back on support of war dependents. In early January 1915 imperial authorities ceased automatic separation payments to war dependents, claiming that domestic peace was at issue. Minister of the Interior Loebell wrote, straddling the issue, "that a benevolent means test for war dependents, perhaps not with quite the same standards as for poor relief, is in order; there are no reservations to supporting able-bodied dependents when they have fallen into desperation as a result of temporary unemployment."[86] The adoption of some form of means testing, officials hoped, would at least give the illusion that state subventions were more rational than before and that the population more equitably bore wartime sacrifices.

But the specter of more, not less, support from the state hung ominously. As government officials staggered on with makeshift policies throughout the war, Berliners and others increasingly held authorities responsible for the dire circumstances. There were, to be sure, expressions of opinion from many parts protesting loss of support to soldiers' wives, including in much of the press, especially from the Social Democratic leadership. At the same time, there were plenty of public voices willing to spell out just how the state might meet these putative obligations to the wider populace. Maverick Social Democrats had from the outset of the war demanded attention to the food question for the sake of all Germans through greater intervention in the market and widespread confiscation of foodstuffs from farmers and merchants. By the first months of 1915, groups from across the political and economic spectrum supported the popular claim that only deeply interventionist measures by the state could return society to order. For some, including representatives of wealthy consumers, agriculture, and commerce, this support was often by way of denying their own roles in the inequities of food pricing and distribution. A columnist in the *Reichsbote* cried crocodile tears for the poor, declaring, "Who wouldn't happily give up cake, when the feeding of the German nation stands in question, through the [lack of the] most important of all foods, bread?" He went on to claim that the ban on cake was hardly an answer to the problem of bread deficiency. He looked to officials to take care of the problem in "more efficacious ways"—that is, ways that perhaps would not take the cake from the mouths of the wealthy population.[87]

Civil servants entered the debate in their concern to maintain social order—and in their concern for their own welfare. Police Sergeant Schwarz argued the case directly to his superiors: "In just such an instance, there is much that could be done" by Prussian and imperial authorities.[88] Upper-level government employees used the daily press to argue against Chancellor Bethmann's perceived timorous approach to issues of food distribution.[89] Economic Councillor Franz Schiftan wrote in the agricultural lobby's *Deutsche Tageszeitung,* "It is absolutely essential that the state take the provision of food for the people into its own hands and actively control it."[90] Demands for aggressive interventionism effectively became mainstream.

The Bundesrat responded by acting on the most compelling specific demands but cast these new measures as unique and limited. A week after Sergeant Schwarz compared the ill fate of the unemployed with that of soldiers' wives, Schwarz noted that the former now received some form of support through the city.[91] Officer Otto Görl confirmed in turn, "The population welcomed the announcement of rent support that would be offered not only to families in which the breadwinner was on the front, but also to the unemployed."[92] Officials had acknowledged as early as October that "public opinion is unified on the point that price ceilings must be set for the most important food items."[93] As the grain authority issued ration cards for bread in January 1915, it set national price ceilings for the first time on a number of foods, including potatoes and legumes. Authorities defended rations and price limits to farmers, wholesalers, and retailers, claiming, "We must not simply ensure that the next harvest just covers current needs but that it creates supplies for next year. . . . Toward meeting the goal of absolutely insuring the people's nutrition, a goal of value both economically and politically, the suggested measures have been established, and the price ceilings must be set."[94] This was a "man-made" hunger; "men" had to address it, unusual as it was, for the privilege of continuing to fight the war. The government would regret this promise, once it was clear that more than propaganda and even occasional rations and price limits would be necessary to make good on the notion. Officials would regret still more the more general expectation, now legitimated, that the state was responsible for the needs of the greater population.

3 WOMEN OF LESSER MEANS

As in the case of bread, the availability of other "most important foods," such as potatoes and pork, influenced popular perceptions, social organization, and political action. These foods also dominated public attention through their fate on the open market and through ongoing acts of official policy to control their distribution. The cost and shortage of potatoes in the winter of 1914–15 transformed shopping into a task riddled with anxiety and rancor. This experience contributed to the rearrangement of social relations along lines of consumption versus production, and of buyer versus seller. As a consequence, a new social protagonist emerged, the "woman of lesser means." The woman of lesser means came to represent the front-line soldier in the inner economic war fought in the streets of the capital city and throughout Germany. She did not fight against her fellow consumers—indeed, she was a symbol of their collective victimization. Rather, she fought against the merchants and rural producers who had chosen profit over patriotism, as contemporaries styled it, largely by virtue of standing in line. By the spring of 1915 the sympathetic perception of the woman of little means lent legitimacy to far-reaching demands both for heavy market intervention and for broad welfare provisions.

THE GREATEST POTATO LAND IN THE WORLD

Due to an early frost in Germany, the 1914 harvest yielded a poor supply of potatoes.[1] Government policy exacerbated the scarcity of potatoes. The Bundesrat attempted to stretch supplies of grain in the fall of 1914 by ordering the use of potato starch in the production of bread. Officials also recommended that farmers use both edible and seed potatoes as a substitute for deficient grain fodder. But as political economist August Skalweit pointed out in hindsight, "The potato, not grain, was ultimately the point of departure for the food shortage."[2] The initial result of the government's unusual pressure on potato supplies was a premium on the lowly tuber. Farmers and merchants responded by raising prices and holding back supplies. By October 1914 poor consumers complained that potatoes, which had nearly doubled in price from their prewar cost of 7 pfennig per kilogram, would soon be completely unaffordable.[3]

This was a serious problem for Berliners, as for other urban Germans. Potatoes were a staple of the German diet as well as Germany's greatest crop. Skalweit observed, "The German is a potato eater; he can stand all else, but potatoes he cannot live without."[4] Potato acreage had grown steadily in the decades before the war,[5] particularly in the eastern German countryside surrounding Berlin. German farmers relied heavily on potato exports for income. Swelling output also represented increased potato consumption among Germans, including in cities, in the form of durable flakes and starch. Likewise, improved freight transportation across the country meant that potatoes could sit in the ground until just before they were needed in urban shops and marketplaces. Concomitantly, potatoes became a customary food; their absence in the winter of 1914–15 represented another sign of unwelcome change on the homefront.

The unavailability of potatoes, due to scarcity and especially cost, was a problem above all for the working classes in Berlin. For members of this population, potatoes were, like bread, not just a common food but a central element in their diet. German workers sang, "Potatoes in the morning, at noon in the broth, in evenings along with their peels, potatoes forever!"[6] They figured traditionally as the main constituent of the hot midday meal. Their virtues for the population of lesser means were many. Potatoes were filling and nutritious. They were an important source of calories, in the form of carbohydrates and protein, as well as of niacin, potassium, iron, and vitamin C, not easily obtainable through other available foods.[7] Their cost was in part the source of this dietary emphasis. Potatoes were far and away the cheapest food available, kilo for kilo.[8] By relying on this staple, the working poor, including unskilled laborers, could survive on wages alone. Thus, the poor felt they were especially hard hit when potato prices rose in the late fall of 1914. Indeed, the simultaneous loss of both bread and potatoes created serious privations for those of lesser means in the first winter of the war. Food scientists had in the fall of 1914 touted the nutritional interchangeability of the two foods. But the equation did not square, those in the streets responded, if both foods were in short supply.[9] If, in light of grain shortages, the potato was "now the main source of nutrition for working-class families,"[10] its own deficiency was all the more keenly felt, even "catastrophic" for workers and part of the lower middle class.[11]

Thus the working population once again felt singled out to bear the burden of wartime shortages as a result, witting or not, of government policy.

Propaganda warning the populace not to overindulge their appetites on potatoes as on bread exacerbated this resentment. Germans employed the potato to represent someone as fat and misshapen, as in "potato paunch" (in wartime, the *K-bauch*) and "potato face," suggesting someone who met the desires of his or her own belly above all else.[12] This association served the interests of the state, as did the prevalent belief that workers, in particular, ate too much.[13] As a result of these circumstances that singled them out, working-class consumers standing in lines registered their rising "dismay" and "disapproval." Police reported menacingly in October 1914, "The patriotic sentiment of the populace has experienced no great change. However, . . . there is definitely significant unrest among the workers in response to the rise in food prices . . . , particularly in the price of the potato, that main food source of the people."[14] Pleas and warnings from municipal authorities to the federal government to cap the price of potatoes and to take steps to control supply also reflected this concern.

As in the case of bread, the government responded quickly enough, once warnings concerning popular discontent grew sufficiently dire. In November the Bundesrat instituted ceilings on the wholesale price of potatoes, setting it at 3 marks per *Zentner* (fifty kilos). This policy initiated the practice of price setting (*Preispolitik*), which, like the institution of ration coupons for bread, soon became the norm for all foods. State tariffs and price supports in the name of the Junker were common enough in the decades before the war, but measures such as price ceilings were unprecedented in united Germany, as was confiscation of bread grains on behalf of urban consumers.[15] The effects of the new policy were, in any case, difficult to discern in the first months after its institution. Farmers responded to the directive by foddering most of their potatoes, even after the Bundesrat, in an about-face, proclaimed this practice illegal. Rural producers found potatoes far more valuable for their weight in pig fodder than in food for people at the price set by the government. As a result, potatoes completely disappeared from city markets, raising the ire of the entire population.

In consequence officials wavered in their policy, sending out rumors in December and January that they might raise the price ceiling. The effect was to aggravate the deficiency immensely. Now distributors joined farmers in the practice of holding back potatoes in cellars and warehouses, confident that the practice would expedite retraction of the policy and that they might then sell their stored potatoes for a higher price. Consumers complained bitterly that merchants carried only seed potatoes rather than those considered humanly edible; moreover retailers, who could still charge what they wished, sold these inferior goods for exorbitant prices.[16] Municipal officials, who themselves could purchase potatoes only at the ceiling price, had no authority to force the hand of Brandenburg farmers; thus the city's own supplies of potatoes, sold through special stands in the municipal market halls, rapidly sold out.

Police observed "great disturbance" among working women, for whom the only option now remained private shops, the proprietors of which presumably acquired supplies by ignoring the price ceilings and passing the costs on to their customers, with interest.[17] By mid-January, Berliners protested both the loss of potatoes and their frustrating experiences in the marketplace. They demanded that the government right the situation and take action against speculators. The contemporary expression "right into the potatoes, right out of the potatoes" (*rin in die Kartoffeln, raus aus die Kartoffeln* [*sic*]), suggesting arbitrary, contradictory, and ineffectual behavior, expressed precisely how working-class Berliners perceived official measures concerning this main food source.

The lack of affordable potatoes, particularly in the traditionally working-class neighborhoods of north and east Berlin, inspired turbulent street scenes that reached a climax in the second week of February 1915. These scenes were not only a function of the vexatious shortages but also a consequence of the circumstances at shops and market stands. In this era before self-service, lines of some length were the norm at busy shopping times. Now, before any given stand, hundreds of Berliners would line up, anxious to reach the front before supplies sold out and tremendously frustrated if they failed to do so. Dramatic tumults erupted particularly in the working-class neighborhood surrounding the Andreas Street marketplace in northeast Berlin, in the shadow of sculptor Gormanski's *Woman of the Working Class and Child.* Political police described with dismay mob scenes in which "thousands of women and children" clamored to purchase a few pounds of potatoes at considerable physical risk as "each tried to get before the next, whereby women ripped the articles from the arms of the next," trampling children in the effort.[18] Such "agitated scenes" took place around the city in working-class areas.[19]

These tumults created precisely the sort of street scenes that the state wanted so badly to avoid. Although limited to particular neighborhoods, the image of these marketplace fracases had the power to affect morale across and even outside the city, including morale on the front, and to give evidence abroad that England's "starvation war" was bringing Germany to its knees.[20] The street's public nature drew widespread attention to all activity in it. After food-related unrest in northwest Berlin in 1910, Police Commissioner Jagow had warned residents, "The street serves only for traffic. Countermanding state authority on this issue will result in the use of weapons."[21] The job of patrolmen in the war years was, as before the war, to prevent disorder in the streets, through forceful intervention if necessary. Officials charged the political police to keep them informed of any such disturbance in the making and moved these informers from socialist political meetings to the streets with the commencement of hostilities in August 1914.

The concern of officials for protest in the streets reveals a number of contemporary sociological beliefs.[22] The first axiom was that the mere fact of collective presence constituted assembly (*Ansammlung*) among those present. Police and others consistently described the wartime food lines as assemblies, composed of one identifiable population or another. A second truism was that the experience of assembly created in turn a sense of common identity, interest, and purpose among the implicated. Officer Diercks suggested that "line-standing," as it was denoted, "elicits almost the impression that many women had found community in standing together before the shops."[23] A third belief was that the image of assembly attracted outside attention, providing moreover a forum for the views expressed by participants. Emphasizing both the social and the performative aspects of such queues, journalists, police, and line-standers themselves cynically dubbed the act of waiting to purchase food as "dancing the polonaise," an activity Berliners accorded significant attention.

Fourth, officials subscribed to the notion of a natural propensity of assemblies to become riots (*Aufläufe*), as a result of the unreason of the street crowd. *Auflauf* also translates as "unlawful assembly," a criminal violation. Thus, officials demonstrated an almost paranoid fear of any populous presence in the streets, including even demonstrations of "patriotic support for the war" that arose in the first weeks of hostilities.[24] Even flag-festooned windows indicating support for the war elicited nervous police reports. Finally, authorities asserted, such riots were de facto political, at least in effect, whether or not in intent. In light of the danger to international image authorities believed such events posed, officials proclaimed in October 1915 that any participants in a crowd even threatening to become a demonstration be subject to punishment, including as traitors to the state, a potentially capital offense.

Such beliefs constituted a series of self-fulfilling prophesies. The state's own concern served to focus broader public attention on the masses in the streets. Officials invested in the crowd in the streets a power to influence popular sentiment and public opinion that belied the limited official political rights provided by Prussia's narrow franchise. It turn, it is clear that the crowd began to win the ability to influence state policy in meaningful ways. Despite their recognition of the dangers, police knew they could not prevent the populace from assembling for food. This is why food lines constituted the central focus of police attention even before unrest began, as evidenced by reports of August and September 1914 noting that food prices and scarcity were "not yet" a problem.[25]

Moreover, police found these disturbances related to scarcity difficult to control through socially acceptable means. The unrest arose from the simple circumstance of many people trying to procure some of the inadequate supply of potatoes. No agent provocateur stirred up the crowd that stopped the flow of pedestrian traffic. Police easily dissipated the crowds that threatened to protest once a shopkeeper declared his or her supply exhausted. But no sooner did they calm one commotion than another erupted.[26] Police urged high-level officials to address the "potato days" with more expansive and long-term strategies, for "the sale of potatoes within Greater Berlin creates a truly dangerous threat to security and order." Officer Dittmann concurred, "Working-class families can no longer continue to exist with the present inflation. . . . The government doesn't concern itself enough with the living situation of the worker. It is no wonder . . . that they are storming shops and taking what they can."[27] Without strong measures "very soon," Officer Paul Hartwig warned, "this situation will not change."[28] The ominous tocsin of these reports was typical in these months. It suggested a level of both food deficiency and threat to order qualitatively different from that which had arisen in previous decades.

By early 1915, would-be shoppers experienced the quest for food as one of battles in the streets, as they lay in wait to storm the shops. They borrowed the notion of an inner economic war from government propaganda, which portrayed German civilians fighting the inner enemy called need (Not).[29] Not referred at once to specific privations and generalized want, to the emergency this want generated, and to the urgency of response. A broad public renamed this inner enemy, in the person of the profiteering stallholder or shopkeeper. During this period inimical and violent relations formed between those who had potatoes and those who wished to buy them, through the experience of the street and the marketplace. Police and press reports provide anxious descriptions of rapidly escalating confrontations, verbal and physical, between consumers and retailers. Officer Diercks informed

"Don't get excited, Mr. Secretary, you'll get your ten rolls, just like always. But now you also must order ten sausages too." The wealthy too contended with merchant schemes. (Ulk, 18 December 1914)

his superiors that "the shortage of potatoes has engendered frightful scenes, bringing about unbearable relations between customer and merchant." [30]

Suspicion of the soldier's wife did not disappear entirely in this period; it returned especially during a moment of tension among consumers in 1916. But conflicts among consumers seemed to recede into the background. Soldiers' wives encompassed growing numbers of the population and growing numbers of mourners, certainly as the war of attrition began in earnest. Moreover, the soldier's wife perpetrated no malevolent misdeed of her own, while poorer consumers saw merchants as actively malicious. These consumers found merchants' perceived profiteering and other chicanery a more irksome problem now; ultimately they seem to have found unity as consumers strategically more effective than division among themselves.

Consumers also battled invisible wholesalers and producers, protesting their offenses from the sidewalks and the streets. Police reported that, along with anti-shopkeeper sentiment, "The view has arisen among the populace that the artificial speculation of the wholesalers is at fault: they have held back the potatoes in order to demand higher prices for them later."[31] As the unrest continued, police repeated the charge in the imperative, suggesting their own belief in its validity. Following the official word, police asserted, "There are quite enough potatoes to be had, as this year's harvest was abundant." But, they concluded, "the producers have held them back in order to demand truly unconscionable prices."[32] Jagow himself set the blame squarely on potato wholesalers.[33]

For shoppers in poorer areas of the city and for the wider Berlin public, the "battle scenes" in the streets became a central focus of attention. Berliners read in all the papers about "tumultuous scenes," "the struggle for potatoes," and "potato battles"; they heard of the street scenes by word of mouth.[34] As police reports assert, the image of an inner, economic war began to eclipse public discussion even of military campaigns. Indeed discussions of the war itself often related specifically to prospects for a regularized food supply (and damage to England's supply).[35] Authorities were in no wise blind to the possibility that particular military strategies might help assuage protesting urban dwellers.

But within the population hardest hit by the shortage and price of potatoes, even economically oriented military news could not divert attention from the immediate circumstances. Commissioner Jagow reported to the interior minister, "The submarine battle against the English merchant fleet has been watched very closely. . . . The confidence in a victorious outcome in the world arena has remained. Those in the lower classes of the population are however less confident, in regard to the food question," presumably convinced that this was an inner war.[36] By the first week in March 1915, police opened their reports with concern over food rather than with the customary reference to military events, or even with the politically charged national conference of left Social Democrats convening in Berlin on the fifth of the month or the "women's" peace demonstration at the Reichstag on the eighteenth.

Until February, officers began their reports by noting the response of "the public" to wartime events before commenting on the reaction of "the populace" to questions of unemployment, housing, and especially food supply. Now police spies began to conflate descriptions of public opinion (bourgeois, cerebral, and rational) and popular sentiment (working class, especially women; emotional; and irrational) for the first time in reports. In an account displaying a significant departure from earlier descriptions, the usually irrepressibly cheerful Officer Arthur Starost commenced his report on 3 March 1915, "The broad mass of the people have demonstrated discontent regarding the rising price of food. The potato question is the most important, the most burning, since the potato plays such an important role for the poorer population." Officer König noted that "the populace" applauded the successful submarine campaign, while "the public" responded with pessimism to a new measure concerning food.[37]

COALESCENCE OF THE *MINDERBEMITTELTE*

The real crisis in basic foods drew the attention of many Berliners and other urban consumers away from the battle front and to the question of adequate nourishment. The experience of attempting to procure enough food each day and being at the mercy of individuals who seemed to withhold available supplies also powerfully influenced perception. These circumstances inspired Berliners to debate the plight of "those of little means." Initially newspapers, organizational tracts, and police reports employed almost exclusively more customary terms of socioeconomic stratification. From fall 1914, police and press reports noted typically that "the working class is ever more united" against the scarcity of bread, and that the price of potatoes had elicited "indignation" and "dismay" particularly among "the working population," "those in worker neighborhoods," and "the workers."[38] Such categories remained in use. At the same time, however, observers began to use other forms of description more frequently. Police reports from December indicate that "the 'potato question'" worried the entire "poorer population," and that "particularly in the lower circles," the lack of potatoes was a "calamity."

In the first months of 1915 "those of lesser means" took hold as a meaningful social identity.[39] Germans had long employed such terms, particularly around issues of subsistence. "Of lesser means" initially implied a disadvantageous relation to wealthier consumers; chroniclers depicted the latter, however, without the comparative dimension, simply as "those of means" or "the rich." "Of lesser means" bore a fortuitous vagueness, useful to describe persons who felt themselves "less well off" and the very poor. The term also described persons of minimal mental resources, pointing up the cultural belief that the poor (as well as women) were inherently unreasonable and incapable of thought that transcended their immediate circumstances. This observable shift in terminology was a product of two phenomena. The first was the attention of urban Germans to the scarcity of food. Berliners recast social categories according to a primacy of consumption and of means, monetary and otherwise. The second phenomenon producing an emphasis on those of lesser means was the emiseration of the population that traveled up the socioeconomic hierarchy. By the time of the potato calamity, police noted that "really deep-running despair and resentment in the populace" was now visible in the *Mittelstand* as well.[40] Terms such as *minderbemittelt* could and did constitute a broadening segment of the population. To look at it another way, the emphasis on consumption permitted social elision across hard productionist boundaries and allowed a new elasticity across a variety of categories, including gender as well as class. This was a function of the new commonality of defining experiences in the lives of those "from the bottom, up to and including circles of the *Mittelstand.*"[41]

"Those of little means" thus came to represent an alliance of interests that crossed prewar class lines to create a new kind of class. The usefulness of the term derived in part from its ambiguity and from its inclusion of an ever broadening population; in some sense, everyone conceived of himself or herself as part of it. This openness differentiated the category from the exclusively constituted population of soldiers' wives. In the coming months and years this ambiguity functioned well to hide differences among constituents, as it served the purpose of putting forth a united front against perceived enemies. High-level officials were keenly aware of this phenomenon and took steps to foster the more customary sense of distinction and distance, for example, among the police and other low-level civil servants from the working-class population. In mid-1915 they assigned police to the category of "heavy laborers," which won them better rations and also greater respectability as civilians in terms of serving the needs of the nation. The category also imputed masculinity to the police at a time when protesters scornfully asked why these able-bodied men spent their days watching hungry women rather than fighting the nation's enemy. At the same time, ironically, the categorization officially grouped policemen with (male) factory laborers.

Police, like journalists, however, continued to employ the nomenclature, even using *Minderbemittelte* interchangeably with "the consumers" and "those desirous of buying." Naturally, the local shopkeeper was also a consumer, both in the sense of providing for his or her own needs and as a customer of the wholesaler who provided the shop's wares, and merchants hastened to make this point. It was the merchant rather than the consumer aspect of the shopkeeper's total identity that others emphasized, however, including impoverished members of the *Mittelstand,* the merchant's former class equals.

Another important transformation in the use of societal categories, both as cause and effect of the emphasis on procurement of food, was observers' explicit feminization of those of little means. Officer Rhein described a scene of "thousands of women" seeking potatoes, adding that "all women as well as men find the government guilty" of brooking these circumstances.[42] Officer Kurtz wrote, "Market halls have been closed to the general public, particularly in the east, and the women can choose only to go to the grocery stores."[43] In alternation with terms such as *Minderbemittelte,* women were identified as the population constituting the long lines for potatoes.[44]

It was women to whose sentiments police and journalists alike attended and whose words observers reproduced. "As all women reported, it hasn't been possible to get potatoes anywhere in the east and northeast of the city since last Friday."[45] Thus, "the great potato privation in Berlin and the suburbs . . . is making women really very depressed indeed."[46] One can easily account for the feminized description. Just as Wilhelmine Germans customarily figured the universal worker as a man, so they cast the consumer as a woman. This feminization was rendered more striking by the greater percentage of women visible in the streets. The time women now needed to spend in the streets in order to procure food magnified this visibility. The participation of men in queues for potatoes and the prominence of men in lines for coal did not revise this generalized image.

At the same time, men felt able to identify with this feminized icon. The earlier animus of the poorer population against various feminized categories was rare to find by February and March 1915. The limiting of unusual privilege in the form of the temporary means testing for separation allowances may have contributed to observers' rethinking these gendered identities as might have the expansion of benefits to the unemployed. This transformation in public perception of female images continued, however, even after separation allowances were reinstated, in March. The new image of the female consumer held no position of exclusivity; it embraced ever growing numbers of the Berlin population (men and women) who felt that they, too, counted among the victimized. Now the prominent feminized role was one with which large numbers of Berliners and even outsiders identified rather than fought against. It may be no coincidence that representations of Germania, following on very male-centered images of the nation at war, enjoyed a resurgence in this period.[47]

By early 1915 the wider public expressed support for those "of lesser

Franz Stassen postcard, 1915. "A call like thunder stormed!" Germania rallies the troops. A strong female warrior leading the troops first appeared as a popular wartime image in early to mid-1915, corresponding to the changing image of women and the war. (BAPK, file 5796)

means" and "the poorer population," as indicated by newspapers and organizational publications of all political stripes. Police reported, "There is generalized vexation noticeable over the rise in bread prices for the poorer population," and "The ever rising cost of foods is creating concern among the entire population . . . in light of the new potato deficiency . . . in the poorer circles of the population."[48] Yet the wealthier population had been reluctant to demonstrate support for demands of the working class before the war began. This expression of affinity between richer and poorer Berliners perhaps developed more easily because *die Minderbemittelte* did not bear the same stigma for the well-to-do bourgeois as "the workers." The feminization of the category was salutary in the same way. Bourgeois Germans imagined the threatening worker who engaged in protest on the shop floor and who voted for the Social Democratic Party (SPD) as male. However, members of bourgeois women's groups tended to cast working-class women as passive sisters who needed to be helped by their social superiors.

The lower *Mittelstand* had always enjoyed the respect and concern of the wealthier classes, at least nominally. The lower middle class represented the backbone of *das Volk,* the rock of German culture. It was important to Germans who defended the class system that the lower middle class not be allowed to slide too deeply in neediness — into the straits, that is, of the working class. Thus, bourgeois observers both joined members of the lower middle class to workers on the basis of available means for consumption and still perceived them as distinct on the basis of their production-centered cultural differences. This paradoxical taxonomy also won "those of little means" the active empathy of wealthier Berliners.

To be sure, the paucity of bread and potatoes exacerbated economic polarization along the traditional class spectrum. Individuals financially well off before the war compensated for bread and potato shortages with more luxurious foods. Germans in many positions attained new wealth under the conditions of war. At the same time, all Berliners claimed they had suffered some discomfort in their efforts to obtain the most normal German foods, and this, too, motivated sympathetic responses for those who suffered most.[49] The liberal *Vossische Zeitung* and other papers denoted the class of injured as "we consumers," casting all consumers as a single interest group — here against the anonymous rural producer.[50]

Urgent, imperative demands for action in the name of *die Minderbemittelte* dominated police reports by early 1915, demands police officials communicated to ever higher levels of authority. Sergeant Schwarz opined in the midst of the potato unrest that "a confiscation of potatoes from producers and wholesalers, as is the case with bread grains, would be very appropriate."[51] He made the observation still more emphatically two days later: "Only a confiscation of potatoes from producers and wholesalers, as with bread grain, can create some change and mitigate the need."[52] Still suppressing such forthright suggestions, Commissioner Jagow himself recommended, "It is absolutely necessary that the population, who have been told of the abundant supplies of potatoes through the press, speeches, etc., be assured that these supplies will not be disturbed." He "urged a proclamation to this effect, in order to quiet the population."[53] By now proclamations were not enough.

The press reinforced this distinction between disadvantaged consumers and their enemies. The Social Democratic papers found the emphasis on consumption-centered categories useful for its own purposes in winning back members, thus continuing its balancing act between supporting the civil peace — indeed touting its constituents' contributions to the war effort — and criticizing state domestic policy.[54] The *Schwäbische Tagewacht* cried, "Defenseless are the consumers now that potato-profiteering has been delivered upon them: the prices that are demanded must absolutely be paid! . . .

A *deep bitterness* fills millions of citizens of the German state."[55] The article decried the war speculators waged against "the consumers," "the *minderbemittelte* classes of the populace," and even German citizens, eliding the categories. The liberal *Freisinnige Zeitung* explicitly differentiated "the consuming population" from "those of little means." But the effect was the same. The paper maintained that the Bundesrat "cares for the needs of those of little means before anyone else. Others besides those of little means are also going without. Is that fundamentally righteous? We think: No!"[56] The article closed by demanding the new Imperial Potato Agency actually meet its goal of distributing potatoes equally.

This collective consumer persona was not only feminine; she was explicitly urban and, in the capital, a Berliner. Democratic activist and publisher Hellmut von Gerlach noted dolefully in the *Welt am Montag* that there were "virtuous . . . and less virtuous producers," whose victims he named alternately as consumers, housewives, and Berliners.[57] Berliners set themselves up against purportedly malicious Brandenburg farmers, the generalized rural population, and Germans in other parts of the country. Berlin lord mayor Wermuth complained via the Städtetag that Bavarians were refusing to share their abundant resources with their neighbors to the north, a notion reflected in popular parlance. As various states and localities (fearful of their own disadvantage) proclaimed new export restrictions, they reinforced for Berliners the vision of the inner economic war.[58]

At the same time, Berliners described this poor, urban consumer as expressly German. The *Berliner Morgenpost* exclaimed, "One could hardly imagine a worse enemy of Germany than this speculation business."[59] The *Reichsbote* equated the "poor consumer" with "we Germans" and "the people" (*das Volk*) against foreign foes as well as internal enemies who threatened the civil peace, establishing an equivalence between protagonists in the military and economic wars.[60]

This generalized empathy toward impoverished consumers bears similarity to earlier moments of subsistence crisis in German lands, France, England, and elsewhere. It also represents a qualitatively new move. In the case of eighteenth-century Europe, scholars have long noted the role of the bourgeoisie in validating the right of poor women to bread for their families. In the case of World War I Germany, poor women consumers seemed to act through their demonstrations — and even by standing quietly in line — as representatives for the interests of the larger urban communities. The support of the urban bourgeois public for poor women's demands for state confiscation of farmers' goods is remarkable. Moreover, the language of this public support suggests that those of lesser means had a civil right,

*"The Inner Enemy." The Dragon Selfishness steals food from Germans' mouths, aiding the outer enemy. (*Simplicissimus, *21 June 1916)*

rather than simply a natural right, to make such claims. The broad public now seemed willing to find working-class Germans, at home as on the front, "patriotic" and ready to "hold out" in the interests of their nation.[61] Public figures demanded that the government respond by supporting these patriots, compensating their efforts and enabling them to play their appropriate part.

At the same time, a sense of fear played a role as much as empathy for and even identity with those of little means, a response that also mirrored eighteenth- and nineteenth-century episodes of unrest. Wealthier consumers were anxious to deflect blame from themselves, avert the spread of unrest, and for many, protect Germany's military position. *Der Deutsche Kurier* defensively asserted that the fault lay precisely in the unbridled urban discussion of food shortages and protests: "To the pleasure of all the readers of the hate- and lie-mongering yellow press abroad, it has been reported: Germany is starving."[62] But richer Berliners responded publicly at least to news of unrest by reinforcing popular demands for official action.[63]

Soon this concern to demonstrate support for those of lesser means spread to representatives of the commercial and agricultural worlds as well. Retailers and farmers hoped to cast off accusations of profiteering. They also hoped to help reimpose order on the streets of Berlin. By December 1914 the *Deutsche Tageszeitung,* organ of the League of German Farmers, asserted that "the nourishment of the people" was a compelling government responsibility. By February 1915, articles pleaded for "greater understanding for the farmer" and for "greater friendliness and understanding among our people" and "the *entire* people."[64] By April the *Tageszeitung*'s pages demanded in the name of "the leading men of German agriculture" that potato rations for the population "of lesser means" be raised, and that this distribution be ensured before the rest of the populace received more.[65] To be sure, this measure put the burden on consumers rather than producers, but the demand for intervention was the same. Likewise, the *Berliner Börsen Kurier,* representing commercial interests, called for the protection of poorer consumers against the profiteering in potatoes.[66] In the midst of the disturbances in mid-February, the liberal *Berliner Tageblatt* published a column demanding state protection of the poor consumer against the outrages of the wholesaler; the negative description of the merchant could not help but further inflame the populace.[67]

Prussian and imperial authorities felt paralyzed. Officials knew that any reallocation of resources or control of distribution would arouse new conflicts, despite protests to the contrary. Moreover, military priority fixed limits on resources available for civilian use. Finally, controlling speculation, even if it were possible, would spell limits to the massive taxes thriving speculators paid, even as the Reichstag voted up war credits again in late March, not to mention injury to the close relation between the state and both industrial and agricultural interests.[68]

Officials recognized the new symbolic significance of the population of lesser means in wartime urban German society. The potato price ceiling of November 1914 as well as the bread and flour rationing of January 1915 acknowledged the need to provide the "population of lesser means" with these goods, "in plentiful quantity."[69] In March the Bundesrat divided the Berlin population according to standards of lesser means and better off (*wohlhabend*), distributing ration cards permitting Berliners in the former category to purchase potatoes at a lesser price—though this strategy that divided consumers against one another soon fell victim to protest.[70] The *Freisinnige Zeitung* castigated officials for their "mechanical" division of the *Minderbemittelte* and the *Bemittelte,* startlingly recommending "generalized confiscation" of foodstuffs, so that the "pain of all consumers might be salved . . . before it is too late."[71] Still Prussian and imperial authorities continued to use the category of *minderbemittelt* in official capacity until the end of the war, in turn reinforcing popular use of the term. By 1915 it was the category by which officials accorded the right to use special municipal sale outlets, offering goods at "reasonable" prices, as long as there were goods to sell. Such means testing did set definite boundaries on who was and was not of little means, but these boundaries shifted throughout the war.

Such a response prevented those of little means from becoming a stigmatic category, serving rather as a description that united the population, despite the crude government reaction, in a positive fashion. Through this means a formally doubly disenfranchised population, composed predominantly of poorer women, secured a remarkable amount of societal power. In an attempt to forestall unrest, Reich officials continued throughout 1915 to demonstrate responsiveness to those of lesser means, expanding the system of rations and price ceilings. Official ability to meet successfully such demands represented an important barometer of general public satisfaction with the state. Herein lay the roots of a dynamic that suggested that the state's legitimacy could rest with the provision of services to a largely noncitizen population, often in conflict with military, agricultural, industrial, and commercial interests.

For consumers who stood in the streets seeking potatoes—largely poorer women whose movements observers so carefully followed—the implications in early 1915 were mixed. These women still faced with dread the daily task of trying to feed themselves and their families, frustrated by new mea-

sures that failed to treat the lack of access, angered by the increasingly rancorous interactions with merchants, and tired of finding and waiting end-
lessly in lines, resolutely defending their place, for food they might not even
procure. Poor consumers expressed cautious optimism with each new measure announced, pleased that officials recognized their circumstances. But
the ultimate failure of these measures substantially to transform prevailing
economic and social relations spurred renewed dismay and pessimism. As
chilling weather and early nightfall continued to thwart the efforts of tired
consumers, poorer Berliners remained quick to anger.

PEOPLE VERSUS PIGS

After the week of intense disruption and unrest over potatoes at shops
in the east of the city, the Bundesrat responded in mid-February by raising
the wholesale price ceilings on potatoes, as it had hinted it would. But something was wrong. No rush of potatoes materialized in shops and market
stalls. As *Vorwärts* stated provocatively, there was still a "potato deficiency,
despite the highest prices."[72] Berliners were furious. All eyes turned to the
farmers, who, it was rumored, continued to (now illegally) feed their potatoes to pigs rather than turn the vegetables over to wholesalers, even at a
higher price. Farmers protested that much of the harvest had already been
depleted, above all through the Bundesrat's own policy of substituting potatoes for grain, for both human and animal use.[73] Furthermore, they complained of difficulty in transporting potatoes to Berlin and elsewhere, as the
military had commandeered rail equipment.[74] Finally, they averred, the
shortage of workers, thanks to conscription, limited their ability to harvest
the potatoes, and much of the crop still lay in the ground at the time of the
first frost. Thus the farmers claimed that through no fault of their own, potatoes rotted in the ground and in silos, rendering them unsuitable for both
people and animals.[75]

The failure of potatoes to return to market following the rise in price ceilings led to the first sustained attacks on the state by street protesters; they
accused officials of indifference, incompetence, and subservience to the politically powerful East Elbian landowners. By the end of February, individuals claiming to represent popular opinion demanded that the state confiscate remaining potato supplies from farmers, challenging officials to prove
their intent to respond seriously to the prevailing emergency.[76] In late February Schöneberg communal leader Dr. Kuczunski asked in an ironically
posed query on the first page of the *Berliner Tageblatt,* "Where does the con-

fiscation of potatoes remain?"[77] In a forum on 4 March 1915, spurred on by popular demand, the Berlin city government pushed the state hard to take deeply interventionist steps, insisting that civilian officials confiscate all available stores of potatoes from farmers, just as military authorities had done to cover the needs of the troops.[78]

Here the government balked. The Interior Ministry stalled for time, issuing an ill-worded brochure directed at urban populations, insisting that "every German man and every German women must participate industriously to watch out for waste within their own families."[79] Officials extricated themselves from their difficult position in mid-March, finally, by publicly entertaining the possibility of ordering the large-scale slaughter of swine, part of a plan that authorities had discussed since late January. Officials hoped this measure would not only bring potatoes back to market but would also force down the price of pork, which had climbed steeply in the new year. Authorities wagered that such a measure would offend farmers less than full-fledged confiscations.[80] Still, this was a difficult step for the state to consider. As officials themselves imagined it, however, German civilians could cause the war to be lost over the food question.[81] The poorer population received the prospect of the slaughter of 9 or 10 million swine (as opposed to the 6 million butchered voluntarily by farmers the preceding year) with more unqualified enthusiasm than the coincident military slaughter in the Carpathians.[82] Poorer Berliners cheered for a "pig murder" (*Schweinemord*) as a sign of the demise of those creatures whose appetite stole food from the mouths of the German people, and as a symbol of death to the profiteering and other "swinish" qualities that marked producers.

Officials themselves had first raised the notion of direct competition between pigs and people. In early February, Center Party representative Matthias Erzberger wrote to the Imperial Office of the Interior, warning, "The pig is the greatest competitor with people because it feeds on that which people need for their own nutrition."[83] Nutritional expert Paul Eltzbacher warned the Reichstag of "the endangerment of our people's food supply through oversized swine stock"; his colleagues figured that "64 million people could eat off the same potatoes required for 10 million pigs."[84] In the 5 March Berlin municipal forum, SPD leader Emanuel Wurm questioned provocatively whether the nutritional needs of pigs or people would be served.[85] Landowners had carelessly played to this image, reinforcing the insult by delivering fodder potatoes to market. Still, by mid-March officials had not moved to make good on their proposal for a "St. Bartholomew's massacre of the swine," as the public demanded.[86] At the same time *Berliner*

Tageblatt editor Theodor Wolff wrote privately of the "long 'sausage' of trenches" that marked the western front, evoking the unpleasant image of the soldiers who filled this sausage, feeding the voracious war.[87] In an editorial titled "People, Pigs, and Potatoes," Hellmut von Gerlach demanded, "What is the story with the *potato,* which our people need as badly as the daily bread if they are not to starve?" Castigating the government for having thus far chosen to "do nothing," Gerlach continued, "Therefore, on with it, honorable government! Full steam ahead! Ten million must bleed on the altar of the fatherland, as soon as possible. And if they won't be led there voluntarily, as evidence has suggested, then the state must force them there. *Without pigs, it's o.k. Without potatoes, it's not o.k.* We've heard enough of pretty exhortations. Let us *finally* see some action!"[88]

As they awaited action, poorer Berliners turned the aspersion around, associating the porcine animal not with themselves but with those who raised it, as well as with those who could afford to eat its meat. The Social Democratic press buttressed this inversion, confirming that the farmers themselves were greedy pigs whose potatoes ought to have been simply confiscated after all.[89] The image worked neatly in reverse and functioned in turn to reinforce popular animus against the new economic enemies, including agricultural producers. The great variety of German associations with "pig," such as "dirty pig," "pig's business," and "pig's mess," suggested a messy business run by sneaky, greedy, and immoral types whose obesity spoke to their eating well.[90] Berliners traditionally referred to neighborhood policemen as "pig buttocks" (*Schweinebacke*), indicating their disaffection and disdain for these figures.[91] Now such terms of abuse took on new significance. Officials referred to the foreign enemy off the record as curs (*Schweinehunde*); the populace turned the insult inward.

In light of the continuing shortages and worsening popular outlook, the Eltzbacher commission counseled that authorities act rapidly in beginning the slaughter.[92] The state had relied on these experts to provide the rosiest predictions regarding German food supplies. Their mid-March report varied significantly from those in August and December, claiming indeed that Germany should never have begun an extended war without food stocks, long-range planning, and structures of control. The March report also officially confirmed that deficient supplies could be traced in part to the malice of producers and merchants alike.[93] Finally, following on the heels of the Berlin city government, the SPD Reichstag faction did, as promised, propose a bill demanding government confiscation of all potato supplies on 10 March.[94] In doing so, they referred to the voice of poor consumers, who in turn likely

"'Care of Youth.' The hungry wanderer: 'Oh to be a pig!'" (Ulk, *9 August 1918*)

came upon the idea of confiscation in the pages of the party's papers. In response imperial authorities agreed at last to the forcible slaughter, ordering that it begin that week.[95] The Reichstag proposal for confiscation was immediately tabled, and the question of confiscation temporarily abated. Officials set the order of slaughter to remain in effect until potatoes returned to the market. This did not occur until May, by which time a full third of Germany's swine stock had been sacrificed.

But the government's victory was short lived, for state measures failed to attend to merchant practices. Potatoes no sooner reached the market than they disappeared again, especially from the poorer neighborhoods. Poorer Berliners protested that now the shopkeepers were "holding back," saving potatoes for "special customers," or storing them until they rotted, in order to drive up prices. The press reported a session of the Conservative-dominated Prussian assembly in which a member claimed, in an effort to demonstrate that news of price hikes were exaggerated, that he knew a Prussian official who had purchased a *Zentner* of potatoes for a mere 3,70. The report met with grave public dismay.[96] Pork itself returned quickly to "fantasy prices," despite its renewed abundance.[97]

The inaccessibility of pork created a new problem for Berliners. Although pork had never held the place of centrality in the working-class diet that bread and potatoes occupied, the meat was still a "most important" food source, symbolically and materially, for the entire population. Bread times, when bread was all one could afford, signified a time of misery, of famine. Berlin historian Ernst Kaeber claimed, "In the last decades before the war, meat was the most important food next to bread and potatoes. This was the case through nearly all of Germany, but was all the more so in the major cities."[98] Food expert Max Rubner, too, claimed that Germans, including the poorer population and urban Germans especially, were meat eaters, for "meat had become in Germany a 'food of the people,' which even the little man took care to eat nearly every day." As Berliners put it, "Better a louse in the cabbage than to have no meat." Meat consumption had jumped from 36 to 52 kilograms per German per year between 1897 and 1912. On the eve of war Germans ate as much as they would eat in the federal republic in 1956.[99] The increase was concentrated, above all, on pork. In 1913 Germans consumed 400 percent more pork than they had eaten in the mid-nineteenth century.[100] Pork was the German meat of choice.[101] In prewar conditions, pork had served in some sense to reinforce a symbiotic class difference. The rich and poor ate different cuts and parts; the same animal served both.

From early in the war, however, "the poorer population" could no longer afford this important source of fat and protein.[102] Meat prices began to rise in November 1914, especially as suppliers could sell it at extremely high prices to the army.[103] Farmers argued that the cost of fodder and the limitations on their use of potatoes as fodder drove up the cost. By February, pork prices had become completely "unaffordable . . . for the poorer circles of the population," which Berliners of modest means felt to be particularly unbearable in light of the concomitant potato deficiency and the high price of bread. Poorer Berliners' inability to afford drippings, or *Schmalz*, which they used most often as a spread for bread and which had risen from 80 to 140 pfennig per kilo, sent poor consumers into lines for jam. In response, shopkeepers raised the price of jam to new heights.[104] The Bundesrat tried to anticipate the meat shortage that would result from limiting potato foddering and ordered all localities of over 5,000 residents to provide inhabitants with coupons for 15 marks of preserved meat. But again the impact was short term.[105]

So once more poorer Berliners moved from despair to anger and "great agitation."[106] Jagow reported to his superiors in May, as the slaughter order was lifted, "The butchers themselves admit that the price especially for pork is unjustifiably high. In any case, the opinion is now widespread that, in this regard, everything is not in order, and that the speculator has his hand in the game." He warned, "It is precisely this conviction that has turned the otherwise general depressed lassitude regarding price hikes into a fiery resentment. To be sure, above all with regard to the worker circles, who are not fearful of the danger of unrest, it is effecting a disadvantageous mood everywhere."[107]

Imperial officials responded yet again, following the recommendation of the Eltzbacher commission, offering "extra rations" of fresh pork specifically "to the population of little means, at the cheapest possible price."[108] The city of Berlin took great strides to build on the imperial measures. In the aftermath of the great slaughter, the city spent more than 14 million marks to create a store of smoked and preserved meats for its residents.[109] Nonetheless, in May police continued to report "unjustified" and even "usurious" increases in pork as well as potato prices and found the municipal stores little relief, precisely because they favored only a limited portion of the population.[110] Official and press reports noted that difficulty in obtaining pork had spread from "lower civil servants and workers" to "members of the middle and lower strata," "the majority of inhabitants," and finally, "consumer circles," portrayed in direct conflict with "userers" and "speculators."[111]

In the summer of 1915, trade sanctions by the neutral countries against Germany cut the supply of fodder, pushing the price of pork still higher; overall, Berliners now spent an average of 40 marks a month on food, in contrast with 23 marks a year earlier. Jagow observed explicitly that concern for those of lesser means was creating broad ill will throughout the population, eliciting for the first time widespread calls for peace.[112] Dubbing profiteers "war extenders," many now asked pointedly, If Germany were doing so well in this defensive war, why was the nation still fighting? Jagow counseled immediate, still more far-reaching intervention, in the state's own interest.[113]

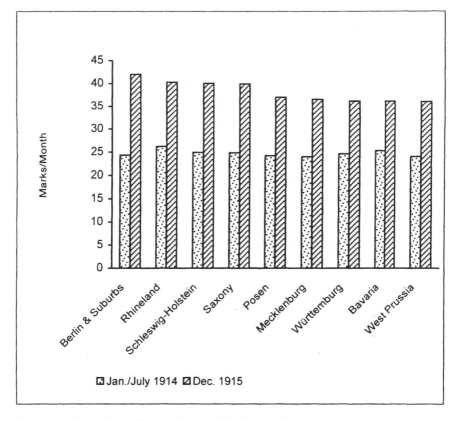

Figure 3.1. Average Expenditures on Food per Month, 1914 and 1915
Source: Zimmermann, "Veränderungen," 428.

PROFIT VERSUS PATRIOTISM

In the course of early 1915 the axis of conflict over food shifted from privilege to profit. From the beginning of the year, poorer consumers and others protested regularly against the "profit-coveting speculator" and his "exploitation of the consumer," rendering an an unjust economy of sacrifice.[114] Police observed housewives searching for affordable pork at shops in the imposing shadow of the city's huge central slaughterhouse off the Landsberger Allee. These circumstances "would be easier to bear if the opinion weren't so widely entertained that the high prices are not a justifiable product of the circumstances and are, rather, for the most part to be chalked up to the arbitrariness of producers, speculators, and shopkeepers, against which the government has made insufficient use of its powers."[115] By late spring the rally against excessive profit inspired public protest against the injustice of profit *tout court,* at least under the prevailing circumstances. In May the Social Democratic *Grundstein* cast the interests of "capitalists" against those of "all other people," claiming that "the salesman had created the neediness of his fellow human."[116] In June 1915 the SPD demanded an "end to the 'profiting-out' [*Auswucher*] of the consuming population."[117] That Social Democrats should make such comments comes as little surprise. But many other segments of the population also publicly proclaimed these injustices.[118] Police filled the pages of their logs with records of such sentiments, from protest in the streets to the ubiquitous press commentary.

Following notions with a long prewar genealogy across the political spectrum, many Germans, including political leaders, were suspicious of the market's purported natural tendency to regulate itself appropriately. The growing absence in these months of any relation between the income of most Germans and the price of food seemed to confirm these suspicions. For increasing numbers of Berliners, it was not government-controlled prices that were artificial and arbitrary, as merchants and farmers had charged. Rather, it was the price set by the wholesaler and the merchant, who "played around with the food supply," that bore these qualities. Presumably, poor urban consumers perceived the fair price to be close to immediate prewar prices, adjusted perhaps for still-lingering high unemployment rates. But consumers demonstrated satisfaction with any ceiling, at least initially, in the hopes that the amount represented a secure price that they could count on.[119] Thus, from the period of the potato riots on, reports of popular opinion are rampant with references to the "arbitrariness" of wholesalers and the "artificial setting of prices" by the shopkeeper.[120] This maddening arbitrariness referred also to the merchants' freedom to impose their own "taxonomies" on the public, via customer lists and "coupons," modeled after government rations but available only to some, determining who warranted food and who did not. Berliners focused particularly on the middleman, a bogey largely visible only through the effects of his misdeeds.[121] Berliners in Friedrichshain claimed to have seen good evidence of this. On a market day in mid-February they observed over 30,000 swine for sale in the main slaughterhouse, while nearby shops stood empty of pork.[122] Middlemen, rumor had it, bought only about 10,000 of these, hoping through artificial scarcity to drive up pork prices. Worse still, the remaining pigs needed to be fed. Whether or not there was truth to this rumor, public discourse cast consumers "in the lower and lesser-meaned population" as victims of the despised trade through middlemen (*Zwischenhandel*).

The idea of profit as evil bears a complicated genealogy, sketched only briefly here. German Lutheranism as well as Catholicism posed a long-standing antipathy to the notion of profit and, thus, to the pursuit of capitalism, as German Städtetag leader Hans Luther noted in his postwar memoirs.[123] For contemporary adherents to social democracy, the case against profit had been developed in full, deriving from theories of both political economy and moral socialism. Among some segments of the lower middle class as well as among workers, the middleman played no defensible role in the economy, particularly with reference to food. Such beliefs, in part hearkening back nostalgically to village-centered economic relationships, remained a more or less recessive tendency for many low- and middle-income Germans, a tendency that revealed itself under particular stresses in the course of industrialization and urbanization. The tens of thousands of poorer recent migrants to the metropolis from the German countryside likely perceived the problem acutely. In light of this, it is not surprising that concern over profit emerged in the battle of consumer interests that characterized the war years, as the number of middlemen burgeoned for any transaction over food. The terms "usurer," "usury," and "usurers' prices" (*Wucher,* also the word for speculation) proliferated in both oral and written descriptions of the food situation. In 1915, Werner Sombart penned *Merchants and Heroes,* disparagingly comparing the English "shopkeeper's soul" with the more noble and heroic German soul.[124]

In light of government propaganda that had expressed the unity of all Germans in the cause of the nation, many urban consumers began to suggest that profit was unpatriotic. That is, within the vision of an economic war, Germans who profited at the expense of their countrymen and countrywomen sundered the ties that bound them and even demonstrated their enmity. Moreover, poorer consumers asserted forcefully that the merchant stood to sabotage the cause of the military war by making it impossible for the consumer population to hold out, despite its willingness to sacrifice. The Social Democratic *Offenbacher Abendblatt* condemned the "business patriots" who exploited their "fellow humans," revealing their coldhearted loyalty to a false leader, the god of wealth.[125] Berlin-based *Vorwärts* provocatively described the situation in terms of historical materialism: "The businessman *must* take advantage of the situation . . . or he wouldn't be a good businessman. . . . [He says,] as a good person, I must give a thousand marks for the Red Cross; I must stick the public for 100,000, otherwise I wouldn't be a good businessman."[126] As Officer Schade expressed grimly a year later, "One endures great difficulties just to survive. As this characterizes primarily the population of little means and the lower civil servants, bitterness toward the rich, the rural producers, and the merchants grows daily. In general," he concluded, "one regards these latter as the most evil enemies who do not possess the slightest glimmer of love for fatherland and for fellow man. The war has provided only a golden opportunity for these types."[127] Protesters, police, journalists, social reformers, and others characterized such practices as governed by a despicable principle of self-interest in a time when civilians claimed they had risen above their own interests.[128]

In response to this sense of exploitation, poorer Berliners issued an ultimatum to the state. In the summer of 1915, protesting consumers demanded that officials confiscate virtually all scarce basic food goods from these traitors and distribute them equally.[129] Such an act would restore appropriate economic relations, protect the German people, and facilitate the prosecution of war. The failure of officials to do so, as police reports represented popular opinion, would cast the state as traitor to its own people — and to the nation. This challenge contained specific demands as to what the state must do, demands that had been radicalized over the preceding months as less severe tactics appeared to have failed. Protesters drew on marginal concepts long in service or on existing concepts that now took on new meaning, calling for redistribution of the municipal burden (*Lastenausgleich*), a "new orientation," and an incorruptible "food dictator."[130] Demand for a food dictator drew on the long-standing desire of radical right-wing Germans for a military-controlled government that could lead the nation successfully through an aggressive war.[131] As popular perception emerged that the military governed efficiently, successfully, and with foresight (as evidenced by, for example, the victory at Tannenberg and the army's relative success in keeping soldiers fed), a broad swath of urban society pinned its hopes on the idea of a strong, uncompromising, and possibly military leader.

As Berliners transformed the content of each notion in popular usage, a new, apparently unified social vision arose. Poorer Berliners wanted a centralized authority that would apportion all foodstuffs "equitably." Protesters' demands, inspiring ever greater acclamation, contained harbingers of both radical left and radical right politics. Through this rhetoric Berliners began to develop a new politics of entitlement, though the bases for this perceived entitlement varied widely among different populations and over the course of the war. For some this entitlement related to basic human needs; for others it was instead (or also) connected to one's contribution to the war effort. Some Berliners based their demands on their identity as citizens or proto-citizens. For others this was also a question of national identity, in an inclusive and sometimes quite exclusive sense. At this moment, however, popular demands and their bases appeared unified, representing the coincident interests of populations regarded as widely diverse when examined through a lens of antiprivilege and antiprofit. As Jagow asserted to his superiors in July 1915, the state must act to throw its lot with poor consumers or it would be seen as against them.[132] The Conservative *Post* averred that it was the state itself that battled the people in the economic war. This normally staunch defender of Wilhelmine politics commented in February 1915, "Unfortunately, the government appears to be more inclined to respond to the wishes of the producers and merchants than to the righteous demands of the consumers."[133]

Commentators thrust the role of bearers of the culture and defender of the nation onto the *Minderbemittelte*. In turn, it appears that protesters in the streets began to speak in these terms themselves. Increasingly, civil servants joined in the chorus, linking hunger and unfair distribution of food to the degeneration of German culture and of Germanness and reporting demands for definitive government measures to end the manipulation of prices. Officer Gerhardt claimed, "For the greater mass of the lower civil service and lower middle class it also represents privation, and this can bring only economic, moral, and cultural downfall as a result."[134] By late summer, poor consumers on the streets, simultaneously empowered and frustrated in their quest for affordable food, began to threaten the state with a call for peace at any price, in the economic and the military war.

4 BATTLES OVER BUTTER

The lack of pork meat and fat in the spring of 1915 put increasing pressure on the supply of butter in the fall and winter of that year. The butter question riveted Berliners' attention in the fall as the potato question had some months earlier, due to the importance of fats, both physiologically and culturally, to the diet of urban Germans and to the scarcity of fats in wartime. The combined insufficiency and high cost of dairy and meat fats and the perceived injustice of their distribution led to the most numerous and threatening episodes of unrest yet experienced in wartime Berlin. These episodes, beginning in mid-October 1915, continued on and off in Berlin for some nine months and spread to cities around the country. Authorities at every level, including military officials, took the unrest seriously and responded both with further interventionist measures and with stepped-up surveillance in Berlin and around the country.[1] Women of little means remained prominent in the new crises over dietary fats. Despite the escalation of protest, police spies, journalists, and other commentators privileged this population as legitimate and reasonable, in contrast with men and youth and in juxtaposition to the government's perceived unreasonable and ineffectual responses. The pressure that women of little means in tandem with other societal groups exerted on Prussian and imperial authorities helps to explain the state's move to a new level of commitment in caring for the needs of the broad urban populace. The butter riots and their aftermath provide an especially clear moment of transformation in relations between state and society, as imperial authorities continued to legitimate demands to serve the populace's needs as Germans while failing to address those demands adequately.

THE FAT DEFICIENCY AS A POINT OF CRISIS

Germans had increased their fat intake tremendously in the decades before the war. This rise was related in part to the increase of meat in their diet. The intake of butter had also grown enormously, nearly matching the amount of meat consumed.[2] Contemporary figures suggest that Germans consumed a weekly average of 275 grams of butter, pork fat, margarine, and vegetable oil, for a total fat intake of about 300 grams a week.[3] (The current U.S. Department of Agriculture recommendation is about 350 grams per week. The increase around the turn of the century should not necessarily be seen as an acquired need only, particularly for hard-laboring Germans.) The rise was particularly notable in urban centers.[4] The dramatic change was a result of the tremendous growth in domestic dairy farming and swine husbandry as well as the rising import of fats, which unlike that of other goods, was not restricted in the last decades of the nineteenth century.[5] In turn, the perceived satisfying nature of dishes prepared with fats seems to have encouraged demand for such products as available and affordable. Germans desired fats also for their association with luxury and modern, urban living. At the same time, fats had quickly become an acquired need, a fact that was integrated into the culture at all levels. The new coterie of nutritional experts generally agreed that fats were the central element in good nutrition.[6] Popular opinion on the eve of war held that animal and dairy fats, specifically in the form of lard and butter, were virtually as fundamental and important to the German diet as bread and potatoes.[7]

This opinion fit well with long-standing notions specific to working-class culture, which maintained that food must be "hearty" and "bodily warming," particularly in the winter months.[8] These qualities were all the more important during northern Germany's cold, wet winters. In this era of affordable and regular fat consumption, at least in Berlin, workers consumed more fat per week than any other segment of the German population.[9] This consumption may have been related in part to factory laborers' desire for fat calories, which relatively prosperous Berlin workers were able to attend to, and which became an ever more urgent need under the exhausting conditions of wartime industrial labor.[10] In local Berlin parlance "fat" was synonymous with "wages"; it went together with bread.[11] This dietary emphasis was not unique to Berlin. Fats and fatty foods fulfilled the three dietary desiderata of contemporary Rhenish workers: they provided a minimum of dietary fat, they aided in the preparation of a daily warm meal, and they could provide a delicacy eaten just for its taste (*Leckerei*).[12]

Thus the German diet in this era, especially in urban centers and including that of the poorer population, relied heavily on fats. Germans most often prepared food with lard, butter, or vegetable fat. Boiling one's food was nearly as unacceptable as having no hot meal at all.[13] Still more important was the role of fat (as lard or butter) as a spread for bread. "Butter bread" (*Butterbrot, jeschmierte Schrippe*) was the material and symbolic center of the working-class diet. It was also important for the lower middle class. Hence the ironic police report in August 1917: "The rations of bread have been raised; therefore the lack of fat is felt more sharply than ever."[14] Raised rations in the most basic foods of the people fueled the need for more fats, despite the cheerful exhortation of the National Women's Service that "eating dry bread makes one's cheeks red."[15] Lard and butter were closely related to each other in the German cultural taxonomy through this identical use.

Berliners consumed about twice the national average of butter, likely traceable to the local dairy industry and, in turn, the north German predilection for dairy fats.[16] Even so, butter in Berlin was more expensive than virtually anywhere else in the country just before wartime ceilings were set and nearly double its retail cost in Bavaria.[17] Bromides such as "She's missing the butter from her bread" telegraphed the essential nature of butter.[18] If "fat" meant "wages," "working for buttered bread" traditionally signified earning the lowest wages. At the same time, butter was an important element in the diet of wealthier Germans, in part because of its association with richness and luxury, as in the expression "It's all in (the best) butter."[19] Butter also symbolized the good life for members of the new *Mittelstand,* white-collar workers who wished to distance themselves from manual laborers.[20] These contradictory notions coexisted harmoniously while butter remained in good supply.

The exigencies of war came into conflict with the widespread demand for butter. The premium on butter increased in the second half of 1915, as it had earlier in the year on potatoes. Pork and pork fat had been expensive and in short supply from early 1915, aside from a brief summer hiatus following the pig slaughter. Moreover, even margarine and vegetable fats had become scarce and had risen enormously in price, rendering them nearly equal in cost with butter in Berlin. As a result, the importance of butter and the concomitant demand for this dairy fat grew greatly in the late summer and fall of 1915, particularly within the working class, which could no longer afford lard. In light of this shortage of meat fats in many areas around the country, butter drew unusual national demand. This agreeable substitution of butter for other, scarce sources of fat in wartime ought to have worked well enough, at least for Berliners. The surrounding Brandenburg countryside boasted more than 700 dairies, including some very large concerns, such as Bolle.[21] Yet even in Berlin butter was scarce by the fall of 1915. Domestic supplies were down considerably, a function of insufficient imported oilcake fodder for dairy cows. The press began reporting local butter shortages by July 1915. In light of shortages, the price of butter rose enormously from summer to fall in 1915. The price increase, which pushed the cost from 2,60 marks to 3,60 marks per pound,[22] rendered the product inaccessible to most of the working-class population as well as much of the lower *Mittelstand.*

The fall in domestic supply does not provide a complete explanation for the scarcity and price increase. Despite domestic production, on the eve of war Germany had still imported one-third to one-half of its butter supply, including from enemy Russia and Siberia, to accommodate national demand.[23] Wealthier Berliners particularly consumed foreign butter, which they perceived to have special cachet. While the product remained available from Holland, Denmark, and Sweden during the fall and winter of 1915, the cost of these imports had risen substantially, in part as a result of new competition with the dual monarchy for these goods. Finally, even these supplies were limited, as the neutral governments restricted exports to ensure their own domestic supply.[24] The loss of imports opened the domestic butter market to wealthier Berliners, which drove up prices of the domestic product and left shelves empty at shops in poorer areas.

Dwindling supply thus inspired merchant response in the form of higher prices. This in turn provoked poorer Berlin consumers to protest at a level that dwarfed earlier wartime unrest. Contemporary figurative associations of butter may have guided public response to the unavailability of the product. When retailers seemed to act deliberately to deprive poorer Berliners of their share of this staple—"to begrudge someone the butter on his or her bread"—the broad public displayed still more outspoken sympathy for poorer consumers than before. The counterpart expression, "not to let the butter be taken from one's bread," prefigured the response of poorer consumers, who fought fiercely to recover what they perceived as rightfully theirs. That one should "get one's fat" would seem to apply both to that which was due those of little means and to the "just deserts" that deceptive shopkeepers warranted.

In light of the cultural as well as physical dependency on such fats, the deficiency of butter, in combination with that of meat fat, "brought about the sharpest and perhaps most bitterly felt change in circumstances of the war."[25] Berlin saw generalized public condemnation of the perceived speculation, and there was widespread demand that the highest-level civilian and military officials take the matter more decisively under their control. Interior Ministry officials conceded that "the solution of no other food question showed itself to be so important, and related to [the quieting of] so many disturbances, as providing for butter."[26]

In the turbulent days between 14 and 19 October 1915, police detailed over fifty displays of "excesses" or riots.[27] These instances of unrest arose primarily over butter (approximately forty-two were reported). The riots were, as in the case of the February potato protests, concentrated primarily in a tiny segment of Greater Berlin, in this instance a radius of several blocks straddling the limits of the city proper (Friedrichshain) and the suburb of Lichtenberg, part of the predominantly working-class "Stralau quarter" on the city's north ring. Three years later this area would be a primary site of the revolution and civil war. One butter riot involving several thousand women took place on 16 October in Oberschöneweide, southeast of the city; by 18 October, riots had spilled into Neukölln and elsewhere. There were also ten episodes at butchers and meat shops, beginning on 16 October; these were concentrated in another established working-class neighborhood in "Red" Wedding.[28] If officials and the wider public feared the crowds primarily simply standing in line in February, they felt greatly threatened by these riots, each of which drew crowds from several hundred to six thousand, as a harbinger of sustained protest around the country.

Concerned parties named several different causes of the initial October riots. Police explicitly cited the high price of butter in eight cases, concentrated in the earliest reports. Prices in Berlin rose some 20 to 60 pfennig just before the protests began, to over 3,40 marks.[29] The failure of police spies to name this cause more frequently may have been based on their belief that the importance of cost in inspiring protest had been well established, and that it was more important to emphasize to their superiors the additional impetus of gratuitous merchant provocation of customers. The primary complaint police identified at both butter shops and butchers was shopkeepers' rudeness. Conversely, in only one of the fifty-odd reports on the mid-October episodes do police describe an altercation among customers themselves. This emphasis on shopkeeper provocation raised once more the specter of the internal economic war, in which consumers were pitted against merchants. The near-depletion of cheaper butter as well as of meat fat at municipal distribution centers in mid-October forced even the poorest shoppers to contend with "free market" prices, also helping push prices up.[30] The serious inadequacy of supplies at municipal outlets also directly caused protest in at least three cases, as shoppers who had waited in line for hours discovered that this butter had run out. Finally, the advent of cold, rainy weather both increased demand for fat and made waiting customers all the more uncomfortable and irritable.

Popular belief that private shopkeepers were holding back on supplies and otherwise tricking poorer customers also provoked protest. Police observed evidence of chain trade (*Kettenhandel*), encompassing what protesters found to be one of merchants' worst practices. In the wake of rapid industrialization, chain trade had referred at the turn of the century to the burgeoning of middlemen in the distribution of a product, arousing suspicion and concern for the product's just price. More than other food products of the time, butter and dairy goods were sold predominantly by a number of large franchises, another type of chain trade. Chain dairies such as Bolle and Assmann, which had replaced small, neighborhood-based establishments, had aroused mistrust from at least the milk wars of a decade earlier. In the fall of 1915, consumers traded rumors that these large dairies were relocating butter from their storefronts and wagons in poorer neighborhoods to those in wealthier locales, where they could both charge a higher rate for this coveted food and maintain or establish good relations with richer customers. This practice helps to explain the concentration of episodes before shops of a particular chain, such as the J. F. Assmann dairy. Unrest before Assmann franchises comprised sixteen of the forty-two named disturbances over butter in mid-October.[31]

The actors in these incidents appear to have been much the same types as those who protested in the February unrest over potatoes. Police and other officials identified participants most prominently as women, women of little means, and women of the working classes. They also characterized adolescent boys and, to a lesser degree, drunken men as regular protesters. This is not a surprising tableau of a food riot. In the contemporary political topos, each of the groups named "lacked reason," that which qualified one for public and formal political life. In the protest marking the first few days of demonstrations against butter prices, police distinguished little among participants. Officer Dittman's report regarding the disturbances on Saturday, 9 October, described the working-class "females" (*Weiber* [derogatory]) who participated in it as violent and coarse, though he did attribute their acts to the unreasonably high prices.[32] This description evoked the characterization of women, found in propaganda, as demonstrating "lack of understanding" and "exaggerated concern" for the food situation.[33] Police described youths and drunken men throughout the period as acting wantonly and "purposelessly" violent, caught up in the "crowd" mentality and the "rabble-rousing" tendencies associated with the "lowest masses."[34] They obeyed no "reason" and were thus controlled with difficulty, as they roamed the streets, hooting and howling, destroying show windows, and plundering goods. In an episode on 15 October, while other Berliners celebrated war hero Paul von Hindenburg's birthday, Lichtenberg police commissioner Max Lewald charged a crowd of several hundred, composed of "women and adolescent boys," with throwing rocks and pieces of coal to break shop windows; the descriptions evoke reports of eighteenth- and early nineteenth-century riots.[35]

After the first day or two of the October unrest, the descriptions changed, as police contrasted the behavior of women between the approximate ages of twenty-five and fifty with that of drunks and young boys (and sometimes "youth"; younger women and girls seemed to straddle the divide). Telegraphing the distinction, Lewald continued: "If, on one hand, it is true that these excesses can be traced to rabble-rousing boys, on the other hand, it must be acknowledged that the constant, astronomic climb in butter and fat prices has fomented an increasingly widespread agitation and embitterment" among the women. He demonstrated the gratuitous quality of the boys' violence by remarking on the sound financial standing of a boy who was arrested.[36]

By the next day, and virtually from that point on in the months to come, police identified only adolescent boys and street youths as the perpetrators in the "senseless" act of breaking windows.[37] Women, on the other hand—at least those not too irrationally old or boisterously young—assembled in protest of some specific grievance. Officer Marschke described an incident on 15 October on the Landsberger Avenue, not far from the Friedrichshain cemetery honoring Märzgefallene, those who died in protest in the revolution of 1848, and site of the annual radical March demonstration. "Before the Göbel butter shop at Landsberger Ave. 54, a number of women protested loudly against the higher butter prices and assumed threatening behavior, so that the manager of the shop closed early, at 6:30 P.M. After that, police easily enough dispersed the protest. However," he continued, "at 8:00 P.M. large crowds gathered anew. Provoked by the loud griping of particular bigmouths, the crowds began to howl, whistle, and even throw a couple of stones at the shop, which broke the shop's show window. When the attending officers attempted to intervene, stones were repeatedly thrown at them. . . . It was 11:30 before peace returned to the street. All in all, about five to six thousand people participated in the [later] riot; the majority here were adolescent boys." Driving the point home, Marschke concluded: "The women, insofar as they participated, responded to valid requests [to disperse and go home], while it was necessary to intervene energetically against the male, in part drunk, participants."[38]

Police rehearsed this scenario over and over, in Wedding as well as in Friedrichshain, emphasizing, moreover, shopkeepers' regular breach of the courtesy due fellow Germans, such as the "*loutish remarks of a merchant*" that rightfully drove women to protest.[39] Indeed, from 15 or 16 October, police attributed the women who they claimed composed the predominant population of protesters with near-rational motivation, acting in understandable and even appropriate fashion to express their rightful concerns and assert particular demands and ceasing protest when demands were met.[40]

Police reports now referred to women alternately as "persons" and even "the public," the term conventionally reserved for the citizen classes. Sergeant Schwarz blends the subjects "the public" and "working-class women" in his characterization of the protests overall; "the public" directly engaged in "rows" with "the merchant," because the merchant had speculated to the detriment of poor women.[41] In contrast, in the face of the "new assembly" of adolescents arriving after the shops had closed, officials "finally called in the mounted police to 'clean up the streets,'" as Officer Hanff rather menacingly reported.[42] Still, while police begrudged these youths little respect, they used the youth violence to demonstrate what could happen if officials failed to respond to women's demands. This paralleled policemen's indications that protesting women offered a glimpse into action that police themselves might be tempted to follow.[43]

Individual riots seemed to follow consistent patterns, as described by police spies. In turn, the dynamic of this period as a whole reflected a regular motif, as lower-level police styled it, accounting at once for events in the streets, for the press and political publications, and for official measures. Police reported a series of assemblies, emphasizing their gravity and relating them to the public mood more generally. They offered evidence of the press's and other public commentary of the day, including Social Democratic recommendations, all of which often seemed to have provided the source of the specific demands voiced by the populace.

Rather than simply summarizing and editing the contents of individual police reports during this week, Jagow passed them directly upward for the first time, into the hands of the high commander and the Prussian Interior Ministry, revealing the urgency they communicated. By the end of October, he sent copies directly to Bundesrat members and even to the kaiser. Authorities were on the whole greatly unnerved by the unrest. The highest-level civilian and military officials responded rapidly to each of the episodes as they received the daily reports, by attempting to meet popular desires in some form. Afterward a brief period of calm ensued, in which political policemen noted the "acknowledgment" and "welcoming" of the measures taken, and quiet would reign.[44] But then new unrest erupted. Police attributed the fresh outbreaks either to the inadequacy of the official response or

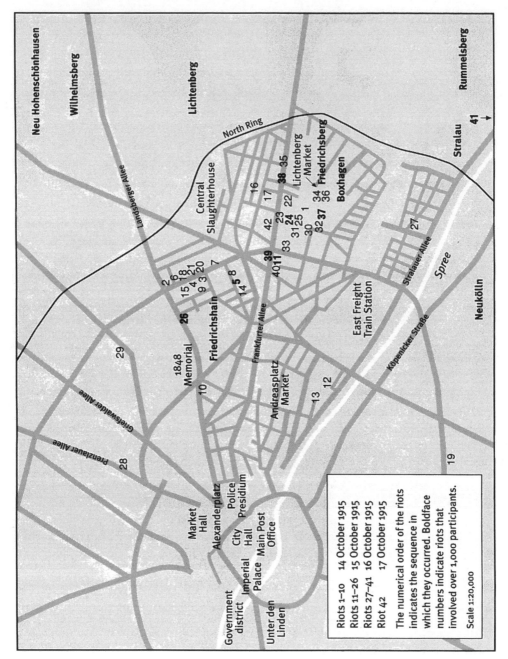

Butter Riots, 14–17 October 1915

to new, equally irksome circumstances. The period between 14 and 20 October offers two cycles of this pattern; officials themselves viewed these days as the opening of a potentially long interval of sustained serious protest.

The first cycle played out between 14 and 17 October, over the cost of butter and the belief that merchants held back butter supplies to drive up prices. Two small incidents of unrest over butter had taken place on Saturday, 9 October, but these did not yet appear to constitute a serious problem. To the chagrin of officials, the Berlin-based *Vorwärts* had published a short piece on 8 October, provocatively titled "A Victory over Consumers," concerning a "butter war" in Münster. The paper then followed on 11 October with an article on "butter riots" in Aachen. The latter item noted that consumers in Aachen protested the "monstrous" price of 2,85 marks per pound —some 60 pfennig lower than the price of butter in Berlin. The article concluded prescriptively, "It is becoming ever clearer that an improvement is possible only if the German imperial government fixes the wholesale and retail price of butter for the whole empire." On 13 October, police observed, *Vorwärts* printed an article on the local rising butter prices, alleging that the sudden high cost could be traced to merchant speculation, exacerbated by the maldistribution of butter among shops, which the government might have prevented.

On Thursday, 14 October, unrest in Berlin broke out over butter. Police detailed ten riots for that day alone; eight, together commanding crowds of several thousand protesters, took place before franchises of Assmann that stood within a four-block radius. Mid-level police officials responded, calling in reinforcements. Mounted police and officers in commandeered motor taxis prowled Friedrichshain between 6:00 and 10:00 P.M. the next evening, the peak times for both women's assemblies and those of adolescents.[45] Authorities also stepped up information control. Officials sped up production in the new Imperial War Press Office, which passed on news stories ready for print to all major dailies for the remainder of the war. At the same time, High Commander Kessel ordered redoubled efforts at press censorship, specifying pointedly that references to "all present and future butter riots" were to be stricken, revealing his concern for the press's role in provoking and maintaining discontent as well as for providing a showcase for protesters' demands.[46]

These measures had little effect on the cycle of protest already in progress. Assemblies before Friedrichshain- and Lichtenberg-area butter shops took place again in full force on the evening of 15 October. The dailies noted that municipal butter supplies were now drained, as in the *Vossische Zeitungs*'s evocative "The Mob Scene before the Municipal Sales Outlets."[47] Police spies commented that this represented the defeat of the city's best effort to avert conflict, and that responsibility lay further up the governmental hierarchy. They also warned that protest itself was beginning to spread, drawing in white-collar workers — including, presumably, their own class equals.[48] It can be no coincidence that police began to differentiate between gratuitous and meaningful protest at this time. Officer Sauer noted that women "continued the tumultuous street demonstrations, which are directed against the shameless exploitations of the German people."[49] Informers noted, moreover, that overall violence in the streets, though not directly related to protests of food prices, was on the rise, a problem not only for police but also for Berliners who spent so much of their time in the streets. Police reported numerous arrests on 15 October, evidence not of deterred but of increased activity. All told, as police cast it, protest was not about to wind down on its own; neither would information control nor increased security make a significant impact. They made their view on the matter plain: "Without a cut in the price of food, calm will not return."[50]

In contrast to Jagow's role some months earlier in aiding high-level officials to delude themselves, the police commissioner himself now minced no words in his communications to Loebell. "Unfortunately one must reckon with the continuation of these attacks . . . as long as these rising prices remain. I don't have to warn you of the importunate effects such events will have inter alia abroad."[51] Jagow asserted that the answer to the civil unrest was not to be found in greater police force but, rather, in political action to remove the sources of protest.[52] The petit bourgeois *Lokal Anzeiger* condemned the rising cost of butter as a product of merchant speculation allowed by the government. The conservative daily *Post* menacingly echoed the rhetoric of the inner war in its item titled "Battle against Rising Costs." The right-wing *Deutsche Kurier* warned still more threateningly of the rising prices and their consequent hardship on the populace.

The Bundesrat responded the next morning, describing in detail plans of the new Reich-wide Price Monitoring Authority (Preisprüfungsstelle, or PPS), which might seem to have represented the kind of expansive government planning the public sought. But now the press stepped in again, little hindered by the narrowly conceived censorship. Numerous papers juxtaposed official press releases on the body with editorial challenges to the PPS's potential for immediate effect as well as its ultimate usefulness.[53] The *Vossische Zeitung* noted acerbically, "Repeatedly we hear asked among our readership, 'Where is the PPS's activity?'" The author went on to offer his own opinion: "There isn't much." The paper called the PPS unnecessarily self-limiting in scope, arrogating to itself only "advisorial" powers, a charge that would continue to haunt officials throughout wartime efforts to control food pricing and distribution.[54]

Protests began again on Saturday afternoon, 16 October, an especially active shopping time after workers received their wages and went shopping for Sunday dinner. Police explicitly detailed another fourteen incidents, involving thousands of Berliners, and announced the spread of unrest to other suburbs. Protesters converged to fill the immensely wide Frankfurter Allee at Niederbarnimer Street, by late evening throwing stones at shop windows from the central island of the avenue. In response to the impressive display of mounting discontent, High Commander Kessel moved that evening to set the retail price of best-quality butter in Berlin and Brandenburg at an upper limit of 2,80 marks per pound. This was 20 to 60 pfennig under the prevailing rate reported in Lichtenberg. The ordinance was another short-term fix, effective immediately through 31 October. But it emphasized the potentially serious criminality of merchants rather than of protesters. The measure threatened failure to comply with a fine of up to 3,000 marks or six months' imprisonment. Kessel added in his proclamation, "Those who hold back butter in order to win excessive profit, or those who limit their trade of butter in order to push prices higher . . . are liable to one year of imprisonment and a fine of 10,000 marks."[55] The high commander, a top-level military official, effectively adopted the argument of protesters, police, and the broad press as to where the fault lay in the economic war. In this way, Kessel was able to abate unrest, at least temporarily.

The ordinance was printed throughout the local press by the next morning, 17 October, signifying authorities' urgent attention.[56] Shops apparently did abide by the ceiling, at least for the day, and the day was quiet.[57] Perhaps the reduced Sunday shopping traffic played a role. Perhaps the lack of unrest can be traced to the fact that shoppers had not just come from a hard day's wage work and looked forward to the traditional Sunday meal with the family, such as it was. The absence of conflict might have been related to attempts by officials to promote a festive mood in honor of the upcoming 500-year jubilee of the Hohenzollern house.[58] Police spies, however, tied the prevailing calm directly to the announcement of the butter ceiling. Here, as after each official measure, police noted *Anerkennung*, meaning acknowledgment, but also approval. Thus police had accredited to women of little means the power and stature to adjudicate on the satisfactory nature of the official act.[59]

Viewing this parable for contemporary protest, police and press reports offered another moral, which spoke to the continuous unrest over the next months, following successive official measures. While the populace acknowledged that officials had followed their specific demands, at the same time Berliners also demanded leadership and coordinated food policy from above, in order to end the cycle of repeated crises. Kessel's measure applied only to a very limited period of time. His attention to butter grades was important but did not make clear how butter was in fact to be differentiated and priced. Moreover, in the absence of imperial intervention in wholesale prices, it soon became clear that the reform, which applied only to retail prices in Brandenburg, had succeeded merely in rendering local retailers unable to afford prevailing wholesale prices.[60] In consequence, butter shortages soon became more intense following Kessel's edict; local retail merchants allied themselves with consumers in demanding intervention at the wholesale level.

Police spies, the broader press, municipal authorities, and Social Democratic Reichstag representatives all pushed imperial authorities to take responsibility for the food situation in exhaustive and anticipatory fashion, each author warning of "women in the streets." The *Vossische Zeitung* submitted, "*Only the central government agencies* have the capacity to take control over all the individual goods, from production on, and to institute real regulation of goods. . . . Any other economic regulation is doomed to remain a palliative on the bigger problem."[61] Jagow's circumspection in celebrating the effects of the new butter ceiling was soon vindicated. By the evening of 18 October, unrest surrounding the "fats question" had begun anew.

EATING ONE'S WORDS

The new cycle of protest and response, lasting from 18 to 20 October 1915, was still shorter than the one before it. Nonetheless, the official attention accorded to the single day of serious protest on Monday, 18 October, demonstrates how closely officials at every level listened to what was said on the streets of working-class Berlin—despite the continued inadequacy of their responses. The angry voices issued, above all, from the streets of Wedding, in a "battle for meat and fat."[62] Although the area sat on the doorstep of Bolle's central dairy off Alt-Moabit Avenue, it was nine cases of protest against butchers on 18 October that police merited with individual reports. Police were once again quick to legitimize protesters' grievances, in this case again, merchant rudeness, and to highlight the potential threat they saw in these demonstrations. The events of this cycle of unrest confirm that the concerns over food were not only about issues of material hardship, though these were important. The protests were also about questions of German culture and who defined it, about what a German should reasonably expect to be able to eat, and about how Germans should treat one another. Finally, this cycle offers some insight into the increasing generalized stress that governed civilians' lives—and especially those of working women—as early as the fall of 1915: a mounting, lasting state of emergency.

The form of protest between 18 and 20 October was virtually identical to that of two days earlier. Police reported numerous instances of "usurious prices" and butchers "holding back" goods advertised as available, but also especially of shopkeepers' "rudeness."[63] None of the police mitigated their reports with comments concerning the strains retail merchants might be suffering, nor regarding customers' discourtesy. In a case drawing nearly 6,000 participants, a butcher had responded to complaints over the high cost of lard, "You should spread shit on your bread."[64] Some demonstrators complained further that the shopkeeper used the familiar form of "you" in making the remark, in both singular and plural, in the latter case implicating the entire waiting public. This surely conjured up the apt Berlin expression "Since when do we keep pigs together?" [*Wo ham wir denn schon zusamm' Schweine jehüt?*], an epithet used when one was inappropriately and disrespectfully addressed in the familiar. Just after police dispersed the crowd, Officer Hanff telephoned news of this demonstration to the police department to emphasize its serious nature.[65] This incident was in turn the source of Jagow's direct memo to Ernst von Berge, chief of staff at the High Command.[66]

Protesters objected to disrespectful merchants at butter shops as well.[67] After the butter price ceiling went into effect later that same day, Sergeant Schwarz observed that, in Friedrichshain and Lichtenberg, "When riots did come about . . . they stemmed nearly exclusively from the impolite remarks of a shopkeeper to the shopping public."[68] Bolle branch shops were relatively free of unrest all along, though Lewald identified Bolle as "the leader in forcing up the prices."[69]

A whole range of self-proclaimed fellow consumers demonstrated sympathy with the sacrifices of custom that poorer Berliners experienced, reinforcing rather than calling into question their Germanness. The *Tägliche Rundschau* cited Professor A. Röhrig's remarks that "the buying public" protested "with good reason" in light of "inferior" available fats.[70] *Vorwärts* in turn cited the *Tägliche Rundschau,* adding, "It's bad when surrogates must be used, worse when bad surrogates, rather than good ones, must be bought." Drawing on comments originally addressed to a narrow professional audience, the first article drew sympathy from bourgeois audiences; the second newspaper article communicated that sympathy back to working-class readers. Poorer Berlin consumers experienced both unexpected attacks on their respectability from some quarters and unanticipated public displays of support from others.

In this context the press emphasized that working women, or women of little means, comprised the population worst affected by the food crisis, a consequence of prewar living conditions that were already precarious, in combination with arduous new challenges in their lives.[71] Indeed, life was hard for such women, beyond food shortages. Rainy, cold weather and hints of coal shortages inspired fear for a second winter of war. There were also the stresses of bearing up under increased rents as landlords distributed new apartment leases on 1 October.[72] Finding and maintaining suitable housing remained difficult, particularly in Berlin as both a garrison city and a city of industry, where a landlord might easily evict a family to bring in higher rent from a single war-industry worker who had come to Berlin from the country-side. Families daunted by increased rents faced relocation, often resigning to share already limited quarters with parents and in-laws.

Casualty lists offered grim evidence of the improportionate number of working-class Germans among the conscripted, though by this time relatively few Berliners escaped the thought that someone they knew might die in action. This fear was another experience that crossed class boundaries and permitted expressions of emotional identification.[73] Poorer residents of the city raced from long lines for food to join the great crowds of Berliners jockeying for the opportunity to see the casualties lists, dreading the appearance of a loved one's name; cries regularly broke the tension as a crowd member's worst fears were realized. Daily pieces in *Vorwärts* about fatalities among young children of poor families left untended at home and even of child abandonment and infanticide speak to the crisis air that hung relentlessly over poorer Berliners. Beyond these acute moments that punctuated daily life in the capital city was the tension that governed all human relationships at a time when circumstances challenged the meaning of such relationships. While poor consumers may have found new common cause with one another, relations among individuals became increasingly strained. Mothers argued with crying children over who should eat what and how much.[74] If wealthier Berliners publicly proclaimed empathy with their poorer counterparts, there is evidence that Berliners and other Germans also felt it necessary to harden themselves to the suffering of others, including those close to them.

Cognizant at some level of the pitched point of stress that informed protesters' quick anger, the Bundesrat intervened once more on the evening of 18 October, ordering that police in Berlin personally deliver a threat to each shopkeeper accused of harassment of customers that they gambled with charges of incitement to riot. Jagow passed on the ordinance, emphasizing the risk of punishment not only for "holding back" but also for failing to "treat the public in the most thoroughly polite fashion." He added that butchers "risk punishment if they refuse to sell fat without meat, if the price board says they have the fat."[75] No longer were shopkeepers' new pricing and packaging schemes to be countenanced. Following news of the ordinance and evidence of police vigilance on 19 October, 20 October passed in relative quiet, apparently confirming once again police assertions that protests would cease when authorities met popular demands.

Yet, although emphasizing the tight link between the price ceiling and warnings to merchants and the cessation of the mid-month riots, Sergeant Schwarz reported on 28 October a continued "cautious and depressed" mood traceable to anxiety over generally unaffordable prices and inaccessible goods. "Even if food prices remain the same, we must anticipate new mass unrest," Schwarz warned, emphasizing that the imminent cold weather intensified popular worries.[76] Thus, despite the immediate calm, officials were sufficiently concerned about the prospect of renewed unrest to pursue further measures. Authorities ensured that measures would not directly impair protesting women of little means or in any way insinuate that authorities blamed them for the unrest. They formulated their ordinances instead with an eye to preventing poor female consumers from "being provoked."[77]

Working together for the first time with civilian Prussian and Brandenburg officials, Berge fashioned a four-part plan to combat unrest in the streets of Berlin, now the high commander's greatest concern. Authorities would "impress upon the press" still more forcefully that newspaper articles must "take a point of view that would ensure public peace and order."[78] Still more important, officials would make clear to merchants the risks of tricking, acting rudely toward, or in any other fashion provoking customers, plastering the warning ubiquitously in sensitive districts. The new ordinances threatened anyone inciting unrest, but in effect it referred only to the press, radical Social Democrats, "rabble-rousing youth," and above all, shopkeepers.

The meeting of such varied and high-level authorities betrays the enormous official concern for this unrest that before the war would scarcely have been cause for notice among higher echelons, especially in restive Berlin. Yet the plan was in large part merely a consolidation of commands that had already been issued in the preceding days. Despite their avid attention, officials remained caught in the fear of doing too much or too little, celebrating the calm after each ordinance and dreading the return of new conflict, as threatened by police and press reports.[79] To be sure, imperial authorities were determined above all to win the war and consolidate the status of the Wilhelmine state. Yet despite some officials' singleness of vision, authorities' strategies for pursuing this vision with regard to the homefront were fatally indecisive and contradictory. Many officials still fundamentally maintained their belief that the war—and their prestige—would be won or lost on the battlefront alone. Prussian and imperial authorities also attempted to maintain good relations with other segments of society traditionally allied with the state and important to the war effort; they feared antagonizing agriculture and commerce by heavy intervention into the market on behalf of consumer interests.[80] Finally, in the midst of this long war, these officials had little interest in assuming new responsibilities.

By failing to take decisive control of the food question, however, they ceded this authority to others. The Berlin populace, which as a whole had long condemned Prussian military power and militarism, began to proclaim its faith in the military alone, calling for a "military food dictator." Military officials such as the deputy commanders around the country already expressed serious doubts about how their military and civilian superiors both were handling the domestic crisis. In November, as protests continued, poorer shoppers demanded and received ration cards for dietary fats, a measure that struck fear in the hearts of the commercial community and that ultimately earned the wrath of wealthier consumers.[81] The kaiser's throne speech of the same month offered vague promises of postwar political and economic reforms, clearly linking the unrest, food shortages, and popular sacrifice to broader calls for political reform. Following popular demand, in January 1916 the Reichstag called for the establishment of a new central food steering committee, as members also introduced discussion of loosening the franchise. Still the pattern continued.

5 ONE VIEW OF HOW POLITICS WORKED IN WORLD WAR I BERLIN

The pattern of unrest, both within a single incident and over the course of the fall and winter 1915; the array of actors implicated in the unrest; and the particular susceptibility of German officials to popular demand all played a role in establishing how politics worked at this point in the war. All of these factors help explain how the Prussian and German governments were brought to the point of acceding to total food control in deference to the needs of the *minderbemittelte* population. Consideration of the interaction of this variety of elements, and of how different segments of the population worked together to pressure the government to act, relies on a wider definition of politics than scholars have commonly employed with reference to this period. Although historians have viewed food scarcity and related generalized discontent as an important issue in World War I Germany, few have paid substantial attention to the food protest, except to draw a dichotomy between the economic grievances of the first half of the war (led predominantly by women) and the political demands of the last half (as expressed by men, on shop floors and battleships).[1] Political historians have limited themselves primarily to institutional forces when tracing the processes of power and pressure as they worked throughout society.

To consider the political influences of broader and more amorphous segments of society, we must adopt contemporary definitions of politics. As Jagow put it to his superiors in November 1915, citing from a Social Democratic newspaper, many Germans found "extraparliamentary means" essential to successfully elicit change. At that time, Jagow asserted, "'extraparliamentary means' mean[t] none other than demonstrations in the street."[2] Such a perspective sheds new light on the wartime imperial government's unprecedented intervention in domestic affairs and deference to the broad populace in shaping domestic and even foreign policy. Historians have long spoken of the limits of "total war" as executed by the German authorities in World War I.[3] But the constraints on state power were, under the conditions of war, perhaps still greater and somewhat different from those that scholars have recognized to date. These limitations highlight differently, in turn, the fractured nature of interests that characterized government and the wider society and that allowed Germany to slip toward civil upheaval. This brings another perspective to arguments about the imperial state's reformability and "modernity."[4]

Food protests in the streets were not sufficient to inspire close government attention and careful response during the war. In this period, forces across the political spectrum and up and down the socioeconomic hierarchy worked together to forge a powerful force in pressuring the government at all levels to respond to the crisis in fats and basic foods. That is, similar protests appeared unified, to officials and to the various protesters. Part of this collective force may be traced to Berliners' and other urban Germans' perception of their common needs as consumers, though, in fact, many public desires were manifested both consciously and unconsciously in competition with one another, which made the government's task still more difficult. But the cooperation, in effect, of self-defined consumers, journalists, professional politicians, and civil servants, including policemen, gave new meaning to the civil peace that authorities feared was collapsing. This unity challenged those who defied the interests of "the people," including speculators and even the government itself. A wide variety of effective political actors actively exploited street demonstrations to press for and elicit imperial intervention in the food crisis, bringing together unlikely segments of society and exercising a "policy of the diagonal" beyond Bethmann's fondest dreams.[5]

GOVERNMENT OF THE PEOPLE?

Bethmann's Conservative government was particularly susceptible to public pressures in wartime. As an administration representing a state that had long fought for greater prestige on the European and global front, Bethmann's cabinet struggled from the outbreak of war to demonstrate the country's strength and at the same time to justify Germany's role in the war as defensive. Both acts were designed to exhibit the virtues of Germany's culture and, relatedly, to defeat the notion propagated by West Europeans that Germany was a savage and barbaric land. Officials managing propaganda still winced at the name of Zabern, a symbol of Prussian militaristic force exercised wantonly against civilians. Yet British propagandists found their greatest source for whipping up anti-German sentiment in atrocity stories from early in the war about German soldiers' brutal abuse of civilians, particularly of Belgian women and children.[6] British forces bolstered the will of Allied soldiers to fight with rumors of German ill treatment of prisoners of war, pushing Germany to enormous lengths to optimize conditions in POW camps, indeed at the risk of stirring up resentment on the homefront. In May 1915, German submarines sank the passenger ship *Lusitania*, which the British construed as a new canker on the German image. This event was still fresh in the minds of Germans at the end of the year, as military authorities planned for expanded submarine warfare, and as civilian officials pressed Reichstag representatives to support new war credits.

German authorities attempted to protect the national physiognomy even at the immediate expense of the civilian population, in deference to what they saw as the long-term rewards. Initially Bethmann's administration felt a powerful impetus to distance itself from problems with the food supply for fear of confirming for the British the success of the blockade.[7] Historically the national government had intervened on behalf of popular interests only in moments of serious challenge, as in the case of Bismarck's reforms of the 1880s. Otherwise imperial officials left such mediations to state and local authorities, to private organizations, and even to party and trade-union efforts. News of the unrest in the streets from late 1914 made this stance increasingly difficult to maintain, particularly as both the foreign and the domestic press used the subject to demonstrate Germany's particular weaknesses vis-à-vis foreign powers: economic unpreparedness as well as an image of brutality. Princess Evelyn Blücher wrote on 11 November 1915, "This morning the English papers are full of the butter riots in Berlin. The accounts are, of course, exaggerated. There is absolutely no question of '200 people dead.'"[8] The incident in the British papers referred to an explicitly political demonstration in Berlin, but the British press apparently found it useful to conflate the protests. It also related the suppression of that demonstration to the "barbarism" shown in the coincident trial and execution of British nurse Edith Cavell.[9]

Bethmann both pleaded with and threatened editors of the domestic press not to report on the several incidents in November and December in Berlin in which thousands of female peace activists and left Social Democratic women demonstrated against the war at the Brandenburg gate and at the gates of the kaiser's palace, eliciting mass arrests in the first instance and police brutality in the second. This brutality appears to have been enough to get Police Commissioner Jagow "kicked upstairs" to ward off bad publicity.[10] Both popular unrest and its violent suppression, especially in Berlin, threatened to confirm international opinion on Germany's weaknesses. It is in part for this reason that the food protests in working-class neighborhoods, which would have been largely ignored by imperial officials in the prewar era and quickly stamped out by local authorities, now took on new importance. The state's initial sacrifice of civilian interests to foreign political concerns, in the form of relatively limited response to the food crisis, came back to haunt the Bethmann government by October 1915.

Perceptions of the effectiveness of Britain's economic war were not the only images that caused the contained Lichtenberg, Friedrichshain, and Wedding protests to capture the attention of officials at every level. These demonstrations over food injustices also possessed the power to threaten domestic enthusiasm for the war, at home and on the battlefront (which might also buttress enemy morale). In the winter of 1915–16, shivering civilians huddling in endless lines displayed their "war-weariness" and their concern that they could not "hold out," particularly against the ravages of the increasingly oppressive food shortages.[11] In light of the threatening alternatives to "holding out," the term became a watchword for officials in monitoring the depths of popular despair as well as discontent. Authorities were also well aware of the direct connection between homefront concerns and morale on the battlefront. As one would-be helpful Berliner wrote to Loebell, "Can the Minister not take the appropriate measures to push prices down forthwith? If it comes to revolts, the effect on the front will surely not be good."[12] Soldiers at the front were clearly aware of circumstances at home, despite censorship, through "letters of lament" from their families, newspapers, and news from other soldiers on leave or garrisoned in Berlin. With pointed reference to the limits of the civil peace, front soldiers quipped bitterly, "We know no butter, we know only jam."[13] Berliners and other Germans asked whether authorities were too incapable or too corrupt to resolve the crisis, or whether the wartime circumstances simply made the provision of all Germans impossible, despite propaganda assurances. Neither message was the one authorities hoped to communicate.

In the fall of 1915 police began again, as they had in February of that year, to note how concerns over food eclipsed news of military affairs. Officer Starost noted, "The entry of Bulgaria into the world war has been generally welcomed. The general mood in the people, however, is seriously compromised by the rise in prices."[14] The political police went further to suggest that the concern for domestic affairs translated into an explicitly pro-peace sentiment across a wide swath of the population, despite military and foreign political successes. Officer Diercks insisted that "through these circumstances [on the homefront], the desire for peace among the population has become ever greater, and the events in the military theaters elicit ever less interest," even, he observed pointedly, for fixed-wage civil servants.[15] Scarcely four weeks later Jagow admitted to Berge and other superiors, "One comes across the wish for an end to the war more often now."[16]

Other members of the "respectable" public warned of a generalized yearning for peace and of a view of military achievements as Pyhrric victories. Noting that a year earlier civilians had hoped for peace by Christmas, Evelyn Blücher remarked on the considerable sharpening of that sentiment by October 1915.[17] Blücher, like many contemporaries, saw the fall and winter of 1915–16 as a watershed in general public opinion toward the war. She noted in November "disappointment at the chancellor's speech," which capital city residents had hoped would demonstrate the government's control of the situation and at least provide incentive for continued fighting. The speech left Berliners and other Germans with a "general depression," as Reichstag representative Eduard David observed.[18] The public's negative response to the speech served as a referendum on the notion that support for the war effort constituted patriotism. The public felt no more salved by the "bourgeois" parties' divulgence of war aims, which seemed to many to render their sacrifices unnecessary, meaningless, and maliciously forced on them.[19] Bethmann's political downfall in 1917, related in part to inability to control the civilian public, stemmed largely from his apparent failure to instill and maintain active enthusiasm for the war and faith in the government's ability to rule successfully. Reaction to his speech in November contrasts sharply with the enthusiastic rally for the Social Democratic Party's "peace interpellation" in the same month, led by "outraged women" demanding food and the return of their husbands. As the capital continued to buzz with news of the ongoing "throngs" of women at butter shops, morale across the city deteriorated.[20]

The incipient loss of support for the war, and the reception of this loss particularly in Britain as evidence that the economic war had been effective after all, compromised the stature of the German state and, potentially, the state's ability to prosecute war successfully. Still more threatening were signs that defeat of the German state could come from within, references flaunted by the press, local authorities, and even the police in a bid to force action by imperial authorities. A defender of the war wrote in March 1916 to warn the police and state authorities of her belief that if dramatic steps were not taken, "the people," and by this she referred "not only to the workers, but to the majority, all the way up to the 'better' public[,] . . . will give up, and there you have the revolution!"[21] If officials had conceived of war in part as a means to distract the German public, unify it against an outer enemy, build national self-esteem, and shore up the government's strength, these purposes were certainly thwarted. Protest against both the military and the "inner" wars inspired explicitly antigovernment attacks, carried out by Berliners claiming that the government might destroy the nation. This slide from a judgment against the war to one against the state itself was a qualitatively new development in the fall and winter of 1915–16.

For the first time officials noted threatening sentiments against the state, "all the more among those otherwise predisposed toward loyalty."[22] The public cast poorer women, or simply "women," at the vanguard of this movement against the government. Evelyn Blücher observed in November 1915, "Women are realizing the enormous burden imposed upon them. They have to do men's work as well as their own, and when they have earned their pay it all goes into the pockets of others who sell them food at enormous prices. Naturally they begin more than ever to say: 'Why should we work, starve, send our men out to fight? . . . We'd rather fight for a more just division of the goods of this earth. . . . The State that called upon us to fight cannot even give us decent food, does not treat our men as human beings, but as so many screws in the great machine of the German army.'"[23]

She finished menacingly, "Everywhere you can hear it murmured: 'We are forced to keep silence now; but wait till the war is over, then our turn will come'" — regardless of the war's outcome. Blücher's words certainly contained no specific reference to what "the women" would do when the war was over. But it is clear that many officials and others worried what such statements might mean. In late 1915 and early 1916 police attempted to distinguish between food protesters and those they perceived as less defensible demonstrators, including organized peace activists, believing rougher treatment of the latter would win public sanction. But the Berlin public itself seemed to conflate these populations as "the women," at least concerning police response. Conversely, peace activists outside Berlin looked favorably upon the city's food unrest, calling for the "contrivance of women's riots after the Berlin model."[24] Beginning particularly in January 1916, police claimed evidence of the growing influence of radical Social Democratic women, all the more in the wake of Zimmerwald,[25] on the exhausted consumers seeking butter and lard.

This scenario provides insight into how women protesting for butter in the streets became a power to be reckoned with, pushing the state finally to organize major interventions in the market on their behalf by early 1916. As poorer women, police spies, journalists, and a widening population felt threatened by the deficiency of necessary foods and the wider context of unjustified deprivation and loss, these societal elements worked together, each drawing on the unique abilities and strengths of the other, to make their case effectively.

POLICE AND POLITICS

In light of government concern for maintaining peace and order on the streets of Berlin—and of authorities' ongoing failure to do so—political police spies occupied a role of singular privilege in putting their own interpretation of domestic events regularly before the anxious eyes of high officials. German police officers saw themselves as planted firmly within the system and as stalwart defenders of the state against its inner enemies, such as Social Democrats and the organized working class. The effects of war frustrated patrolmen, who felt their own inability to control the increasingly unrestful crowds; political policemen resented officials' not-quite-sufficient responses to their grievous reports. Police were also acutely aware of their own wartime privations, a sense that led them in the winter of 1915–16 to find common cause with those they watched over. Political police officers used their reports to warn officials of this predicament and to make their own interests loudly heard.[26] Law enforcement officers now dropped the formula of "alleged" causes when describing the "emeutes that arose among the shopping women," stating the causes affirmatively and challengingly.[27] From the first months of 1916 Sergeant Schwarz and even Police Commissioner Jagow were increasingly less willing to suppress such references in the reports they passed upward. Officials observed this phenomenon with concern, well aware that defection of militia and security forces to the rebel side was historically an important element in successful revolution.[28]

It appears that Berlin police spies slowly became aware of the value of their position in portraying this unrest, with potential import for their own concerns, all the more as their reports rose in increasingly unexpurgated form into officials' hands.[29] Police used their reports to construct a particular scenario in which they began to maximize certain qualities that aroused fear among their superiors in the domestic administration, giving full weight to the "excesses" practiced by women of little means while legitimizing what they presented as the women's demands. As the winter of 1915–16 wore on, informers increasingly claimed that women physically threatened shopkeepers, damaged property, and occupied shops.[30]

In this context it is worth noting that despite the generally positive characterization of women's unrest in contrast with that of youth and drunks, on the national level in this period police charged women with far more crimes against property than youths.[31] Moreover, as sympathetically as police portrayed these women, reports reveal that protesting women in Berlin and elsewhere increasingly exercised violence against patrolmen, an activity men seem to have practiced most often before the war.[32] In the October riot in Oberschöneweide, women threw flower pots at police. Well outside Berlin, in Schneidemühl, a middle-class teenager reported in her diary seeing women in the marketplace banging on shop windows demanding food. When a "rude" policeman grabbed the collar of a woman seeking milk, she jerked away and hit him full in the face with her jug.[33] In general such women did not seem to respond mutually to policemen's proclaimed empathy. Plainclothes political police may have been spared some of the violent reactions, but protesters were aware of who they were, despite changes in personnel as the war progressed. As Officer Sauer rather hyperbolically put it, they were the only men in the marketplaces, as the rest were on the front.[34] Police attempted to harness this violence to induce officials to act.[35]

Police used numerous leitmotifs, however consciously, to communicate the urgency of their own concerns. Officer Ludwig wrote in December 1915 that despite the momentary calm, high officials had better read the writing on the wall.

> For there are innumerable families who are going day after day without butter or other fats, and who are forced to eat their bread dry and to prepare their food without cooking fat. . . . Government measures have been declared inadequate. . . . Even good, faithful patriots have begun to turn into pessimists, and the thought that Germany could be brought to its knees as a result of its internal economic defectiveness is continually gaining ground. The current deplorable state of affairs and the insufficient countermeasures by high authorities are characterized as the best agitator for social democracy, and with grave concern one awaits relief, which can only come in the form of a better and more equal distribution of all foods.[36]

Ludwig warns of the potential for further riots, even when all is quiet in the streets, thus maintaining a level of high tension and urgency. Ludwig blurs the lines between worker and civil servant. He spells out the ominous terms of the inner war, placing police in the threatening position of patriots who must fight against the state in defense of the German people.

Like his colleagues, Officer Ludwig exhorted authorities to intervene more forcefully to avoid further threat to civil peace—indeed, according to left-wing Social Democratic desiderata, as spelled out in *Vorwärts* and other party organs. Officers varied between two forms in expressing these demands. The first, offered in the passive voice, as in Ludwig's report, gave the impression that there were objectively clear and obvious paths that must be taken if further unrest were to be averted. The second tack was to formulate specific demands as though shopping women had voiced them, though they may or may not have done so. In this way, police won the ear of high officials with what may have been their own particular vision of what should be done, without taking any ownership of the ideas. At this stage police were unlikely to risk making such statements on their own authority, nor was Jagow likely to have passed these statements upward.

There were other subtle displays that call into question the motives of low-level police as they carried out their duty. Officers stated often that they were unable to control the crowds that gathered outside shops, claiming that only imperial intervention would effect the desired results, even as they also noted how easily they dissipated groups of women. Evelyn Blücher observed the general belief that police "hated . . . drastic measures toward women," though this had not been a strong concern in years past.[37] Jagow periodically questioned the activity of both the political police and patrolmen, as on 20 October: "I would like to request enlightenment as to how a window pane was broken in the presence of a uniformed officer."[38] Some observers suggested that police actually encouraged women to initiate these and other questionable strategies.[39] Police consistently used the image of "unprotected show windows,"[40] eliciting the vulnerability of merchants and of officials as well, just as, for waiting customers, the windows represented a taunting scene of goods of which many could not partake.

Police spies played on the relation between the inner peace and an inner war and the relation of both to the military war. Officer Kurtz reported on 14 October, "The urgency among the populace grows daily. The press at the municipal sales outlets is life-threatening. The indignation and anger of those who stand in line for hours to receive nothing — and these number in the hundreds — is indescribable. Disparaging remarks regarding the government . . . are the order of the day." "Disturbances of the peace," he concluded, would not let up without serious intervention.[41] Police began to write of "little troops of women" in the streets, referring alternately to "poor consumers" and the still more explicitly political protests for peace. Such troops "advanced" toward Unter den Linden (where victorious soldiers traditionally marched), leading Berliners in the fight for peace, against the government.[42]

Police thus played, consciously or not, on the dominant contemporary sociology of crowds in an age of rabid bourgeois phobia of mass upheavals and assemblies. Police exploited these notions, manipulating the belief that crowds grew "contagiously." Lichtenberg commissioner Lewald warned, "Circles which have till now stood at a distance will come to take part and will contribute to the spread."[43] Jagow himself worried that "the danger remains that these excesses will be repeated, and will grow even larger and more widespread."[44] Street-level political police intimated that excesses might ultimately grow to include themselves. Police made ominous references to riots that had radiated around the city, though in this period they did not document many. Political police elsewhere, deputy commanders, and others made authorities only too aware that unrest had extended around the country as well. It is hard to tell to what degree women outside the working class joined in actual street protest; early on, at least, such women tended to rely on individual strategies, from getting themselves on "customer lists" to calling on local patrolmen to contend with a deceptive merchant. Officials assigned political police to observe in almost exclusively working class areas, and reports, for example, from the police commissioner of Charlottenburg, an area of mixed-class population, to the Berlin police commission, are very rare. Police may have been fabricating the spread of protests or embellishing on rumors for their own purposes. At the same time, considering the nature of these "riots," which grew so directly, at least initially, out of the experience of trying to shop, any group of Berliners that shopped for themselves at public markets might indeed have engaged in such protest.

Officers claimed that women were easily subject to "losing their wits" under the urgent conditions officials allowed to reign, "in their excitement threatening now to finally tell their men on the front about the circumstances [involved in getting food], regardless of the consequences."[45] After all, police noted, "One often hears the claim [from the shopping women]: 'Our men are good enough to let be shot to death, but us, they let starve.'"[46] Police often cast these women simultaneously as a canny group that could play their politics respectably or play hardball, according to necessity. They suggested that the women's "spontaneous shouts" about telling their husbands might have represented a conscious threat that protesters would refuse to play the game of the civil peace any longer in the absence of official resolution of the crisis. Likewise, the official spies trumpeted the warning of women of little means that they would revert to "self-help" if assistance from other quarters were not forthcoming: "It is exactly the poorer population that is very infuriated by the prevailing rise in prices, and one intimates that one will engage in 'self-help' if the government doesn't intervene against the usurious prices."[47] By early 1916 police reported popular "acknowledgment" ever less frequently, withholding these signs of hope for authorities that their incremental measures might produce calm and order.

They noted, conversely, that although the frequent riots were not planned demonstrations, the "hours-long, often fruitless wait of housewives" made women "easily vulnerable to the influence of political provocateurs" and "offer the extreme radical position considerable material for agitation."[48]

THE PRESS AND POLITICS IN PUBLIC

Police employed mood reports to establish their own concerns (as well as those of the women on whom they reported), especially regarding the inadequacy of food supplies. Like the police, members of the press used their own particular abilities, in combination with the powers of protesters in the streets, both to distribute information and to make demands on the state. News reports of a government decision, or lack thereof, believed to have adversely affected the fate of poor consumers often resulted directly in protest on the streets—at least this was the connection made by police spies. At the same time, news of circumstances on the streets, as rendered in the press, elicited grave concern from around the city, inciting further unrest in some quarters and outspoken pressure on officials from others. The connections between press reportage, police observation, and popular demonstration, among other sources of communications, were intricate and mutually reinforcing.

Like the police, the press published specific demands on the government, which were then viewed by the wider public as well. Police aided, in turn, in bringing demands in the press to the attention of authorities, at the latter's own request, using relevant articles to support their own representation of a public crisis. Demands for government response stemmed from the particular political persuasions and more specific interests of the various papers. By the end of 1915, however, demands had virtually converged in urging coordinated and thorough imperial intervention in regulating the food supply, in the interests of the fair distribution of the most important foodstuffs. The wider press seems to have picked up recommendations according to the agenda that had appeared for some time in the Social Democratic dailies, though the exchange of editorial opinions was active in all directions. Newspapers of all stripes regularly cited one another, often as sources of authority and certainly implying an unusual sense of fundamental unity among them. This unity and mutual reinforcement worked almost exclusively concerning the food question, one of the most prominent issues of the day. In turn, it appears that members of the populace (as well as the police) often formulated their own demands through recommendations in the press. Yet the great attention to food in the Social Democratic press likely arose initially from that party's desire to maintain the waning attention of the civilian working class, which had made its general concern over food issues quite clear.

The press acted as a conduit for communications in all directions, by virtue of its effective alliance with the consumer population. These included opinions directly from the public, though these were fewer for poorer Berliners than for others. The *Berliner Volkszeitung* cited a woman reader from working- and lower middle-class Tempelhof writing in response to butter merchants' "arbitrary" habit of rounding up sales prices, particularly as consumers could buy only in small amounts: "In a time when the plagued housewife must reckon with every penny[,] . . . it would be most desirable if, through your much valued paper, the officials might be informed that they should force the shopkeepers themselves to pay better attention to pennies and stick to the fixed price ceiling."[49] The end result was to broaden the range of public voices. Jürgen Habermas has spoken of the power of the press as "publicity," a literary terrain for open debate over politics and society, though he accounted narrowly for the range of actors who had access to this tool of communication. The wider press effectively provided public space (though limited, to be sure) for poor, disenfranchised consumers to engage in the political debate at some level. Indeed the press worked better for consumers in many instances than for officials, with their new, expansive propaganda apparatus. This is clear from press and popular responses to Kessel's and Bethmann's respective press conferences in October 1915 concerning the price increases.[50] Newspapers also directly validated and imputed political import to popular demonstrations. If Jagow revealed this perception to his superiors, it was the *Volksfreund Braunschweig,* along with papers in Berlin and other cities around the country, that communicated to and confirmed for the great public that street protests were now a primary site of politics.[51]

This was the case despite government efforts at censorship. In the press clampdown of 14 October 1915, Berge expressed a concern for the provocative quality of a wide range of publications. Minna Cauer ran up against censorship of her magazine, *The Women's Movement* (*Die Frauenbewegung*), because of military authorities' explicit concern to limit "polemic and scaremongering among women."[52] The censor ordinance of October came after the horse was out of the barn, however, concerning the riots in progress.

The phrasing of the ordinance did little, moreover, to quell further unrest or control responses to it. It did not prevent references to women spending night after night waiting to buy at the municipal meat authority or to deputations of women sent to speak with municipal officials or to the still-rising costs, particularly of fats. It did not disallow reports on the inequities in the distribution of fats, the alleged speculation by wholesalers and retailers, and the deficiencies in the government policy that responded to these issues.[53] Indeed censorship left a press image of the beleaguered consumer as patient and forbearing, while the government itself appeared to be unreasonable, erratic, and operating under suspect interests. Social Democratic and "bourgeois" newspapers alike reported on the conditions under which women of little means suffered. *Vorwärts* described poorer Berliners attempting to purchase lard at municipal sales sites, underscoring the limits of local-level efforts and the failures of government measures to date. "They all . . . hundreds of persons, mostly women . . . take upon themselves the grievance of a sleepless night in the open air and the risk of a cold rain shower in order not to be too late for the sale, which takes place only from 7 to 10 A.M." The article continued, "We could have wished that Lord Mayor Wermuth had been there another half hour. Then he could have heard the complaints and desires of the disappointed women, who left empty-handed after another sleepless night full of hope and patient perseverance."[54]

The liberal *Berliner Tageblatt* described the "Night Camp on Thaer St." as women and veterans, demonstrating great "willingness to sacrifice," settled in to wait until the municipal sales outlet opened in the morning. Of all the requirements to be able to shop at the municipal sites, the foremost was "patience, a lot of patience." The article asserted, moreover, that although the municipal outlets were now supposed to be accessible only to the poorest consumers, government regulations prevented many of them from that access. But, the author noted, "one hears no complaint here, not a single angry word. One is used to harder things than this nightly wait under the open sky. . . . They who freeze here and wait also contribute to helping the Fatherland hold out for victory!"[55] *Der Deutsche Kurier* noted that in the face of such urgency, "the broader view," of which such women had been impressively cognizant, "disappears," and—as was "completely humanly explicable"—"discontent finds room to enter."[56]

Like policemen, the broader press portrayed women of lesser means as resolute and enduring, patriotic, and as rational as circumstances allowed. Like German soldiers, poorer women would take up a fight forced upon them, though it was not of their own choosing. On 8 October *Vorwärts* cynically proclaimed the "victory over consumers." In the midsts of the riots, the paper continued the motif: "In Berlin, thousands of persons battle daily for a tiny quantity of meat or lard. To be sure, this battle is not fought with weapons of violence nor even with sharp words. But isn't an impropor-

Part of the street scene: women digging a subway line, 1915. (BAPK, file 1573)

tionate expenditure of time and strength, a stubborn perseverance on chill fall nights, also a battle?"[57] Here was no reference to food riots, but the threat of poor women's potential to do battle, as well as their quiet tolerance, was forceful all the same.

These scenes bring home the degree to which the dozens of Berlin newspapers had the power to create a picture or theater of the street for millions of Berliners as well as for the millions of readers outside the city. Photographs and contemporary paintings speak to the variety of types and images on the street: thousands of soldiers on leave, in transit, or home on disability; children and teenagers who spent more time in the streets; wealthier Berliners who still strode briskly about in business suits or filled the city's sidewalk cafes; families in mourning clothing whose numbers grew during each year of the war; and women delivering mail, running streetcars, and even digging new subway lines. Yet the press's image of the streets in which newspapers claimed to reproduce the sights and sounds and equally tangible emotional distress that journalists observed created a surprisingly focused portrait. *Der Deutsche Kurier* averred, "We make all possible sacrifices for our troops in the field, and for our beloved fatherland; but we overlook all to easily that which lies near." The paper concluded evocatively, "Whoever looks with open eyes into our daily life and knows how to listen cannot fail to recognize the imminent danger; and whoever doesn't want to believe it, should go where the poorest live."[58] This must have drawn powerful responses even from readers who still managed comfortably under the prevailing conditions; certainly it frightened officials.

Berge's revised censorship policy of 21 October proscribed any explicitly provocative text in the press. However, it seemed that inspectors on the whole took a relatively relaxed view of what this censorship encompassed. Authorities argued vigorously in this period about appropriate censorship, as many officials asserted that the press could function as a kind of "safety valve."[59] The combination of official indulgence of certain topics and censorship of others worked against state interests. In any case, the censorship failed to stem other important forms of information and communications, including handbills and leaflets and photographic postcards, as well as the intensified traffic in oral communications as so many spent time in the streets.

As a rule, contemporary newspapers featured the food question less prominently than many Berliners might have deemed appropriate, at least among the growing circle of those who spent much of their days in pursuit of adequate food. Even so, at least one or two newsbriefs on some aspect of the food crisis appeared in virtually every issue of most of the daily papers, from "Food Prices in Berlin" to "A Contribution Regarding the Rise in Butter Costs" to "The Imperial Government's Food Policy."[60] In contrast, events such as the 500th anniversary of the Hohenzollern house on 21 November 1915 and the normally well celebrated birthdays of the kaiserin and kaiser in October and January, respectively, received very little press, either in advance of festivities or afterward.[61]

As the urgency of the food crisis grew in these months, the juxtaposition of piece after piece on the food question in the dailies was in itself a powerful statement, sketching the rise of one problem after another. On 19 October *Vorwärts* began to publish such articles on the front page, with a feature titled "Price Ceilings for Butter," an article commending the responsiveness of the high commander. But on 27 October the lead article in the Social Democratic daily, "Meat Cards and the Rising Cost of Meat," called for implementation of this new far-reaching measure. Beginning with the butter riots, *Berliner Tageblatt* and other papers moved all news on food to the first page of the second section, a traditionally important page for domestic news. *Vorwärts* now devoted its regular column "Political Overview" to report on the food crisis.

Naturally editors demonstrated thereby their interest in attracting a mass readership. This presence across the press kept questions over food on the front burner for the entire population, however. By early November, though, newspapers treated the daily flurry of new, limited, sometimes arcane official measures with confusion and disgust rather than welcome. The *Vossische Zeitung* hinted at the frustrating effect of such news in its article of 5 November, "On the Meat Card, Again." Likewise *Der Tag*, on 15 December, printed "The Provision of Food, Again." *Vorwärts* reported on 31 December, "It's Enough to Make you Scream!" Both *Vorwärts* and *Vossische Zeitung* regularly reported the official announcement of a new ordinance on an inside page, with a small headline; then within days they would run a second piece criticizing the ordinance, often virtually repeating the headline, in larger type, in an article closer to the front page. On 22 October *Vorwärts* announced the Bundesrat's plan to fix wholesale butter prices, as Berliners had long demanded. Then, on 23 October, the paper observed, "So we have a new food ordinance from the Bundesrat. This time it's about butter. It doesn't regulate the prices directly but, rather, extends complete power to the chancellor." So, *Vorwärts* commented in exasperation, "We must raise doubts as to whether the planned measures will indeed bring a *notable cut in prices.*"[62] Poorer Berliners begged for relief, which they envisioned by early 1916 as all-encompassing official control of food production and distribution. When not proclaiming their shared distress, wealthier Berliners demanded the problems of food be taken care of and removed from sight, away from enemy eyes and away from their own. Such press pieces contributed to the public's ever more skeptical response to the "surgical" strategies authorities had pursued to date in narrow and literal response to popular demand.

The wider press kept up the onslaught, from the twin fronts of demanding the state take up particular measures and condemning authorities for their failure to implement a plan for total control of food production and distribution. Newspapers of all manner cast acts of municipal and provincial governments, such as local retail price ceilings and municipal sales outlets, as sincere but necessarily limited by the scope of influence. The papers depicted Imperial acts, in contrast, as too little too late. The press questioned the interest of the state in protecting poorer consumers and thereby once more established the responsibility of the imperial government to do so.[63] Newspapers challenged the government's assertion that there was no single, simple response to control the rising prices. *Vorwärts* claimed to give voice to the "opinion of the greater portion of the population," asserting on 11 October after some isolated protests that "the high prices would have been completely avoidable through appropriate [imperial] measures and could still be moderated. One certainly thinks in general that the imperial government doesn't care to do anything against the so-called unavoidable evil."[64]

Beginning in this period the Social Democratic press hinted at an alliance between itself and other sectors of society, such as the Berlin municipal government, as well as the bourgeois press, against the threat of speculation.[65] It posited the central government, conversely, in an unstable position, poised to fall in with the economic enemy but possessing the ability to redeem itself through strong and rapid action.[66] *Vorwärts* observed that while other countries took care of their own populations, Germany took care of its producers of grain and livestock.[67] The *Correspondendenzblatt* suggested that "unfortunately, the Bundesrat has used the means of price ceilings and confiscation *with too little scope*" and concluded that "for the present high prices, unfortunately *the government is not entirely innocent.*" Proving the Social Democrats' point, the *Berliner Tageblatt* reprinted the piece verbatim on the first day of the butter riots.[68] Outside Berlin the *Offenbacher Abendblatt* sought to identify "who is the enemy who is starving us." "One ought not to forget that the obsession of the foreign press with the German food emergency was made possible, first, through the guilt of the German government and those circles that participate in the food speculation. Why does one hesitate, then, to tie the hands of the speculator, wherever he is, and thereby get rid of the speculation?" Bringing home the disaster of the government's early propaganda, the paper reinforced the terms of the inner war: "It is a fact, *there is enough food in Germany,* and the enemies who want to starve the German people are to be found not outside of, but in the country itself."[69]

The press asserted that the central government's leadership regarding food issues was at least as important to the future of Germany as that regarding military strategy. Members of the press thus treated partial, grudging responses by imperial authorities as courting disaster, in the form of domestic unrest, international derision, and the consequent breakdown of the military effort. So, despite the Bundesrat's promise of some form of price regulation, *Vorwärts* editors insisted on 19 October, "*A change can only come if a single price for butter is set for all Germany.*" The article ended, "*If we communicated to England the price that we pay* [for butter], *we would receive, as the prices themselves also deserve, insult and ridicule.*"[70] *Vorwärts* went further the next day, setting the wide range of societal opinion on the side of the consumer, against the government, and indicating officials' role as followers rather than as leaders. "Just as with the bread and potato question, the government has, in the provision of fats, waited so long that drastic acts were no longer to be avoided in response to the climbing discontent of the populace."[71] "*But what does the government do now?*" the article asked. It provided "half measures," with potentially catastrophic results. The bourgeois press loudly echoed these condemnations.[72] Such criticisms strengthened public belief that only total government control would resolve the crisis.

Newspapers frequently reported opinions from the front lines to cement this argument, as in the rightist, National Liberal *Tägliche Rundschau*'s article of 19 November, "Warning from the Trenches." This piece made explicit the link between the war on the fronts and the battle at home and reminded authorities, in the words of a soldier, of just "how important the mood at home is for morale on the battlefield." Notably, the soldier's letter implicated the newspapers themselves, as well as letters from home, in shaping this "great influence." "But it was quite disturbing, for me as for my comrades, to hear of the news over high prices and the shortage of food. The blood rises to one's head when one imagines that behind the front, turncoats are exploiting our inhuman sacrifices to fill their sacks of gold, and that they are enriching themselves out of the neediness of women and children."[73] Altogether, the press's role indicates the remarkable limits on the ability of the German state to control public expression as well as to assume a forceful leadership role on some issues, an image at odds with a prominent view of that state as effectively authoritarian, even under the Bethmann regime, all the more as it moved toward total war.

HOW POLITICS WORKED FOR WOMEN OF LITTLE MEANS

The best evidence for the limits to state control is the power that poor, disenfranchised consumers accrued to influence government policy. The police and the press, among other societal forces, used women of little means to evoke a certain view of reality. Complementing one another's abilities, these forces impressed upon the imperial government the need to intervene in the inner, economic war. These various interests cast demands simultaneously in their own names and in the name of those of little means. The line between these entities was blurred, and for the duration of the war, this blurring strengthened the power of the demands, arrogating influence to poorer women as well as to police and the press.

Women of little means were not mindless pawns in this game, however. The police and the press in particular did these women the service of both recording and legitimizing their voices—at least some version thereof— and set up poor consumers as a force to be reckoned with. Yet these voices issued from the women themselves, who exploited, consciously or not, their own dual power of legitimacy and threat. Though these women did not know exactly what officials heard, they knew they got action. Police themselves suggested that these poor consumers came to recognize the meaning others invested in their unrest and "play[ed] the game" themselves. Officer Diercks noted, "The thought is widely heard that it was only through these riots that the authorities were forced to intervene, and thus this method has been recommended, directly or indirectly, as the standing mode of operation."[74]

Poor women created their own open-door policy. In Rhenish Solingen in October 1915, "some 200 women advanced from the woods to the city hall, where police held them back. A delegation of five women was received by the deputy mayor, who promised he would take care of providing cheap potatoes and coal. But the women weren't satisfied with that. So then they negotiated the matter and came to a preliminary agreement that a general raise in the subsidy rate would be initiated. Then the women selected a new deputation, which met with the provincial district magistrate, to take up these suggestions with him. A similar incident played out in Weyer as well."[75] The reporting newspaper concluded pointedly, "It has however not yet come to acts of self-help," notifying officials that the public was still willing to invest authority in the German state, provided it acted quickly and comprehensively. Since an article in *Vorwärts* referred to Dresden rather than to Berlin, officials permitted the paper's report that "*a delegation of women from the Dresden working population* presented their grievances regarding their urgent need to Lord Mayor Blüher. He promised in turn that all would be done that lay in his power to do to mitigate the food emergency and rising prices." Blüher "assured them particularly that women, too, would be called up for the municipal food committee and in the various price monitoring committees."[76]

Thus perhaps it is of little surprise that poor women remained relatively cool to the campaigns for universal suffrage that bourgeois women's groups and the majority Social Democrats continued to carry out during the war. Poor women had found a meaningful if temporary way to make politics work for them and to establish their perceived rights in the system, even if the food scarcity remained. In the midst of war they had little interest in the abstractions of voting rights, though the franchise was consistent with their demands for representation and responsiveness. Their focus now was on very specific, concrete measures on the part of Prussian and imperial authorities. Yet such demands were not only implicitly political; they were also potentially radical in terms of the transformed relations between state and society that they embodied, both for the particular moment of the war and beyond. Poor consumers themselves asserted that their demands represented a more general set of interests (even though officials sometimes responded with measures explicitly to the advantage of these working-class shoppers). They convinced adversaries as well as allies of the power of their threat. By November 1915, merchants had expressed their own concern to municipal officials that authorities act on behalf of those of little means in order to secure their own livelihood and personal safety.

In response, imperial officials both acknowledged and legitimated the notion that street protesters should set the agenda for official action. High-level authorities noted, for example, "the populace expects that those of greater means limit their butter intake, in order to mitigate the effects of the shortage on the circles of little means."[77] On this basis, in mid-November State Secretary of the Interior Clemens von Delbrück announced a series of meetings to discuss state management of an equitable national distribution of butter. These talks resulted in the establishment in mid-December of a national butter distribution authority, which would operate through the Central Purchasing Authority (ZEG), which functioned previously only to seek out foreign goods for import.[78] All Berliners seemed to receive this news of national-level treatment of the issue with satisfaction, though it was unclear at this point exactly how authorities would interpret "equitable" distribution of any foodstuff. This pressure from below in turn decisively influenced military strategy in, for example, forging a path to Turkey, a source of wheat.[79]

The flip side of this remarkable government responsiveness was the limitation on the state's ability simply to quash with violence the irksome unrest that had taken on so much meaning in the course of the war. Police themselves strongly resisted violence against women during this unrest; they consistently emphasized in their reports that they had not used weapons in dispersing crowds of women even when it took hours to accomplish.[80] Despite their belligerence toward patrolmen, poorer women now insisted that police were there only to protect them, to punish abusive merchants, and even to control soldiers on leave, who believed their status permitted them to sail to the front of food lines.[81] Gendarmes in this era did carry swords and often pistols with blanks. From mid-October 1915, authorities sent in reinforcements on horseback and even in motor vehicles to scare protesters. But the protected position of female food protesters, which was all the more secure after the public censure of police in the incidents on Unter den Linden, offered women license to proclaim their views as emphatically as possible, a freedom of which they amply availed themselves. Later in the war, when Hindenburg attempted to call out the military to silence protesting women, public aversion to such responses was even stronger. Protesting women loudly proclaimed they were writing their husbands and brothers in battle with news of their treatment, asserting their connection with men on the front, as strugglers in common. Censorship of such letters was spotty, and the press in turn publicized soldiers' responses, contrasting their own relatively positive treatment by enemy governments. It is clear that such women began to perceive themselves as in a position to make big demands on the government.

6 A FOOD DICTATORSHIP

Following on the October butter riots, 1916 opened in Berlin
and other German cities with a resounding cry for total centralized control
of food supplies that would guarantee the "fair" and "equitable" distribution of food. The "food question" was "the only topic that all of Germany
[was] discussing."[1] Paradoxically, the government's ability to institute firmer
control, specifically over food distribution, became the litmus test of the Wilhelmine regime's "reformability." The government accepted the challenge,
announcing early in the spring of 1916 the inauguration of the War Food
Office (Kriegsernährungsamt, or KEA), under the auspices of the Prussian
Ministry of War, to oversee all food distribution. Many Berliners publicly
rejoiced at the establishment of the KEA in May 1916, the culmination of
seven months of nationwide popular demand. But the public soon perceived this office to have failed in its mission; the cycle of government response followed by failure ran its course now on a grand scale. A bitter and
unrestful summer followed, concluding with popular support for the new
Supreme Army commanders' determination to expand their powers over
domestic affairs. Acclamation for a "dictatorship" led by new Supreme
Army commander and war hero Paul von Hindenburg in August must be
seen as support for a "food dictatorship," a "militarization of the pantry,"
a "positive state" that would intervene forcefully and effectively to see to
the nutritional needs of civilians as it did those of soldiers.[2]

Government officials and the general public alike debated the merits of
a military food dictator and simultaneously more democratic control, making for strange political bedfellows. As a further paradox, those most concerned to relieve civilian suffering during this period of rapidly spreading
hunger failed to do so, while those least concerned may have best succeeded.
These circumstances turned contemporary political labels and presumed
agendas on their heads throughout 1916 and generated broad, engaged debate on food scarcity, German politics, and the appropriate relationship between state and society. The military administration exploited popular concern to mobilize civilian resources for military plans. But as the domestic
crisis proved intractable, military leaders faced a greater challenge than they

had bargained for. The new leaders strengthened censorship and ordered violent police and military intervention in all public political activity. Authorities strategically exempted food riots and "women's protest," however. The effect was to elevate this dissent to ever greater importance, reinforcing the right of these women to adjudicate the government's success or failure. As Germany entered total war, it was far from a time of political complacency and fixity on the military goal. It was, rather, a time of extraordinary openness and flux.

THE ROAD TO TOTAL CONTROL

In response to the street riots and generalized public chorus of concern that continued from October 1915, Prussian officials announced plans in March 1916 to institute an office that would establish total and enforceable control of the food crisis, providing for equity in distribution. The KEA symbolized a qualitatively new step in the distribution of food.[3] Though the Ministry of War was a civilian office, Berliners initially saw the KEA as the realization of the military food dictatorship they had demanded. Poorer Germans voiced admiration for the military leadership's apparent determination and effectiveness in securing adequate food resources for the population under its control, which to date had been constituted by soldiers. This seemed a marked contrast to the hapless policies pursued by the Bundesrat and by Imperial State Secretary Delbrück. Aggrieved consumers expressed hope that the KEA would emulate military officials' successful appropriation of raw resources for the war effort and their ability to consistently feed soldiers. Wittingly or not, hopeful civilians failed to recognize that the security of food for the troops and other resources for the war effort existed largely at the expense of the domestic food supply.[4]

Poorer consumers hoped that if military or quasi-military authorities controlled both military and civilian food distribution, they would not distinguish between supplies for soldiers and for civilians. They wished that, as in the military, officials would conceive of civilian food provisioning in terms of reciprocation and enabling a contribution to the national effort rather than as poor relief. The conception of how officials provisioned civilians remained as important as the actual material benefits poor consumers sought, even as food became more scarce. Germans voiced hope that the KEA was a sign of new and appropriate relations between state and society, and evidence of internal governmental reform as well as of the food dictator Berliners now seemed to agree was necessary.[5]

The KEA was founded, at least in part, on the apparently genuine concern of some officials (including in the Prussian war and interior ministries as well as in the less influential Reichstag) for the plight of hungry Germans. Officials also expected that the KEA's programs would quiet popular disturbances. At the same time, although authorities promised the KEA would lead authoritatively and single-mindedly, Prussian and imperial officials proposed an institution with an eye to inclusive leadership. The KEA executive committee was chartered to include representatives of the trade unions, the Social Democratic Party (SPD), urban centers, and bourgeois women's groups. Women's groups participated in the form of a special committee on the provisioning of women, implying that women presented a discrete provisioning problem. Officials hoped this move to include presumed representatives of the populace would be received as responsiveness to popular demand. There is no question that this maneuver also allowed for the diffusion of blame in the event of failures.

The broad set of organizations, offices, and parties represented on the board of the KEA engendered conflict among its members, despite the agency's presumed singular mandate. Outside pressures also burdened the office. Outspoken Prussian agricultural minister Klemens von Schorlemer and his minions worked successfully to prevent a Social Democrat from occupying the KEA's director seat—in the interest, Schorlemer claimed, of serving "the *whole* people."[6] At the same time, Supreme Army Commander Erich von Falkenhayn resisted putting General Wilhelm Groener in charge, another potentially popular move, precisely to diminish the KEA's pressure on the military administration. War Ministry officials placed the agency under the stewardship of Conservative Adolf von Batocki, former administrative head of rural East Prussia.

National Women's Service member and later War Office Women's Bureau chief Marie-Elisabeth Lüders observed other potential pitfalls in the set-up of the KEA. "Through the Bundesrat proclamation of 22 May 1916, the power [to control food supplies for the civilian population] was transferred 'within certain limits' to the chancellor, who handed them over also 'within certain limits' to the KEA, to provide for the nourishment of the people."[7] She noted that the army was still separately provisioned and retained priority claims on agricultural production. Lüders added that, as a Prussian office, the KEA had no formal jurisdiction over other states. Indeed protesting the vested interests this new Prussian-centered authority, state and local governments maintained intranational export bans, although these governments had in many cases joined the chorus for centralized control. Moreover, planners of the new agency never clarified the KEA's relationship with the various Prussian and imperial authorities. Schorlemer used the imperial Bundesrat to keep KEA hands off the interests of big agriculture. Conflicts between agriculture and interior ministry officials and other instances of "departmental particularism" tied the hands of KEA authorities at each juncture.[8] The KEA frequently battled its own ostensible ally, the Imperial Office of the Interior.[9] In contrast with the popular vision, Interior officials and other high-level authorities hoped to use the KEA to regularize market relations and thereby avoid a controlled economy. As Lüders concluded, "Establishment of a 'dictator' was not, then, realized."

The result was that the KEA was only very limitedly successful in its mission of total control. The KEA moved to coordinate the innumerable offices at every level that collected and distributed "most important" foods around the country. In the months after its founding, the office also organized the controlled distribution of many additional foods. But General Groener privately registered disgust for the limits of the agency's power, by both plan and temperament. He described in his diary the "bloodless creation of holy St. Compromise" concerning the jurisdiction as well as the leadership of the office. Groener added, "Batocki doesn't want to get on anyone's bad side . . . everywhere nice, everywhere flexible. . . . 'Dictators' aren't cut from this kind of wood." As summer 1916 wore on, Groener grew more assertive in his opinion that the agency must be given more transcendent authority—if only to save the German state.[10] Like its predecessors such as the Price Monitoring Authority, in the end the KEA had insufficient power to enforce its own regulations. Especially by midwar, moreover, authorities lacked both the personnel to oversee individual trade practices and the moral authority to demand compliance. Private entrepreneurs skirted new regulations nearly as easily as they had in the past. In response to the KEA's limited immediate effects, popular support for the authority faded within weeks after the office's inauguration; public airing of the many conflicts surrounding the agency's jurisdiction quashed expectations almost from the start.[11] The populace found Batocki all too clearly heir to Delbrück's legacy of ineffectual leadership.

Poorer Berliners demonstrated a state of renewed bitterness in the summer of 1916, as many suffered compromised health for the first time since the beginning of the war. Surveys by the War Committee for Consumers' Interests showed many urban Germans at 40 percent of prewar levels of food intake, 25 percent below Eltzbacher's standard of necessary consumption. Health official Max Rubner claimed in retrospect that many working- and lower middle-class Germans were eating at closer to one-third of prewar consumption, identifying this period as the first interval of serious malnutrition. Ernst Kaeber reinforces this judgment specifically for Berlin.[12] Dr. Alfred Grotjahn described Berliners as appearing "ever more Mongolian" in the spring of 1916, with cheekbones jutting out and skin hanging in folds.[13]

Berliners pursued a variety of individual and collective strategies to address their predicament. Wealthy residents observed with some amusement their gardens filled with noisy chickens and planted with every vegetable. For their part, working-class Berliners attempted to grow potatoes and keep them secure on plots dug near railroad tracks and in the Friedrichshain and Hasenheide parks. They tried to keep goats on the tiny balconies of their tenement apartments, but such efforts were difficult to maintain. In July lower civil servants formally protested their circumstances for the first time, presenting Bethmann with an urgent petition for aid. Metalworkers (still a predominantly male population in mid-1916) threatened work stoppages throughout the summer in consequence of insufficient food, making very direct the connections between consumption and production.

Food-related unrest in the streets of Berlin and throughout Germany returned with a vengeance. Police and deputy military commanders characterized "women" as "in a terrible mood," protesting loudly for "peace at any price." They noted, too, the particular interest of radical Social Democrats in these women and, in turn, the former's success in turning out 25,000 demonstrators in Potsdamer Platz on 27 June, demanding, among other things, the release of Karl Liebknecht from custody. Desperate women filled the streets, now actively demonstrating with signs and banners demanding food and peace, as in artist Franz Wimmer's drawing, "We Want Peace."[14] While the high commander's office confidently opined that factory workers would resist any major, extended radical action, "on the other hand, the widespread street demonstrations must be prevented at all costs," in light of their ominous potential.[15] Officers described demonstrators ever more insistently as both working class and lower middle class. Around the city and particularly in heterogeneous Charlottenburg, police now felt obliged to arrest numerous women in the spring and summer of 1916 for acts of verbal and physical violence against police and against the state.[16] As official failures grew more monumental, so did the frustration of the populace, which, having assigned the Wilhelmine government the responsibility of ensuring basic needs, wondered aloud whether this government was capable of doing so. Police warned of increased popular attention to the new Spartacists and other left Social Democrats and foretold the rise of a revolutionary threat. Police Officer Schade reported fearfully, "Everything pointed to the notion that, with the end of the war, there would be active agitation against capitalism and against the government."[17]

Broader political turmoil drew on this focus. In June, even as officials sought approval of new war credits, Reichstag members across the political spectrum threatened a vote of no confidence for Bethmann, some for his failure to preside over the domestic crisis, and others for the distraction from military efforts. Political organizations from Spartacists to peace groups to the ultra-right Free Patriotic Union held formal demonstrations, calling for an end to the war or for the installation of a military government. They converged on the idea that "Hollweg *soll weg*," that Bethmann must resign.

It is clear that Prussian and imperial authorities were listening carefully to "the street," as officials put it, on the food question, in decisions over Bethmann's future and replacement of the Supreme Army Command (Oberste Heeresleitung, or OHL) as well as in discussions of possible new military aggressions and expanded submarine warfare.[18] Bethmann responded with efforts to heighten the powers of the KEA, but with little result.[19] Batocki promised at the same time to open KEA discussion to the scrutiny and judgment of the wider public; the promise was a remarkable signal of the transformation in political culture.[20] But in July *Vorwärts* claimed that the decision-making process in the KEA still took place behind closed doors.[21] In the midst of this domestic turmoil, in August Romania entered the war on the Entente side. This signaled Chief of Staff Falkenhayn's failed negotiations with that country, which was an important potential source of grain. Overwhelmed, the kaiser immediately appointed Hindenburg chief of the OHL. This seemed an inspired move among so many political blunders. One of the few remaining popular figures in government employ, Hindenburg was perhaps most admired for his ability to "get things done." The prospect of Hindenburg's takeover temporarily revived popular calm and cautious hope. Though Hindenburg was clearly committed to continuing the war, Germans believed they were finally getting their "*military food* dictator."[22] This image was no accident but was, rather, the product of the careful grooming of Hindenburg by aide Martin Bauer.[23]

Hindenburg hit the ground running. He invested imperial officials with emergency powers over the Prussian ministries, giving Groener, a military official, command of the War Ministry and the KEA beneath it.[24] The OHL itself took on powers heretofore reserved for the civilian administration, including jurisdiction over the economy. OHL leaders formally solicited extended authority from the kaiser, claiming that the civilian administration was losing public confidence because of the food crisis.[25] To be sure, by the winter of 1916—17 virtually all foods were produced and distributed through official coordination—at least in principle. But regardless of its tough talk, the OHL hesitated to alienate its erstwhile allies, refusing, for example, to make the KEA an imperial office, as the much maligned Batocki had recommended.

On top of this, rumor spread furiously in the early fall of 1916 that Prussian and imperial officials had disseminated false propaganda from the beginning of the war, domestically as well as abroad, concerning the abundance of national food supplies. Urban Germans responded with rage; rural Germans, with bitter contempt. This widespread controversy took place simultaneously with angry popular debate of the state's true war aims. Germans asked themselves whether officials had lied about both to trick them into war two years earlier, virtually ensuring a food crisis.[26] The two topics were closely linked in new public demands for open, responsive governance, by which measure the Wilhelmine state appeared to have failed miserably. SPD Reichstag representative Philipp Scheidemann responded in October 1916 to popular outcry: "In the provisioning of food, many grave errors have been committed. The worst is that the people were not told the truth in the first place."[27] He challenged the state, including the new military leadership, to make good on its promises in order to save itself. Meanwhile police reported, "The lower classes of the people look on the coming winter with great worry. . . . One casts complete blame on the KEA. . . . In the poorer circles . . . [the KEA] has been characterized as an establishment that not only deprives children of their main foods, but also entrenches this undernourishment." Officer Dittmann concluded, "In general one hears from these circles and beyond still further cries for a rapid peace."[28]

Police spies confirmed popular accusations that, as a result of this misguided official policy, the state itself might have subverted the chances for military victory, guaranteeing, rather, an "unfavorable peace."[29] Noting the price increase of 1,000 percent and more of some foods, by December the *Tägliche Rundschau* proclaimed, speaking in the name of "even those among us who don't eat potatoes," that Germany's insistence on its adequate food supplies was "a very lie-filled truth, a two-sided sword, an instrument of hari kiri. . . . [Further,] the serious mistakes of the KEA's price policies are in part responsible for the *construction* of the terrible situation."[30] The article concluded menacingly but ambiguously, "Now whatever food is left (and there's doubtlessly something) must be handed over to the consumers." Officer Görl reported that "women," including even those "from functionary circles," were engaged in "the most provocative talk against the authorities in question."[31] Observers around the country joined Officer Görl on the eve of the catastrophic winter of 1916—17 in predicting dire consequences for the Wilhelmine state, precipitated by women protesting in the nation's streets.[32]

FOOD DISTRIBUTION, THE NEW ORIENTATION, AND THE GERMAN POLITICAL ECONOMY

Administrative failures in the first half of the war concerning the most important foods had led to the belief widespread in Berlin that only total government control of all foods could ensure equitable distribution. This emphasis on control permitted segments of the population with vastly different perspectives and interests to unite, at least publicly, in advancing a solution to the food problem. This solution challenged the Wilhelmine government to demonstrate at once its forcefulness and its responsiveness to the German people. It also engendered broad, urgent discussion of Germany's political economy and the nature of government intervention, with implications beyond the war economy. In response, beginning in the spring of 1916, the press and other public bodies hinted at the possibility of a "new orientation" of the government that would provide the prospect of measures appropriate in scale to respond to the new obligations and relations developed in war, including particularly around the food question. This notion, which Social Democrats had advanced in the years preceding the war, and which Bethmann himself had entertained without result, now referred to a wide range of proposed reforms, including increased representation of the working class and of women at all levels, from universal franchise to labor and party representation on industrial boards.[33] In the wake of the late 1915 protests, SPD representatives pushed for this new orientation as the quid pro quo for their loyalty to the civil peace and for their efforts to hold their constituency in line, despite the strained domestic conditions.[34] Police, the press, private organizations, and a wide array of actors in the public sphere commented on the idea. Weighing the risks, Bethmann announced cautious and ambiguous plans for a "political new orientation."[35]

Some quarters responded privately and even publicly with concern, recognizing that this might well be a discussion about long-term structural changes. Many Germans expressed fear for the "rationalization" of governance and of society, anticipating heated interwar debate across the continent.[36] *Germania,* the premier organ of the Catholic Center Party, worried that "political new orientation" could not be separated from a complete "economic new orientation," and that, together, they represented threatening changes for the country.[37] The Center Party took a decisive stand against the policy, allying itself with "the right" against such a "one-sided and exclusive orientation toward the left."[38] From outside Prussia, Bavarian minister president (and future chancellor) Georg Graf von Hertling registered his concerns for the apparent favoring of urban as against rural interests in the pursuit of "socialist principles."[39] Commercial interests sounded a note of alarm in response to an article in the March 1916 edition of the Social Democratic *Internationale Korrespondenz*, which made clear the radical potential of the new orientation.[40] Business interests generally questioned whether the current "war socialism" might not devolve into peacetime socialism.[41]

The idea of prevailing conditions as war socialism appears absurd in light of the tremendous profits capitalists gained through arming and feeding Germany, all the more in a government under Hindenburg's control.[42] Nonetheless, whether through hope or fear, contemporaries across the societal spectrum identified prevalent government practices in this fashion and entertained the notion of the survival of the practices beyond the war. Economist Albert Hesse noted that "the question of whether the war has brought us closer to socialism now takes clearer shape," but he concluded that the long-term implications for the economy were still open.[43] Detractors aided supporters in bringing the new orientation to the attention of all Germans and linking it to a potentially more radical agenda for political and economic reform, further legitimating such notions.

At least as many officials and community elders remained more worried that the government would not exercise sufficient control over food distribution for the duration of the war, with tragic implications for the war effort and for domestic peace. On the eve of Hindenburg's accession to power, General Groener wrote remarkably in his private record, "On the domestic front, the government [should] pursue Social Democratic practices. Without state socialism, we won't make it through. Therefore, no more waiting: get to it."[44] His aide within the KEA, Robert Merton, observed that, all the more once the Third Supreme Army Command ruled, "the movement of the war economy from right to left has been treated respectively as a dangerous or a welcome omen regarding the 'new orientation,' and fought for more or less on these terms."[45] Merton made his own position clear in an October 1916 confidential position paper, asserting that a new order of "total control" was essential to the basic nutrition of those of little means, currently threatened by officials' pandering to interest groups, inside and outside the government.[46] Merton observed the growing nervousness of "agrarian-conservatives" by the late fall of 1916, finding imperial officials less "trustworthy" allies than they had been in the past. The *Deutsche*

Tageszeitung wrote, "Without a doubt, the majority of current measures for the war economy have a strongly socialist cast."[47] Yet, the author continued, this was strictly temporary reform from above to forestall greater demands from below. Therefore, the writer urged the paper's conservative readership to submit to these changes.

Military officials followed their civilian predecessors, however, down the road of promising reforms, then pursuing them only in limited fashion, ultimately validating the reforms while advertising their own shortcomings in realizing them. In October 1916 Hindenburg's new state secretary of the interior Karl Helfferich confusedly assured anxious Reichstag representatives (a large percentage of whom were Social Democrats) that his acts were guided by the prevailing "state of emergency": "What I'm saying has nothing to do with any new orientation." He indeed suggested such reforms would best come after the end of the war.[48] Authorities expressed concern for the "multiple hostile encounters" between Helfferich and the Social Democrats.[49] Helfferich's intransigence was enough to arouse popular nostalgia for Delbrück, who was regarded as incompetent but sincere. Prussian officials noted privately that "The [SPD] journalists . . . now urgently demand *acts* of the new orientation; [the limited response] creates doubts as to whether the chancellor has indeed the power to pursue these acts, over inflexible wills."[50] These "skirmishes" in turn incited "endless" public exposition over food control and a new orientation, reaching a zenith by late fall and extending well beyond the capital city limits.[51] The result was, the *Breslauer Tagewacht* charged, that indeed "the previous indications regarding a new orientation are no longer adequate for the masses; they want to see where it will go. The mistrust . . . is growing rapidly throughout the masses."[52]

Until late 1916 the populace in the streets had commented little specifically on the new orientation, insofar as it represented expanded franchise. Now, however, poorer consumers grew angry at what appeared to be a fresh example of false responsiveness. This was of concern to the OHL, which required a relatively compliant civilian population for its new military plans. Thus, despite pressure from some high-level Prussian officials, under OHL direction imperial authorities attempted to evince a more convincing display of commitment to reform, exhibiting a conciliatory facade to labor and the SPD in late 1916 as well as to its more traditional partners in negotiation. By the end of the year imperial officials were forced to act on some of their new promises, such as their extensive agreements with trade union officials that provided for special food supplements and factory canteens as well as for greater representation in the decision-making process generally. Moving beyond the immediate military interest in the war factories, the OHL hoped to use Georg Michaelis, director of the Imperial Grain Authority and confidant of the new military leadership, to convince Berliners and other Prussians of the leaders' sincere commitment to a military food dictatorship, as related to the new orientation. These acts had the effect of further legitimating the rhetoric of new orientation and of other broad political and economic reforms. Moreover, as war raw materials chief Walther Rathenau warned Bethmann and imperial Interior officials, by late 1916 it was clear that the controlled economy would undoubtedly continue after the end of the war—whatever the government in power.[53]

In turn, poor urban consumers helped to establish the philosophical validity of opposition to the free market that inspired public embrace of both a new orientation and a forced economy, with ends very different from those envisioned by Conservatives on the eve of war.[54] The rhetoric of "artificial" and "arbitrary" distribution in reference to free-market trade and profit returned with force to popular parlance by mid-1916, in contrast to the liberal view that a "free" market was the most "natural" way to regulate trade. Police spy Schiller reported in May 1916, "The arbitrariness with which the butchers acted against the shopping public in the last week . . . only contributed to fanning the flames between the poorer class of people and the propertied." As a consequence, he continued, "one hears everywhere that 'peace' is the only solution; with help from the men returning from the field, the women hope to transform the relations that constitute their miserable living conditions."[55] Schiller reinforced the position of these women as leaders whose husbands and sons on the front would return to act as their aides.

The *Berliner Volkszeitung* emphasized the degrading effect of the free market, provocatively demanding in May that butchers "let Berliners feed [*fressen*] on their meat in peace" and claiming that "Berliners hereby express their gratitude for the opportunity to eat meat already half eaten by rats and mice."[56] Hans von Berlepsch, former Prussian official and head of the Association for Social Reform, spoke to the inappropriateness of market trade, which wounded one's sense of justice, with potentially dangerous effects.[57] Soon the press across the board questioned the legitimacy of free-market activity; as *Der Tag* posed the question, "Is this allowed?"[58]

By the second half of 1916, buoyed by both street-level protest and the government's own renewed insistence on its commitment to controlled food distribution, many among the greater public questioned why a shopkeeper should be able to determine the price of his or her goods generally or which goods and how much of them he or she sold. Why, in other words, was he or she justified in acting to maximize profits in any context? In this setting the specter of bread versus cake, the lack of fats to spread on bread, and the holding back of potatoes, meat, and butter all returned to haunt officials.[59] In October police belittled butchers' claims that they were abiding by market practices: "The notion that the butchers aren't getting enough meat lacks any support whatsoever. . . . As any number of people [have to] let their meat cards expire because of the high price, the butcher can scarcely be in the unpleasant situation of being unable to satisfy his customers."[60] Officer Rüschel closed a report by noting that the only thing one could be sure of was that butchers were up to no good, deciding for themselves who should receive meat.[61] Berliners also asked why farmers, with whom city residents had direct contact at the weekly markets, should be able to choose how much to bring to market. In light of this new thinking, the *Berliner Volkszeitung* refashioned a market-based argument to suggest that the sale of cake instead of bread was "completely uneconomic . . . and stands in *no relation* to the value of the ware." The author concluded emphatically that the new administration must correct this injustice. The value of a ware must be calculated relative to the product's ability to fill the needs of certain populations.[62]

Poorer consumers complained in late 1916 that it was equally artificial and unnatural that the richest and best-connected Berliners had privileged access to food merely on account of money and social status. This was a new order of thinking, a step beyond impugning soldiers' wives for undermining prewar socioeconomic arrangements. Interior Ministry reports indicate that "it [was] considered particularly noteworthy" that "well-off" people still had access to all manner of foods due to insufficient control of the market.[63] The petit bourgeois *Berliner Volkszeitung* inflamed readers in December 1916 by reporting on a discussion in the Prussian parliament in which representatives claimed that "'only the most enormously rich'" could afford goose simply "for the pleasure of the palate." Goose, normally a luxury or feast-related item, was prohibitively expensive for the working and lower middle class even before the war. But by Christmas 1916 goose symbolized desperately needed, "bodily-warming" fat as well as protein. The author asserted the "widespread opinion," which he shared, that this distribution was not right.[64] The panoply of food distribution bureaucracies likewise reported to their superiors "inequities" in consumption deriving from a still-prevailing "artificial" market system, above all in the major cities.[65]

Still, the broad public admonished with exasperation, officials insisted on governing through "half-way" measures.[66] As a result, official measures tied the hands only of those who required protection. Most Berliners did not

"Her Majesty, the Saleswoman: 'Would anyone perhaps like anything?'" (Vossische Zeitung, *11 May 1916*)

condemn the controlled economy, at least publicly; they condemned its poor execution. SPD leader Otto Braun asserted that the plan for distribution of potatoes, the most plebeian of foods, "serve[d] only the minority."[67] "Meatless days" and "unity sausage" provided little relief for poor consumers and little evidence of equalized distribution; wealthy Berliners dined on truffles and caviar or bought up extra meat the day before at uncontrolled prices.[68] *Vorwärts* reflected popular animus with its sarcastic piece "To Each an Egg," repeating the wording of a proclamation hung around the city.[69] The author noted that many Berliners did not even receive their one egg because of a system that worked against those who tried to work within it. Prussian Interior Ministry officials acknowledged that the populace found new measures, such as fixing ceilings on cheese or providing coupons for potatoes when the products had long disappeared from the market, absurd and even malevolent.[70] The press supported popular fears that "half-baked" government measures actually promoted profiteering and mal-distribution, as in the *Norddeutsche Allgemeine Zeitung,* which taunted, "Miss, would you like a little butter? You can have as much as you want."[71] In this way, those against the controlled market and those who deplored the execution of this market converged in condemnation of the government.

"Deeply embittered" consumers protested that authorities had explicitly organized and institutionalized a "dual system" that seemed to many to maximize the injustice, creating the "socially undesirable situation in which the poor were languishing while the rich had excesses."[72] Officials themselves had introduced the notion of a dual system through a plan to satisfy the basic needs of all without sacrificing the privileges of the wealthy. By late 1916 Berliners blamed the dual system for the disappearance of coffee, jam, and sugar. Germans considered coffee and jam essential to making bread without butter edible. Sugar was vital for making bitter turnips palatable in the absence of potatoes. Consumers in the streets ridiculed Prussian efforts in August to set up the War Profiteering Office (Kriegswucheramt, or KWA), accusing officials of promoting hoarding themselves.[73] Yet poorer Berliners continued to make demands on authorities, maintaining their belief that officials still could and would provide for their needs and regularize distribution if only they could see the error of their ways. Poorer Berliners continued to assert their own patriotism, which police and military authorities reinforced.[74]

At this point in the war, being first in line, running fastest from store to store, and pushing ahead the most effectively held no greater merit than greater wealth for most Berliners as the means to distribution. The *Berliner Tageblatt* deplored "the 'right of the stronger elbow'" that supplanted "equitable distribution."[75] The *Berliner Morgenpost* noted that in the daily "onslaught" before bakeries, the weak or ill were at the mercy of the bakers; indeed, they were required to ask for special treatment.[76] Capital residents insisted they should not submit to lawlessness and disorder that emerged in the streets because of weak leadership, they should not have to compete in the virtual battlefield that was the market, and above all, they should not have to depend on the mercy of the enemy. Police found this privilege to the fleet of foot the surest source of dangerous rioting in late 1916; Officer Schrott reported "pure consternation" over the "virtual race to the door," creating a "mob . . . among which often one may hear the most vile, destructive rhetoric against the government."[77] By now Berliners seem to have widely accepted that the distribution of food ought not to be based on any form of competition at all.

In this context the civilian and military administrations struggled with

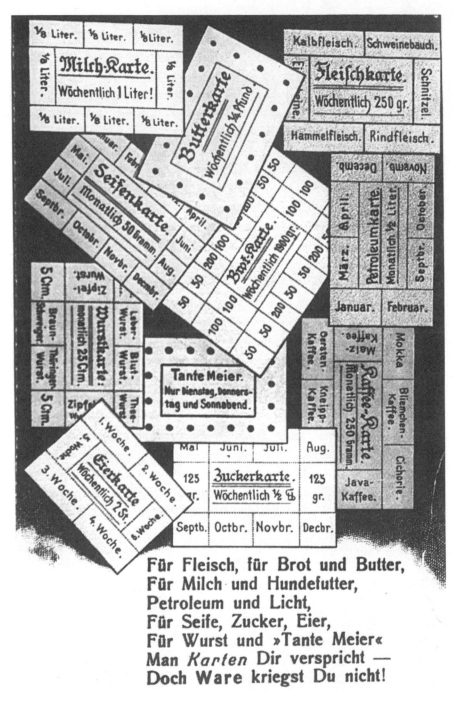

Für Fleisch, für Brot und Butter,
Für Milch und Hundefutter,
Petroleum und Licht,
Für Seife, Zucker, Eier,
Für Wurst und »Tante Meier«
Man *Karten* Dir verspricht —
Doch Ware kriegst Du nicht!

"They promise you cards. But goods you won't get!" (BAPK, file 1578)

widespread demand for a new orientation at the end of 1916. The League of German Women's Groups (BDF), moderate Social Democrats, and other social reformers urged authorities to announce plans for new political rights that reflected the contributions and sacrifices of both women and men.[78] Others voiced a far more radical vision of societal transformation.[79] The radical Social Democratic Women's Conference that took place in October (along with a secret Berlin women's meeting in late September) spelled out in great detail the relationship between peace, food provisioning, women's work, and the transformation of domestic political relations.[80] By early 1917 the future of the war, the chancellor, and the kaiser himself were wrapped up with these demands for reform. At the same time, the new year marked the formal establishment of the Independent SPD, which explicitly dismissed the existing regime's potential for meaningful reformability.

NEW TRUE GERMANS AND THE BATTLE OF THE MARKET

For many urban Germans, by 1916 not just the market but the market economy represented a battlefield. Prussian and imperial officials characterized public pressure for total government as informed by a "distribution fanaticism," a demand for "equalization" between consumers and producers, inspired by "war psychosis."[81] The deception of authorities and their refusal to realize fully their perceived promises constituted a swindle that ill rewarded and even maligned the steadfast patriotism of urban Germans. Asserting their own unity, Berliners claimed that Prussian and imperial officials allowed inner enemies, now identified as farmers, residents of other cities, and even other German provincial governments, to flourish in the battle of the market economy. At the same time, urban German consumers not only challenged the appropriateness of a market economy for Germany; they also asserted a vision of popular sovereignty, claiming themselves to be the real site of the nation, which the government must serve or spurn at its own risk.

Berliners' public demand for total government control of food distribution drew on a presumed shared assumption that the artificial market economy exposed them to inimical forces. A columnist in the *Tägliche Rundschau* denounced Bundesrat officials as pandering to interest politics and obstructing measures for the good of the whole — as represented by Berliners. "Here there is obviously skulduggery at play," the columnist wrote, "and the call for patience in the name of patriotic interest is only aiding and abetting the swindle."[82] He concluded menacingly that even in the United States, with its "unrestricted freedom," there were lynch laws for scoundrels, and that the Bundesrat "traitors" should likewise be brought to justice in Germany. The *Berliner Tageblatt* contrasted the government's treachery with the patriotism of Berliners. The author noted that the foreign enemy was well aware of the "stirring patience" and "great sacrifices" of Germans and especially Berliners, which German officials seemed to snub rather than reward. The article continued rather disingenuously, "It's not as though the deficiencies here were more sensitive elsewhere but, rather, that here the *inequality* of the distribution—less a deficiency of food than of *organization*—is particularly palpable."[83]

Although poorer urban residents of Berlin and other large cities condemned the access of wealthy and well-connected individuals to food, urban populations as a whole continued to cast the enemy outward. Despite new revelations that German food supplies were not as abundant as authorities had once maintained, Berliners united in their condemnation not just of farmers but of the German rural population more broadly, as "artificially privileged" precisely in their ability to escape regulation. Robert Merton of the KEA identified the battle between urban and rural populations over the question of government control as the most contentious in the inner war in the fall of 1916, stemming from "psychological as well as material" sources.[84] In one of his first reports, new Berlin police commissioner Oppen confirmed that, in the capital, it was "the widespread view that Berlin was far more poorly situated for food than those in the country."[85] Lord Mayor Wermuth emphasized that "while in the country meat pots remained full, Berliners struggled for a weekly ration of half a pound, marking a slow starvation."[86] A cry arose throughout the capital against the "self-helping" or "self-provisioning" rural consumer. Berliners were "wildly jealous of the self-provisioner. This jealousy had not coincidently contributed to the growth of the highly undesirable opposition between city and country."[87]

But as in the case of soldiers' wives, the fault, Berliners claimed, lay with the Prussian and imperial administrations. The greater Berlin public complained that state policy focused only on controlling consumption within the cities themselves while leaving consumption in the countryside to its own resources. In this way, too, officials instituted a dual system in which the good Germans were controlled while loyalists to greed and profit were given free reign.[88] Social Democratic Berlin municipal representative Paul von Hintze concurred: "The closing off of great states and other parts of the country from import into the big cities must be done away with; it must not be that the latter languish while those in the countryside come away well from it."[89] According to KEA guidelines, growers had to be given the advantage with the product of their own labor because it was counterproductive to "bind the mouth of the hand that feeds."[90] Michaelis tried to defend government efforts, explaining attempts to help farmers relearn the Christian ethic, changing from "Give us this day *my* daily bread" to "*our* daily bread."[91] Yet once more superficially deferring to popular demand, the KEA responded to the unrelenting call for total control over countryside as well as city by rationing many foods for rural consumers in December 1916 and January 1917, though rural populations received more than city dwellers. In response German farmers predictably expressed their own deep concerns for the government favoring the cities.

This new rationing plan infuriated Berliners all the more, for, they claimed, it suggested that their counterparts in the country actually deserved the greater portions to which they had earlier helped themselves.[92] Capital residents saw the distribution question not only as a touchstone for the government's reformability. Berliners also viewed it as a referendum on who contributed more to the nation—who was a better symbol, indeed, of Germanness. Officer Klonicki wrote that poorer Berliners painfully contemplated the new ration distribution, particularly as food prices still rose "usuriously . . . while the government does nothing to restrain these inner enemies of our fatherland."[93] Klonicki's report called into question the Germanness of the rural population while, typically, equating the urban population with the population of lesser means. His colleague Schade found likewise that as "the population of lesser means and the lower civil servant" found difficulty in just surviving by late 1916, "the bitterness grows each day against the rich, rural producers as well as against the businessmen. In general one regards these as the worst enemy, who don't possess the least glimmer of patriotism and love of one's fellow man."[94]

Both Liberal and Social Democratic representatives weighed in with attacks on Agricultural Minister Schorlemer, as intercessor for the interests of Junkers with little concern for "distributional equity." Right-wing Social Democrat Robert Schmidt observed the egregious "inequalities" in distribution between urban residents and those living in "surplus areas." This sharp contrast "permits the conclusion that Mr. von Schorlemer has no idea about the situation with our food. It would be advisable for him to take a look from time to time at the working-class neighborhoods of Berlin and to look at the crowds that gather before the shops. . . . He could also have seen just how well a working-class family makes out with these rations."[95] Emanuel Wurm put it more simply, repeating the rhetoric of the previous year: "The pig gets the potato, the people get the fodder—the turnip."[96] By year's end the broad urban populace blamed Schorlemer for having swayed Hindenburg from a policy of total, equitable control, which the populace had initially imputed to him, to one of differentiating among and privileging various populations, such as rural residents, through sins of both omission and commission.[97] Though Berliners perceived these policies as politically motivated, nonetheless they felt their sacrifices slighted and their patriotism impugned.

Berliners believed that the state ignored their sacrifices not only with respect to rural regions but also vis-à-vis other areas of the country. Capital city residents felt that, as Prussians, they suffered relative to Bavarians, who still seemed to have adequate reserves of fat, and in comparison with residents of Württemburg, which had maintained its food export bans to other states of the country.[98] The local press trumpeted the perceived disparity in regional provisioning, which further incited popular concern. Newspapers warned that officials' measures exacerbated the effects of the "ridiculous" trade bans—comparable to the blockade itself—which thrived among the German states and even among districts in Greater Berlin. The *Berliner Tageblatt* warned, "*This must* have an embittering and agitating effect. Examples of this will soon be countless; they grow so from day to day."[99] The populace was all the more furious at authorities' differentiation between Berlin and other industrial centers, such as the Ruhr region, as well as the contrast of Berlin with cities that were clearly lesser centers of war production.[100] Berliners proclaimed that conditions in east Prussian cities were the worst, and Berlin was the worst of these. This sentiment was manifested in each region of the country, as the new monthly reports of the deputy commanders make clear.

In this poisoned atmosphere Berliners joined other Germans in adopting anti-Semitic language in the course of 1916, a habit that became particularly entrenched after the end of the war.[101] Greater numbers of Germans in turn found such language, long a marginal discourse, useful in deflecting blame. New and preexisting radical right organizations began to generate and disseminate anti-Semitic propaganda by early 1916, specifically tying Jews to the nation's food woes.[102] In March the anti-Semitic Reichs-Hammer-Bund issued a statement detailing the Jewish sources of the economic war visited upon the German people.[103] By mid-year, mainstream Germans around the country began to accept and employ this explanation, though irregularly. The peak of public anti-Semitic expression in mid-1916 seems related to the strength of the sentiment that control of distribution was handled poorly, rather than to the actual subsistence crisis that arose in the subsequent winter. In Berlin, anti-Semitism was also related to the influx of refugees, some of whom were Jewish, from the East from the beginning of the war, putting pressure on already strained resources.

The notion of "the Jew" worked well in public discourse because of the figure's perceived quality as apart from, alien to, and even inimical to the German nation. "The Jew" figured primarily as the commercial middleman (*Geschäftsjude*) who brought urban consumers (and even retailers) to their knees through his allegiance to profit. This idea had a long pedigree, including Berliners Albert Stöcker and Heinrich von Treitschke among its supporters.[104] Oppen reported in August, "The blame for the present food relations is directed primarily against the producers and the middlemen, who are all of them designated as speculators and war userers, among which one supposes they are predominantly Jews."[105] He warned his superiors that the onus was on them to control this source of misery. It was "Galician Jews" who held back eggs from the people in Berlin, Oppen reported, modifying the category to intensify the perception of the merchants as aliens.[106] Jews made a fine foil for popular frustrations, as blaming them seemed least injurious to the putative public unity at a point when the end of the civil peace entered active discussion. When some cast their Jewish co-nationals as being opposed to Germans, the integrity of German unity appeared intact, while this inner enemy seemed closely aligned to the outer enemy. Protesters absurdly observed Jews' "advantage" as consumers as well in not so keenly feeling the absence of pork or the inability to purchase goose, because they did not celebrate the Christian holidays with which Germans associated the fowl.[107]

Consistent with a long-evolving process, some Germans associated "Jewish" not only with a particular religion or even "race" but, rather, with the act of profiteering. In turn, the term "Jew" was used to represent anyone who engaged in such activity. The "Jewish gouger," a term without necessary reference to the background or heritage of the person in question, graced popular rhetoric. Berliners referred likewise to the "Jewish double-talk" (*Judenquatscherei*) with which such merchants deceived poor consumers.[108] The victims of the Jew's ploys were, variously, Germans, the people, those of little means, women, and children. Use of "the Jew" worked alongside class and other antagonisms. Police hinted at their agreement with "the word in Berlin . . . that only Jewesses and the wives of munitions workers can afford goose now."[109] Social Democratic leaders "recognized with great clarity a certain anti-Semitic strain among the workers, which is traced to the supposed or actual heavy participation of the Hebrew population in war contracts, to incidents of speculation [*Wucher*], and to their role in the press (also *within* the army)."[110]

Some Germans identified "the Jew" as one of the worst consequences of the government's lack of sufficiently broad and thorough control.[111] A member of the radical Reichs-Hammer-Bund wrote in November 1916, "It is unfortunately quite certain that wide circles of the German people, including also rural dwellers, great landowners, and peasants, have been infected by the prevailing profiteering epidemic that originated among the Jewish war producers, profiteers, and 'chain' merchants."[112] Charging the government with failing to stem this profiteering, the Bund called on the church to pursue the anti-Christian enemies of the fatherland. A policeman warned his superiors in April that prevailing policies permitted a Jewish poultry retailer to offer "soup bones . . . of such inferior quality that even the women of little means out to buy something refused them."[113] Many Berliners asserted that, in the absence of sufficient government control, Jews were able to wriggle out of the draft because of their suspiciously won riches and because of their "connections," which "normal Berliners" lacked. *Vorwärts* reported that the "'opinion [was] widely held among the people'" that "in the war industries, there were particularly many '*Jewish* shirkers.'"[114] This also left Jewish food merchants free to insult and trick Germans without repercussion.

Prussian and imperial officials did not shy from employing such notions themselves. Anti-Semitic epithets may have actually aided imperial officials in acting on urban demands for control by drawing on the support of the growing radical right forces, including in the countryside. Bethmann and Delbrück invoked anti-Semitic language in their well-publicized conflict over the future of food control.[115] In August the high commander whipped up the already heightened sentiments through a temporary ban on publication of the *Berliner Tageblatt,* edited by Jewish liberal Theodor Wolff. Though the ban stemmed officially from Wolff's liberties in a column questioning the inevitability of war as a general principle (the paper also regularly annoyed officials with its insistent pro-intervention stance on food), authorities countenanced the popular viewpoint that Wolff's "Jewishness" played a part in his willingness to question the nation's role in war.[116] On 19 October the Imperial Budget Committee resolved to determine how many among those who had "avoided the draft" thus far were Jews.[117] In the fall of 1916, imperial authorities released information on the controversial "Jew Count," figures compiled in the process of taking the national census. In doing so, Philipp Scheidemann claimed, officials had pandered to popular opinion in the worst way, using the results of the census to encourage the rising anti-Semitism.[118] Certainly from 1917 on, state propaganda and the Conservative press alike attempted to use these domestic divisions to rally support for the war, naming the new revolutionary Russian leaders as Jews with "connections" and with dreams of conquest on German soil.

Officials' strategy backfired. In the second half of 1916 many Germans countered that the ongoing food crisis proved the government itself was Jewish, as well as a defender of Jews. This was a sign of the state's own inimical relation with the German people and the German nation. Conservative Party leader Kuno Graf von Westarp denounced the "Bethmann-system," the chancellor's systematic missteps on the provisioning issue, as benefiting the nation's Jewish enemy. Police Officer Lobiecki noted the popular analog: "Recently one can hear it said everywhere that Germany can defeat its outer enemy; but, in contrast, the inner enemy (this refers to the KEA and the Jews) will bring the people over the edge, and that's not far away anymore."[119]

Such rhetoric helped many view themselves as true Germans: those who sacrificed for and even represented the nation. This sentiment corresponded with a concept of German nationalism that rose to prominence in wartime. Drawing on Hegelian notions, Germans overall had before the war acceded to the notion that the state was the site of the German nation; it was the obligation of German subjects, therefore, to serve that state. In the decades before hostilities broke out, various public figures had introduced discussion of popular sovereignty as it existed in France and the United States. Though it remained marginal, the idea was particularly popular among the radical nationalist groups that sprouted in the 1890s, as they voiced their dissatisfaction with the Wilhelmine regime by declaring the death of the state nation (*Staatsnation*) and the birth of the people's nation (*Volksnation*).[120] But it was the wartime experience that brought this notion to the fore and gave it widespread legitimacy. Beginning in August 1893, as Germans had prepared to dedicate the new Reichstag, debate arose over the appropriateness of the inscription the architect had planned for the building's grand pediment: *dem deutschen Volke*, "to the German people."[121] Ultimately officials decided to leave the field blank for the time being. As *Vorwärts* suggested, an open field meant that a fitting inscription could be added "when the appropriate time comes."[122] It is no coincidence that this time came in August 1916, when imperial representatives determined that *dem deutschen Volke* offered an appropriate homage to the new mood of popular sovereignty, arising from the sacrifices of nationals both on the front and at home.[123] The state must serve *das Volk;* failing that, the state, too, would reveal itself an inner enemy.

If *das Volk* represented the nation, who represented *das Volk?* As Berliners cast it, it was still in midwar the woman of little means, a figure without formal political rights but with great symbolic power as the leader on the right side of the economic war and of the war over Germany's future. Yet at this moment in late 1916 new ambivalence arose over this figure, as Germans faced for the first time the question of what actually constituted equitable distribution. The very different views on this issue revealed the fault lines in the coalescence around the woman of little means. Those fault lines and the significance of the various views of equitable distribution are taken up in the next chapter.

7 SOUP, STEW, AND EATING GERMAN

From early in the war, some politicians and reformers advocated a system of mass provisioning of prepared meals (*Massenspeisung*) for the nation as the most efficient and effective way to ensure Germans' nutritional needs. Authorities reconsidered mass dining in spring 1916 in response to the popular demand for total control. But the idea of total control at the level of the consumer divided Berlin consumers against one another, threatening the collective voice of the *Minderbemittelte*. Authorities' own ambivalence toward public kitchens and mass dining halls reinforced public concern. Working-class Berliners expressed cautious interest in a public kitchen program if it were to serve them on the basis of their contribution to the nation rather than according to their neediness. They required a program that allowed them to "eat German," following prevailing mores. If poorer Berliners were to embrace a program of mass provisioning, it must bear no resemblance to prewar soup kitchens. Berliners and other urban Germans adhered to these stipulations resolutely, even through the catastrophic "hunger winter" of 1916–17, which truly threatened the health of capital city residents.

At the same time, discussion of how to realize such a program rent the fragile unity of Berlin consumers along class lines. Members of the working class on the whole demanded that the public kitchens should be a centralized enterprise in which all participated; lower middle-class Berliners particularly rejected this means to control the economy. The result was that public kitchens, located in the neediest areas, failed to attract clients despite their relatively consistent offerings of affordable food. However, mass provisioning in the form of factory canteens, which burgeoned in the fall and winter of 1916 commensurate with Hindenburg's efforts to drive up munitions production, thrived, perceived as rewarding those who worked for the nation. Here once more the interests of the Supreme Army Command (OHL) and at least some working-class women seemed to coincide, as other political alliances fell apart. In response, by early 1917 it was lower middle-class women who led the demand for more controlled provisioning for all. This dynamic sheds light on the paradoxical war and postwar relations between the German working and lower middle classes.

PUBLIC MEAL HALLS

From the first years of the war, public kitchens and mass dining in some form played a role across Germany in local efforts to provision the population. Especially in the western industrial cities, municipal authorities had expanded the existing system of soup kitchens (often opened in response to the prewar inflation of prices on basic goods) early in the hostilities to supplement the provisioning of soldiers' families, the unemployed, and others designated as "of lesser means."[1] In Berlin the National Women's Service, under the umbrella of the League of German Women's Groups (BDF), had by midwar established a number of public kitchens for use particularly by soldiers' wives; private charitable organizations also opened facilities specifically for the lower middle class. Few potential clients took advantage of these kitchens on the whole.[2]

By 1915, however, both the Städtetag and individual Social Democratic Party (SPD) Reichstag representatives had pressed for some public system of mass dining to be expanded nationwide. Social Democrats such as Richard Calwer and Elisabeth Engelhardt took the lead in espousing a centralized national system. They believed that imperial-level sanction of such facilities could make them palatable to potential clients. By early 1916 police reported hesitant but rising popular interest in such a system as part of the desired official control of food distribution. Many higher officials were quite pleased with the idea of widespread public kitchens, hoping that the system might aid the new War Food Office (KEA) in quelling popular protest. Moreover, this total organization of food distribution seemed administratively efficient, in contrast with the hugely cumbersome existing machineries of distribution. Military authorities offered approval, in part because public kitchens might save laborers time away from work that was otherwise lost to shopping and preparing meals.[3] The Prussian ministers of agriculture and commerce both expressed enthusiasm. They noted, as would consumers, that public kitchens concentrated control on consumers rather than on producers and merchants.

By early 1916 the Prussian Interior Ministry moved enthusiastically to realize such a system, in light of new popular mandates for total control. The ministry placed the burden of responsibility, however, on local authorities and local private welfare organizations. On 14 April 1916 Minister Loebell ordered all greater municipalities to integrate and augment their existing systems of soup kitchens (*Volksküchen*), which in most cases predated the war. While in principle this localized level of execution made sense, from the start the program bore the earmarks of the failures of earlier programs. The KEA would oversee the operation, but aside from administering a one-time grant of food and monies to the kitchens, the KEA restricted itself to an advisory capacity. It was open to question where the food for this initiative would come from on an ongoing basis. This strategy augured poorly for popular acceptance of the program, all the more because of the role of communal and private authorities in prewar soup kitchens.

The interior minister designated Berlin as the site of a fully developed pilot program of prepared food outlets beginning in summer 1916, in recognition of the residents' particular need and of their power to protest.[4] Prussian-level authorities offered the insight that, hunger notwithstanding, the cultural connotations of the system would be crucial to its success.[5] Interior Ministry officials and the high commander agreed that Berlin-style "stew cannons" (*Gulaschkanonen*) should form the prototype for the new public kitchens. The virtually unique example of successful municipal public kitchens early in the war, in Hamburg, was based on stew cannons, which held about 1,400 portions each. SPD officials noted that Hamburg had already served 165,000 portions this way by July 1916.[6] More to the point, these rolling carts had long existed in Berlin and were accepted as a sometimes necessary convenience. Their nature suggested mobility from one neighborhood to the next (though they remained primarily in working-class neighborhoods); their familiar form suggested a meal that was taken home to be eaten around the traditional German "family table"; and their very name invoked comparison with military field kitchens rather than with poorhouse soup kitchens.

But the Berlin city council, the local Central Office for People's Welfare (Zentralstelle für Volkswohlfahrt), and the Central Organization for the Well-being of the Working Classes (Zentralverein für das Wohl der arbeitenden Klassen) together drew on another precedent.[7] Hans Luther, Berlin city councillor and chair of the Städtetag, conceded that his task was mandated by popular mood as much as by Batocki, and that his response had to meet popular satisfaction.[8] Still, city authorities feared that food trucks, which the populace seemed to endorse, would by their nature encourage new queues in the streets, spurring the "assemblies" and "disorder" officials hoped to dissipate.[9] Stew cannons already existed on a small scale in Lichtenberg, the very center of the recent unrest.[10] Theodor Wolff argued in conversation with Mayor Wermuth, moreover, that the stew cannons could never meet prospective demand—more than half a million per meal, he imagined.[11] For their part, the private organizations championed their own traditions of soup kitchens with mass dining halls.

Wermuth and his subordinates thus set about instituting a system of ten main kitchens supplying a network of stationary eating outlets. The kitchens and outlets would have a far greater capacity for production and distribution than stew cannons and would provide the opportunity for clients to eat on-site as well as to purchase food to take home. Wermuth also proposed that to improve equitable distribution, sites should be chosen by determining where the greatest need and demand for these kitchens existed. Thus in May and June 1916, all interested residents had to register their desire to participate in the new program in mass dining. This selection process revealed circles of interest concentrated in traditionally working-class neighborhoods. The very concentration of the facilities along with the proposal that they be housed in schools, churches, and private institutional buildings reinforced early public perceptions that they were more like soup kitchens than army mess halls or field kitchens.[12] Plans seemed to reflect the requisites of the standing, popularly disliked Elberfeld system of public kitchens, keeping programs as limited, localized, privatized, and inexpensive as possible.[13] This in turn dampened working-class enthusiasm for the program even before the first facility opened in early July.

Working-class consumers sought a different sort of equitability of access. They offered hopeful suggestions to save the system by better sharing it with those of higher socioeconomic standing. Working-class consumers demanded the widespread dispersion of these state-run facilities around the city, which would communicate an anticipated clientele of all Berliners, not just poor Berliners. *Vorwärts* buttressed this view, reasoning that "when each person must take part in public dining, then no one can feel degraded by participating."[14] On this point local authorities turned a deaf ear. High-level officials pursued other measures that had the effect of stunting popular interest. In the first weeks of the meal hall program, Prussian and municipal authorities together determined that use of the kitchens would count against one's weekly rations of meat and potatoes.[15] Thus while on the one hand not everybody was compelled to use this system, on the other hand it also did not provide a supplement to existing rations. Yet this latter was how some residents had resigned themselves to private soup kitchens in the first years of the war, insofar as they had used them, as an alternative to the black market in augmenting inadequate basic rations.

Wermuth addressed this conundrum, claiming that the city could not both provide the kitchens with quality food and fill all Berliners' rations through retail sales, though early propaganda intimated this might be the case.[16] The lord mayor argued that the intent of the new program was, rather, to maximize quality and minimize the stigma of the public kitchens. Yet his very aversion to encouraging use of the kitchens over retail outlets bespoke his own prejudices. For while he did not want the kitchens to be "an institution of lesser quality food," neither, he admitted, "do we want all families to be removed from their own hearth."[17] In this admission he reflected the sentiments of many women of the lower and upper middle class. Skalweit claimed, "Most women were reluctant to demonstrate their neediness on the open street, where a woman's neighbor might recognize her."[18] Such thinking served as both cause and effect. As National Women's Service member Agnes Harnack noted in retrospect, "part of the population of women" would not eat in these institutions as they were constituted. "They wanted to maintain their pride, that which divided them from the lowest level of the population," she explained. "They would rather starve inside their own four walls than be seen going to a people's kitchen."[19] It is likely from the context that "part of the population" referred primarily to lower middle-class women as well as possibly some wives of skilled workers. The public meal hall reflected the limits of the unity of Berlin consumers.

Wermuth had thus fallen into the very trap others had hoped to avoid through the use of stew cannons. For despite planners' emphasis that meals purchased at public kitchens might be brought home for consumption, the physical connection of the kitchens with mass dining halls created for many Berliners an unbreakable conceptual link between the two. Detractors used this link to stir up concerns for the further loss of the bourgeois custom, central to proper German living, that the family enjoy the warm midday meal together, around the table at home. Many community leaders spoke of public kitchens with their associated dining facilities as promoting the demise of the family, along with the drop in the birthrate, the rise in sexually transmitted diseases, the poverty of the lower middle class, and the entry of women into the workforce. Some bourgeois reformers helped ring the death knell for this form of mass dining, claiming such facilities were, as always, acceptable for the poorest working class but hardly suitable at any time for respectable Germans, above all at a moment of crisis for the nation and its culture. The preexisting terminology reinforced the message of the facilities' physical structure and location. The common term "mass feeding" itself did not necessarily suggest dining on-site, but historically at least, the term connoted public eating as in poor relief. As Hans Krüger of the KEA executive committee noted, *Massenspeisung* was "not a pretty word."[20]

The general term "feeding of the people" (*Volksspeisung*) aroused still-greater suspicion, with its quasi-class-specific resonance that in this context served to divide rather than to unite Berliners. Prospective lower middle-class clients registered doubts about the program. Authorities' distinction between working-class kitchens (*Volksküchen*) and those of the lower middle class (*Mittelstandsküchen*), following prewar practice, only reinforced reemergent class divisions. The dining halls available clearly accommodated fewer people than the attached kitchens could feed (indeed, some claimed this further stigmatized consumption in the dining halls). *Vorwärts* thus sought to soothe anxieties, noting that while the dining halls themselves were terribly pleasant, their capacity at 500 communicated their limits relative to the number of portions kitchens could produce. This, the newspaper claimed, confirmed planners' presumption that most people would want to take the food home.[21] The working-class women who used these services on the opening day of the program did, for the most part, pick up the meals for consumption at home.[22] Yet the regrettable link between public kitchens and mass dining halls seems to have further poisoned the idea of mass provisioning for potential lower middle-class users.

This was no less an issue for prospective working-class clients. Eating a warm midday meal at home with the family (*familiäre Tischgemeinschaft*) represented not only unity with other Germans in some bourgeois ideal of national culture; it was also a cherished if long threatened working-class custom, providing the proper setting to reconstitute the family physically and conceptually as well as offering respite from the work environment.[23] The interruption of the family table through the introduction of factory work had been for decades a point of tension. On the eve of war, working-class women who did not labor in factories themselves often brought the midday meal in baskets to their husbands, whose break did not accommodate a trip home to eat. While it might seem that public dining halls provided the same possibilities for affirmation of the family in principle, reformer Else Zodtke-Heyde observed deep working-class suspicion of such an idea.[24] Under the new wartime circumstances, even if the whole family—such as it was—might gather in a dining hall, it was not adequate to reproducing the family table. Now the differentiation with their bourgeois compatriots seemed an unjust slight. For this reason, too, working-class consumers viewed the new public kitchens with disaffection. These consumers charged that officials had once again instituted a dual system whereby those not forced by poverty to use the system were free to choose better options, a disparity that protesters found deeply unjust.

Poor, hungry Berliners expressed their disappointment with their voices and with their feet, despite the still-rising shortages of meat, fat, potatoes, and bread, of which food rioters complained grievously in July. In the first week of the mass dining program, which opened on 10 July, the entire system of Berlin public kitchens, which boasted the capacity to feed 250,000 clients, served only 6,400 participants.[25] The initial lack of coordination between the private Central Office for People's Welfare and municipal officials did not help matters. The Central Office opened facilities on their own, depriving those halls of the official imprimatur potential clients sought. At the same time, police warned authorities of the signs of renewed unrest and generalized dissatisfaction among the "working population," due to both continued shortages and continued inequities of distribution, particularly at this point just before the harvest.[26] Lower middle-class residents of the capital who refused to use the public kitchens themselves complained ironically that these facilities were sapping the supply of meat and potatoes available to the wider public.[27] In their view this represented the advantaging of the few over the many, though they eschewed suggestions that they take advantage of the kitchens' bounty.[28]

Authorities at all levels attempted, in their rhetoric at least, to contain damage to the prestige of the incipient program by casting public discussion of mass kitchens in the most positive light. Hans Luther stressed that although the new system drew on the structures of prewar communal and charitable aid, its integration into the "common economy" and its purpose in serving "the *Volk* at home," like soldiers on the battlefront, made it qualitatively different from prewar programs.[29] In a speech before the Berlin assembly, Wermuth made his case that officials should "go all the way" with this program, averring pointedly that the system "was not poor relief" but, rather, a necessary and positive step that all Berliners ought to take in order to maximize available resources.[30] He and other municipal authorities stressed the national emergency to which all were vulnerable, identifying precedent in earlier wars and occupations.[31] Wermuth claimed the facilities were thus designed to serve disadvantaged *Berliners,* rather than "the poor" alone, for he added, "No one doubts anymore that Berlin has been hit hardest by the prevailing inequality in the distribution" of food.[32] The mayor's statements appear intentionally ambivalent, offering the possibility that the program, while assuredly temporary, was somehow a vanguard of the new orientation and of new social relations. Wermuth's statements also signaled his concern to close the rift among consumers, indeed by emphasizing instead the deep tensions that had opened between urban consumers and rural producers.

Throughout July Wermuth distributed proclamations via the press and public kiosks, encouraging use of the facilities among capital residents and proffering official approval of Berliners who purchased their meals at these sites.[33] Wermuth and other city officials took pains to note that authorities guaranteed the food supply at the public kitchens, at least in principle. To the city's credit, food seems to have been fairly consistently available at the facilities, at least at first, though difficulty in estimating usage led to both waste and shortages at individual sites.[34] City officials emphasized that the program represented official response to protesters' own grievances. They noted that clients need make only one stop for food, which was considerably more pleasant than waiting all night in lines before either private shops or municipal sales outlets. Wermuth played, above all, to working-class women, claiming, "We're beginning in terms of dining the thousands; soon it will be the tens of thousands, for those bound to work who can no longer cover both the procurement and preparation of meals every day."[35]

Grain Authority director Michaelis also put his weight behind the program, bringing with him, moreover, the cachet of the respected new military authorities now set to take power, with whom he had close contact. Michaelis penned a column that appeared on the front page of the *Berliner Tageblatt* describing his mid-July visit to the first of the new meal halls, which opened in the working-class Humboldthain area of Berlin. He commented on how well the program was executed, how good the food was, and how easy it was for clients to use.[36] Invoking the magic comparison, he explicitly likened the food to that in army mess halls (from our perspective certainly emphasizing the specificity of the moment). Like Wermuth, he emphasized that this program was for all Berliners and claimed to expect, in turn, widespread and heavy participation.[37] Despite repeating the desired mantras, Michaelis, too, acknowledged that authorities targeted the program particularly at working-class women, in the misguided belief that such a strategy would win this population's approval.[38] Calling the public kitchens a blessing for "busy women" in particular, he noted that it would be impossible to cook the same quality food at home as cheaply.

As Wermuth had done, Michaelis intimated that the intended user at public kitchens spent her day doing work that contributed directly to the war effort. This was both practical recognition of the wartime realities and an attempt to cast public kitchen clients as they wished to be seen. It was more than this, however. To whatever degree it was part of a conscious propaganda campaign, such commentary began a decisive move in high military echelons to praise and reward civilian women less for their willingness to sacrifice as consumers and more as producers for the war effort. Although civilian officials continued to speak of women's contribution as consumers, Michaelis suggested a link between women's productive work and the new mass dining.[39] The rhetoric anticipated military authorities' plans in the fall and winter of 1916 to press civilians, above all urban women, into service in the expanding war industries. KEA official Lucien Wiernic, who would soon supervise the provisioning of war-factory canteens, noted admiringly that public kitchens in Berlin could serve 15,000 portions across the city within the fifteen minutes allowed for the midday break in some factories.[40]

Much of the press also lent its strong support to public kitchens, elaborating on officials' praises and acknowledging planners' attention to potential users' concerns, in addition to printing official propaganda on the program. Papers from the *Deutsche Tageszeitung* to *Vorwärts* commented on how technologically advanced the kitchen equipment was, emphasizing how rapidly the sparkling machinery could peel potatoes and prepare vegetables and meat for cooking (intimating, indeed, that there were meat, potatoes, and vegetables to be had).[41] This was certainly an effort, in part, to distinguish the new facilities from old-fashioned soup kitchens, pointing up their modernity and newness as well as their responsiveness to busy women. The *Tageszeitung* pointedly evoked the image of military mess halls, citing an eye witness's perception that "the pot-bellied polished brown kettles stood like a company squadron alongside one another in the middle of the bright hall."[42]

The *Tageszeitung, Vorwärts* and the *Berliner Tageblatt* all observed at the same time how "attractive" the facilities were, "with flowers of different colors on every table."[43] *Vorwärts* noted that one should be able to procure meals to go in "ten to twelve minutes," altogether "a welcome convenience and relief for wide circles of the population."[44] "Wide circles" referred to "the plagued housewife, who until now has spent nearly the entire day 'on the streets,'" and who "can now use her time in more useful and appropriate fashion." The article concluded by "expressly noting" that "participation in the public kitchens does not constitute the acceptance of charitable acts. The provisioning is much more conceived for all classes of the population." Lack of time rather than lack of money seemed above all to mark intended participants; the presumption was that their time was spent in the service of the nation.

But meal halls concentrated in working-class districts and yet open to all, housed in schools and run by charitable organizations, left hungry Berliners unmoved. Wermuth described a sanguine vision of the future, but the present he created seemed to be set up for working-class women on the basis of their need. He hid poorly his prejudices that the structure of the program remain largely as it was. Publicity photos (more often of the dining halls than of the kitchens or take-away counters), with their ranks of fiercely smiling middle-class servers (and empty tables or tables filled with working-class women), likely did little to dissuade potential clients that the facilities were glorified soup kitchens that separated users from true Germans.[45] Despite the press's apparent conviction that the new program of public kitchens was intended for all, potential users remained dubious. Patronizing descriptions of the tablecloths and flowers only made readers aware that the reporting journalists visited the facilities solely on a professional mission rather than as users. Lower middle-class women remained unconvinced, bourgeois women had other options, and working-class women consequently refused to use them.

EQUITABLE DISTRIBUTION AND OBLIGATORY PARTICIPATION

In September 1916, coincident with the move of the Third OHL into power, the program stood at a crossroads. From early in the summer many working-class Berliners had argued that participation in mass dining should be not only widespread but mandatory. This would allow the system to sustain its claim to controlling distribution equitably through a single process that applied to everyone, and as the means to demonstrate that meal halls were truly respectable and German. In early fall, Hans Berlepsch wrote, "among the workers in the big cities, one is generally convinced that *forced mass dining for everyone* would be the only way to satisfy a feeling of justice in the shortage of food" and to prevent "those of little means" from "bearing the full blows of the shortage."[46] A year after the Berlin butter riots and subsequent unrest, Berlepsch and others emphasized visible vulnerability to radical politics and protest among even those with the "greatest will to hold out." In the best tradition of imperial politics, many officials urged Hindenburg and Loebell to institute obligatory participation in mass dining, in order to maintain control from above. Obligatory participation of the entire population would be a truly radical step, whether from below or above, however, though its political implications would be ambiguous.

The broad public offered strong and very mixed responses to the idea of obligatory participation as the debate came to the fore. The issue moved various societal interests to dispense powerful rhetoric surrounding liberties, rights, and compromised justice at this confluence of national-cultural and politico-economic crisis. Once more the variety of interests and political ambiguities made for strange bedfellows. Officials at every level were split on the issue of forced, universal participation.[47] Proponents included the new OHL leaders, Michaelis, KEA staff members, and many liberal and Social Democratic representatives.[48] Social Democrats, drawing on prewar recessive views on the potential virtues of mass dining, claimed explicitly to represent this view on behalf of "women."[49] Commercial and agricultural lobbies found themselves convinced by Richard Calwer's argument that tight control of consumption would permit a more open market in the arena of production and distribution; Calwer hoped that farmers, in turn, would be induced to grow more.[50] Spurning the disorder on the homefront, the new military authorities sought means to exercise their control on civilians. Coupled with recognition of the new labor exigencies of the September 1916 Hindenburg plan, the OHL looked with keen interest at forced mass dining. Michaelis wrote in favor of an enforced program on the basis of the deficiency particularly of fats, which had rendered cooking at home very difficult, and because of the inequality of distribution promoted by the growing black market, which authorities had been unable to control.[51] Other officials supported the idea as the only means to economic rationality under the prevailing circumstances.

With Hindenburg at the helm, the lobby of proponents was a powerful one. But the KEA, as the negotiating agent, was not known for its forceful action; moreover, it was divided within itself on the issue. In his urgent October memo calling for new interventions, Robert Merton expressed his own concerns against this "extreme" route, characterizing *Volksküchen* already as "the absolute of forced consumption."[52] Städtetag members expressed fear for the enormous prospective onus on the municipalities. In a compromise move, in late October 1916, the KEA issued guidelines that all cities with populations over 10,000, and particularly those in which munitions workers were concentrated, must at least create access to prepared meals in public kitchens.[53] *Vorwärts* warned that officials had better act quickly and decisively to implement the plan, such as it was, before it lost the popular support it had and went the way of other hapless "half-way measures."[54] But in the end, the KEA instituted no mechanism for enforcement of the guidelines, and little action ensued.

Supporters sought other means to encourage widespread voluntary use of public kitchens. Prussian officials attempted to reverse the damage of earlier policy decisions, facilitating the use of the meal halls by moving the requisite advance registration to the meal halls themselves, rather than at a separate office. (About the same time, however, Berlin officials pushed the weekly sign-up and payment to Fridays — one day before payday.) Local administrators worked to ensure that the dining halls were open without fail.[55] Greater Berlin authorities made headway in September and October in coordinating the use of potatoes and other scarce foods among all metropolitan-area kitchens.[56] At 40 pfennig per full portion (1 liter of stew), the cost of the food was not subsidized, but clients did not have to pay for overhead or for the now exorbitantly priced fuel required to prepare a warm meal.[57] Most important, the food was available.

It was the disastrous 1916 potato harvest, unforeseen when the public kitchens were erected, that drove up the numbers of participants, however. By October, as the deficiencies of the newly harvested crop became evident, about 55,000 Berliners (of a population of 2.5 million) took advantage of the institution.[58] By December the total jumped to about 80,000 public kitchen clients per day. The *Berliner Morgenpost* cast the rise in use of public kitchens as proof of how terrible circumstances were in Berlin.[59] At the same time, that only 3 percent of the population used the facilities under the circumstances is impressive testimony to their disinclination to participate in the program, a disinclination stronger even than that in most other cities.[60] Berliners continued to stand in long retail and municipal hall lines and protest on these sites more faithfully than they frequented meal halls. In the Ruhr and other industrial cities faring as poorly as Berlin, deputy commanders noted that "the ethical considerations have fallen away almost entirely. The 'war kitchens' are considered the only way" that residents of these areas "will make it through winter to next spring."[61] In some locations, however, particularly Berlin and Magdeburg, Germans responded with such strong aversion that the deputy commanders expressed fear that civilians would simply starve.

Worse, from the OHL's perspective, police linked the renewed protest in the fall of 1916 ever more tightly to the prospect of radical political and economic change, far overtaking Bethmann's new orientation, for the war and beyond. Officer Schade warned, "The standard of living among the *Minderbemittelte*" — here explicitly including lower civil servants — "has been pushed to unbearable circumstances." He depicted the specter of revolutionary upheaval.[62] With fresh news of the slaughter on the Somme, protesters now demanded that the war end immediately. They tied both their own suffering and the battlefront slaughter to capitalist interests, to which they claimed the government deferred. Throughout the fall, police spies reported with alarm the rising strength of the Spartacist and other radical left movements (led by "radical females") and their influence, above all, on hungry, working-class women.[63] The reported incidence of women's threats and violence against police officers, which had risen greatly since the 1915 butter riots, intensified yet again, superseding prewar levels for the first time with 1,224 episodes in 1916 (compared with 986 in 1915, likely concentrated at the end of the year).[64] Despite censorship, the press broadcast the multiplication of these riots in working-class Berlin with the onset of winter, a function mainly of the "inequities" in distribution.[65] Press and military reports on conditions around the country echoed these worried pronouncements.[66]

Such reports brought the OHL and other parties back to the issue of obligatory public kitchens. SPD party tracts now approved Calwer's plan, claiming that total participation in the system was the only reliable means to rational use of available goods—and, paradoxically, to salvage the existing system. Groener's own antipathy to forced participation notwithstanding, his diary through the fall and winter indicates the consistent connection he made between the possibility of victory, the "worker question," the extremely poor mood of the people, and the decision to move to ever greater economic intervention in whatever form necessary.[67] Under the pressure of these conditions, in December Hindenburg and Michaelis demanded that Batocki create a "universal system" of mass dining. Hindenburg recognized that such a move might have to be at the expense of the field marshal's extensive plans to appropriate resources just for munitions workers.[68] He may have been more concerned about the unrest over food than is commonly thought.

Many voices from prominent spheres still responded vehemently against proposed forced participation in public kitchens and mass dining halls, regardless of conditions in the streets. Many Berliners were uneasy at the prospect of this degree of control over their lives at a time when the OHL was making plans for unprecedented management of civilians' labor in the interest of weapons production. Skalweit called the notion of "publicly feeding the entire nation a utopia, grown out of a war psychosis, blowing remarkable hot air off the brains of doctrinaires and fanatics."[69] Wermuth adamantly rejected the KEA proposal, citing financial riskiness for the big cities despite promises of imperial subvention.[70] Some critics found the idea "unthinkable" based on the twin fears of actively ushering in the new orientation and of announcing Germany's economic vulnerabilities abroad, though these voices seem truly out of touch with the prevailing realities of the street.[71] Others suspected a conspiracy. The *Tägliche Rundschau* asserted, "The popular belief . . . gradually spreading in the capital [is] that this [artificial worsening of food shortages] is taking place according to plan, in order to *make* the entire population submissive regarding public eating."[72] The columnist claimed simplemindedly, "Such draconian measures we can do without. One must simply say to us truthfully what creates this urgent need, and we'll resign ourselves to it." Robert Schmidt asserted, as his fellow Social Democrat Calwer had frankly admitted, that mandatory public dining was a way to loosen restrictions on the Junkers and shift increased restraints to the beleaguered consumer. Thus, "for the rural producer, no limits. For the rest of the population, *further* limits."[73]

Despite the potential economic gains for powerful rural producers, *Deutsche Tageszeitung,* the organ of the League of German Farmers, publicly expressed reservations to obligatory mass dining on cultural grounds: "Take note that the German housewife strives to cook at home when she has the necessary food. Indeed, one must not try at all costs to raise the statistics of those who use public meal institutions."[74] The column followed precedent in spuriously connecting the purchase of food at public kitchens and eating in public dining halls; indeed, the paper claimed that German women must prepare — and would insist on preparing — that food themselves. BDF leaders demonstrated considerable anxiety for what they perceived as the complete breakdown of the German family, through the war and its unprecedented casualties and now through the combined economic and political pressures that forced women into war factories. Despite their own involvement in public kitchens and their acknowledged interest in pushing working-class women to work in war-factory jobs, BDF leaders lobbied against regularized use of prepared meal programs.[75] Yet by early winter, at a time when many women in the capital worked mandatory double shifts in the war factories and found neither food nor coal at the market, public kitchen facilities might have been the only way for some women to ensure a warm family meal, whether in a dining hall or at home. This virtue of the public kitchens was buried in the rhetoric, however.

Opponents as well as supporters claimed to represent the views of German women. Robert Merton protested that just as authorities had "sealed up" the farmer's silo and butter machine, leaving a "policeman in his henhouse," so government measures such as public kitchens now sealed up the stovetop and stew pot in the household, forcing the German housewife out of her kitchen. "The one is an intervention in the business economy, the other in the economy of the household, and it remains to be seen whether the psyche of the consumer will bear this burden, particularly when at the same time the psyche of the grower would be simultaneously relieved of its burden."[76] August Skalweit condemned government assumptions concerning the efficiency of obligatory community kitchens. With perhaps dubious consequences for those he claimed to champion, Skalweit insisted that "all knowledge has shown us that nobody runs a household so thriftily as the good housewife" — "the *good* housewife!" he added.[77] The response of Theodor Thomas, Frankfurt public kitchen advocate, that German housewives did not understand enough about nutrition to ensure proper eating habits under the existing conditions did little to aid his cause in encouraging the embrace of public dining facilities.[78]

It is hard to know to what degree women in general and working-class women in particular agreed with this characterization of their sentiments toward cooking at home, as opposed to the more clearly and commonly expressed desire to eat at home. Reformer Agnes Harnack claimed to have overheard women worrying, "'My husband wouldn't like to see that.'"[79] This was hardly clear evidence for women's general disaffection either for eating food cooked outside the home or for mandatory participation, particularly in the context of Harnack's reported hearsay in late 1916: "'Man is the strong one; we don't have any work; now we don't even want to cook for ourselves?'"

Some enthusiastic SPD party officials further fueled the argument against obligatory mass provisioning when they demanded in the fall and winter of 1916 that imperial authorities enforce universal use of these public kitchens in the name of equal distribution, for "equality might only be achieved when the entire people ate out of *one* pot."[80] In December *Vorwärts* demanded to know, "Why should the one who has the bigger wallet be able to feed himself differently and better than the greater mass of the population?" While this was by midwar virtually a mainstream public sentiment, it was, for many, another thing entirely to claim, "If it is clear that a regulated distribution of food is necessary, in whatever form, then there must be equality of food for all."[81] Those who now identified themselves as *minderbemittelt* had long joined forces in demanding "equitable" distribution and had questioned the right of the bigger wallet or even of the stronger elbow. This tenuous unity among poorer consumers was based in part in the ambiguities of what equitable distribution might mean. As working-class consumers adopted this new rhetoric of equal distribution, they found themselves at odds with members of the lower middle class. It may be no coincidence that during this period, police reports and other official documents used the term *minderbemittelt* almost exclusively in reference to "working-class women" and as distinguished from civil servants' wives and other lower middle-class women.[82] While the petite bourgeoisie and working population had been able to share their unhappiness over the inequities of soldiers' wives eating cake and over the very wealthy squandering pork, now that control among consumers seemed potentially imminent, some members of the lower middle class protested revealingly that they deserved more than workers for their place in the nation.[83]

Obligatory participation in mass provisioning in no way necessitated equal provisioning, though it did demand that authorities decide the issue one way or the other. In army mess halls the differentiation of quantity and especially quality of food by status was carefully preserved; in the navy, this was all the more the case. The system of specifically lower middle-class and functionary kitchens, both private and public, made great efforts to offer material acknowledgment of the relation between status and food. Calwer and Engelhardt explicitly repudiated the necessary connection between obligatory participation and equal apportionment, calling indeed for a three-class system through which food would be allocated according to one's socioeconomic status before the war.[84] Such a system would indeed have preserved the prewar hierarchy far better than the existing official system of ration cards. But by late 1916 street protesters themselves trumpeted the link between obligatory participation and equal distribution. In this instance their power to decisively shape the issue worked against implementation of the program altogether.[85]

THE DEMISE OF PUBLIC KITCHENS
AND THE RISE OF FACTORY CANTEENS

Cultural strictures contributed to the demise of high-level plans to institute centralized mandatory mass provisioning. Therefore many seriously malnourished Berliners and other urban Germans found themselves unable to take advantage of a still relatively dependable source of nutritious food in the depths of the hunger winter. In turn, the kitchens themselves became increasingly less dependable, even as they spread around the city. If working-class enthusiasts of obligatory provisioning had contributed to dooming their own case, however, lower middle-class opponents of the plan succeeded in promoting official endorsement of an alternative plan for provisioning, one that left them largely out in the cold. In light of divided public opinion, as well as in view of the resistance of Wermuth and important Prussian ministries, the OHL and imperial authorities gave up the idea of mandatory and even centralized provisioning of table-ready food for Berlin and other large cities and put their energies into other plans.[86]

In the first months of 1917 hungry women remained resigned to running helplessly in the bitter cold from municipal sales outlet to retail shop and to protesting violently in the streets, still finding this more respectable than mass dining.[87] Although use of the public kitchens actually increased steadily through February, it did not grow commensurate with worsening material conditions. By the end of the year there was some greater willingness

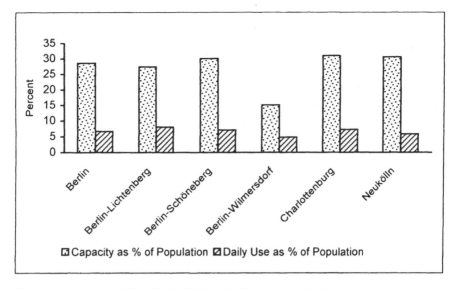

Figure 7.1. Capacity and Use of Public Kitchens in Greater Berlin, October 1918
Source: Skalweit, Kriegsernährungswirtschaft, *51.*

among Berliners to send children to special breakfast and dinner programs because of the coincidence of rising scarcity, municipal takeover of children's programs from private charities, the climbing number of women working in the munitions factories, and the lesser concern for social stigma in the case of children. Particularly by the new year, however, many school-based breakfast and lunch programs shut down along with the schools themselves in face of the "coal holiday" or "cold holiday" that accompanied the hunger winter.[88] Through the end of the war, working-class Lichtenberg boasted by far the highest number of public kitchen users. Yet even Lichtenberg participated at less than twice the percentage of Wilmersdorf, an area of few working-class residences, in which residents were far wealthier on average and public kitchens far more scarce. Participation was comparably low in lower middle-class areas, such as Steglitz, though by early 1917 petit bourgeois Berliners claimed they fared far worse than those in the working class. The press and public figures continued to emphasize Berliners' common cause, particularly in contrast with rural populations.[89] Ironically, urban residents across the country bitterly noted the absence of public kitchens in rural districts entirely.[90]

Public kitchen enthusiasts continued to bemoan low participation rates in large cities around the country, though the numbers varied from just over 1 percent in Halle to nearly 18 percent in Hamburg.[91] Hamburg consistently served nearly the same number of portions as Berlin, for its population of

Children fill the streets for a stew cannon (fall 1917). Adults continued to avoid meal halls. Captured English tanks rolling through the streets drew far less interest. (BAPK, file 1578)

less than half the size. Contemporaries viewed the variance as closely related to the specific regional cultures and the language of local propaganda,
though they remained unable to deploy this knowledge to good effect.[92] In
comparing the figures, it seems clear: the larger and more expansive the program, the more comfortable Germans felt participating in public kitchens
and dining halls. This was not an issue of capacity. Nowhere did clients ex-
haust available supplies. After peaking at 152,000 participants per week in
February 1917, use of the halls fell steadily in Berlin; capital residents evidently found no solace in the neediness of so many others like themselves.[93]
The decline after February was likely related in part to the arrival in the city
of the crop of new potatoes, though poorer Berliners objected that they still
had no access to the tuber. In March officials held a huge symposium attempting to address the system's deficiencies.[94] But by August 1917 most of
the public meal halls in Berlin were closed, despite the still-calamitous food
shortages; by the revolution, few remained in operation.[95] The mores of
bourgeois Germany were remarkably effective in keeping truly hungry
Berliners away from public kitchens.

Other features of the public dining system also drove poor consumers
away. The *Berliner Morgenpost* claimed that public kitchen directors turned

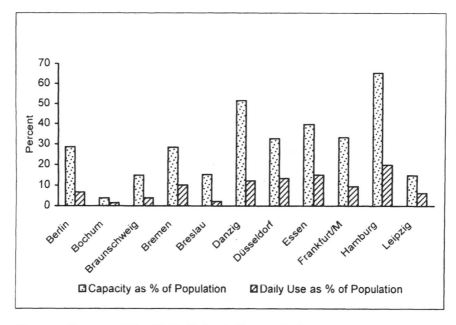

Figure 7.2. Capacity and Use of Public Kitchens in Germany, October 1918
Source: Skalweit, Kriegsernährungswirtschaft, *51.*

away many potential users for the first time in December for lack of sufficient food. Under the voluntary system, public kitchen directors were paralyzed by the same unpredictable access to goods that individual consumers
faced, as well as by inability to anticipate usage.[96] Under these circumstances
public kitchens had no greater ability to produce good quality food than the
average poor consumer (though they regularly had fuel with which to cook).
As a result, many patrons complained throughout the turnip winter that
meal hall food, though for the most part still available, was simply inedible.
The press, including publications that supported use of the meal halls, helped
propagate this image, doing more to dissuade users than to change the menu.
The *Berliner Allgemeine Zeitung* opened a piece on public kitchens with high —
if qualified — praise: "The *municipal mass dining* is, in spite of its many deficiencies, a *terrific act.*" The piece continued, however, to remark upon what the
author considered serious inadequacies, such as porridge one day with sugar,
the next "with liverwurst thrown in."[97] Clients also complained that the
steady offering of "mass cow" (*Massenkuh*), or stew, communicated soup-
kitchen offerings and moreover made for a diet that was far too "liquid";
there was too little meat in it.[98]

What did "edibility" mean in this context? Porridge with liverwurst or
stew with little meat seems like a feast compared with what was available at

shops for disadvantaged consumers, especially rutabagas, or "swede turnips," which were "disgusting" in officials' own eyes.[99] Even though they were normally used for fodder, the turnips did not seem to project as gross an insult as prepared porridge. Outside Berlin, too, the *Kölnische Zeitung,* attempting without success to compare such food to army rations, reported claims that public kitchen fare was "simply inedible" and "produces nausea."[100] The *Tägliche Rundschau* did not help matters with its charge that civilian kitchens started with the food left over from military larders.[101] The notion of edibility became a sign for what Germans should or should not have to eat, in terms of both class respectability and national honor. One Social Democrat had spelled out a direct relationship between "tastiness" and stigma months earlier, claiming that as long as participation was not obligatory, "it will be necessary to make the meals still tastier than ever."[102] Obversely, he wrote with revealing ambiguity, "when the wealthy *have to* take part in the program, then the food *will* become good everywhere!"

As the new year opened, starving working-class Berliners were not entirely without alternatives. The Third OHL had from the start demonstrated vulnerability to civilian disorder. While military leaders were impressively restrained in invoking police and military force against protesters, especially in Berlin, the leaders demonstrated few political concerns for responding with authoritarian tactics, such as a controlled economy, for the sake of quiet in the nation's streets. But the OHL lost interest in enforcing obligatory mass dining as the leaders focused on deploying civilian forces to fulfill their military plans. These plans for accelerating weapons production drove them to differentiate among consumers according to their own vision of contribution to national interests. They wished to lure workers into the munitions factories and to prevent them from collapsing from hunger at their worksites. Hindenburg's subordinates thus turned their attention to the question of food for armaments laborers.

Those who toiled in the war industries were able, and strongly urged, to use factory canteens, a recourse that authorities and clients alike succeeded in portraying in a positive light. Factory canteens, like public kitchens, were not especially well used before the war, but they did not share the particular stigmatic history. Throughout 1916 officials had encouraged munitions workers to patronize factory canteens. The new OHL went still further in this effort, pressing industrialists to build new canteens, allocating meat and potatoes for use in these facilities, and looking away as industrialists dealt on the black market to stock their kitchens. If before the war and in early war such worksite facilities offered little appeal, pulling workers away from the family table, for the second half of the war, factory canteens were far more popular than public kitchens.

This was in part a real issue of food quality. Lord Mayor Wermuth complained that the military was sharing its food supplies directly with factory canteens; though this lightened the municipal burden, it appeared unjust even to the mayor.[103] The connection between quality, taste, and respectability was clear. Oppen noted in October, "Many of the heavy industrial factories feed their own workers to the latter's complete satisfaction in their own kitchens."[104] He observed that other firms simply brought in food from the public kitchens, "but this practice finds little acceptance, as the workers do not find this food tasty enough." Officer Meier likewise bitterly observed, "It has been noticed that at least fifty percent of the workers in question do not, however, dine at the firms on the meals of municipal kitchens, as they are not in sufficient distress."[105] But the figure of 50 percent participation in those factory canteens alone that served public kitchen food is nearly ten times the percentage of Berliners who ever took advantage of the *Volksküchen*. This figure is all the more notable in light of the fact that armaments workers were some of the best-paid laborers in town. Many skilled male munitions workers in particular might have fended for themselves with some success on the black market.

In the factory canteen setting, workers felt they were being compensated for their much needed contributions to the war effort—whatever they felt about the war itself. The fact that the OHL had directly arranged for privileged access and special rations for these canteens, and the fact that workers sat beside soldiers who had been called back from the front for the high purpose of munitions production, reinforced this idea.[106] Thus, workers themselves considered the cafeterias a project discrete from that of public kitchens. Moreover, munitions workers had hopes that, as "war-requisite workers," they could expect canteens to get still better, provisioned by the new War Office, rewarding both their work for the war and their "discipline and calm."[107] As Officer Josef Meier pointed out, in contrast to the public kitchen phenomenon, patronage continued to increase at Berlin war-industry works. Indeed, he perceived the expansion of factory canteens as a product of worker demand, as did apparently the workers themselves.[108] From the late fall of 1916 workers kept up pressure, through shop-floor protests and labor negotiations, for new and expanded canteens throughout the city.[109] These new worker efforts coincided with the massive influx of working-class women into munitions jobs, under pressure from Hindenburg. Working-class women in particular were relatively enthusiastic about the factory canteens, despite the drawbacks of eating on-site in terms of procuring food for the family, and by the new year they were putting their energies into making this system work for them.

The largely though not exclusively lower middle-class poorer Berliners who had fought public kitchens won a Pyrrhic victory. As the experiment in public kitchens was conceptually exhausted by the end of 1916, the OHL and workers alike pinned hopes on the viability of worksite kitchens. High-level authorities left lower middle-class women and those men who were not forced to work in munitions largely to their own devices and to private, charitable endeavors.[110] Despite increasingly urgent reports on the desperation of the lower middle class and of civil servants in particular, officials offered little response. In December, the same month in which authorities granted all munitions factory workers extra rations of coveted fat, they cut normal rations of potatoes and butter, and Batocki put on the back burner a petition submitted by civil servants for special rations. "Normally rationed" Berliners no longer had sufficient coupons to purchase more than one portion per day at public kitchens even if they cared to.

In response, the greater urban, lower middle class turned its attention to attacking the "narrow" clientele base that dined in factory canteens; in doing so, they attributed to such facilities still-greater cultural cachet. As in the fall of 1914, when lower middle-class women expressed their resentment of the purported privileges of working-class soldiers' wives, now they complained of the unfair privileging of "the working class" and of working-class women in particular through canteens.[111] The imperial League of the German Lower Middle Class (Reichsdeutsche Mittelstandsverband) argued once again that the privilege undermined the prewar hierarchy, putting large portions of the working class in a better position than their petit bourgeois counterparts.[112] The league argued against war workers' greater effort for the nation and warned of the lower middle class's "great resentment and rancor." For the moment at least, the new military administration turned a deaf ear. In the context of military officials' new appreciation for the laborer's contribution to the war effort, it was no social advantage to identify oneself as *mittelständisch*. This renewed split between the lower middle class and the working class based on the latter's newly advantageous position reflects a well-rehearsed view of World War I history. Impassioned battles over methods of food distribution offer fresh perspective on how this split took place, and how it coexisted with new social constellations that pitted urban Germans collectively against the country's leaders.

8 FOOD FOR THE WEAK, FOOD FOR THE STRONG

The consensus of the broad self-defined population of little means over controlled distribution showed signs of wear in the second half of 1916, as the issue of food control among consumers brought to the fore the question of what constituted equitable (*gleichmäßig*) distribution of available food supplies. As Berlin entered a season of severe shortages above all in fats and potatoes, defenders of lower middle-class interests particularly began to assert the importance of differentiated food distribution that recognized their prewar class position. Other groups, from social reformers to proponents of redoubled military efforts, concurred that equitable distribution of food might best be achieved through differentiated rather than equal apportionment. Authorities at every level responded with policies in the summer and fall of 1916, creating and augmenting existing special allowances for the ill, pregnant women, children, hard laborers, and even soldiers' wives. Beyond the system of public kitchens and factory canteens, these supplements supported the particularly weak or the especially strong. But, as in the case of mass dining, Berliners and other urban Germans were uncomfortable accepting provisions on the basis of their presumed special weakness. They were little more prepared to countenance these benefits for others. In consequence, by the time of the catastrophic turnip winter of 1916–17, the neediest Berliners suffered without special high-level government aid, as the scarcity continued to divide the population of poorer Berliners.

Germany's new military administration delighted in the prevailing mood that allowed officials to attend specifically to the needs of "strong" Germans, allotting food supplies first to hard and hardest laborers (*Schwerarbeiter, Schwerstarbeiter*), then to munitions workers overall in the course of the winter. This coincided neatly with Supreme Army Commander Hindenburg's plans for both accelerated military production and exploitation of civilian labor. This system of supplements rewarded a significant population of poorer urban women on the basis of their strength and contribution to the nation as military producers. In contrast with supplements for the weak, this system was highly successful in providing its beneficiaries, among them hundreds of thousands of women, with extra rations of coveted meat and fat along with potatoes and bread in the winter of 1916–17. This new position of strength through labor power also aided Social Democratic and women's reformers in making a compelling case for the need for a new orientation. At the same time it brought working-class women in close contact with more radical socialist men and women in the latter's campaign to end the war.

The ravages of the turnip winter spurred the "normally rationed," including lower middle-class women and working-class women outside the war industries, to reverse course by early 1917 and protest differentiated distribution of any sort. General Groener noted a "great pressure toward equality" in these months.[1] If supplements kept war workers relatively well fed, the new system contributed to the slow starvation and deterioration of health among the broader population of poor consumers. Working women's new, in some respects salutary relationship with the state and nation came simultaneously with the prominence of an invidious culture of selection, which challenged the right of the weak and other Germans outside the war factories to state aid for survival. This story continues to chronicle the development of ambivalent relations between the working and lower middle classes, identifying the effects of the new, crooked cleavage created by munitions factory supplements.

FOOD FOR THE WEAK

In the summer and fall of 1916, public rhetoric reflected a growing trend in defining equitable food distribution as differentiated, both in amount and type of food. Representatives of lower middle-class interests made this clear in their opposition to forced participation in public kitchens, which they interpreted as an equalization of distribution. Outspoken Berliners, from member groups of the League of German Women's Groups (BDF) to civil servants' lobbies to street protesters, argued for controlled distribution based on a variety of perceived special needs. In light of the ever worsening scarcity in German cities, authorities responded by according particular groups privileged status on the basis of publicly recognized deficiencies. These groups included, variously, the ill or infirm, the aged, pregnant women, infants, children, and war dependents. Officials constituted these populations collectively as weak, authorizing ration coupons particularly for milk at a time when recipients of normal provisions often found no milk at all.[2] War Food Office (KEA) distinctions in both amount and type of food dispensed in this way drew on the new science of nutrition as well as German custom.[3]

Gender as well as class and age played an important role in creating the rhetorical and bureaucratic taxonomy of weakness and in determining who received which foods. Germans often associated weakness with women, although the ill and infirm as well as children and the elderly were usually ungendered categories in public rhetoric.[4] One might more accurately speak to the lack of masculinity in the characterization of weak populations. The explicit feminization is obvious, however, in the conceptualization of pregnant and nursing mothers. Mothers of many children were weak by association.[5] Women's perceived dependent position in the family linked soldiers' wives and their supplements tenuously with the discussion as well. There was popular support in the fall of 1916 for an increase in separation allowances (particularly now that the category encompassed such a large percentage of German women), an increase under discussion in the Bundesrat from early in the year.[6]

Conventional wisdom associated women with milk, the food of weakness; women both provided it and required it. Wilhelmine Germans conventionally perceived milk to be vital for all weak populations. Milk was yet another basic food, sustaining and nourishing.[7] Hence the north German expression "She doesn't have much to crumble into her milk," indicating poverty. As with bread, it would seem to suggest that milk was the very least one should have. But in the main, Germans saw milk as imparting its nutritious qualities to those incapable of digesting meat.[8] It was not associated with men. *Milch-* as a modifier derogatorily suggested something effeminate as well as juvenile (or premasculine), as in *Milchbart,* "milk beard" (adolescent beard), or *Milchgesicht,* "baby face."

Yet the ill, pregnant or nursing women, and "families" (as some denoted mothers with many children) often had difficulty from late 1915 on in purchasing this vital fatty food.[9] Although the region surrounding Berlin was self-sufficient in milk and the city should not have suffered deprivation of this food, a number of factors discouraged its steady flow into the city. Milk, as opposed to most other foods, was big business in Berlin. Three large dairies, Bolle, Schwarzkopff (unrelated to the munitions concern), and Viktoriapark, provided most of the milk that served the metropolis. These dairies controlled the retail shops and familiar horse-drawn carts that sold their milk as well as butter. Until the outbreak of hostilities, price wars among the dairy-owned shops, other stores, and farms that sold directly to consumers distinguished the milk market in Berlin.[10] The war brought with

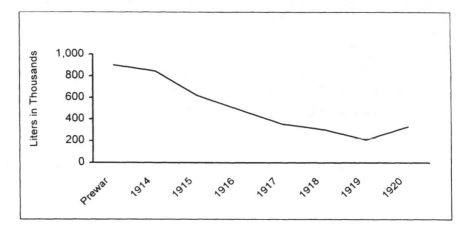

Figure 8.1. Daily Delivery of Milk to Berlin, Prewar–1920
Source: *Skalweit*, Kriegsernährungswirtschaft, *217.*

it a "civil peace" among producers and sellers of milk, however. Bolle and Schwarzkopff combined in 1915, and the major dairies collectively pushed prices from the wide range of 12 to 26 pfennig per liter to 33 pfennig and higher by late in the year.

Berliners protested the price rise along with that of butter.[11] City officials responded in November 1915 with a retail price ceiling on milk of 30 pfennig per liter. In the pattern that had become the rule, producers immediately withdrew the product from the metropolitan market. Prussian officials also helped instigate the new milk scarcity by encouraging (the more lucrative) butter production in response to the frightening display of popular protest against butter shortages in October 1915; butter was not associated with either the especially strong or weak. Prussian-level authorities also encouraged the slaughter of cattle in the face of both fodder and meat shortages; farmers responded willingly, as beef carried no price ceiling.[12] In consequence of these various measures, by early 1916 the milk supply available to individual consumers had dropped to 20 percent of its prewar level.[13]

In response, the municipal government considered raising the price ceiling on milk, speculation that naturally further inhibited supply. Although demonstrators in the streets continued to concern themselves primarily with the price of butter, meat, and other foods, working- as well as lower middle-class women now registered their concerns for both milk scarcity and high prices as well, adding that the higher cost would most hurt the weak as well as the poor.[14] The press joined the chorus to protest the fate of the weak at the mercy of milk producers; newspapers kept up a steady supply of stories of speculation and deception.[15] In response, municipal authorities determined in July 1916 to pursue policies of differentiated distribution of this product to ensure the flow of milk to the weak. Städtetag officials, who by midwar concerned themselves almost exclusively with matters of food distribution, drew on Berlin's precedent, wrangling throughout July over how to define those populations requiring milk in order to forge a policy consistent across the country.[16] These officials decided only the certifiably ill, women in the seventh or later month of pregnancy, and nursing mothers warranted aid.[17] In a controversial move, Städtetag representatives accorded children, including infants, only "milk preferred" status, signifying they might fill their rations only after the "milk required" population had done so. This was a meaningless category in light of scarce supplies.[18] Berlin authorities adopted these guidelines. In midsummer Charlottenburg took the further step of providing women in advanced pregnancy with a "control" card, sending them to the front of the line at dairy shops, an especially useful measure.[19]

The protests over milk scarcity and the particular burden on the weak drew imperial officials into the discussion. In mid-1916 authorities instituted a central Milk Provisioning Office modeled after the imperial Butter Provisioning Office. The Milk Office was supposed to coordinate policy with the Berlin Fats Authority, which began rationing lard in the same month. In August the Milk Office announced its first measures, responding to capital residents' demands by ordering dairies to deliver milk to the city. Despite their interest in maintaining their retail outlets, dairies reacted by selling from the train stations. Irregular deliveries offered the advantage to residents in the vicinity of the two principle milk delivery points, the freight stations in Tiergarten and Schöneberg. This left the shortage still "very tangible."[20] Government efforts to promote sales of powdered milk ("cow in a bag") brought little relief, as even these supplies were scarce. In response to this chain of events, the Milk Office, too, turned to regulating consumption. It issued imperial-level ration cards across urban Germany in late August, following upon the long-awaited meat card and superseding the Städtetag rationing system. Imperial authorities evidently had different criteria for determining who belonged in the weak and needy categories and what their needs were. The Milk Office rationed whole milk as follows:

women in the last two months of pregnancy, up to .75 liters per week;
children through two years, up to 1.00 liter per week;
children three to four years, up to .75 liters per week;
children five to six years, up to 1.00 liter per week;
ill, with doctor's note, up to 1.00 liter per week.[21]

The Milk Office designated children aged seven to fourteen years for milk-preferred status.

Still, weak populations found it very difficult throughout the fall of 1916 to obtain the milk to which they were entitled.[22] The term "up to" was telling; ration cards, even those issued at the behest of the highest levels of government, still did not guarantee supplies. Police and press reported that the "weak and pregnant," "families," and "women and children . . . were forced to stand for hours in the freezing rain to get, if they were lucky, a few drops of milk."[23] The Berlin Fats Authority issued a new set of ordinances in late October, claiming to account realistically for existing supplies though doing nothing to increase the supply into the city. Rather, the office tightened regulations regarding certification for illness and removed the "preferred" status for children above six.

The military administration now entered the arena. Following upon measures that emphasized consumers' competition with one another rather than greater control over supply, the high commander announced the right of those with special coupons to go to the head of lines for milk and other foods throughout Greater Berlin. At the same time, Berge qualified the perquisite, ordering still more stringent control of these privileged categories. By "control" he indicated that officials at all levels, including policemen on the streets, be given the prerogative to determine whether the bearer of a certificate rightfully possessed it. Indeed, he intimated a connection between the degree of patrolmen's vigilance and the level of indignation of the waiting crowd, emphasizing the importance of maintaining public calm and responding to popular demand, no matter how changeable.[24] The result was that few of the certified weak were able or even willing to take advantage of their position, all the less as the freezing fall and deadly cold winter befell the city.

Numerous factors militated against the potential benefits of the system. The administration of special privileges for the weak was a great onus on municipal authorities; functionaries responded by discouraging applicants.[25] Considering the work involved in getting certified, individuals with the strength to pursue the certification may have been the least in real need. Perhaps most important, it appears that the population of poorer Berliners that did not have "privileged" status, official or otherwise, demonstrated increasing ambivalence by late 1916 toward this preferential treatment, though many had pushed for differential provisioning only months earlier.[26] This was due in part to the direct competition imperial authorities set up between resources for the weak and the normally rationed. These were distinct from the special stocks from which officials provided supplements for hard laborers and war-industry workers.[27] In consequence, particularly in cases where the affliction or weakness was not immediately visible and obviously genuine, it appears that the waiting population on the street was unwilling to accept the validity of the official certificate or to permit the privilege. The *Berliner Tageblatt* ruefully noted, "One 'stands' again, now once more for milk," and that the strongest and most aggressive were the ones to get it.[28] In the face of these new popular pressures, officials worried for the potential "abuse of the concept 'sick.'"[29] August Skalweit characterized milk distribution in this period as an extreme case of lack of coordination among authorities in providing for special populations. But the changeability of policy may be attributed in part to rapidly changing views of who deserved what on what basis.[30]

It seems those standing in line had to be able both to feel empathy with the privileged individual and to appreciate his or her difference, in order to suffer the latter's advantage on the spot. By the late fall of 1916, during which many Berliners worked long hours, ate little of sustaining value, and spent exceedingly cold nights in food lines, everyone felt sick. Officer Münn observed, "The health of many women has been seriously compromised by the hours-long standing . . . incit[ing] the most excited mood among the populace."[31] Outbreaks of influenza and tuberculosis in the winter of 1916–17 only exacerbated already grave conditions.[32] Indeed, the flip side of the denunciation of special treatment was that, by late in the year, most families had at least one member who could reasonably have claimed rights to milk. In response, despite protests of the Central Agency for the Feeding of the Sick, officials continued to tighten qualifications for certification; by November it was virtually impossible to be declared ill. Städtetag officials reworked the definition of "sick"—and of "whole milk."[33] "Exceptions are to be granted only in the *most urgent* cases," the Price Monitoring Authority of Greater Berlin announced. "And these exceptions are to apply generally to the allowance of preference cards only to those in advanced pregnancy."[34]

Overall, however, pregnant women fared little better than the sick. Throughout the war, Germans regarded pregnant women more ambivalently than recent historical work might suggest.[35] Pronatalist voices were weak in Germany during the war, when measured against competing opinions. In October the League for the Protection of Mothers (Bund für Mutterschutz) petitioned both the Reichstag and the Bundesrat for better provisioning of milk and bread to pregnant women, with little effect.[36] The BDF devoted some attention to wartime benefits for pregnant women to ensure the future of the nation.[37] Some members even chastised women for a perceived "birth strike" in the course of 1917, as pregnancies carried to term plunged from over 1.8 million in 1913 to about half as many in 1917.[38] But BDF member organizations focused on encouraging middle-class women in particular to become pregnant. By the fall of 1916 the BDF was most interested in pressing working-class women into war factories to demonstrate women's national contribution as workers. Government propaganda urged women to serve the nation through war-factory production even at the expense of parental obligations.[39]

Many Germans now looked dubiously at women's protruding bellies. Lurid newspapers stories of soldiers returning home to find their wives in bed with lovers, rumors of rural women's fraternization with foreign farm laborers, and pamphlets about the threat of venereal disease even on the homefront created suspicions concerning pregnancy, all the more as Hindenburg sent ever greater numbers of men to the front.[40] As the new military policies drew hundreds of thousands of women into war factories, visions of women's relations with prisoners of war in the factories (by consent or under force), betraying both husband and nation, arose in the fall of 1916.[41] There is some evidence poorer women resented their pregnant counterparts for more or less voluntarily increasing demands on the food supply.[42] There was no societal consensus on the virtues of "producing children for the nation," during the war at least; there is good evidence that this ambivalence survived the armistice under the economic and social conditions that marked the postwar period.[43] Pregnant women comprised a population characterized by weakness; support for pregnant women's special needs waned in the late fall of 1916, as propaganda under the military leadership emphasized total mobilization for war.

The "working, childless population" and parents with adult children demonstrated little more sympathy for young children than for pregnant women, and little interest in their special provisioning.[44] Many families with few children now actively protested the perceived advantages of those with many, whose rations they claimed to be improportionate to their needs.[45] One woman wrote in fury to Michaelis that whenever a baby was born, the family would rush to register the child in order to receive bread rations for the newborn.[46] On the eve of war, working-class women on average had more children (three or more) than upper and lower middle-class women (between two and three).[47] Many seem to have exaggerated this difference, rendering equivalent working-class families and those with many children and raising again the specter of unequal class-based burdens or privileges.[48] Naturally, having many children was a financial burden, all the more in light of soaring food prices and the difficulty in procuring well-paying work;

"Those in possession of milk cards will be taken care of first!" (Ulk, *12 November 1915*)

"child-rich" women complained bitterly that their special needs and contributions were not acknowledged.[49]

The category of children created the most strained debate among officials, as the German public and authorities alike argued over whether children required more or less food than adults, and what foods they required. Among great differences in apportioning food for the weak, officials at all levels seemed to agree on leaving out children aged six to fourteen years.

When in November the Berlin Fats Authority withdrew even "milk-preferred" status from such children, they ordered that milk left over after rations be turned into butter to appease the broader population (and the dairies as well).[50] In August 1916, August Müller, Social Democratic member of the KEA executive committee, had given a speech identifying families with many children and hard laborers as the two populations the KEA was most concerned with helping.[51] In the coming months, officials raised the rations of hard laborers, but the KEA cut children's rations overall from three-quarters to one-half of the adult allotment, even as the latter shrunk in size. Many mass provisioning programs for children shut down in this period.[52] Children were badly affected by the shortages, distributional chaos, and greed that marked apportionment of the food supply, experiencing the hunger winter on top of the wartime deprivations to which they had already been subjected.[53] Pictures from this era reveal emaciated bodies and other physical irregularities among children. By later in the war and postwar, photographs show stunted growth, illustrating only one aspect of the deforming experience of the war.[54]

Soldiers' wives formed the most difficult special category for officials to classify, being neither clearly strong nor weak. Bundesrat members debated increases in their allotments throughout 1916, resulting ultimately in successful passage. In June, as August Müller addressed an audience of consumer advocates, he was taken aback by shrill attacks on the proposed increases in separation allowances.[55] Soldiers' wives requesting aid, numbering nearly 145,000 in Berlin in late 1915, comprised a still larger cross-class population by late 1916.[56] Still they remained a symbol of division among consumers, a symbol that reemerged when consumers competed with one another. This popular ambivalence remained in place, although soldiers' wives maintained their allowances.

In the end it appeared that neither the especially weak nor the wider population of lesser means received much milk, despite the fact that butter also remained limited.[57] Even as authorities stepped up prosecution of black-market operations, the populace believed officials looked aside as cafés, still frequented by wealthier Berliners, found sources for milk and cream.[58] The Berlin Fats Authority made Bolle/Schwarzkopff and Viktoriapark the sole official distributors of milk supplies in Berlin. Though in principle authorities carefully oversaw this distribution, some consumers viewed this strategy as appointing the fox to guard the henhouse.[59] While military authorities lent personnel to combat abuses of milk ration coupons, these officials were far more concerned to ensure the privileges of the strong, that is, those who worked in the war industries.

By late 1916 authorities sacrificed the interests of the weak to the concerns of both the normally rationed public and the differently privileged. In November 1916 imperial officials centralized the entire system of milk and fats distribution. Their first step was to cut milk rations still lower, at the same time working to increase fats supplements for the hardest laborers and munitions workers.[60] The broad populace had shown itself unwilling to "privilege" mothers, increasingly the greater proportion of working-class women not in war factories, while with the accession of the military regime to power, officials showed far greater interest in women's productive rather than reproductive capacity. Without significant effort to maintain its availability, milk, food of the weak, largely disappeared from general public access altogether during the winter of 1916–17—along with the public discussion of it.

In the contemporary cultural context, milk did not make the weak strong; it maintained their weakness. With this understanding, the new lack of commitment to benefits for the weak held disturbing implications. Military authorities intimated their sentiment that the German nation had little interest in supporting this weakness but looked, rather, to buttressing what they considered to be the country's strength.[61] The Meat and Fat Committee tried to emphasize the responsibility of milk producers to ensure the supply particularly for weak populations.[62] This propaganda was drowned out, however, by that of military authorities demanding meat production, including the slaughter of dairy cattle, to feed heavy laborers as well as the troops. Much of the public mirrored this sentiment. *Vorwärts* reported impassively in November on the League for the Protection of Mothers petition demanding better provisioning for mothers and infants. Perhaps not surprisingly, the paper took a far more activist stance in an article on the same page, purportedly about "provisioning the people," in which the editors urged that military officials directly provide meat and fat for factory workers.[63] This coincidence of military and popular opinion was fateful.

FOOD FOR THE STRONG

Meat and meat fat were food of the strong and able. Public discussion never noted a lack of milk for civilian men but, rather, their lack of meat or fat. If looking like "milk and blood" indicated a woman's beauty, and thus health, to seem as "meat and blood" signified a man's hardy appearance, and therefore health. "Meat" was associated positively with the flesh of men, as in biblical references.[64] When associated with women, Germans used it universally in a derogatory fashion. Women could be "a piece of meat," vulnerable prey for prurient male interests.[65] For a man to marry was to "hang a piece of meat from his neck."[66] Batocki expressed deep concern for the lack of butter and milk for the normally rationed and for the weak and sick. But he deferred to military pressure to attend to heavy laborers, who must have fat for their work and could not be expected to get it "through cottage cheese."[67] It seemed workable that many men would receive their fat in meat fat (and butter on bread) via military apportionment, while women, children, and the infirm received priority for milk resources. But the productions of milk, butter, meat, and meat fat lay in conflict with one another.

Some poorer women found a way out of this conundrum. The categories of special privilege were initially gendered terms, coded as strong and weak populations. As women in Berlin entered the munitions and weapons workforce in great numbers, the policy regarding special supplements lost some of its negative gendered overtones.[68] Large numbers of women benefited as war-industry workers from special supplements of potatoes and of meat and meat fat, the most coveted products throughout the turnip winter. In turn, the principles authorities formulated to give theoretical coherence to the policy of special supplements came to represent a more ambiguous gendering of the notions of strong and weak. They also offered a new way of regarding women's contribution to the war and the nation, with potentially positive implications for women more broadly.

There were few official categories of special privilege through the first half of the war; early popular response to soldiers' wives was one indicator of the public's disaffection for such treatment. However, in July 1915, a full year before the city granted specialized milk supplements, local Berlin authorities offered additional bread rations of 100 grams per day, an increase of 50 percent, to hard laborers on the basis of their perceived greater physical need. The Imperial Bread Ministry provided for the additional bread required. Metropolitan authorities never spelled out conditions for eligibility for supplements, but in practice they dispensed the coupons to men only. The KEA took over the issue of bread supplements in June 1916, nationalizing the program, spelling out specific jobs that constituted hard labor, and adding the designation "hardest laborer." Hard laborers continued to receive an additional 100 grams, while authorities granted hardest laborers an extra 300 grams per day over the normal ration of 200. Hard laborers also qualified for twice the potatoes of their normally rationed counterparts, receiving 1,000 grams per day.[69] The jobs imperial officials designated as hard labor make clear their hopes that supplements would entice workers into war-industry factories, helping realize War Minister Adolf Wild's new production goals in 1916. General Groener noted, "While it was true that it was up to Batocki to make decisions, one remained cognizant of the constant military influence."[70] The list contained exclusively positions normally held by men. The KEA was not always successful in providing for the additional rations, and the bitter unrest of the summer of 1916 spilled over into the Berlin metal industry. Wild narrowly averted a massive strike in June with his promise of more secure food supplies to hard laborers.[71]

Paul von Hindenburg's ascendance to power in late August brought with it the ambitious weapons production program that bore his name, a part of the field marshal's sweeping plans for expansion on the eastern front. Supreme Army Commander Hindenburg, along with Erich von Ludendorff and Max Bauer, looked to homefront resources to help realize these plans, trespassing previous limits of military jurisdiction.[72] In September Hindenburg ordered rural Germans to produce and turn over larger yields of meat and potatoes in order to ensure supplies for the hard-labor supplements. The Supreme Army Command (OHL) hoped thereby to coax still-greater numbers of workers into the munitions and weapons industries as well as to maximize productivity and to avert protest. Berlin was a stronghold of the munitions industries and home base for the great Deutsche Waffen- und Munitionsfabriken (Muna).[73] Other firms outside the industry, including Siemens, AEG, Borsig, and Thyssen, retooled works for munitions production. With a single-minded interest in winning the war, the Third OHL made clear its prejudices in caring particularly for urban war-industry factory workers. (This did not include all war workers, such as the women who sewed uniforms, but only laborers producing munitions and weapons.)

The new military leaders did not rely on enticements alone. In October 1916 OHL leaders drafted an auxiliary service law (*Vaterländisches Hilfsdienstgesetz*, or VHDG), to force all civilians between fifteen and sixty to work in war-industry factories. The OHL was only too aware that in order to meet its production goals without a massive recall of soldiers from the front, it would need to attract urban women, by far the greatest potential labor force, into munitions.[74] Military leaders hoped to leave tens of thousands of troops on the front through women's munitions labor.[75] Bauer was keen on forcing women into war factories and drafted the VHDG with language explicitly including women in this "patriotic obligation." The notion of an obligatory "national women's service" had existed for years.[76] But the inclusion of women in the VHDG, widely perceived as the ugliest aspect of this distastefully coercive edict, became the focal point of controversy over ratification of the law. The powerful State Secretary of the Interior Helfferich drew on the "traditional" social and moral objection to women's formal participation in military service.[77] Many munitions industrialists claimed they could only honor their contracts using male workers, including skilled laborers reclaimed from the front. Trade union leaders were concerned for the dilution of skill among the workforce, a long-standing issue focusing on women as "dirty competition" with skilled male workers.[78] Social reformers led a public clamor against the idea on the basis of moral degeneration and breakdown of the family. Military as well as civilian authorities also feared working women's "uncontrollability" and even willful proclivity to create disturbances, of which the streets seemed to offer continued evidence.[79] By some estimations the inclusion was nugatory, as there were more women seeking than finding jobs, though the law was largely about controlling industry as well as workers.[80] But many women argued they would take no job voluntarily that prevented rather than aided them in getting food, such as working a twelve-hour shift in a factory might do. Still, in order to save the VHDG from total defeat, the OHL redrafted the law without explicit reference to women. The bill was passed in this form, set to go into effect in December 1916.

From the OHL's perspective, however, "the entire remaining civilian population including women were to be militarized by this plan," drawing on "every available ounce of energy and determination."[81] Thus the military leaders had to work harder to bring the women they required into the war factories, to increase their "*willingess*" as well as their "*ability and consistency.*"[82] In mid-fall of 1916 the government sponsored training courses for women, instructing them in skills shop-floor supervisors were disinclined to teach them.[83] Military authorities pushed reluctant industrialists to redesign large factories, with the intent of opening up whole shops to a feminized labor force.[84] They worked closely with bourgeois women's groups, which showed themselves eager partners in the goal of demonstrating women's commitment to the nation and the national effort. BDF president Gertrud Bäumer expressed her conviction that "German women would be proud and happy to take up their responsibility to the patriotic auxiliary service, if the law also dictated it to them"; without the legal obligation, they were all the more pleased for the opportunity to demonstrate their "own patriotic consciousness."[85] These middle-class women planned to exhibit their patriotism predominantly by pressing working-class women into war factories. Some lower middle-class women also joined the war-factory labor force, but this population overwhelmingly stayed away or entered the rising numbers of white-collar positions associated with the production increase.[86] The OHL was well aware of the BDF's interest in reforms after if not during the war as the flipside to this patriotic consciousness, particularly in the form of women's suffrage. But the leaders did not concern themselves with these interests for the moment.

Officials were quick to accept the offer of the BDF and the National Women's Service (NFD) to act as intermediaries—to realize the mobilization "of women by women."[87] They were pleased to limit contact with working-class women and to leave to semiprivate volunteer forces the task of administering this new bureaucratic tangle. In mid-December General Groener called for women's groups along with trade unions and other associations to organize women's work through the National Committee for Women's Work in the War (Nationaler Ausschuß für Frauenarbeit im Kriege, or NAFFIK).[88] Soon after, Marie-Elisabeth Lüders took over directorship of the Women's Bureau (Frauenreferat), a direct subsidiary agency of the new and powerful War Office.

NAFFIK and the Women's Bureau adopted a three-pronged approach to steering working-class women into war service, offering placement, practical aid, and moral support in the form of widespread propaganda.[89] To this end the bureau generated a manifesto covering the totality of working women's lives, treating their health, morals, and family situation.[90] This agency instituted a gamut of services for working women. This included both a factory and a home inspectorate, peopled by volunteer women from the BDF organizations, as well as from the Social Democratic Party (SPD), affiliated with the NFD. This hierarchy of services attempted to meet many needs that arose for working-class women as they undertook to balance factory jobs with family responsibilities, even as schools closed and public transportation shut down for lack of coal.[91] Some of these services such as job training and child care, insofar as they actually existed, did help make possible women's factory work, though bureau activities also constituted an unprecedented invasion into working-class women's lives.[92] One might say that these middle-class women now acted as auxiliary to the working-class women who served on the shop floor as much as to (male) government officials or even to men on the front.

But potential laborers in the streets who were not legally required to enter or remain at the factories made it clear that no job without the explicit promise of food could be worth the time lost to scouring the streets for new stocks brought into the city.[93] Higher authorities heard this message through a variety of channels. Lüders argued to her superiors that "no one could fight two wars at once." Members of NAFFIK asserted, "Women must strengthen men's backs, and must therefore remain strong themselves."[94] Military officials responded directly to this concern.[95] The OHL refused both BDF and SPD entreaties to reinstate protections for working women that authorities had lifted in August 1914, including banning women from working with certain dangerous materials.[96] But in late October 1916 officials revamped the list of positions eligible for supplementary rations, and it now included jobs regularly filled by women. More explicitly, the published list contained the addendum, "Female workers, insofar as the preceding guidelines apply, are to be treated the same as male workers."[97] Hundreds of thousands of women along with men became eligible for potato and bread supplements, just as officials cut the normal rations in late 1916.

Arms industry workers could procure their rations directly at the factories with a far greater success rate than on the open market, including the still-greater allotment of meat that officials granted to Berlin workers above those who worked outside the capital. The high commander's staff carried through plans to open canteens in all Berlin-area factories, for the entire workforce.[98] Officials had once conceived of these same canteens as part of the system of public kitchens, open to all. Now, under the control of the high commander, the dining halls, in tandem with supplemental coupons, were the mark of the "worker as soldier," as an Interior Ministry report put it, open only to war-industry workers.[99] In December the new War Office took over allocation of these extra rations, relieving the much maligned KEA of control over the program. Because of the status of the War Office as an arm of the OHL, these special rations delivered the desired cachet of ascribing quasi-military status to recipients.

These programs and policies confirmed the ironic words of trade union officials: "The military dictatorship has demonstrated itself to be in many ways far more understanding of the urgent need of the people than the [civilian] bureaucracy."[100] On this very confined terrain, military officials appeared to have responded to the fondest wartime hopes of poor urban women. Military authorities provided relatively well for some poor women's most fundamental needs, on the basis of their contributions. If Oppen observed that many women perceived their noninclusion in the VHDG as a slight, these women surely found solace both in propaganda emphasizing their pivotal place in the national mission and in military officials' material rewards for their voluntary entry into the factories.[101] Women responded in turn. By mid-1917 some 3.5 million women across the country had joined the munitions labor force. By the end of the war these numbers had risen to about 6 million.[102] Within Prussia, women workers relieved over 64,000 combat-ready men for return to the front, about twice the number freed by civilian men through the VHDG.[103]

Yet while the strength of women was recognized and rewarded, officials did not treat them the same as men. Policy makers suggested that it should be possible for women to achieve "hard laborer" status for jobs in which men would be ineligible for extra rations, on account of women's "more delicate nature."[104] As Lüders put it, "Women are no men!"[105] Thus, women were rewarded for their "strength" and "weakness" at the same time or, as one SPD leader put it, for how they had worked to overcome their natural weakness in order to contribute to the fatherland.[106] Such women were like wounded veterans, going beyond the limits of their individual bodies for the nation. SPD leaders made the case for the extra support of women in these "hardest, most greatly bodily taxing efforts," even as they expressed the concern that women not be made to take over traditionally male jobs in large numbers. KEA officials indicated the view that it was more difficult for women than for men to perform certain tasks, defending women's greater rations for some jobs as greater energy spent.[107] By early 1917 officials compensated workers with calories for labor that "harms the nerves; comes close to fire, poison gases, or moisture; is executed in dark, wet, or cold; or taxes muscles and tendons." They also recompensed laborers for working on Sundays, nights, or swing shifts and for working hours that made shopping difficult, of special concern to women.[108] New KEA guidelines divided the population of special needs into men and women, on one hand, and the explicitly weak, on the other. Correspondingly, officials did not grant these women milk supplements, which would maintain their weakness, but accorded them extra meat or meat fat, to make them stronger. Women soon climbed to 25 percent of the hard-labor force.[109]

By the new year the OHL had virtually replaced the category of "hard laborer" with that of "munitions worker" (although these were only partially overlapping categories), allocating increases in special supplements henceforward primarily to munitions workers and hardest laborers only. Munitions workers like hardest laborers received 1,000 grams of potatoes, or double the normal ration. When potato rations were cut in February 1917 (and the normally rationed still had trouble filling their quotas), munitions workers still maintained their advantage proportionately.[110] By early 1917 all munitions workers also received crucial extra rations of meat and fat as well, while all "weak" Germans had lost their extra rations of milk. Military authorities allotted munitions workers 42.9 grams of meat and 14.6 grams of fat per day, compared with 35.7 and 8.9 grams, respectively, for normal rations and about one-half these amounts for children.[111] Munitions workers ate more of the food that made them German and made them strong. Where heavy laborers outside munitions work received supplements, these were often in practice in lesser amounts than those accorded to munitions workers. Correspondingly, those who lost ground as hard laborers inside and especially outside the war industries were predominantly men.

By early in the new year, in the armaments industries overall women comprised over 50 percent of the workforce by some estimates. This contributes to evidence that those women able to pursue such work found their most urgent demands met.[112] The percentage of women climbed still higher if one subtracts the number of hardest laborers in munitions, who would have benefited wherever they worked, as well as reclaimed soldiers, POWs, and foreign workers, who worked outside the system of special supplements.[113] The percentage and absolute numbers of women among munitions workers were higher still in Greater Berlin, climbing to 172,000 in early 1917 (as compared, for example, with Düsseldorf's 97,000).[114] At the same time many munitions workers began to demand the right to determine the distribution of food supplements within individual factories themselves, hoping to minimize the remaining distinction between munitions workers and hardest laborers in these works.[115] These special supplements saw large numbers of working-class women in munitions factories through the devastating winter, even as weak populations lost their special supplements, as heavy-laboring prisoners of war lost their extra rations, and as farmers and rural populations lost part of their "self-provisioning" allotments.[116]

The OHL valued women's — and civilian men's — labor power. Military and industrial policy concentrated on systems of personal delivery, ensuring to the greatest degree possible that only the worker him- or herself consumed the designated rations. Military officials searched workers as they departed factory canteens to ensure they took nothing out with them.[117] This meant that wives of male munitions workers did not benefit from the latter's status, outside of their higher wages, which were of lesser use than in previous years. Women working in war factories still had trouble providing for children and other dependent family members. Workers, presumably men and women both, fought fiercely for the right to feed dependents, and officials felt pressured to appease them.[118] One KEA official admitted that women in munitions factories were "*often not in a position to buy food in their free time,* food which was for the most part minimal to begin with." The official warned his superiors to "redress this terrible situation," for women in war factories at least, if they were not to leave the factories altogether.[119] Under the guise of a narrow social policy (*Sozialpolitik*), military officials worked with the trade unions and the Women's Bureau to ensure that women in war-industry factories would, in principle, be able to procure food for family dependents as well as to eat relatively well themselves.[120] The wages of female munitions

State weapons factory, 1916. (BAPK, file 1578)

workers rose rapidly as well, in contrast with the wages of women in other employ. Their wages constituted an increase over their prewar pay even greater than that of their unskilled male counterparts in the war factories, above all in Berlin.[121] SPD leaders and others now publicly argued that women ought to be still-better compensated in light of their contribution and their needs, despite trade union concerns for maintaining men's position.[122]

There is no question that the military administration's responsiveness to women as well as men in the factories was motivated by the OHL's annexationist military vision. The move from rewarding hard laborers generally to all munitions workers could hardly have been more transparent. At the same time there is no doubt of OHL leaders' personal lack of concern for German women and even of authorities' outright misogyny, which affected women's lives in many ways for the worse.[123] The OHL's labor policies naturally reflect the administration's general negotiations with industrial and trade union leaders as well as the specific interests of the new female war workers.[124] It is nonetheless clear that despite their protests to the contrary, military authorities responded to popular pressures as well, including those of working-class women. These pressures worked especially effectively in discussions that tightly linked production and consumption.

Moreover, if, as trade unionists suggested, the OHL was better able to re-

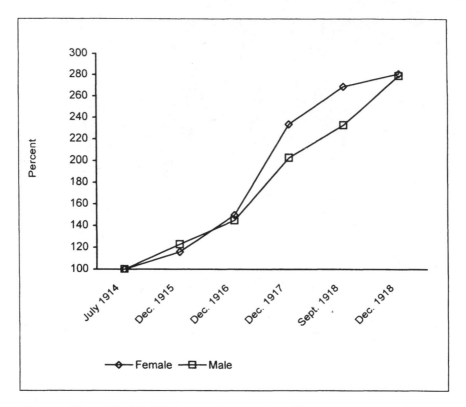

Figure 8.2. Wages of Unskilled Workers as a Percentage of 1914 Wages, 1914–1918
Source: Zimmermann, "Veränderungen," 373.

spond to popular demands than civilian authorities were, it is also paradoxically the case that the military authorities liberated working-class women
from some of the constraints of Wilhelmine mores, with lasting consequences for the postwar years. The OHL shunned the traditional view that
women had no place under military purview—and thereby no comparable
avenue for demonstrating their commitment to the nation.[125] Military
officials valued women for their productive capabilities, if in the crassest
way, providing women with a direct relation with the state rather than one
mediated through husbands or children. Despite necessary deference to
both trade unionists and industrialists, military authorities overran the concerns of both groups for the influx of women into jobs previously reserved
for men. This engendered consequences in terms of new relations between
state and society, despite women's overall forced retreat from these positions after the war.[126]

These authorities refused to reinstate protections on women's labor that
had in many ways limited women's employment and bespoke the pater-

nalistic stance over working-class women that both bourgeois women's groups and trade unionists held. The OHL's sheer disdain for working-class women — for their concern over exposure to harmful chemicals and explosives and for their responsibilities to their families — is manifest. A 1917 gunpowder explosion in Hennigsdorf that killed and injured dozens of women was only one of many incidents. This is beside the point in this context, however. Because of the societal ambivalence over women's work in war factories, because of the power working-class women thereby accrued for their voluntary entry into munitions and other war work, and because of the ever greater potential of women to protest with threatening ramifications, military authorities had to respond directly to these women on the basis of their strength and what they had to offer. In turn, whatever officials' own cynical sentiments toward these women were — and despite the fact that these direct benefits were short term — the broad public recognized the labor power of women as well as their ongoing sacrifices as consumers. In consequence, the public supported special advantages for both male and female munitions workers at a time when authorities dropped supplements for other populations with little protest.[127] As important, women gained social power from this role — power with ramifications for the postwar state.

Imperial officials negotiated in this period to redefine the concept of need to fit the changing allocation of scarce food resources. KEA executive committee member Adam Stegerwald noted, *"The informing assumption must not be 'to each the same' but, rather, to 'each his own': that is, that which is necessary to life and to the sustenance of one's capacity to work."* [128] He equated survival and productivity, or perhaps individual and national survival: "The distribution of the limited amounts is now especially difficult, as each person does not require the same amount to live on and maintain the strength to work. There is *a difference in the productivity and in the use of strength."* Military authorities likewise paradoxically defined need according to "what our troops absolutely require and what the interior cannot do without."[129] The code word for the military's new defining principle was *Leistungsprinzip* (productivity principle), cast in Ludendorff's war productivity law in the early fall of 1916.[130] Hindenburg presented the matter less ambivalently in a private memo of September 1916, suggesting one should abide by the principle "Whoever does not work shall not eat," including "countless thousands of women and girls running around doing nothing, or pursuing the most useless employ."[131] Military officials attempted to apply this principle as the vast population of the normally rationed, without the resources to obtain food illegally, began to languish through both inadequate and unfillable ration coupons.

Almost 200,000 primarily working-class women in Greater Berlin alone found a means to feed themselves in a respectable fashion through the depths of the turnip winter. The role of women as military producers as well as sacrificing consumers and activists also contributed to the positive public image of poorer women in the country's urban centers. But this relatively salutary arrangement between working-class women able to work in war factories and the new OHL came at great cost. In the virtual famine of the unprecedentedly cold winter of 1916–17, many residents previously designated as weak and even the normally rationed without unofficial outlets for food began to starve. Increasingly this included family members of war-industry workers. Military policy indicated that such populations were unworthy of high authorities' concerted aid to survival. However, by early 1917 poorer Germans within and outside war factories recoalesced to demand a new equalization of food distribution, cementing their collective identity as urban consumers in a struggle to survive enemies of the nation.

The turnip or hunger winter of 1916–17 was not the only time of true hunger during the war for much of the population. But it represented a low point, which many families scarcely transcended for the remainder of the war and beyond. The freezing, wet fall of 1916 destroyed the new potato crop, including the tiny plots Berliners had planted for themselves. In late August Romania had entered the war against the Germans, cutting off this rich source of wheat before deliveries from the summer's harvest. Coupled with extreme shortages of virtually all foods, Germany experienced a subsistence crisis. Aside from its lack of nutritive value, a diet primarily of swede turnips—the infamous "Prussian pineapple"—and other deficient food sources created serious gastric disorders for many poorer Berliners and other Germans. Nutritionist Max Rubner called the diet one of "slow starvation."[132] As prices of basic foods increased 800 percent or more over prewar costs across the nation, millions of Germans without special resources or outlets survived on an estimated 700–900 calories per day, one-half to one-third of the allotted normal rations (ca. 1,985 calories), on a diet almost entirely devoid of protein and fat.[133] During this same time munitions workers were allotted 3,072 calories per day, and they actually received some meat, fat, and potatoes.

Deputy army commanders described scenes of starving Germans in cities around the country; wealthier Berlin dwellers wondered how the poor survived at all and warned of serious popular reprisals.[134] Asta Neilsen, newly arrived in Berlin from Denmark, described her horror when a skele-

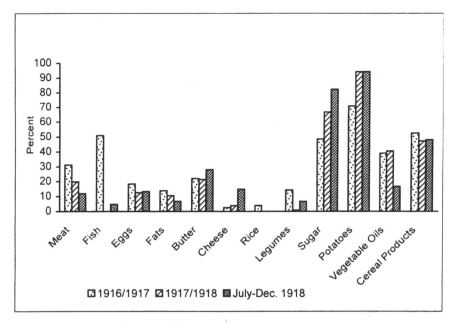

Figure 8.3. Rations as a Percentage of Peacetime Consumption, 1916–1918
Source: Zimmermann, "*Veränderungen,*" 457.

tal horse collapsed in the street. "In an instant, as though they had been ly-
ing in ambush, women armed with kitchen knives stormed out of the apartment buildings and fell upon the cadaver. They screamed and hit one another to get the best pieces, as the steaming blood sprayed their faces." As
latecomers arrived to collect remaining blood in cups, the women disappeared as quickly as they had come, "pressing the conquered lumps of meat
to their breasts" and leaving only some bones behind.[135] Berliners shared
with their rural counterparts only the sentiment that circumstances were far
more favorable under the enemy governments:

> Aurora, aurora, England still has no great need,
> France still bakes fresh rolls,
> Russia still eats pigs' feet,
> Germany has nothing but "jam" and fodder turnips.[136]

The winter of 1916–17 was unusually severe, not only for the lack of
potatoes, bread, fat, meat, dairy, and other foods. The early frost that had
ruined the potato harvest turned into an unprecedentedly cold, wet, and bitter winter, particularly in northeast Germany, as temperatures plunged to
−25° Fahrenheit.[137] The only virtue was to keep at bay the strong smell of
one's neighbors against whom one stood pressed in line during this time of

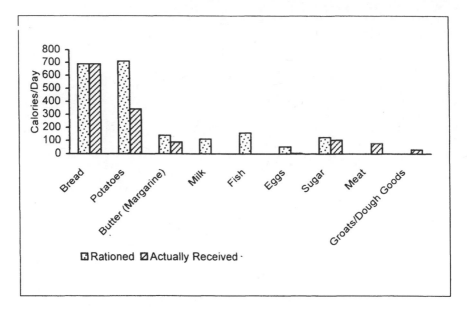

Figure 8.4. Rationed and Average Actually Received Food in Germany, Winter 1916–1917
Source: Rubner, "Ernährungswesen," 15.

no soap, no fuel to heat water, and a diet of turnips and some cabbage.[138] Standing in line for food was simply unbearable, but necessary. Police and the press reported "the standing" as more than ever a dominant "daily image in Berlin street life."[139] Collapsing from hunger and cold in food lines, in the streets, or before casualty lists was a prominent symbol of the era.[140] Many families had no fuel to cook the "disgusting" and "hated" swede turnip, much less fats to cook it in; the military commandeered the petroleum and coal that working-class and lower middle-class Berliners used to cook and heat their homes.[141] Heinrich Zille's contemporary portrait *Standing for Coal* depicts children in pursuit of a task they could now accomplish on their own because of the tiny allotments. Children waited in the cold at freight train stations hoping to snatch fallen briquettes.

The reduction of domestic fuel supplies resulted in deep cuts in the operation of public transport, leaving the poorer population in particular to expend still more time and energy on the cold streets, now without streetlights, many of them trudging for hours through snow to and from work. Shaking in worn clothing they could not replace, poor capital residents wrapped their feet in newspapers to prevent the snow from creeping in through worn shoe soles.[142] Police stopped streetcars en route to save fuel, forcing thousands of workers into blinding storms to walk home.[143] Stores closed early for lack of heat and light, even as those who labored in war fac-

Fantasy postcard, 1917. (Preziosi Postcards)

Searching through garbage for heating fuel, 1917. (BAPK, file 1578)

tories worked ever longer hours. Berliners joked bitterly that authorities ought to establish an imperial snow office; then the stuff would disappear immediately.

Workplaces were often no better heated than the homes of the poor. Women outside the war industry described laboring with numb fingers and watching ice crystallize inside workshop windows, while those employed in the makeshift shacks that often comprised new munitions works alternately froze and sweated.[144] For those of lesser means—encompassing an ever greater portion of the population, despite war-industry perquisites—life was survival at best.[145]

Under these circumstances thousands in Berlin alone succumbed to the flu epidemic that arrived with the new year, along with outbreaks of tuberculosis, typhus, cholera, and dysentery.[146] Life in the city was far more precarious than in the countryside. The number of deaths in Brandenburg increased nearly by half from the eve of war, while Berlin and a few other large Prussian cities bore mortality averages far higher still than elsewhere in Prussia and in the empire overall. Among young women the death rate was the highest. Across Germany about 700,000 civilians died directly from malnutrition during the war, as civilian death rates climbed.[147] These conditions belied the distance of the military war's theaters from German soil. The war-

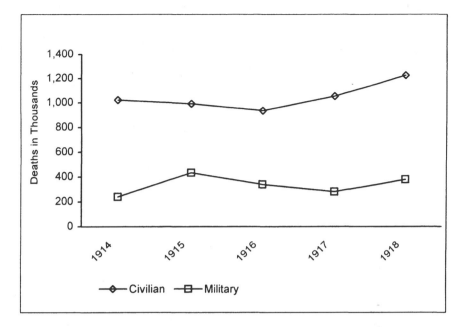

Figure 8.5. Civilian and Military Mortality Rates, 1914–1918
Source: Roerkohl, Hungerblockade, *360.*

time experience was etched on the faces of the poor; young women appeared as old.[148] Capital residents received with dread news of Hindenburg's accelerated advances on the eastern front in December, while the Allies rejected Germany's offer of peace in the West and international opinion blamed Germany for a war of aggression. Berliners manifested their longing for peace ever more sharply.[149]

In their zeal to pursue national requisites that transcended "selfish" individual needs,[150] the OHL redoubled efforts to ensure that war-industry workers did not share their food allotments with their families or dispense with them in other "inappropriate" ways.[151] Military authorities promised greater supplements of meat and fat to factories that could guarantee this. They siphoned off the highest-quality goods from public meal halls to these canteens and looked away as industrialists built up their supplies with illegally acquired foodstuffs.[152] Looking at the official calorie charts of the era, it is clear that authorities did not suppose that all munitions workers physically required the extra food energy, relative to either the normally rationed population or to heaviest laborers. The heaviest laborers were believed to expend less than 800 calories per day more than light workers; heavy laborers, 500 calories more; and munitions workers, just over 600 more. By contrast, the amount of calories allotted for each privileged category far exceeded these differentials: heaviest laborers received up to 2,000 additional calories per day.[153]

Those outside the war industries effectively competed with the military government for food. Batocki offered little hope to a delegation of civil servants submitting a formal request for raised rations, though Prussian and metropolitan officials made small concessions.[154] Weak populations unable to enter war factories struggled on their own. Individuals who were institutionalized, the most purely dependent on the ration system, were in the most precarious position, and here there is evidence of widespread starvation.[155] Wounded and shell-shocked veterans outside lazarettos had difficulty filling their coupons and, moreover, often found less sympathy among police and other officials than did most normally rationed women.[156]

Beyond food deprivations, children as a group suffered enormously. Family relations eroded still further under the strain of the turnip winter. Many women with children in Berlin and elsewhere who began munitions work did not find (or did not like) the promised services in caring for and feeding their children. Prewar sources of formal care, such as they existed, were overfilled or closed, while other neighborhood or family caregivers could promise only to keep children with them in the streets.[157] Some women had sent children to live on farms through BDF-sponsored programs (where they worked as farm laborers), but farmers had little interest in accepting new children in the winter. The press ran still more frequent stories than it had earlier of young children left alone setting fire to their apartments or falling off balconies. Sheer neglect, as thousands of youngsters huddled for hours on end without adequate food or heat, was the far more serious problem. By late in the winter of 1917, women with young dependents began quitting the war factories, leaving behind older women and especially younger girls without their own families. But women outside munitions work had little to offer their children, whose own special rations had dried up. Older children often worked in factories themselves, as they had before the war, but their wages as well as rations failed to increase as had those of adults. Children not in factories spent much of their days in the frigid streets, competing for food with unsympathetic adults.

Though ration coupons still promised a sustaining if monotonous diet, they were on the whole meaningless scraps of paper for urban Germans without wealth or connections.[158] On the whole the largest cities offered the least supplies to fill rations, and Berlin was worse than others.[159] Less vital but still important, the population of the normally rationed had no official, positive relationship to the state or to the rest of society. For many, this represented a rude transformation of their former identities. Wives of lower civil servants no longer felt rewarded for the contributions of their husbands. Mothers of many children lost status marking their contribution to the nation through their progeny, a notion with some purchase before the war. Men of the lower middle class, as of the working class, insofar as they were not drafted for combat or deemed indispensable in their positions, were bound to work under the VHDG. They thereby removed some of the burden for their wives and female family members but made little direct contribution. Men designated indispensable were rewarded for this status by normal rations only; civil servants felt forsaken and unimportant. Only after the most ominous warnings did imperial officials pronounce political policemen "hardest laborers" in November 1916, deferring to the value of their role in quelling unrest in qualifying them for the maximum supplementary benefits.[160] Notably, Berlin municipal authorities and many neighboring communal governments refused to acknowledge this higher level of support for policemen, denying that they played a difficult or important role in quelling the unrest of starving, freezing women.[161]

Berliners receiving normal rations did not suffer these circumstances for long. By early 1917 lower middle-class women championed the equal distribution of foodstuffs, a reversal in their demands of a few months earlier. For "each believes he is doing everything in his power in the service of the employer and the fatherland, and each believes therefore that he has a claim on a special food supplement."[162] The "housewives of Steglitz" and "otherwise dependable social circles" joined again with working-class Berliners, at least those who did not work in munitions factories, now in active protest against what they perceived to be their abandonment by the state.[163] Together they chanted, "The poor deliver the bodies, the *Mittelstand* has to retreat, and the rich profit from the war."[164] In the same spirit this population attacked ration supplements given to POWs, who were, after all, not even German. In response, illuminating the OHL's sensitivity to unrest in and out of the factory, despite the need for the labor power of POWs, and in defiance of official concerns for international reputation, military authorities cut back extra supplements for hard-laboring POWs in early February.[165] Here officials demonstrated how diet could make the strong weak.

By the new year, these protesting populations elicited renewed public support. In November 1916 the petit bourgeois *Berliner Volkszeitung* commended, as did most other papers, the extra supplements for war workers, "precisely as much a question of our [German] existence as the suffering of our brave soldiers on the front."[166] One month later this paper made a very different argument. In "Who Is Buying the Golden War Goose?" the paper played on the similarities between "heavy laborer" (*Schwerarbeiter*) and the "enormously rich" (*Schwerreich*).[167] Lower middle-class women themselves grumbled bitterly that female munitions workers could eat goose for Christmas dinner when they could get nothing at all, echoing the protests against separation allowances two years earlier.[168] But demonstrators won greatest public support with their renewed attacks on farmers, merchants, and the KEA; most Berliners continued to believe, with some good evidence, that but for unchecked profiteering, there would be enough food at least to prevent serious hunger.[169]

Women in war factories also began to argue for an equalization of benefits, at least among munitions factory workers. They were successful in this mission over time. In a notable move to pacify women munitions workers in particular, the KEA and the War Office issued new regulations in January 1917, against ambivalent trade union response, proclaiming that entire factories, rather than individuals within a factory, would be authorized for supplements.[170] In a move he had refused in December, by early 1917 Batocki authorized increased fat rations to all munitions workers, including those not classified as hard laborers. Women working in munitions successfully pressed industrialists to demand an equalization of government meat supplements among war-industry workers.[171] By the fall of 1917 the category "hard laborer" would be entirely replaced by "munitions worker," while hardest laborers received little more. Lucian Wiernik, who oversaw the provisioning of the factory canteens, wrote that it was important that authorities provide for munitions workers as equally as possible, lest one excite their natural irrationality.[172] He urged, too, *"that the workforce be allowed to have a role in the distribution of food to as great a degree as possible."* [173]

In early 1917 the protests of female munitions workers began to merge with broader calls for equalization of distribution outside the factory among the wide range of poorer Berliners, as women in and out of the factories mixed in the streets, all the more as growing numbers of women munitions workers felt forced to leave the war factories to care for dependent family members.[174] In January General Groener observed in Berlin and elsewhere that of all the "more or less serious conditions" that inspired unrest, foremost among these, after sheer want, ranked the perceived "unpurposefulness and injustice of the distribution of food supplements." He concluded, "It appears very doubtful whether the continuing emphasis of the KEA to deliver food preferentially to the munitions workers and, among these, the heavy and heaviest laborers is the appropriate choice." [175] Protesters focused collectively on the government's perceived failure to distribute controlled food equitably and to prevent profiteers from taking advantage of

Germans at their most vulnerable. The broad range of poor women, outside and within the munitions factories, made their case plainly and vocally, in advance of the better-known April labor strikes. The early 1917 unrest proved a last challenge to the government to make good on its implied promises.

9 THE END OF FAITH

The collective power of Berliners of lesser means returned
with a vengeance in the late winter and spring of 1917. They coalesced in
calls for equal distribution of food among themselves and demanded the
government address both official measures and private acts that compromised this equality. Poor urban consumers riveted their attention on the
black-marketing that blossomed in this cold winter, largely displacing conflicts among themselves once more. The renewed street protest was closely
tied to the shop-floor unrest of February and April. The well-studied strikes
of April 1917, which began in Berlin metalworks and spread around the
country, have often been perceived as the first sign of serious political unrest in Germany. Scholars have often interpreted the strikes, like the revolution of November 1918, as a popular revolt against the attempted tyranny
of a government that had imposed total war on German society. But popular fury throughout the war arose as heatedly from the inability of Prussian
and imperial officials to impose their authority as firmly and as effectively
on the food question as many would have liked.

In spite or perhaps because of the single-minded focus of the Supreme
Army Command (OHL) on winning the war, civilian and military authorities
reacted with redoubled responsiveness to street and shop-floor protests
alike, committing the highest officials to the tasks of equalizing food distribution and prosecuting speculation. In turn, as late as the fall of 1917, Berliners and other Germans still maintained some faith in the government's good
intent, if not in its ability to execute it, and this, along with the promise of
peace negotiations in the East, kept Germans from following the revolutionary path of their eastern neighbors. Indeed, poor urban Germans wanted to
believe that officials represented their best chances at getting food. Nonetheless, government food scandals rocked Berlin in the fall and winter of
1917, pitching residents into numb despair. By the end of the year, hope
even for officials' good intentions was wiped out by the image of cynical authorities who indulged in speculation themselves at the expense of just distribution among the larger population. Even as Foreign Office authorities

announced renewed prospects for peace in the East, poorer Berliners concluded they should no longer place any faith in the Wilhelmine regime.

PEACE, FREEDOM, AND BREAD?

The year 1917 opened to desperate calls for an equalization of food distribution, by working-class and lower middle-class Berliners and especially by women, on and off the shop floor. Groups of normally rationed protesters in Berlin as well as in other cities continued to decry special rations for the ill or for children.[1] But the focus now lay elsewhere. Women in the war factories demanded an equalization of rations among munitions workers, and the normally rationed called for the equalization of rations overall.[2] One after another, the deputy commanders reported renewed unrest around the country, including concerning the continued "privileged treatment" of war-industry workers—and especially hardest laborers.[3] Hardest laborers sought to retain their special supplements; still, they too joined the campaign for equalization by protesting differences in supply among the various factories.

By the early months of the year, however, these segments of the population began to turn their wrath away from one another and toward what they all perceived to be the far larger enemy under the controlled economy: profiteering in all its forms. Profiteering was, of course, the long-standing wartime enemy of poor Berlin consumers. It was first in the course of the fully controlled economy that, correspondingly, the black market burgeoned as a full-scale alternative to buying regulated foods.[4] Police reports were full of incidents of "hoarder trips" taken by so-called hoarder men (including likely many women).[5] Berliners observed dealings "roundabout" and "through the back door," as officials ordered police to vigilantly prosecute such activity.

For patrons of the black market, even this horrid period passed without more than discomfort and considerable expenditure of time, money, and energy, despite Michaelis's avowal that "everyone, even state ministers," was only barely surviving on turnips.[6] (As sailors stationed in Kiel noted, they too would like to eat their turnips in the fashion of the officers: with lots of meat.)[7] Evelyn Blücher, like those outside the capital, wrote of great dinner parties thrown by high society during the peak of the crisis over meat and fat. Those with stores to spare claimed they would rather feed them to their friends than hand goods over to the authorities, despite the protest many had made publicly on behalf of the poor.[8] Evidence of such polarized access

"The Nightmare of the War Profiteer," that is, peace on earth. (Kladderadatsch, 31 December 1916)

to food supplies qualifies aggregate figures offering evidence that Germans ate more than rations allowed.[9] Still even wealthier Berliners complained of regional disparity, calling for redistribution of goods from the agricultural areas of Greater Berlin, as well as other areas of the country, especially Bavaria.[10] Concerns for such "underdistribution" brought in protests from around the city: from Steglitz, a district of functionaries, and wealthy Schmargendorf, Südende, and Zehldendorf as well as from Friedrichshain and Lichtenberg, offering an impressive, apparently united urban consumer front in deed now as well as in word.[11] In part for this reason, poorer Berlin consumers continued to focus their animus primarily on the seller rather than the buyer of black-market goods and to deflect blame out of the city altogether.

The press continued to reflect and reinforce the anxieties of poorer Berliners, running daily pieces on the black market in the first months of the year. Newspapers delivered warnings to the hoarding farmer, the greedy middleman, and the retail trickster, challenging their "patriotic disposition."[12] They provoked readers with titles proclaiming farmers' views: "We'd Rather Feed the Pigs with It."[13] They boldly proclaimed the existence of massive hidden supplies, preserved, foddered, sold on the black market, or even allowed to rot, spurring poorer consumers to unrest by the relentless repetition of such accusations.[14] At the same time, many newspapers provoked fury by continuing to accept advertisements from black-market sellers.[15] The damning

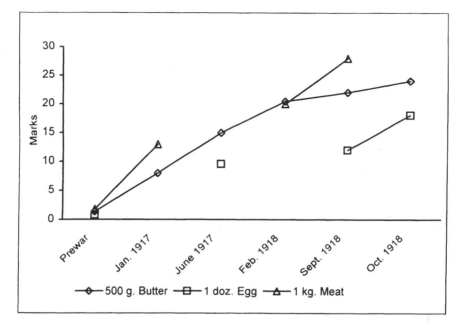

Figure 9.1. Black Market Prices in Greater Berlin, Prewar–1918
Source: Materna et al., Geschichte Berlins, 540.

articles passed easily under the censors' eyes. Military authorities allowed such pieces to appear as long as they did not directly attack the state or fatherland.[16] Yet the press indeed excoriated the government and its various arms for their failure to suppress the speculation. The *Reichsbote* expressed deep vitriol against the "*shameless* hoarders and profiteering *merchants*" who traitorously preyed on economically vulnerable women. The paper judged most sharply, however, officials' "gentle treatment" of these traitors.[17] The *Berliner Tageblatt* offered wholehearted support for a Reichstag representative's admonition to his colleagues and "the government" for the failure to fulfill their premier obligation, provisioning the people.[18]

Police as well as the deputy commanders around the country helped maintain the pressure on their superiors. Police observed popular appreciation for authorities' bid for peace in the West and, failing that, their subsequent pursuit of unrestrained submarine warfare as a move to break the blockade (and an appropriate act of vengeance).[19] However, they noted, "an enormous portion of the population doesn't care about the war at all any more" and exhibited a growing lack of faith in the military as well as the civilian administration.[20] Poor prospects for food created a broad "hotbed" for antiwar sentiment.[21] In the wake of the split in the Social Democratic Party (SPD) and the conference of left-wing SPD women, policemen expressed new fear

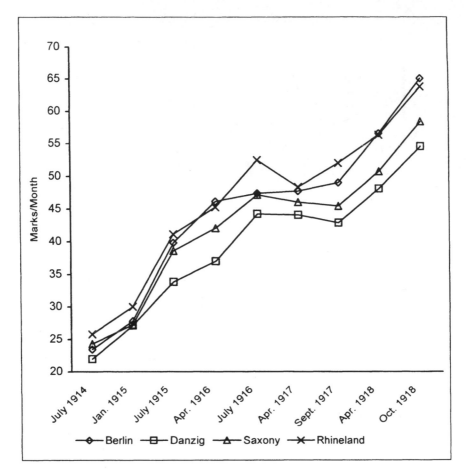

Figure 9.2. Monthly Worker Expenditures for Food, 1914–1918
Source: Zimmermann, "Veränderungen," 463.

for the effect of "radical women" on the street protesters.[22] It is indeed clear that Spartacists and independent Social Democrats turned their attention increasingly to the desperate women in the streets demanding food as a central potential mass revolutionary force. The annual March demonstration, populated by radical women and youth, gained greater attention and interest than in previous years. Participants held aloft a large, bright banner that vilified the kaiser: "Curse the King, the King of the Rich, who can't know our misery, who won't rest until he has exacted the last from us and lets us be shot like dogs."[23] Police observed the scene but declined to intervene.

Demonstrators still vehemently protested merchant trickery and treachery and the offices that failed to control such activity. They deplored merchant policies that forced them to buy one-third of their bread supplement in flour (if flour were to be had) or one-third of their coal allotment in useless coke.[24] In mid-March women, expressing deep "hatred" and "resentment," created unrest in the central market hall that required reinforcements to put down, as they protested against the expensive fish that adorned the market stalls in place of the cheaper fish that was advertised.[25] The scene recalled the old Berlin legend of the "women's band" that was supposed to gather to end a great famine by fishing together at night on the Spree River.[26] But there was no fish for these shoppers, and no end to the famine.

Street protest over government failures was matched by disruption on the shop floor, in a series of one-day strikes in Berlin metalworks on 3 and 10 February. Workers struck over wages, food supplies, and the general "food calamity," as well as perceived failures by the ZEG to stem profiteering. At the time of these first broad wartime strikes in Berlin factories (soon repeated around the country), women constituted the majority of war-industry workers. Munitions worker Martha Balzer noted with pleasure the widespread press response in February to "the demonstration of Britzer women," the more than 500 women, predominantly but not exclusively from the war factories, who stormed the communal offices of this working-class suburb adjoining Neukölln, claiming to be "speakers for the people."[27] Balzer observed the extra ration cards protesters exacted from communal officials, more evidence that only continued protest brought desired ends.

In contrast to their relatively positive representation of the street protest and even of the shop-floor unrest generally, police responded dismissively to the participation of hardest laborers in the strikes, claiming that they ate better than anyone else in Berlin.[28] Police conflated protest on and off the shop floor in the battle for "equitable" distribution, making a case for the "generalized agitation" rather than for the interests that divided the populace. Groener responded in early March, recommending special supplements be targeted to the population of protesters, above all women, children, and adolescent youth.[29] In turn, although the OHL's foremost commitment was to producing munitions, officials reacted more responsively to the demands of street protesters than of war-industry workers, better to the demands of general munitions workers than of hardest laborers, and better overall, by some measures, to women than to men.

Despite the OHL's "radical militaris[m],"[30] Reich- and Prussian-level authorities continued to announce measures that sounded impressively earnest, vowing to revamp the system of special rations and to institute a general principle of equal food distribution that truly reckoned with both legal and illegal forms of special privilege. In the first months of the new year the KEA and military officials adjusted special supplements to flatten distribution, despite concern especially among men in the war industry.[31] Officials were just as responsive to popular condemnation of food speculation, despite their reliance on Junkers, speculators, and wealthy consumers for political and material support. In December 1916 the KEA had issued an edict in its most forceful language to date, banning "food profiteering, food displacement, and chain trade."[32] Early in the new year, the Berlin police commissioner charged the War Profiteering Office (KWA) to execute the sense of the edict.[33] Governor of Pomerania Wilhelm von Waldow launched a national initiative claiming a more dependable way for localities to purchase and distribute goods for their residents, easing tensions between city and countryside. Prussian officials set up a revamped Potato Office with greater authority to oversee production as well as distribution.[34] Feeling fresh power, Batocki publicly demanded the KEA be given enforceable control over policy on a national level. Prussian ministers overruled their colleague Schorlemer's objections to provide new powers to the Prussian Commissariat for the Provisioning of the People, giving it the control that the KEA had lacked over all Prussian civilian agencies concerning food. They put in charge of it former head of the Grain Authority Georg Michaelis on 21 March.

Berliners were hopeful despite a fresh snowfall. Perhaps at long last they had their food dictator and evidence that the government would respond properly and effectively.[35] Working-class Berliners looked favorably toward Michaelis. They perceived him to be a forceful proponent of government control over food, as in the debate over public kitchens, and a successful adversary of agricultural particularism. Above all, poorer Berliners perceived the new powers and prestige of the commissariat as an important sign of the responsibility and obligation officials seemed to accept for the fate of the population. In this context the populace appreciated Michaelis's close ties to the military leadership. Unfortunately, his appointment in late March came simultaneously with an announcement of a prospective 25 percent cut in bread rations, following closely on the cut in January.[36] Attempting to take hold of the situation, however, Michaelis spoke before the Berlin city assembly, spelling out a plan for controlled, equal distribution of bread. He announced that, this time, war-industry workers, including hardest laborers, would bear an equivalent reduction in their bread rations. In this way he cast a positive light on this dreaded measure for the broad population of poor consumers, even at the risk of renewed shop-floor unrest. Indeed, new measures throughout the remainder of the year removed virtually all privileging of war-industry workers, including hardest labors, as particularly strong or as offering unusual service to the nation.

Authorities now embraced equalized distribution generally. Michaelis described the system of differentiated distribution, in retrospect, as one that simply was not working. "One tried it," he noted, "with a system of supplements for heavy and heaviest laborers and the sick[, and with] special supplements for the elderly, women in childbed, children, etc. The administration became ever more complicated. Each worker claimed to be a heavy laborer." Correspondingly, members of the general, normally rationed population asserted that each person warranted "special supplements."[37] At the same time, Michaelis acknowledged ruefully, "women's wallets were filled with food ration cards of every kind, but the rations were often so minimal that it wasn't even worth picking them up."[38] Military officials concurred. Berge observed, "A simplification of the system of heavy, heaviest, munitions, and special laborer supplements is urgently desired, especially because . . . regulated differentiations and fair apportionment isn't possible. This is eliciting pitched discontent and jealousy among the workers without supplements." He finished with the popular recommendation that "all defense worker supplements . . . be abolished, and in its place the general rations of the 'non-self-provider' should be raised."[39] Bundesrat officials agreed to a new meat card that would equalize distribution of this product among all Germans. The Städtetag put together a new system of benefits explicitly for the population of lesser means, acceptable because of the open way the category was defined.[40] Through this new equalization, women lost the opportunity to be characterized as especially strong. But the broader urban populace read this change as acknowledgment of the needs and sacrifices of the greater population, as consumers and as producers alike.

Michaelis took a stance no less energetic toward profiteering and deception, promising reform of both the KEA and the ZEG and demanding "unified action" by military officials nationwide, through the deputy commanding generals.[41] Batocki followed enthusiastically with demands that, following KWA efforts, officials redouble efforts to prosecute speculation and confiscate goods generally, on behalf of disadvantaged urban residents, "without regard for the implications for after the war."[42] Berge's office banned "hoarder trips," proposing to install precious military forces at all train stations, conduct regular searches, and recommend heavy penalties against transgressors.[43] Kessel promised a "search through the villages" to ferret out sources of food to bring into the city under official aegis.[44] Officials moved concertedly to draw in the churches and private organizations in generating massive propaganda against black-marketing and hoarding.[45] The KWA announced the prosecution of over 24,000 cases of profiteering to date, claiming to root out another 4,000 cases each month.[46] The KWA and

Police bring suspects, all male, for questioning about hoarding and reselling. (BAPK, file 1578)

Michaelis announced that Berlin police now pursued black market offenders as a primary task, protecting the populace rather than defending the government against the populace.

Bethmann weighed in with specific promises for domestic political reform, even as the OHL put a new request for war credits before the Reichstag. On 27 February Bethmann publicly committed to the pursuit of peace, democracy, and bread; the link between these concepts was tight and transparent, at least for every poor urban consumer. Bethmann elaborated plans for the new orientation of domestic politics he had so vaguely spoken of a year earlier. The kaiser made his own direct pledge, acknowledging a new low in the regime's legitimacy.[47] In his Easter edict on 7 April, the kaiser promised revision of the Prussian three-class voting system. People in the streets responded generally with satisfaction, though they voiced their hope still for immediate, visible changes in their circumstances. The government's continued acknowledgment of its obligations toward its subjects may have prevented revolution at this point in the war in Germany, as it took place in March in Russia.[48]

The press reported some policy successes as the winter waned, observing that in contrast to speculating "hoarder men," on the whole, residents returning to Berlin by train carried food only in their own bellies, having managed, "as the Berliners say, to have eaten themselves silly."[49] Police claimed satisfaction that they had apprehended the shadowy (male) figures who lurked in the toilets of meal halls scalping bread and meat coupons.[50] And yet, despite reforms, new offices, and prosecutions, black-marketing still flourished. This was in part a function of authorities' very success in "representing" urban consumers. High-level officials failed to call forth (if they ever had) the moral imperative that might spur farmers to turn over all their goods to authorities, and merchants to sell to poor consumers at fixed prices. Farmers, especially Junkers, were little pleased to be characterized as enemies of fellow Germans, above all by a regime they felt had deserted them and privileged urban dwellers, above all Berliners. One Pomeranian farmer claimed she would much rather sell her cows than "slave away" to produce butter for Berliners.[51] By the spring of 1917 most farmers had relatively little investment in the war and even in the incumbent regime.[52]

Authorities ran up against the practical problems of redistributing black market food once they did confiscate it, moreover. The press spread the rumor (often true) that when government agents did seize provisions off trains, they left foodstuffs on the station platform indefinitely, where they simply spoiled. This was certainly not the kind of equality of distribution for which Berliners had hoped. In early April tons of goods sat in the station of the Alexanderplatz city train just outside the central market, "leaking fluid," emitting rotten smells, and thoroughly enraging thousands of passersby as police stood around protecting the goods. Worse still for authorities, every Berlin paper announced the news; Dr. Carl Falck of the KWA found it a public relations nightmare.[53]

In this context authorities themselves dreaded the response of Berliners and others to news of the revolution in Russia. Berliners paid close attention to the revolution, as much in light of renewed prospects of peace with that country as in terms of following Russia's example. Authorities noted that "news of the role played by industry workers in the movement in Russia has made an impact on German workers, for they believed they can spread their influence considerably further, in both their own factories, and on the political leadership."[54] But hungry capital residents remained at least as attentive to the specifics of officials' latest food policy successes and blunders, despairing that Michaelis could not avoid the decrease in the bread ration (despite equalizing the burden) set to take effect in mid-April. Where was the bread in the "peace, freedom, and bread" Bethmann had promised? Officer Kurtz believed indeed that "interest for the events on the fronts, the revolution in Russian, and America's declaration of war [was] completely suppressed by the concern for food." This was not political apathy but, rather, continued investment in a different kind of politics. He repeated the familiar message: "The view remains firm that food would remain in sufficient supply, if a just system of distribution from the producer to the consumer were imposed. This belief has become all the stronger by the observation that food is consistently available on the black market, at usurious prices."[55]

A sudden drop in the availability of potatoes on the eve of the cut in bread rations brought about "the worst imaginable mood all around."[56] Poor consumers around the country joined Berliners in condemning what they feared to be efforts by authorities to patronize protesters with vacuous promises and "*false* pacification."[57] Then delegates of Berlin metalworks and other works declared a demonstration strike for 16 April, the day after the cut in rations was to take effect.[58] The result of Michaelis's promise to cut bread rations equitably was to provoke hard and hardest laborers to join their "light-working" counterparts in the factories and protesters on the streets, indeed taking on Bethmann's mantra as their own. Workers were little impressed by Batocki's new guarantees to the trade unions to provision workers; many resented the erosion of their special position.[59] Many on and off the shop floor complained that the kaiser's edict did "only half the job," in part because it deferred the explicitly political rewards until after the war, but more centrally because it came without the bread that the kaiser had promised they deserved.[60] Michaelis nervously demanded to hear immediately and directly all reports of unrest and strikes that arose specifically from food difficulties, while Spartacists disseminated their brochure titled *Hunger,* encouraging still more radical tactics.[61] Hindenburg stepped in to recategorize political police once more, despite the movement toward equality, to ensure that they received at least as much as any of the workers who might protest—though this strategy had the potential to backfire.

Officials now moved to bring protesters more directly into the project of control and distribution. Workers' deputies met with the Berlin city council, along with Wermuth and high-level government officials, on Friday, 13 April. The authorities promised that all food, including previously unregulated luxury goods, would be under strict government control and that they would, moreover, establish new mass dining halls "without differentiation by status or type of work." On the eve of the planned worker walkout and broad demonstration, set for 16 April, Groener announced plans on behalf of the War Office and State Commissariat to appoint workers to run the business of the Distribution Office, including determining the method of distribution. In contrast to the military leadership's interest in personalizing delivery of food, the new plans explicitly allowed workers (here men) to take food home to their wives, whose own sacrifices required this.[62] Though the scheme was a gambit to put the onus of food distribution on workers' shoulders as well as a last desperate attempt to ward off potentially catastrophic unrest, once more the highest-level officials seemed to be espousing democratization while promising greater control. In response, worker deputies promised to try to prevent unrest, though they claimed workers now lacked all faith in the government.[63] But this claim is open to some question.

On Monday, 16 April, more than 200,000 metal-, munitions-, and other workers failed to show up for work or walked off their shift, by wartime standards a formal act of unprecedented size. Demonstrators from many factories, including numerous war-industry works, spread throughout the city. Most struck specifically "against government measures on the food question," though the food question remained intimately connected to issues of relations between state and society.[64] A large portion of the striking factory workers failed to join the formal demonstration that shop stewards had planned for 9:00 A.M.[65] But there were plenty of impromptu gatherings in the streets, by factory workers and others. Oppen noted with regret that there were many attacks on bakeries, particularly in the sensitive area between police headquarters (the "red fortress") in Alexanderplatz and government buildings.[66] Many groups succeeded in moving close to the inner sanctum of the municipal, Prussian, and imperial government, demonstrating in the thousands in Leipziger Street, just short of the Kaiser-Wilhelm bridge spanning the Spree River near the imperial palace, and in Alexanderplatz, site of the city's central market, where police could not deter people from gathering. Police prevented most demonstrators from reaching Wilhelm Street and Unter den Linden, though radical Social Democratic youth pushed their way through.[67]

Workers felt pleased with the day's events. The walkout had been planned as a demonstration strike, and the great majority of workers intended to return to work by Tuesday or Wednesday. As a demonstration strike this action seemed to indicate for many the potential of successful response; it was a warning communicating a set of demands that strikers believed officials could and might meet. Particularly after the Friday night meeting before the strike, many workers felt that their message had been successfully expressed. At the same time many men in particular were nervous about remaining off the job, as military officials had quietly threatened to send strikers to the front lines. Most strikers showed little immediate enthusiasm for the suggestion of a fresh walkout on May Day, in protest against poor treatment of radical labor leader Richard Müller.[68]

Although *Vorwärts* was interested in denying the political aspect of the April strikes,[69] for most of the protesters it appears that demands were political in the most specific and immediate sense: in having a voice beyond the franchise, in asserting the need for better representation, and in claiming their rights above commitment to a free market and demanding confiscation and redistribution of property to ensure basic needs. These demands were in certain respects more radical than those expressed by the shop stewards, which included a non-annexationist peace, extension of the franchise, and liberation of political prisoners. They were also demands that authorities had already afforded legitimacy. Strikers and demonstrators within and outside the war factories were heartened by "the willingness to oblige on the part of the government."[70]

There are many reasons to see the April strikes as closely related to the ongoing protest in the streets. The latter was not epiphenomenal; the pattern established in making specific, material demands and retreating when those demands were met formed the model for the April strikes as well. The two sites of unrest did not feature distinct populations but, rather, populations that flowed from one location to the other.[71] At least half of the strikers were women, who were also well-represented at meetings to plan for the strikes.[72] In the days before the strike, working-class women in the streets who were not war-industry workers discussed the participation of their husbands as well as their sons and daughters in the prospective unrest.[73] In Berlin, women appear to have formed the majority of protesters overall, though distinct populations were difficult to observe. The greater number of women makes sense in terms of women's majority in the local metal and munitions industry, their immunity from conscription, their ongoing presence in the streets as consumers, and finally their greater numbers generally on the homefront. Continued public (and police) support for poor women protesters in the streets may have prevented observers from publicly condemning the strikers, though some lashed out at strikers specifically while defending consumer protesters.[74] Oppen noted that this large-scale unrest exposed a process of "political fermentation" throughout the city, spreading from street to factory and back, that would become increasingly visible in the coming months.[75]

To protesters' relief and, for many, vindication, Michaelis still appeared to be listening, directly acknowledging opinions of protesters from both the shop floor and the streets. This was the kind of dictator poor urban protesters had hoped for: one who would use his enormous power to represent their interests. On the heels of the strike, Michaelis issued all-new, overriding principles of food distribution, which metropolitan officials attempted to follow, entirely reshuffling and simplifying the existing process. By early May, imperial officials erected a new food distribution office for Greater Berlin.[76] The State Distribution Office (Staatliche Verteilungsstelle, svs) quickly began its work in earnest, defining its task as the "equitable provisioning of the population of Greater Berlin with food and other items of daily need."[77] Branch offices opened around the country, following nationwide unrest, offering workers representation on their boards.[78] Broad segments of the populace perceived this step as legitimation once again of both greater control and a more participatory government. The *Reichsbote* reported that the revamped system of supplements was "especially well received and gratefully acknowledged by those — for example, the munitions workers — who no longer receive many special rations," while the normally rationed were thereby able to avoid public kitchens.[79] Police, too, reported general cautious "content" by early May.[80]

Yet once more the hopefulness faded in the following weeks, as basic foods still remained in short supply. The mayor of Charlottenburg reported in June that potato deliveries to both public kitchens and factory canteens were cut by half, but this cut was not followed by apparent greater general availability of the tuber at private vendors or at municipal sales outlets.[81] General Heinrich von Scheüch, soon to assume the position of war minister, noted that German workers continued to express resentment for the unequal distribution of food within the factories. Scheüch warned of the compromise of popular "resistance" to both disease and unrest that might permit serious outbreaks at any moment.[82] In turn svs officials in Berlin voiced concern for the response of hard and hardest laborers to the changes in the supplements.[83] At the same time, "the unequal treatment" between war-industry workers and their non-war-industry counterparts was still "creating great unrest . . . dissolving the advances that the introduction of the term 'munitions industry' brought with it."[84] Exasperated authorities responded that it must be made clear to workers "that no more can be given them, and that their own wives and children will suffer at the raising of any special supplements," reconfirming that productive labor was not to be the only measure of national contribution.[85] As shipments of raw supplies necessary to factory production (including the war industries) dwindled and arrived inconsistently, moreover, industrialists laid off many workers, beginning in the spring and summer of 1917. Layoffs included above all women workers, who now lost any remaining privileges and swelled the ranks of the normally rationed.[86]

SUBSTITUTE PEOPLE

Poorer consumers became all the more convinced that black-marketing remained the real culprit, as the new equalized distribution of products under official control brought little relief. This suspicion was exacerbated in the summer of 1917 by the problem of substitution. Authorities had promised to compensate for the cut in bread rations by increasing rations in other foods such as potatoes, meat, fish, vegetables, and eggs. Consumers found none of these foods easily available or affordable in early April.[87] This was not the first substitution problem. In the preceding months police and the press had reported consumers' frustration that even swede turnips were no longer available, though propaganda continued to urge their consumption to compensate for the lack of potatoes.[88] One resident of Leipzig observed dryly that she did not mind eating rat; it was rat substitute she objected to.[89] For poorer Berliners, the chicanery, cultural affronts, and actual health threats posed by the burgeoning market in ersatz or substitute foods, not to mention absence of the original items, brought them yet again to the point of protest in the summer of 1917.[90]

The notion of "ersatz" was relatively positive at the outset of war. Military leaders expressed enthusiasm for the potential contributions of science to the war effort. In light of the embargo, they were thrilled that scientists could provide them with ersatz, or artificially produced, fixed nitrogen for gunpowder. Many officials hoped that the new science of nutrition could ease the burden of the economic war by providing ersatz foods. As early as 1915 national commissions on ersatz coffee and tea had regulated the traffic of the various products sold under these names. This seemed harmless enough. As Germany had no imperial markets in bean coffee, most of the population had never drunk anything but domestic coffee, made from inexpensive chicory and sugar beets (though naturally for them the latter was "real" coffee). Other substitutions emerged with the first shortages: potatoes for bread, and vice versa; margarine and jam for meat fat and butter. The population accepted the substitution of one food for another when they recognized a limited gap between the nutritional and sociocultural values of the two foods. Attitudes toward this gap relaxed of necessity as food grew more scarce. In August 1916 women rioted violently in Kattowitz, shouting "Bread! Bacon! Fat! Potatoes! Away with jam!"[91] Now, one year later, consumers in Berlin happily accepted jam as a bread spread.

Serious problems surrounding ersatz foods arose first in the turnip winter, in the form of thousands of food substitutes, the most prominent of which was the loathed swede turnip. In early 1917 the swede turnip constituted the primary food in the households of most Berliners, a substitute for most other foods. There was no regular means to prepare the indigestible fodder turnip, and nothing was available to improve the root's much hated flavor. Officials and private organizations encouraged urban consumers to think broadly about the turnip as mousse, cutlets, or pudding, offering recipes composed of increasingly few ingredients. This propaganda made Berliners all the more "bitter," as reports tellingly characterized the situation, when even the turnip was not available for purchase by the spring and summer of 1917. If this was moreover the most infamous example of an unwelcome substitution, it was not necessarily the worst. Berliners traded jokes about ersatz foods, from the uses put to old battle horses (which probably were eaten) to mattress stuffing to ration coupons themselves.[92] A woman worker from Lichtenberg described the substitute goods as dangerously fraudulent and the government's propaganda as likewise so, from assertions about the nutritional value of saccharine to the promotion of soap powder that exploded in her kitchen.[93] Women responded cynically to ongoing government campaigns to collect genuine gold, iron, money, and even the hair off their heads, while everything they took in was artificial and inferior. As officials concocted schemes to extract protein from dragonfly wings, resourceful tradespeople cut often injurious "stretchers" into good food and watered scarce milk for infants until it was a "transparent blue."[94] Merchants thereby reinforced divisions between themselves and urban consumers, recalling the fears of food adulteration that had constituted one of the few common concerns among consumers across class lines before the war had broken out.

The case of coffee provides one example of how products sold as substitutes lost their relation to the original item. Officials constituted coffee as a "most important food," against the advice of the food experts, due to its cultural role in the German diet. Just before the institution of the KEA in 1916, the Bundesrat established the War Committee for Coffee, Tea, and Substitute Goods. Germans had to drink coffee with their *Stulle*, or coffee break sandwich; it was as basic an accompaniment to bread as the bread's spread. (For many workers, it might alternately be a pull of schnapps, although authorities did not find this a problem for the "German" diet. Beer production, in Bavaria a most important food, was banned in northern

Germany first in the summer of 1917 to encourage land use for more nutritional crops.) Conversely, one did not normally drink coffee without eating a roll or like product, reinforcing the connection between coffee and food; to desire a cup of coffee signified the expectation of bread. Germans of all classes drank coffee (bean or chicory) for breakfast, in the afternoon, and often before retiring. Virtually the national drink, Germans consumed it above all in the big cities.[95] The product contained no nutritional value or, in working-class chicory coffee, even caffeine. Yet Germans did not celebrate the drink for its warmth alone. Most herbal infusions were "tea" and, therefore, not acceptable substitutes. When substitute teas were offered on the market, people often refused them, not just because they tasted disgusting "but, rather, because 'the German doesn't drink much tea, and is rather used to his coffee.'"[96]

Based on the cultural importance of coffee, its scarcity by the second year of the war had caused no small uproar in Berlin. The KEA acknowledged "the meaningful influence that coffee and quasi-coffee drinks had on the general morale of the population," also noting that a warm drink helped make repetitive food, potatoes and dry bread, edible.[97] In 1916 officials had planned to set aside roasted grains for use as substitute coffee. But the entry of Romania into the war closed off these supplies and set the production of coffee in competition with that of the bread with which coffee was drunk. The KEA attempted to take control of the situation, publishing lists of permitted substitutes for coffee (including ground walnut shells and corn powder) as well as for thousands of other food products — from 837 certified forms of substitute sausage to over 3,500 approved pseudo–soft drinks.[98]

By the early spring of 1917, however, officials had lost control again. Berliners had entered the phase of "ersatz ersatz," or "surrogates" (*Surrogaten*). In the absence of common substitutes, substitutes for the substitutes were used, which were often illegal and of ever more dubious quality. Capital residents decried foul products merchants sold as ersatz coffee and as substitutes for all other foods. Skalweit notes, in perhaps an overly generous spirit, that "made up in nice packages, they offered the German housewife at least the pleasant deception that she was enriching the supply of her kitchen."[99] But merchants offered replacements on the basis of some physical approximation, with increasingly little concern for taste, nutritional value, or safety. They packaged and sold yellow powder of indeterminate origin as dried egg; white powder, as dried milk. Washing soda mixed in starch constituted butter, sold under one of the new "fantasy names" — and at fantasy prices. The *Berliner Volkszeitung* lamented, "Coffee has disappeared, the finer substitutes have disappeared; only the price, the price, has remained."[100] Surrogates contributed to the upheaval and disorientation of the war experience, as nothing was what it seemed to be, and the "good" and the "bad" were indistinguishable.

As of spring 1916, officials required producers of substitute products to list contents on their packaging. Consumers consequently expressed outrage when they discovered the contents of the products they purchased, inasmuch as they were actually listed. Ash constituted 85 percent of a product offered as ersatz pepper; many substitute foods contained the "indigestible remains of animals."[101] Yet many desperate consumers continued to buy these products, inducing the onset of "substitute sickness," a syndrome representing the combined effects of insufficient nutrition and the consumption of many nonfood and even toxic items.[102] In August 1917 Oppen himself deplored the sale of bread "in part so bad, that in many cases it has caused intestinal disorders."[103] Consumers began angrily bringing their flour to authorities to be inspected for its content.[104] Officials outside Berlin reported similar stories in understated fashion: "If one is to imagine that one is later to eat this grain as bread, it is little wonder that the aggravation in the populace grows ever greater."[105]

In light of these circumstances, the term "ersatz" took on new meaning.[106] While before the war it had signified simply a substitute, it had now come to mean "fake" or "artificial," "inferior substitute," and even "wretched." Berliners were by now extremely sensitive to artificial dealings on the market, activity that did not conform to government regulations.[107] The press characterized officials themselves as "unconscious provocateurs" for allowing merchants to offer such artificial goods to "the German housewife" and rendering necessary the use of substitutes in the first place.[108] The quality of the goods moreover seemed to constitute the identity of those who consumed them. If swede turnips rendered Berliners equivalent to animals, ash pepper suggested they were less than animals. Those who manufactured and sold surrogates had the ability to determine this identity.

Women working in munitions were disturbed by another association with the term "ersatz." In cooperation with the trade unions, who sought to codify women's place in the factory as temporary, the OHL designated these women "substitute workers" (Ersatzarbeiterinnen) for men at the front. Fellow workers and managers increasingly subjected women to this reminder on the shop floor.[109] National Women's Service volunteers themselves adopted the notion of women workers as a "female substitute army."[110] As "ersatz" came to mean "inferior" or "second-rate," this promoted tensions within the factories.[111] In late 1916 and early 1917 working-class women felt strongly needed and wanted, at least by the OHL. Bourgeois women played an auxil-

*"What's this, Lehmann old crank, you a wanderer with lute and mandolin?" "Quiet, man, it's a sham, so I can hoard eggs and butter underneath for interested parties." (*Berliner Illustrirte Zeitung, *6 December 1917)*

iary role to their productive work. By mid-1917, as factory owners began laying off women for lack of raw materials to produce munitions, and as the trade union leadership gained greater negotiating power with the OHL, the role of working-class women as munitions workers lost some of its luster. Labor leaders were successful in halting some new efforts to refit factories to accommodate a growing female labor force, on the basis of women's "substitute" nature. By the late summer of 1917, as industrialists let even more substitute workers go, they advertised the need for *Facharbeiter*, skilled or "qualified" workers with a sense of "quality." Officials leaked the term "pile of second-raters" (*Ersatzhaufen*) to refer to the straggling reinforcements now called up to the front—those not "man" enough to have been sent earlier.

The notion of the ersatz food came to be used as a metaphor for the depreciating quality of life overall. The term "fake person" (*Ersatzmensch*) arose in this period, signifying someone in wretched condition.[112] The term evoked both the poor state of the individual, waiting for "real" life to begin again, and to the way one felt as a result of eating ersatz foods. By the summer of 1917, as ersatz and surrogate goods were another rallying point for poor urban consumers, members of the "ersatz" labor force joined their counterparts outside the factory gate in ever greater numbers. Berliners and urban Germans still retained some desperate hope in the existing regime's intent and ability to transform their miserable lives. But this experience suggested yet again that even the highest-level officials were simply incapable of controlling the domestic crisis as the war continued to drag on. Poor women in the streets of the capital wondered aloud about the purpose of fighting the war for Germany when the lives of so many Germans, on the battlefront and on the homefront, were thus ruined. A girl from Schneidemühl reported in her diary that her mother and brother returned from a visit to Berlin in July "wretchedly thin and pale." Fortunately for her family, her grandmother was able to revive them with thick pea soup and bacon cracklings; most Berliners lacked such opportunities for relief.[113]

In light of this deepening misery, it was at the height of the summer of 1917 that Berliners began to envision the agonies of a fourth war winter even while the sun's heat beat down on their heads during their daily queues. In July German troops battled Americans alongside Frenchmen and Britons, and Italy and even Russia showed no signs of immediate retreat; despite passage of the peace resolution in the Reichstag, poorer Berliners feared they had to plan for the worst. The experience of the preceding winter left such an indelible impression on Berliners that they spent much of the summer of 1917 in coal lines talking about it.[114] The combination of deficient food and fuel along with the ignominies of surrogate foods was more than many people felt they would be able to bear again. Deputy commanders reported in July, "The matter is very serious. The population won't go along with another winter without sufficient coal. To starve and to freeze is just too much."[115]

Berliners tried to store up coal, wondering if an end to the war would even change the circumstances. But even in these warm months they most often failed because of direct competition with the war industries, which burned the fuel voraciously year-round, as well as with the bakeries.[116] The deficiency of coal continued to wreak havoc on municipal transport. In turn, coal dealers themselves, along with food merchants, claimed difficulty in transporting supplies from train stations, while consumers lacked access to public transportation to carry the goods long distances themselves.[117] Adults wore out their cardboard shoes walking these distances, while children trudged barefoot beside them.[118] Officials responded directly to popular complaints once more, issuing nontransferable ration cards for coal in July. Still, coal to fill the often coupons remained unavailable except on the black market.[119]

The summer of 1917 held other ominous prospects for the *Minderbemittelte* of Berlin. In June landlords began complaining of high taxes on their mortgages, as the city sought sources to help fund the swollen range of services it now attempted to provide. Landlords threatened to subvert the city's intentions by passing these costs on to their tenants, including the wives and mothers of soldiers, whom it was technically illegal to evict.[120] Poorer families remained concerned about being forced out by high rents, to make way for single men and women who came from outside the city to work in war-industry factories. Berge refused the request of local mayors to ban rent increases, demonstrating little of the concern he had for rising food prices.[121] On 1 July, as many landlords announced new rates to begin 1 October, poorer Berliners had a new burden of worry in anticipation of the coming fall and winter. Soldiers' wives and other war dependents in Neukölln banded together in early July, warning of a rent boycott for which they thought they might have better popular support than they had had in the fall of 1914.[122] In response Bundesrat officials quickly reported efforts to better enforce existing controls. But in the end council members did nothing on the matter, at least for the current lease cycle.[123] Their attention seemed focused almost exclusively on questions of food and demands of the broad population of poor consumers on those issues.[124]

Poorer Berliners resorted once more to protest, with a new intensity, urgency, and "a certain heated frenzy" matching the warm summer days.[125] Erupting first in mid-May, in the streets and on the shop floor, food demonstrations and unrest became more sustained during July, spreading across the country. Officer Schrott reported, "The market halls are daily stormed by hundreds of women. . . . It often comes to wild [*wüste*] rows, lootings, and even to blows. . . . There is great tension and hatefulness among the people."[126] The Alexanderplatz market, near government offices and next to police headquarters, was the site of daily, violent "battles" over food.[127] Police noted with bitterness that anyone with money or connections avoided the public market altogether, relying on new, illegal "delivery companies."[128] By this point in the war, anyone on the streets or in marketplaces was likely a protester, lacking the resources to pursue other means to obtain food.

Demonstrations in the summer of 1917 were indeed considerably more violent than they had been at any time in the war to date. Officer Schneider observed a typical "stormy scene" in the weekly market in Lichtenberg, as 300 women gathered at the stand of greengrocer Haase of nearby rural Marzahn, "indignant over the high price . . . and excited to the extreme." As women attacked the stand, Haase "saved himself only by fleeing quickly. However, the women pursued him, howling and screaming, till he sped up to a tremendous gallop, and the women gave up the pursuit." [129] Would-be consumers demonstrated such fierceness that many farmers themselves stopped coming to market, particularly in Lichtenberg and in the northeast section of the city, where this violence was most concentrated. [130] The summer unrest also regularly included trips by women to local offices of official agencies to express their demands directly and to exact a direct reply. As a recurrent practice, this represented a quantum escalation in confrontation. Lichtenberg police commissioner Lewald reported typically, "Several women left the [Viktoria] market for the city hall to demand bread and potatoes. . . . They asked where they could buy bread. . . . Then they went down the street to the baker and violently took thirty breads without paying for them." [131] Such descriptions evoke the period before the French Revolution at a point when hungry women demanded that representatives of the king and state directly provide them with bread. [132]

Spreading out from Berlin and its central suburbs, unrest encompassed the wider region, including small towns and villages. Officer Borchert reported acts of assault and battery by women in Niederschöneweide, southeast of the city and home to many AEG workers. In an area relatively quiet since the October 1915 butter riots, women now stormed the offices of local authorities demanding to know the whereabouts of potatoes and why other areas had gotten some. [133] Borchert reported the women then hitting a shopkeeper with his own broom and insulting a policeman for his "fat belly" (no vacant affront in those days), which, Borchert added, was an accurate epithet. Observers reported regular "crass remarks" and "direct imprecations" against the government, civilian and military, for the failure to totally control supply and to end the war, which protesters asserted authorities had promised to do. [134] Theodor Wolff observed that the government must now provide "real representation of the people" if it were to survive. [135] This was the government's last best chance. [136]

Police and others now characterized even this violence as "reasonable." Lewald described the protesters first storming the magistrate's office, then "violently" appropriating bread, as "rationally thinking women" whose "patience in bearing these cares [was] exhausted."[137] He opined that it was "high time" for officials to absolutely ensure adequate supplies to the "broad masses of the population." Though he often found it necessary to edit his own very charged remarks in mood reports by this period, Oppen let stay his own assertion that officials were bringing Berliners to their last vestige of reason.[138] From outside the capital, the *Bremer Bürger Zeitung* reported most sympathetically on the psychological toll that maldistribution, substitution, and the prospect of more of the same took, especially on the population of lesser means.[139] The article warned that both the injustice and the actual physical deficiencies resulting from this maldistribution destroyed the "reason" of "otherwise rational people." Police contrasted such protesters with others — such as shell-shocked soldiers — acting through lack of reason though contributing nonetheless to the "frenzied" street scene.[140] They declared to their superiors that "discussions with thoroughly reasonable women confirm[ed] that a portion of the population [was] truly starving."[141]

Official and private observers in Berlin and across the country expressed "little wonder" at this unrest and "surprise" that these "understandable" protests were not worse.[142] *Der Deutsche Kurier* explained that "women and girls" crowded before the various market stalls had to constantly negotiate small confrontations, "because there is no other possibility."[143] The paper urged KEA and Privy Council officials to observe these "images of the market" directly and to try to buy goods there themselves — and then to take action as appropriate. Recalling their earliest reports just after the Berlin butter riots, deputy commanders claimed that Germans exercised "astonishing patience"; police warned, however, that popular faith in both civilian and military officials, now nearly two years after the October 1915 unrest, was severely eroded.[144]

Police expressed their own diminished faith ever more poignantly. Hertzberg, police commissioner of Charlottenburg, wrote to Oppen with concern regarding the truly "serious character" of the summer riots, imploring him to dispatch additional manpower.[145] But political police observed in the riots of June and July 1917 that their uniformed counterparts were conspicuously absent. Officer Schneider called it "noteworthy" that only one uniformed policeman was visible at the market at the time of the scene at Haase's produce stall, and that this officer was "otherwise occupied at the cherry stand."[146] Describing the same scene, Kurtz noted that "the women" explicitly "used the momentary absence of police at the marketplace to really give Haase a taste of their fury."[147] The low profile of uniformed police in the marketplace may have been caused by more than simply insufficient forces (and even interest in pursuing their own sources of food); indeed, two plainclothes political policemen were stationed to watch the Lichtenberg market. Whether from sympathy, apathy, or fear, police were clearly reluctant to intervene as shopping women expressed their wrath, storming market stands and officials' offices in turn. Police reported ill response to their attempts to assert authority; demonstrators ignored, mocked, and even assaulted the gendarmes.[148] Still they continued to describe their own role as defending poor women in the streets, a function simultaneously of direct orders and of their growing distance from their high superiors. Policemen prevented men, including veterans, from walking to the front of the line.[149] They arrested merchants for acting "impolitely" and thereby further "straining the nerves" of poor shoppers, even as those shoppers exhibited violent behavior.[150] Military officials considered replacing police with military personnel to better impose order by controlling the women themselves, but they feared that common soldiers would be little less sympathetic to protesters.[151]

Earlier, police and other observers had defended marketplace protesters on the basis of their economic demands, though the effects had been political.[152] Now officials and the broad public increasingly characterized protests and unrest on the streets and accompanying demands themselves as explicitly political. This view of women's strategies to get what they needed during the war sheds light on the standard political history of the era. It explains why working-class and lower middle-class women appeared indifferent to the question of voting rights, promoted by the League of German Women's Groups and, above all, by the Majority Social Democratic Party as the primary political question. The notion that the vote was not a very meaningful political tool under the prevailing circumstances may also have contributed to the mild response to the kaiser's 1917 "Easter edict," though hungry women considered it an important symbolic gesture. A demonstration for franchise reform called by the socialists for early July also fizzled out for lack of popular interest.[153] Social Democratic representatives forced the matter before the Prussian parliament in November 1917, demanding evidence of the state's intent to repay the country's workers for their contributions to the nation and to the war effort. However, as Officer Dittman noted, "the broader mass of workers view[ed] the whole affair without much interest" by the time the proposal was debated in the spring of 1918.[154] Poorer women were more concerned about food for the moment than about a formal political right that could not even be exercised in the foreseeable future. It was also clear that they wielded considerable power and control without this formal and abstract right, and where that power failed them, the vote was of little use.[155]

The highest German authorities found still more impressive measures to communicate to urban consumers especially the seriousness with which government viewed the plight of the people; these measures also reinforced official commitment to steward domestic as well as diplomatic matters. In August the OHL, with the help of the Reichstag, steered Bethmann out of office for his inability to control — and appear to control — the domestic situation. The civil cabinet and military leadership moved Prussian food commissar Georg Michaelis in as chancellor, in part on the basis of Michaelis's perceived expertise on the food question, his reputation as a strong proponent for tight controls on production and distribution, and his image as champion of the cities.[156] Customarily viewed by historians as a puppet of the OHL without independent political standing or qualifications, Michaelis's role as chancellor may be better understood as a symbol to the populace of the urgency with which the highest civilian and military leaders viewed the crisis on the homefront.[157]

Michaelis had his work cut out for him. Oppen questioned in a draft report of late July, "How much longer can this ever growing pressure to rebellion be held back!"[158] Continuing in a statement he would excise from the final version, Oppen wrote, "The broad masses of the population are riveted to the food question. . . . The greater population is inclined to think the continued sacrifices for further battles are simply not worth it and any peace is better than a continuation of war." As chancellor, Michaelis took quick action. He began by replacing the weak-willed Batocki with Wilhelm von Waldow, who in turn set to work to combat black-marketing, the *"greatest pestilence of the people of this world war."*[159]

In September and October 1917 Berliners and others watched, waited, and hoped once more. Most groaned as the OHL ordered new military forays, as Admiral Alfred von Tirpitz announced the foundation of the Fatherland Party, committed to peace only with annexations. They applauded as Reichstag representatives voted down a bill committing to such a peace, resolving instead to continue negotiations with Russia and Ukraine — negotiations for peace and for wheat.[160] At the same time, new rent increases took effect on 1 October. Imperial officials announced another reduction in the butter rations and declared the cessation of fat allowances altogether. Rumor spread that KWA officials spent their time searching schoolchildren for smuggled food at the train station.[161] Police announced still-deepening popular anger, especially within the civil service.[162] Capital residents threatened that they could not hold out for one more war winter.[163] Then Berliners read the news that military officials were pushing Michaelis out of office before he ever had the chance to make good on the expectations accreted to him as food dictator.[164] Authorities attempted to sweeten the pill with methods they had used before. Waldow announced an October appeal to black marketeers to cease their activity, followed by threats of stiffer penalties. He announced the sudden discovery of fruit that had been "lost" between rural Werder and Berlin.[165] Berliners would soon see it, in the form of jam, as a substitute bread spread.[166] Poorer Berliners grudgingly welcomed this news. This was a step in the right direction, at least, of actually getting food on the table, pathetic as it seemed.

Waldow's jam thus bore the weight of enormous expectations in the fall of 1917. Though not a central food, jam was at once a symbol of the government's new control over goods, an acceptable substitute for butter and meat fat, and a sign of the potential of new bread as peace negotiations continued with Russia and Ukraine. But the jam failed to appear after all. With the advent of cold weather, capital residents were beside themselves. Berliners discussed the missing jam as intensely as they did the new revolution in Russia.[167] It was the missing jam that set Berliners moving "above all in a radical direction."[168] Ludendorff himself linked food unrest in Germany directly with the Russian Revolution, claiming now that military interests demanded calming of the domestic unrest.[169] To this degree Ludendorff, too, was hostage to popular pressures, despite his claim that he remained free of such concerns. Although Ludendorff may have thought in terms of swift and peremptory police and military action against unrest, it is important to note the limits of his ability to put such a plan in place.

The expectations officials themselves created had once again induced the deepest disappointment at their failures. Government propaganda "awoke in the Berlin population . . . belief that a regulated distribution of jam would take place." In mid-November a single distribution of jam occurred. Then nothing. "Again, one was left with nothing to spread on one's bread," Officer Faßhauer concluded.[170] Residents of working-class Neukölln in particular were all the more enraged when it appeared that other districts of Greater Berlin had received more jam than they, despite promises that the bread spread would be equitably distributed.[171] In response the Neukölln city council wrote to Waldow pressing for "measures that would ensure the equitable distribution of remaining food supplies, as well as the combating of profiteering."[172] Berliners questioned their own wisdom in continuing to put stock in officials' promises and felt angry for having accorded authorities their vestigial faith.

The jam fiasco was only the most prominent of numerous scandals that made headlines in the fall and winter of 1917, in Berlin and around the country, accumulating evidence not only of the ineptitude of the new authorities but also of their cynical corruption. The *Bremer Bürger Zeitung* reported on the August "potato exposé," citing a Hanover newspaper on an event in Bochum. A member of the Bochum city council revealed that authorities allowed a farmer to turn over half his potatoes for later use in schnapps production.[173] The *Berliner Morgenpost* ran an article titled "The Surplus Food Supply: Excess in the Munitions Industry," which presented new evidence of official maldistribution in the war factories.[174] Berliners voiced their conviction now that the government simply could not fulfill its responsibilities to the populace, despite what really seemed to be officials' best efforts. Poorer consumers charged that officials themselves were creating new problems through their stupidity, lack of vision, and inability to coordinate and execute plans. Berliners read with horror of a scandal over butter in which several communal officials in Berlin-Friedrichsfelde were convicted of playing an illegal role themselves in the evident "displacement." With impeccable timing, a fresh cut in butter rations followed on the heels of this news, reducing official rations from 50 to 30 grams per person per week (about 2 tablespoons) — as available.[175]

Before the implications of the butter scandal sank in, a new disgrace erupted, freighted with the rapidly accelerating lack of faith in the government and suspicions concerning officials' good intentions. At the end of November 1917, Neukölln city leaders presented a confidential position paper to the KEA, alleging that high-level officials had allowed some communal authorities to exceed legal price ceilings in their attempts to buy up food; this explained the unequal jam distribution. Indeed, the paper argued, Neukölln officials themselves had been regularly forced to transgress price ceilings to get any potatoes and other basic foods for their predominantly working-class population, because of the "greed of merchants," cultivated by the military regime.[176] *Vorwärts* got hold of the piece and published it prominently in a special supplement under the title "Collapse of the Waldow System"; a follow-up article suggested "things were getting crazier and crazier."[177] With the help of the press, the public interpreted the accusations as evidence of high officials' thoroughgoing betrayal of urban consumers, whose suppliers (private and public) were evidently forced to compete illegally for food supplies. Waldow himself soon emerged as more actively pernicious than his hated predecessor had ever been.

The populace had long suspected such abuses of the system, but concrete evidence of the corruption and mismanagement spurred the deepest dismay and despair. The defense of communal officials, that they felt they had to overstep the price ceilings in order to ensure supplies for their own residents, little impressed those in the streets. Lacking the means to engage actively in the black market, poorer consumers had staked their claims in the potential of the high officials to make the controlled economy work, to fulfill their needs, and to legitimate their relationship with the state. Officials hastened to ensure consumers that their confidence, such as it was, was still warranted. Authorities tried to spread the message "through the entire Berlin press" that they continued to fight hard and successfully against both the outer and inner enemies of the German people, though newspapers now showed little cooperation.[178] As for direct propaganda, one deputy commander observed that by December, those responsible could not always commandeer the paper on which to print such communications.[179]

The Neukölln exposé was pivotal to a transformation that took place in Berlin in December 1917, a culminating moment offering a final and dramatic bit of evidence of consumers' worst fears. The government had at best demonstrated "impotence" in performing its duties.[180] Now—finally—a large population of working-class and lower middle-class Berliners lost faith in the existing regime's ability and even willingness to act on their behalf and in their interests. "The people held steadfastly to the idea that the government . . . acted itself as a profiteer, offering wares to the people at enormous prices," police observers noted of this time.[181] New relations between state and society remained legitimate, but the reigning government lost authority to participate in that relationship. If poor urban Germans had retained some shred of faith in the government's willingness to represent them even as the new liberal government fell in Russia, they now began to think differently. Recognizing the gravity of the situation, the kaiser hurried to voice his own condemnation of officials who were involved in the Neukölln scandal, in the form of a pamphlet that quickly reached wide distribution.[182] The public demonstrated only greater outrage, taking the kaiser's condemnation as a sign of admission of official corruption. By the first week in the new year, the magistrate in Berlin urged the kaiser not to release further copies of the pamphlet—advice that Wilhelm followed.[183] It was too late; the damage was done.

Now the law of the land was "everything through cheating," Helmut von Gerlach claimed, charging paradoxically that *the black market has become the normal form of traffic in goods,* with the aid of the government itself.[184] Gerlach averred that the new chancellor, Georg Graf von Hertling, was intimately involved in the system of corruption and flouted Bundesrat orders to permit his native Bavaria to withhold food from the rest of the country. This was the legacy of 1917 for the final year of the war. Just as women of little means had played a leading role in negotiating the domestic responsibilities of the German state, so were they essential in signaling the end of trust in the competence, good faith, and legitimacy of the Wilhelmine state.

10 GERMANY FROM WAR TO PEACE?

The year 1918 opened to a mass strike in Berlin. But for much of the following months, Berlin and other German cities saw little of the sustained street-based protest that had marked the previous years of war. It is perhaps on this basis that historians have drawn the connections from the April 1917 strikes through the January 1918 unrest to the revolution of November 1918 that overthrew the Wilhelmine regime, attending little to the long-standing protest in the marketplace. But if the popular demands of the April and January strikes helped pave the way for the October reforms, pushing for change within the system, in many ways, the ongoing mass consumer-based activity was key to the November revolution, above all through its resolution by 1918 that the existing regime was unreformable.

The change in strategy by women in the streets reflected their virtually complete lack of faith in the efficacy of the prevailing governmental structures and in the good intentions of the men who filled the positions. Although poorer women continued to attack the government verbally on a daily basis, they no longer focused on imploring officials to fulfill their promises. Instead they committed themselves to a policy of self-help, eschewing their own part in the compact broken by the government. Theft and attacks on property spiked in the last year of the war, as the moribund official economy left many no choice and no interest in pretending otherwise. As poorer women left off their demands, officials worried about their potential to overthrow the regime. Authorities' own recognition of their inability to provide for Germans' basic needs was an important part of the government's retreat from authority in October 1918.

FIRST ONE MUST FEED ONE'S FACE, THEN COME THE MORALS

The year 1918 opened to popular incredulity and despair at the depths of officials' perceived treachery, in the form of the Neukölln exposé (the aftermath of which dragged on for months) and other scandals in and around the country.[1] These scandals symbolized the Wilhelmine regime's total irredeemability and left the broader population in numb apathy as authorities announced imminent peace with Russia and Ukraine. Rumors of ever greater official travesties of justice now flooded the streets as well as shop floors, and poorer Berliners no longer accorded official announcements any legitimacy. Officials described the darkest mood in the streets and the related threat of a mass strike and nationwide demonstrations in the second half of January. Berliners who continued to spend their entire days in the streets in search of food exhibited little hope that officials would negotiate the peace in the East, and still less hope that such a peace would manifest itself in bread for them. The effete administration responded to threats of a mass strike and demonstrations with efforts to fortify security forces, but police asserted increasing unwillingness to intervene.

As poorer Berliners became ever more mistrustful of official press releases and of any press report of government intent or action, they demonstrated growing reliance on rumor.[2] Berliners repeated hearsay that Poles were getting food that should have come to Berlin.[3] They anxiously discussed the rumblings concerning new factory layoffs.[4] They groaned at the sensational scandals outside Berlin.[5] They spoke animatedly of the Fatherland Party, the Pan-German League, and their influence on the government and wondered at hints of Ludendorff's resignation.[6] They regularly transmitted word that negotiations with eastern powers had broken down, despite official announcements of ongoing progress.[7] The spread of rumors reinforced the sense that officials had proven themselves allied with the enemies of poor urban Germans. Berliners furiously noted that the city's magistrate had supposedly bought up herring supplies as a meat substitute; the herring never appeared, giving rise to accusations of further "bluffs and stupefaction of the *Volk*."[8] Noting that Greater Berlin's borders included publicly owned agricultural areas, Berliners suggested that the metropolitan government was actively complicit in driving up prices for its own profit.[9] It went without saying that the new chancellor, Hertling, was an impostor, like Waldow favoring farmers against the interests of starving urban Germans (especially Prussians).[10]

The lack of faith in official press releases and the presumption that any positive news reflected government influence increased popular interest in other forms of information and communication, along with word of mouth.[11] Police claimed to detect increasing popular interest in the leaflets and pamphlets disseminated by the Spartacists and by the Independent Socialist Party of Germany (Unabhängige Sozialistische Partei Deutschlands, or USPD), such as "Men and Women of the Working People," "The Hour of Decision," "Long Live the Mass Strike," and "On 28 January the Mass

Strike Will Begin!" As important as communications on the homefront, moreover, was the active traffic among civilians and soldiers, through censored letters, through the press, and via men on leave and garrisoned soldiers. The demands of men on the battlefront to their superiors in turn reflected not only dissatisfaction with their own lot (particularly among sailors) but also their grave concern for circumstances on the homefront. There is evidence that soldiers on leave were anxious to return to the battlefront to escape conditions at home.[12]

While police reported popular indifference to positive news concerning the peace process and to new campaigns to prosecute speculators, Berliners in the streets remained considerably more reactive to negative press reports.[13] They were little pleased with stirrings of a new major offensive on the western front.[14] Press reports provided "The Newest on the Neukölln Memorandum," as municipal, Prussian, and imperial authorities publicly "went on the warpath" against one another to defend themselves; this generated public dismay throughout Berlin and across the country.[15] Even reports in the foreign press provided grist for the rumor mill, as well as offering testimony of Germany's unfavorable image abroad. The Swedish *Dagens Nyheters* upbraided "a food dictator like Waldow, who seeks to prevent metropolitan authorities from providing food for the undernourished masses."[16] The paper tied Waldow's misadventures directly to the strikes and demonstrations of late January. The Amsterdam *Morning Post* observed Germans' feelings of deep betrayal by the government, all the more among working women.[17] Although the average Berliner had no direct contact with the foreign press, formally illegal moreover from 1917, such news trickled in through different sources, including the domestic press, which indicates once again the limits of wartime state control.

The traffic in information among the press, the populace, the police, high officials, and others provides continued evidence of the active network of communications operating in the society. Newspapers now regularly cited poor urban women directly in their pages. The *Berliner Lokal Anzeiger* trumpeted the complaints of many among its readership, such as an "old woman" in Berlin who despaired that official measures actively prevented her from filling her rations.[18] Another reader provocatively predicted through the newspaper that the economy was not likely to improve even after the war ended.[19] Oppen addressed the Greater Berlin State Distribution Office (svs) in early February through an urgent, hand-carried letter concerning rumors in the streets that another reduction in bread rations was imminent. If this were false, he wrote, would the svs not use the press to communicate this to the populace? And if it were true, he added, would the svs please be kind enough to let him know directly? The SVS quickly responded that no cuts were planned—at least not until April—by which time officials were banking on the separate peace to bring in new grain from Ukraine and Romania.[20] As Officer Görl ominously informed his superiors, however, their concerted efforts to control the spread of invidious rumors through the press and otherwise were no more effective than their measures to provision the population. Once the peace treaties in the East were actually signed, rumors began immediately that the grain was all diverted to Austria due to German governmental incompetence.[21] By early April, rumors concerning a new reduction in bread rations returned with fresh energy.

Berliners perceived circumstances in early 1918 to be the "peak" of the food crisis, during which only the most "terrible," "inferior" items were available for those of lesser means—eliciting a correspondingly "terrible" mood.[22] Conditions were little better than they had been during the preceding horrid winter, and the quality of available food diminished throughout the first months of the new year.[23] The jam promised in the fall as a "regularly available" foodstuff remained absent, despite Oppen's ongoing exasperated entreaties to the War Food Office (KEA); consumers in the streets had in the meantime long given up on that prospect.[24] At the same time, working-class and *mittelständisch* Berliners heard through rumor and observed with their own eyes that "for the wealthy, everything could still be gotten."[25] The omnipotent merchant decided all; the government was "in control of nothing." The official economy offered no goods to buy.[26] The black market worked marvelously—it was the functioning system—at prices above those the great mass of Berliners could afford. In many respects this reflected only an exacerbation of the prewar polarization of distribution. But this "free market," in which poorer Berliners had just managed to compete before the war, now had no place for them.[27]

Poorer Berliners had invested their hopes in the official economy. Now, they agreed, "whoever doesn't follow the regulations belongs in prison. Whoever does, belongs in the nuthouse."[28] The honorable were punished for their efforts while "crooks run about at large."[29] Refusing to be "victims of the money bags," poorer Berliners followed the exhortations of the Spartacists and others to resort to self-help—as they chose to interpret the notion. This described poorer women's activity in the streets as they struggled to overcome the obstacles merchants and the government put in their place. They employed the black market through barter where possible, but for the most part they simply "helped themselves" where they could find goods.[30] The *Berliner Volkszeitung* had adopted this rhetoric to explain Neukölln's own actions in late 1917.[31] Now this described poorer women's

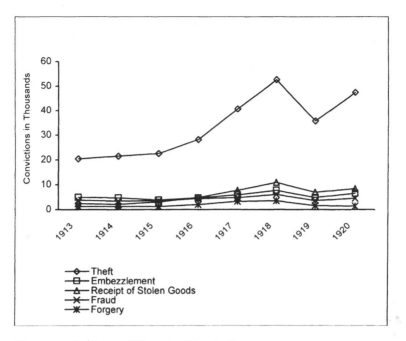

Figure 10.1. Convictions of Women for Crimes in Germany, 1913–1920
Source: *Liepmann,* Krieg und Kriminalität, *156.*

activity in the streets as they struggled.[32] With the new year, poorer consumers were no longer concerned with the criminality of their acts, except insofar as they might be fined or imprisoned, an incursion on their ability to provision themselves and their dependents. Theft rose enormously, far higher still than during the turnip winter of a year earlier.[33] Break-ins increased, and wealthier Berliners nervously implored authorities to find fuel to light the now extinguished streetlights at night. For the majority of women in the marketplaces, the cover of night was an unnecessary luxury. Women marched up to and took what they could get from market stalls where merchants paraded their own illegal acts with impunity.[34] Poorer women were no longer going to act as victims of the illusion that law and order in the economy actually ruled.

This was a painful step for many women, working- and lower middle-class alike, accompanied by the deepest despair, fear, and anger. In turn, many stall-holders at the weekly markets ceased coming and sold their wares through other means. Women had to become still more resourceful in finding and obtaining sources of food. Poorer women felt their ability to hold out, insofar as they would succeed, would be the product of their own mean scavenging.[35] They could not help but continue to attack the government's "impotence," "in the crassest terms."[36] They shouted, "Enough with the

Butchering a horse cadaver in the street, 1918. (BAPK, file 1578)

murder at the front, down with the war! We don't want to starve any longer!"
and "When Wilhelm stands in the crosshairs, or stands in line for potatoes,
then the war will end," rendering an equivalence between the experiences
on the battlefront and the homefront. To men on leave from the front they
added—in messages that reached the front lines—"Finish up already with
that ridiculous war, we're croaking of hunger!"[37] They responded with the
bitterest "ironic laughter" to news of a new campaign to thwart speculators.[38]

This new response, however, though loud and querulous, demonstrated
none of the demands of the three preceding years of protest. Women of
lesser means and many others now lacked all faith that authorities at any
level could or would respond meaningfully. Gerald Feldman and Richard
Bessel have made the case for the populace's deep hatred of the controlled
economy.[39] Only now did the masses of civilian urban Germans discuss
the virtues of removing the controlled economy altogether, as authorities
seemed so much more adept at losing food than at finding it.[40] This was no
food dictatorship, only a blood dictatorship. But there is evidence that these
Germans continued to believe that a controlled economy was in principle a
good tool for ensuring equitable distribution, however defined. The controlled economy would have to be under the stewardship of a different government, however, a prospect they now talked about more and more fre-

quently. As the kaiser "forced them to eat garbage" and even to starve, women in the streets caustically wondered aloud about how life would be under occupation by England or even France.[41] As the snow fell thickly about them, Berliners cast off as ridiculous the High Commander's new "shoveling ordinance," which called upon all residents to help clear public paths.[42] Insofar as civil society remained intact, it was outside any obligation or relationship to the state, except an inimical one. The state no longer had any right to call upon capital residents for anything.[43]

Police warned authorities now of a real threat of revolution.[44] The "limitless speculation on the backs of the populace" made the masses ripe for the entreaties of "radical elements."[45] Informers noted that women continued to play a key role within the USPD and Spartacist movements as well as among those who stood susceptible to their influences. The Social Democratic "women's reading evenings," which police had closely monitored throughout the war, now became a source of considerable alarm to authorities as a seedbed for revolutionary activity.[46] They cautioned their superiors about plans for a mass strike at the end of January (in coordination with similar actions already taking place throughout Europe), emphasizing the vulnerability of women workers in particular as they fought layoffs and reduced wages. At the same time, police observed female consumers' resistance to radical forces as they focused single-mindedly on procuring food.[47] At this point police distinguished between women who played a central role in planning for the late January strikes and those outside war factories. It appears that the latter had few expectations for the results that strikes might produce, though they hoped cessation of weapons production might forcibly alter the government's military plans.

Officials' own reaction to the prospective strike demonstrated differences too. They responded listlessly to police warnings, promising to make good on planned new shipments of potatoes to the factories, offering the possibility of new special supplements, and suggesting the virtues of raising official price ceilings. They no longer made a pretense at offering far-reaching or even meaningful measures other than undoing their own policies, hoping perhaps to divide the populations that united in protest against the government.[48] Not surprisingly, such measures failed to stem the walkout that began at 9:00 A.M. on Monday, 28 January, in Berlin, with some 100,000 participants. Strikers declared the formation of a workers' council and elected delegates. Officials reacted with a hard line. Berge forbade all strike activity in Berlin on 29 January, although even as the edict was announced, officials expressed the expectation that it would not be followed.[49] Although majority Social Democrats in Berlin had come out against the strike, the high

Munitions workers strike, January 1918. (Bundesarchiv Koblenz 183/52518/3)

commander banned publication of *Vorwärts* for three days.[50] Police arrested Wilhelm Dittmann and other USPD leaders as Oppen prepared to send in armed police and military forces.

Police observed, however, that the street scene in the capital appeared fairly calm, although the city seemed crammed with people. Police estimated the number of strikers, concentrated in the war industries, at 185,000 for the week, though the Independent Social Democrats put the number much higher. Sergeant Schwarz reckoned those in the street altogether at 700,000.[51] The movement spread throughout the country, encompassing about 4 million. On Thursday, 31 January, demonstrations of several thousand participants each took place in Treptower Park, Humboldthain, and Jungfernheide. Armed police dispersed the demonstrators without incident.[52] Several dozen strikers engaged in more violent behavior on Thursday and Friday, including an attack on streetcars operated by drivers who refused to walk off the job. Jumpy policemen responded, shooting revolvers into the air. In the process a number of strikers and police were injured. Stenographer and new USPD member Martha Globig claimed police waved their swords about impotently in the general area of a demonstration in Charlottenburg as demonstrators and passersby shouted to them, "You idler [*Strolch*]! Aren't you ashamed of yourself?"[53] Police arrested 148 participants, including 36 women, 84 men, and 28 "youths."[54] Gendarmes then locked down potential meeting places. In the course of the day, numerous protesters attacked police, leaving the latter extremely nervous. While officials never called out military forces against the strikers, four mobile rifle brigades paraded with all their trappings down Unter den Linden on Sunday. Officials treated strikers with less care for appearances than they had with marketplace protesters, though the populations overlapped.

Authorities braced themselves for more, but the worst was over for now. By Saturday, 2 February, all was peaceful again in the streets. Sergeant Schwarz noted that the unremoved snow drifts nearly prevented the demonstrations from taking off in the first place; fresh snowfall may have curtailed the unrest.[55] Lack of hope for positive results was also an important element in the movement's dissolution, despite the threat strikes posed to weapons production. Known radicals mixed with several hundred men and women in the Alexanderplatz market on Saturday, but no further disruptions materialized. Some lower middle-class observers condemned the strikers, particularly the men who participated in what they perceived to be a gratuitous gesture. Still, they reserved their greatest disgust for the government for bringing on the disorder.[56] The strikers themselves followed a far less ambitious agenda of activities than that originally suggested by the USPD. They demanded (once more) equitable food distribution, especially of fat, or at least of its substitute, jam; a rapid resolution of the peace in the East; and more consistent movement toward universal franchise.[57] A delegation of council representatives met with Hertling, though with no conclusive results. In the meantime Supreme Army Command (OHL) leaders added several of the striking factories to the number of those under direct military control. The movement petered out completely of its own accord by the evening of Monday, 4 February. Like the April 1917 strike, this disruption was an amalgam of immediate material demands and longer-range political implications. It was little different from the food demonstrations long in practice, except that some strikers may still have maintained faith in the possibility for responsiveness from the regime in power.

Despite the relatively quiet denouement of the strike, officials were considerably shaken by the general activity in the streets, in light of the staggering numbers and the potential that they imputed to them.[58] Though ultimately limited, many perceived the activity to presage civil war. Acknowledging the role of the USPD in calling the strike, Undersecretary of the Interior Bill Drews noted in his report to the kaiser that the Independents had no strong base in the working class. The lack of conclusive gains from the walkout and demonstrations, despite new government promises, did little to modify popular circumspection toward the USPD immediately. At the same time, however, Sergeant Schwarz took to heart a statement by the Majority Social Democratic Party ([M]SPD) in Nuremberg: "If the war goes on much more, then the great impatience demonstrated today by the women and men workers *will not be peacefully put down a second time.*"[59] Police agreed that the most worrisome implication of the strike was that the radical left might soon make significant headway into the broader working population.[60] As the January strikes had not brought about improvement in the circumstances of workers and others, officials began to fear more powerful, enduring, and revolutionary civil unrest. Sergeant Schwarz concluded, "*The main consequence of the strikes is not the meaningful work stoppage but, rather, the sharpening of the internal political situation.*"[61]

Authorities kept close watch on Berlin. By mid-February, rumors of plans for a new strike at the end of the month abounded, despite the resolution of peace at Brest-Litovsk on 9 February.[62] Police continued to fear the prominent role of women in the shop-floor protest.[63] Near the end of the month, Officer Adolf Palm reported his conclusions that the USPD had "worked zealously in secret and provocative form, particularly among the women, in order to ripen the masses for their ideas and plans, before the mass strike in the munitions works. The women then took part in an outstanding way in the strike itself, as well as in the demonstrations on the street." Women also figured prominently among the smaller number of activists engaging in violent riots. Palm added that the USPD was "now trying to set the stage to continue the uprising in the factories. Here again the women are playing a definite role."[64] He observed their success to date in inciting rioting, above all among other women; here he presumably referred to the greater masses both within and outside the war factories. But, Palm concluded reassuringly, for the moment, "women don't want to know anything more about a new strike and, for the time being, are not interested in street demonstrations either." Officials perceived that women held considerable power to determine the course of unrest.[65] Palm was fairly accurate in his predictions. But police attributed this calm after the strike—despite continued vandalism and growing direct attacks on police—to continued hopelessness among women of lesser means, as "the people no longer accord[ed] its faith for the assurances and promises of the government."[66] This was certainly little guarantee of lasting quiet.

If the ongoing fear and despair continued to bring poorer consumers together in the streets, their effect was more corrosive within official circles. Prussian and imperial authorities demonstrated worry for the apostasy of lower-level civil servants; they argued angrily among themselves about how best to survey and respond to what they perceived as a brewing storm of unprecedented proportions.[67] In July Foreign Secretary Richard Kühlmann, leader of the German delegation at Brest-Litovsk, warned before the Reichstag that officials needed to satisfy the populace domestically, producing a political victory at home as well as military triumph abroad. He was forced to resign for his efforts, at least according to popular perceptions.[68] Word of the possible dissolution of the Prussian parliament over the franchise reform question further fractured official circles, though the populace continued to express disinterest in machinations at this level. Political police adopted an increasingly reckless tone in their descriptions, warning of dire consequences as women of little means continued to seek methods to protect themselves and their families from starvation.[69]

THINGS FALL APART

With the advent of summer, poor consumers expressed their fear in a shrill chorus, as they had in the same months in 1917, despite the new peace with Russia. Industrialists continued to push female munitions workers out of the factories and into the streets. More than ever before, wealthier capital residents asserted a bond with poorer consumers, represented in the desperate figure of the "Berliner Hausfrau."[70] In a June article titled "The Snubbed Berliner," the *Berliner Allgemeine Zeitung* wrote of the end of capital residents' "patience of the lamb." "We Berliners," the paper proclaimed, could no longer bear the "unprecedentedly bad relations" in society, exacerbated by the "deceptive" hopes the government and magistrate had created.[71] Police, too, predicted truly radical activity from masses of Berlin housewives, warning that women's new strategies of self-help closely mirrored those called for by the USPD and the Spartacists.[72] Informants expected unrest that would not be put down, "especially in the market halls and other public retail sites."[73] Despite the activity's unorganized and even largely individual nature, officers proclaimed its revolutionary potential.

In turn official responses, particularly from the military regime, seemed to demonstrate acceptance already that they would soon be deposed (at least temporarily). The summer of 1918 marked Ludendorff's incipient designs for the *Dolchstoßlegende,* or stab-in-the-back legend.[74] Historians most commonly tell this story in terms of military, diplomatic, and labor defeats, but Conservatives identified the failed controlled economy as a basis for blaming the Social Democrats, a strategy radical nationalists proved willing to pursue.[75] For other officials, the lack of concerted new response did not indicate their misunderstanding of the gravity of the situation or of the expectation that the state should resolve the crisis. Rather, it seems to have represented their own acceptance that the reigning regime was simply incapable of fulfilling these responsibilities. Relations among officials grew more rancorous still, and authorities aired their dirty laundry defensively, taking the tone of a postmortem.[76] In June the Bundesrat announced the dreaded new reduction in official bread and flour rations, explicitly recognizing that the separate peace brought no relief.[77] Weekly internal government surveys of available foodstuffs now included black-market supplies and transactions in the totals, acknowledging the failure of the controlled economy.[78] The conviction of communal officials as a result of the Neukölln investigation did not improve the image of the authorities. Indeed, following the adjudication the Bundesrat ordered that transgression of official price ceilings simply must sometimes be allowed.[79] Meanwhile, new evidence of government corruption came to light each day.[80]

Poorer Berliners now demonstrated "utter indifference" in response.[81] They were "self-provisioners" in spite of themselves, and the government no longer had anything to do with it.[82] They claimed that, especially if this year's harvest were again poor, they would simply end the war on their own. They would create a "bread peace," a "peace at any price" by the fall, though they surely had little specific idea of how they were going to do this.[83] In July police conjectured that USPD and Spartacists plans provided the most likely means to answer the "stomach question."[84] Deputy commanders around the country corroborated that internal order was entirely disintegrating, marking 1918 from other war years. The activity of "working women, especially family women" was evidence of the dissolution.[85] July was a key month: things began to change, and to fall apart.[86]

In July the "soul of the *Volk*" in the streets asked but one question: When is peace coming, and with it, food?[87] In August that population sought ways to answer their own question.[88] Berliners responded with interest to rumors and local press renditions of a *Münchener Post* story of working women who disrupted closed-door negotiations among Bavarian government and trade union officials to demand that the authorities declare peace on the spot and provide food.[89] The various authorities attempted to placate the women, but the left-leaning SPD paper commented, "The women were smart enough to decide for themselves the right thing to do." The article reported new plans for a great women's demonstration in Munich to force an end to the war; poorer women in Berlin took note of suggestions that they follow suit. As in Munich, Berlin women shrugged off efforts by the trade unions to mollify their anger and scoffed at the SPD's assertion that speculators, not the government, were at fault. Police reported the "wildest rumors" taking flight in the streets; the very ambiguity of the projected plans seemed to make them all the more ominous.[90]

The USPD and the Spartacists attempted to focus the fury by calling for a new mass strike. Radicals stockpiled weapons, storing them in crates such as those in the Lichtenberg flat of Margarete Wengels and in Cläre Casper-Denfert's apartment in Charlottenburg. When police investigated a tip that Casper-Denfert was storing armaments, she convinced the police that the many crates in her room had been filled with fruit that had been shipped to her from outside the city. The police were easily satisfied that she had been engaged in the illegal shipping act (they themselves had done the same) and pursued the tip no further.[91] Avowed radicals and the broader hungry populace interacted in the streets. Women continued direct and indirect communications with their husbands and sons on the front, now calling for them to simply come home.[92] The radicalization of soldiers and sailors must be seen in this broader context. Like the connections between the overlapping populations in the streets and the war-industry factories, the links between the homefront and the battlefront were tight and critical.

News of the harvest trickled in late in August, promising a yield little better than that of the preceding years. Police warned superiors that a broad population of Berliners and other urban Germans intended somehow to enact a general peace and even to follow Spartacist aims to bring down the government.[93] Spartacists in turn focused attention around the country on women workers.[94] Authorities proposed the last wartime food measures, weakly following up on their earlier proposals for new special supplements for munitions workers, civil servants, and "families" — virtually special supplements for all, the largely symbolic scenario many had demanded a year earlier.[95] Functionaries made plans for new, more "psychologically fitting" propaganda, bringing the government's early sterile strategies full circle.[96] Meanwhile, the street population burgeoned day and night with Berliners in search of food. Desperate, on 2 September the high commander issued a new threat of heavy punishment for potentially seditious acts.

Berliners reacted with demonstrations around the city, making clear their rejection of Kessel's right to impose any such sanctions on them at this point. Police reported a meeting of 1,100 on 8 September led by "radicals," both men and women, to determine an explicit course of action.[97] Representing the (M)SPD and Free Trade Unions, Friedrich Ebert and Carl Legien issued a "memorandum on the food situation," defending the KEA against public accusations that this office raised prices only to coax farmers into producing and thereby stooped to the use of profit rather than public good as a means to increase production. Hertling himself hotly denied the charges, a denial that could only have come out of these peculiar wartime circumstances.[98] Attempting to distance themselves from the ruling regime while trying to prevent its complete demise, (M)SPD leaders called their own nationwide demonstration. They demanded that the regime successfully institute a system of total food control, a demand that held a surreal resonance at this point. A rancorous debate over lifting price ceilings broke out in the Berlin senate on 13 September, while Wermuth issued a blanket apologia, charging to the last that higher officials had doomed the city to this fate.[99] USPD members, Spartacists, and others announced plans for a German communist party and issued a manifesto that set as a goal the "liberation . . . of humanity," achievable not through franchise or parliamentary reform but only through communism.[100]

The imperial and the Prussian governments emitted strong signals of a regime in crisis as well as acknowledging the wartime transformation of state and society.[101] Hertling and his deputy Friedrich von Payer both gave public speeches in the course of the month assuring the populace of their unwavering efforts to effect peace and government reform. The kaiser visited Krupp laborers in Essen to reassure working-class Germans of his commitment to their provisioning. The Bundesrat announced a return to full bread rations on 1 October, though with no indication of how these rations would be filled. Hindenburg addressed the German people directly, promising his commitment to their welfare. The OHL announced it would no longer pursue a "victory peace"; on 29 September the military leaders sued for peace in the West. On 30 September Hertling, a symbol of accommodation with rural interests, stepped down, leaving no immediate replacement. The government in Berlin determined to raise price ceilings after all, which led to a fresh increase in prices of up to 250 percent and rendering those very few foods that had been available now officially inaccessible.

The kaiser hurried to install Prince Max of Baden as chancellor on 3 October; Max in turn announced the appointment of (M)SPD leaders Scheidemann and Gustav Bauer to his cabinet (thus far following Ludendorff's own designs of making the SPD "eat the soup that they had served").[102] Baden immediately responded positively to Woodrow Wilson's Fourteen Points as the basis for peace in the West; he announced plans for franchise reform, new civil rights, and new power to the Reichstag without delay. The great majority of Berlin and other urban newspapers blazoned the changes triumphantly. The broad populace adopted a somewhat more circumspect attitude, in light of both its more immediate concerns and its lack of faith that these new politicians would fulfill their promises any better than their predecessors had within the existing political framework.[103] On 7 October a national conference of the Spartacists and radical left took place in Berlin, calling for armed revolution and the widespread creation of councils. They announced plans for a huge demonstration to take place a week later, on Monday, 14 October. Police braced for action, particularly in Lichtenberg and Neukölln, strongholds of the new left, as well as within the two Schwarzkopff works, north and southeast of the city, respectively.

The fourteenth came and went with few disturbances of the peace. On the fifteenth the radical members of the women's reading evening met, including Martha Globig, Cläre Casper-Denfert, Käte Duncker, Mathilde Wurm, and many others, led by "the old familiar Joffes," the "extreme radical" Käte Rauch. The group broke up to distribute leaflets calling for a demonstration the following day. The demonstration began at the Reichstag about 3:00 P.M. on the sixteenth with a group of several hundred. Police with swords descended to "cool off" the demonstrators, but the latter reconvened within the hour. Joined by onlookers (including those strolling in the Tiergarten, likely not the poorest Berliners), both men and women, the numbers quickly mounted, to several thousand by some accounts.[104] There appears to have been some confusion as to the specific demands of those present; police claimed the demonstration descended into a general "hullabaloo." Members of the Pan-German League appeared at the "iron Hindenburg" statue, shouting insults and attempting to provoke violence. Rauch, Wurm, and others led demonstrators down Unter den Linden, past the Interior Ministry and the Soviet embassy, demanding peace. They were cut off by police armed with swords and pistols five blocks down at the Charlottenstrasse, just short of the kaiser's palace, and ultimately dispersed; several women were injured in the process.

The demonstration raised the general level of tension in the city, though police claimed that the aims of the demonstration remained unclear to most of its participants. In a singularly unsympathetic report to the kaiser, Oppen declared that the USPD exaggerated its own strength, deluded by both the mischievous riffraff and the "hysterical females" who participated in their demonstrations.[105] Pan-Germanists observing the demonstration suggested that participants, especially the "females" should be sent to the trenches.[106] The leaders held "reading evening" again that night, as Mathilde Wurm — along with her husband, Emanuel, who was deeply engaged in the food question — pressed for a new demonstration with clearer and more concrete demands, and one that would better draw on the crowds of angry women in the streets.[107] But police observed, probably rightfully, that no party could at this point claim the faith of great numbers of the populace. Overall the masses still sought primarily concrete, immediate strategies for provisioning, all the more in light of the imminent burden of demobilization, and were wary of investing their faith in any authority.[108] It appeared that,

even as peace was realized, feeding oneself would become still more difficult before it would become easier.

The next days continued the impasse. The Spartacists named 22 October
for the new demonstration, though this date passed, too, without serious
unrest, as the hunt for food continued in the streets. The Prussian parliament brought the franchise reform to a vote, though its inconclusive results
necessitated a new vote set for a month hence. On 26 October Ludendorff
stepped down, eager to dissociate himself from the military defeat. Those
who remained in power in the new reform government seemed confused
and paralyzed. The *Deutsche Tageszeitung* observed the fear for "the popular
mood," bespeaking not only immediate circumstances but the cumulative
effects of the preceding four years.[109] Drawing on the now commonplace
imagery, the Berlin Food Union warned the Distribution Office that the
food situation in the capital was worse than ever, fast eroding any remaining popular "power of resistance"; this referred to both the incipient flu epidemic and Berliners' ability to hold out for the reform government to demonstrate its greater ability than its predecessors'.[110] One Berliner wrote
police urgently of the "epidemic of Bolshevism" that had infected a wide
population, including, above all, women.[111] Oppen also singled out women
in reporting the lack of faith even in the new government (if, he claimed,
overall in the USPD and Spartacists as well).[112] Radical youth began violent
protest in the streets of the capital, resulting in mounting arrests in the last
days of the month, mirrored by unrest around the country. On 3 November the uprising in Kiel began, as sailors refused a last sortie.

The uprising spurred new action across the country and new interest
particularly in the council movement, the closest political corollary to the
self-help in which poorer urban civilians were already engaged. The role of
women in this movement, though little studied, was significant, as photographs and other sources suggest, though poor women were the leading
victims of the flu epidemic that took hold with full force.[113] USPD leaders
charged Käte and Hermann Duncker specifically with organizing women
for revolution.[114] Beyond women's activity at the moment of "the revolution," however, we must acknowledge the changes brought about by women
protesters and their observers for four years up to this point. The high commander's 7 November edict banning councils went unnoticed. Oppen's
claim that he still controlled the city belied the reports of his subordinates.
Protesters ripped the epaulets from the uniforms of government troops in
the streets; these predominantly working-class and lower-middle-class soldiers began ripping them off themselves.[115] Policemen handed their weapons over to workers.[116] In northeast Berlin and Lichtenberg, women in the

Revolution, 9 November 1918. (Karl Dietz Verlag)

streets and marketplaces turned on police with their market baskets and their fists, on the same sites where revolution violently continued four months later.[117]

On 9 November, workers still in the factories joined other Berliners in the streets. Women from the Mansfeld works painted "End the War!" on the streets of central Berlin with paint taken from the factory.[118] Thirteen hundred sailors from the north joined the melee in the capital. Many converged in Lichtenberg, mingling with the crowds.[119] The High Commander's Office ordered police to use weapons to disperse the masses; then the issuing officer reversed himself and resigned. The police had no interest in suppressing the crowds, whether from fear, lack of loyalty to the regime, support for some of the popular demands, or even commitment to their new role in protecting "the people." [120] The government had largely disintegrated even before the arrival of the sailors. The kaiser, pushed into abdication, explicitly charged those who had governed under him to "protect the German people from the threatening dangers of . . . starvation," as well as from anarchy and foreign rule.[121] Max stepped down from the chancellory. Ebert stepped in as "provisional chancellor" as Philip Scheidemann declared a republic, among competing claims for a new government.[122]

The *Kaiserreich* had fallen. The war was over, the revolution had begun, and Berliners and their conationals around the country entered a new era, during which the scarcity, cost, and maldistribution of food would remain a prominent factor. The acts of high officials and of police, as those of protesters, suggest that the revolution was the culmination—though certainly not the only one possible—of the protests of the preceding four years and of the political relations that had developed during that time. The Wilhelmine government acknowledged its defeat, above all, in guaranteeing the possibility for its subjects to support themselves. The Interfractional Committee, the USPD, and councils alike would, at least temporarily, make their appeals on the basis of the demands that women of lesser means had advanced ever more insistently throughout the war, fighting for a just distribution of material goods and of political power. How Germans continued to sort out these problems after the war, and how they attempted to govern themselves more generally, is closely related to the experience of the civilian population in the war years.

CONCLUSION

As Understate Secretary Delbrück noted in retrospect, "There can be no doubt that whether or not the government succeeded in provisioning the population, particularly the broader masses, at prices affordable to them, would have a decisive impact on the course of the war."[1] More than this, the first years of the war saw important transformations in relations between state and society, as a product of the intersection between food, identity, and politics. These changes did not "cause" the revolution. However, in conjunction with the prevailing material conditions, they served to create a set of public expectations about the role of the state that had much to do with the government's loss of legitimacy among the wider population, and with the political landscape that emerged after the revolution. In light of these wartime relations, we must reconsider standard views that the government, particularly under the military dictatorship, ignored the immediate needs and demands of its subjects in its fanatical militarism, deferred them all to the postwar period, or attempted to respond solely through a social imperialist agenda. The civilian and even the military administrations were forced to make impressive efforts to meet popular demand during the war, and not only through such institutionalized representatives as the Free Trade Unions. They acknowledged a new set of obligations toward the entire population, though their efforts were often defeated in the crossfire of competing interests among the state's close traditional allies. These efforts are testimony to the kind of societal power that consumers of little means — women in particular — won under the social, economic, and political conditions of the war.

The ability of the so-called population of lesser means to wield such power begs the question of what constitutes politics, who are political actors, and where they act politically. It also raises the issue of what comprises a political act, in terms of intention, actual demands, and effects, of individuals and collectives. Historians have often treated the wartime food riots as economic and therefore not of political significance. But German officials in World War I considered popular cries for food, tied up with demands to force an end to the war and of the civil peace to be highly political. The calls of this population were largely motivated by what might be characterized as economic exigencies. But was it less politically significant to condemn the starvation of civilians than the slaughter of soldiers on the front?

Poorer women protested not only the absolute deficiency of food but also the various taxonomies of distribution that distinguished among the population, based on one's societal "value." In turn, Berlin consumes challenged the justice and the morality of a free market, under the conditions of war, but with wide-ranging political implications. They asserted a whole range of new government responsibilities, based on an effective notion of citizenship, and demanded that authorities heed their voices, including by heavily intervening in the society and economy on their behalf. Those of little means—women in the streets as well as the political police who observed and "represented" them and the others who included themselves in this grouping—did not clearly articulate a longer-term political vision. Indeed it was the ambiguity of their demands for the long run that permitted widely divergent groups to unify against the status quo as they did. Hungry Berliners were able through a variety of means to communicate their need for bread to officials at every level, and to convince these officials of the need to respond; they were practicing an effective form of politics—even if they were not always getting food. And this, in turn, helps us to understand politics and political change in the larger sense in World War I Germany.

The wartime transformation in relations between state and society anticipated the foundations of the successor Weimar state.[2] The surrender and armistice represented renewed upheaval in the lives of all Germans, due not least to the rapid, poorly planned demobilization.[3] There was no relief regarding import of foodstuffs, as the blockade remained in place until after the conclusion of the Versailles Treaty in June 1919, also contributing to the ruin of the domestic harvest of 1919. In a concrete sense, the war did not end for the German homefront with the signing of the armistice.[4] The notion of economic war perpetrated by both external and internal enemies was even more lasting, surviving the lifting of the blockade in July 1919 and marking Weimar society and politics.[5] Ongoing and even aggravated food shortages naturally spelled continuities with wartime policies under the new regime. It is clear that the new policies, of the council movements as well as of the Berlin coalition, reflected the legacy of German political culture as it had developed during the war. Such policies and principles applied not only to food distribution but to a far wider range of political and economic issues. Within and outside government, German life in the years following the war mirrored homefront politics, including its contradictions.

Historians have well documented the effects of the postwar inflation including the terrible food shortages continuing through the hyperinflation of 1923.[6] Germans continued to speak of efforts to hold out under unbearable circumstances.[7] The results of failing to do so include soaring suicide rates and legion societal violence. Contemporary medical experts attested to the serious compromises to the health of the German people, particularly women and children.[8] Political leaders of all stripes considered provisioning the population, in righteous, "equitable" fashion, their first order of business. This was a premier "obligation" in their eyes and represented the primary means by which jockeying powers could establish their legitimacy.[9] It was the foremost issue on which the new republican coalition in Berlin worked in both grateful and fearful contact with the workers' and soldiers' councils.[10]

The apparatus of provisioning constructed for the special purposes of wartime remained overall in place. The office of the Prussian commissar for provisioning the people was elevated to a republic-level office. The War Food Office was renamed the Imperial Food Office, and continued its duties with much of the same personnel. The War Committee for Consumers' Interests (KAKI), which had started out as a private "cartel of consumer interests,"[11] was given full governmental status and renamed the Imperial Committee (RAKI), a harbinger of the public service politics of the new government. On the local level, the various council movements won considerable legitimacy for their role in channeling foodstuffs to needy populations. The consumer reigned, too, in the myriad private organizations formed to lobby for and oversee government efforts. The German Union for the People's Provisioning (Deutscher Verein für Volksernährung) and the umbrella Central Federation of German Consumer Organizations (Zentralverband Deutscher Konsumvereine), demonstrating new self-confidence and prestige, actively corresponded with the highest officials and boasted long lists of publications. Such organizations paralleled the strength of the prewar associations that had represented, above all, productive economic interests and their accommodation by the regime.[12] As a petition of the Imperial Committee stated in May 1919, establishing the Consumers' Chambers and the representation of consumer interests in the council movement, "The economic policy of the old government was one-sidely dominated by producers' interests. The new economic policy must be oriented toward consumers. This must be in the first instance because one calls for collective efforts precisely upon those circles represented by the great mass of consumers."[13]

Political leaders accepted this onus, although they were well aware of its broad implications and of the political conflicts and traps for which they thereby set themselves up. Officials bespoke their willingness to maintain a controlled economy (*Zwangswirtschaft*) indefinitely after the war, although some made assurances that this would exist only as long as "necessary."[14] They did this because—if done effectively—a large portion of the urban population continued to feel that a controlled economy was indeed necessary, although Wilhelmine officials had failed to achieve it. This was a question of "public morality."[15] For the council movements, Independents, and after January 1919, German Communists, it posed no political problem to claim that other interests must defer to a government's premier obligation to meet the most basic needs of its citizens. For the other political parties, including the Weimar coalition (Social Democratic Party, German Democratic Party, and Center Party), this position meant confronting agricultural and commercial interests. It also sometimes meant countering demands of many demobilizing soldiers. These leaders defended their policies in terms of political exigency, including the need to ward off Bolshevism, another threat to vulnerable Germany.[16] Politicians believed that the masses would be attracted to whichever leaders could provide food. In comparing the food policies of Independent Emanuel Wurm, Majority Social Democrats Robert Schmidt, Richard Calwer, and August Müller, and Center Party figure Adam Stegerwald, one finds remarkably consistent principles and deep commitment to this obligation of the new government.[17]

The rhetoric of political leaders demonstrates starkly that they envisioned themselves as "serving Germans." This is clear as well among some who entered politics in the wake of the wartime experience, including erstwhile newspaper editors Theodor Wolff and Helmut von Gerlach. Officials cast these Germans, moreover, predominantly as urban consumers, often poorer female urban consumers.[18] It is important to see attacks on the Weimar government—that it was overly centralized and served primarily the cities, the nation's workers, and, above all, Berlin—in the light of officials' own vision of fulfilling obligations born of the war.[19] Conversely, officials sharply admonished farmers as well as merchants for anticonsumer practices, often impugning the latter's patriotism as well as threatening their property.[20] In response, even as they attacked the planned economy, farmers, merchants, and others appropriated the rhetoric used by government officials. The local agriculture organizations of Silesia wrote to authorities in April 1919 announcing their own difficulties in holding out because of the forced economy, though they claimed local farmers had "fought on the front lines against the external enemy, and now against the inner enemy, defending against every attack."[21] The Craftsmen's Chamber of Graudenz wrote likewise to the new government in Berlin that "one must put oneself in the soul of a butcher or baker, who for four years of war made big, possibly the greatest, sacrifices for the Fatherland in every regard"—and who now saw his very existence threatened by proposed communalization and redistribution schemes.[22]

Perhaps most telling of the new political culture was the initial envisioned (if not the actual) role of policing and the maintenance of order under the new regime in Berlin. Officials charged police to control the orderly distribution of food, in the name of the new German citizen. To reinforce this power, officials made the War Profiteering Office independent of the police administration, providing it with greater autonomy of action; they gave the Prussian State Commissariat its own special police forces.[23] In addition, authorities established the Imperial Commissariat for the Surveillance of Public Order, commissioned virtually in the service of defending citizens' food rights.[24] Officials noted with irony that this office represented a kind of "class police," protecting against the "maldistribution" that wealthier consumers and merchants might hope to reestablish.[25] Trade through middlemen remained a criminal offense.[26] At the same time, a far less sanguine picture of police in practice arose in the postwar months and years, also as a function of wartime influences. Many officers saw their role as crushing privilege. But there is no question that police and authorities above them feared the disorder that consumers could and did continue to perpetrate.[27] Although People's Commissar for Public Security Emil Eichhorn dissolved the Berlin political police, officials established a new force only weeks later in the winter of 1918–19.[28] Despite officials' assertions to the contrary, in Weimar as in Wilhelmine Germany street protests were political. They were also potentially politically and physically dangerous. The confrontations between police and the men and women of eastern Berlin and Lichtenberg in March 1919 offer considerable evidence of this.[29]

Early Weimar food policy cemented the link between the wartime political transformations and the more general political and economic changes represented by the new regime. The new constitution began with the statement, "The German Reich is a republic. Political authority emanates from the people."[30] If officials viewed urban consumers as representing the citizen, the German citizen now represented the nation. As a German, the citizen was entitled to have his or her most basic needs met. The example of food provisioning in wartime was central to the proposed structuring of the welfare state.[31] Beyond universal franchise, formal and informal politics drew on citizen participation, in the ruling coalitions, in the Reichstag, but also through direct referenda, in the new welfare and other administrations and commissions, and in corporatist relations between industry and labor. For their part, leaders of the local councils worked to maximize participatory democracy as a primary goal alongside provisioning the people. At the same time, framers of the Weimar constitution sought to provide for the strong, forceful, and effective leadership wartime protesters demanded, for example, in the position of the president of the republic. Despite, or perhaps because of, the disastrous consequences of Wilhelmine authorities' wartime food redistribution policies, contemporaries observed a new "openness" to socialism, or at least one version of it. A critical mass of Germans accepted heavy state intervention in the interest of a basic equity among citizens, as a consequence of the war experience.[32]

Yet the legacy of the war years was contradictory. This emerged most clearly in the crises of Weimar, as political leaders tried to act out the freshly formed political visions.[33] The wartime conflicts over defining equitable distribution that temporarily fractured the coalition of those of lesser means presaged the contradictions postwar officials confronted. Under circumstances of unemployment and rising inflation, once more German officials asked, On what basis ought aid to be offered? When one had to choose, should one award aid based primarily on absolute need or on greater perceived deserts, such as sacrifice in the war? If the latter, how ought sacrifice to be measured? How did the sacrifices of urban civilians measure up against those of veterans, particularly disabled veterans? Did loss of a family member add significantly to one's sacrifice beyond four years of enduring the burdens of economic and total war? How should the government adjust for the postwar circumstances of pensioners, civil servants, and others on a fixed income as related to working-class Germans? Framers of the Weimar constitution attempted to balance forceful leadership and representation in a way that seems to have spoken directly to the wartime demands of protesters. But how would this balance fare under new challenges to the state?

Historians have often identified the Weimar Republic's lack of legitimacy from its inception, born of military defeat and baptized by the Versailles Treaty.[34] Still, the Weimar coalition won 76 percent of the vote in January 1919. I suggest that this support was based largely on the new regime's visible efforts to conform to the new terms of political culture that had emerged in wartime urban Germany. Conversely, an important part of popular disenchantment with the new state, apparent already in the 1920 election, was its inability after all either to transcend the contradictions named above or to make choices and pursue them with determination.[35] Weimar policy toward working-class women speaks to the contrarities of the wartime heritage as well as to the difficult choices the new regime continued to face. As demobilization began, hundreds of thousands of women were thrown out of war factories to make way for the returning men. Weimar authorities viewed this policy benignly, deferring to the agreements of organized industry and labor. At the same time, the new government policies did not inscribe women in a system of entitlements related only to their role as mothers and wives.[36] The new constitution also specifically asserted the equality of men and women under the law. Women's valuation specifically as workers, as consumers, and even as street activists, as well as through private bourgeois organizations, had a meaningful influence on Weimar policy in this way.[37] The heavy appeal uniform among parties for the new women voters in early Weimar elections reflects women's sheer numbers as well as organized women's groups substantial efforts to establish women's place as citizens. But the imagery itself bespeaks the position poor urban women won during the war, despite the desperation they suffered, to represent the nation.

The political legacy of the war was rich in possibilities, including popular sovereignty, representative government, and participatory democracy. Naturally some Germans had championed these notions before the war, but the homefront experience transformed them and helped push them to the forefront. At the same time, many other less attractive political ideas also emerged with strength as a consequence of the homefront experience of food scarcity. Indeed the line between these different political notions was often startlingly thin. Ultra-right groups conjured up images of the nation, centered in the *Volk,* that fought an inimical state, with deleterious results.[38] Participatory politics in the most immediate, physical sense was expressed through the desperate politics of violence that mirrored the last year of the war, when Berliners and other Germans had lost hope in the power of the Wilhelmine regime to govern and had lost faith in a functioning society.[39] Right-wing direct action groups recalled this sense, urging "Berliner self-protection" and "no surrender of weapons."[40] Food riots became bloodier in the postwar years. And if the horrors of the regime that followed Weimar can be traced in part to a need to overcome the experience of mass death and human suffering, this must be related to the violence of the homefront experience as well to that, albeit very different, of the battlefront.[41]

In turn, authorities' dread of the power of this violence, predating the war but most powerfully realized in the wartime unrest, marked the Weimar regime from the outset. Fearful of the revolutionary challenge in all its manifestations, Ebert and Scheidemann quickly demonstrated willingness to turn to the traditional military authorities and to revert to the most violent police methods to forestall what they perceived to be attacks on the new state. Authorities very much feared both plunder and demonstrations for

German Democratic Party election poster, 1919. A woman with open arms leads the people and the nation forward. Negative male images represent competing political parties. (Reprinted from Heilfron, Die deutsche Nationalversammlung, *164*)

food. By November 1921 officials charged the municipal police, in cars and bearing guns, with preventing attacks on food shops by whatever means necessary.[42] By contrast, wartime Wilhelmine authorities had prosecuted disorderly behavior, at least over food, with an astonishingly light touch. New paramilitary forces took it upon themselves to simultaneously fight against the terms of the Versailles Treaty and against food unrest in the streets.[43] If Germans across society were now willing to accept some form of socialism and socialists, Social Democratic leaders regularly asserted that socialism represented "nationalism" and a policy of "order."[44] The willingness of large populations during wartime to invest their trust in a military government and other leaders who promised "total control" also had potentially dangerous ramifications.

Further, the new vision of "the German" and "the German nation" was as exclusive as it was inclusive in Weimar Germany.[45] Wartime politics helped spread a radicalized version of the nation's inner enemies, just as it fostered the notion of a *Volksgemeinschaft* among those of lesser means. The imperial commissar for surveillance continued the habit of the political police in reporting regularly on "the battle against inner-political adversaries," in the form of merchants, farmers, non-Berliners, and non-Prussians. Performers in Berlin cabarets sang of *Schieber* and how they exploited the people, referring to profiteers and corrupt politicians alike.[46] Naturally Bavarians, Mecklenburgians, farmers, and small-town dwellers experienced these same divisions; as Ludwig Finckh wrote in January 1919, conflating the new government and the capital population, "To the spirit of Berlin another must be opposed, *the spirit of Germany!*"[47] Such divisions would be another central element in Weimar's downfall. Fault lines of class also deepened even among those of lesser means, as the new government, like its predecessor, failed to satisfactorily address equitable distribution among consumers. Relations of consumption remained as important as those of production, often dividing people within classes while, as during the war, white- and blue-collar workers often stood together now. In an effort to emphasize the unity of the national community, many groups tried to find "appropriate" internal enemies. It is in the context of food scarcity and profiteering, that virulent anti-Semitism, first pervasive in the war, spread in the immediate postwar period and marked the politics of Weimar.[48] Likewise, paranoid nationalism that distrusted all outside powers and eschewed transnational interdependence grew out of the experience of the economic war as well as out of the terms of military defeat.

Wartime politics on the homefront forged new links between consumption and production, between identities as consumers and producers, and among consumption, production, and citizenship. Before the war, these elements had been tied. Activists frequently perceived the relationship in terms of women's consumer-based ancillary support for men's labor action, or of consumer-related pressure brought to bear for production-related ends.[49] The war highlighted how shop-floor activity could be directly related to and supportive of demands concerning consumption, even in the modern period. The ubiquitous early Weimar strikes and other job actions embellished this pattern, as food shortages continued. Three thousand railroad strikers brandished signs in 1920 bearing the complaint, "The minister stuffs his face with meat, the workers eat the bones."[50]

Forced cuts and shifts in consumption had a direct impact on production, bringing consumers and producers (often the same people) together in common cause. Workers expressed concern in early 1919 over cuts in both vinegar production and vinegar rations. Defending their interventions, authorities argued that those of lesser means required vinegar to spice up their food and to make pickles—particularly in the absence of fat—and that the workers affected, both blue collar and white collar, were likely to protest in disorderly fashion the 50 percent cut in production.[51] As during the war, this combination of interests seems to have spurred unrest at unusual moments, such as during a period of layoffs. In turn, the connection to food elicited surprising public support for strikers, all the more if officials responded violently to the strikers. Local authorities urged officials at the republic level to guarantee food distribution so that local workers could work —and thus loyally serve the fatherland and their fellow Germans.[52] Conversely, officials noted the need to support workers in establishing viable relations of production, "precisely for the point of all production—the consumers."[53] The government now urged that prices be set specifically according to workers' wages, rather than according to producers' or merchants' costs (not to mention desire for profit).[54]

Thus, outside as within formal politics, the legacy of the war years on the homefront was significant and helps to explain the potential of the Weimar Republic as well as its pitfalls. Far from representing a figure from the distant past, the poor protesting female consumer emerged with force in the first man-made famine of the new century. Hunger continues to influence politics, though the nature of its influences is indeterminate. The larger question, then and now, concerns rethinking the nature of politics itself. This study tries to contribute to such efforts.

NOTES

ABBREVIATIONS

ADF   Allgemeiner Deutscher Frauenverein
ADW   Archiv des Diakonischen Werkes, Berlin
AFDG   Archiv des Freien Demokratischen Gewerkschaftsbundes, Berlin
BAL   Bundesarchiv, Berlin-Lichterfelde
BANK   Bezirksarchiv Neukölln, Berlin-Neukölln
BAPK   Bildarchiv Preußischer Kulturbesitz, Berlin
BLHA   Brandenburgisches Landeshauptarchiv, Potsdam
EVK   Evangelisches Zentralarchiv, Berlin
GStAPK Geheimes Staatsarchiv Preußischer Kulturbesitz, Berlin-Dahlem
HLA   Collection Helene-Lange-Archiv
IML   Institut für Marxismus-Leninismus, Zentrales Parteiarchiv der Sozialistischen
        Einheitspartei Deutschlands, Berlin-Lichterfelde
LAB   Landesarchiv Berlin, Berlin
PPB   Provinz Brandenburg, Repositur 30, Berlin C, Titel 95, Polizeipräsidium
Pr. Br. Provinz Brandenburg
Rep.   Repositur
SAB   Stadtarchiv Berlin, Berlin
UBD   Ullstein Bilderdienst

INTRODUCTION

1. BLHA, PPB, Nr. 15810, p. 284, mood report, Jagow, 15 May 1915. All translations are my own unless otherwise noted.

2. Ibid., Nr. 15809, p. 18, report, Rhein, 17 Feb. 1915.

3. Ibid., Nr. 15815, pp. 128–29, report, Ludwig, 6 Dec. 1915.

4. "Zur Ernährungsfrage," *Reichsbote,* 4 Jan. 1916.

5. "Die Teuerung und ihre Folgen: Hilfe für die Bedrängten," *Der Deutsche Kurier,* 15 Oct. 1915.

6. BLHA, PPB, Nr. 15813, p. 9, report, Gerhardt, 3 Sept. 1915. In describing the population in the streets, I often use the term "poorer Berliners" or "poorer consumers" to provide a sense of this population that increasingly crossed class boundaries.

7. Cf. Winkler, *Von der Revolution,* 27–33.

8. On the development of German "social politics," cf. Tennstedt, *Sozialgeschichte der Sozialpolitik;* Gerhard A. Ritter, *Social Welfare;* Steinmetz, *Regulating the Social;* Abelshauser, *Weimarer Republik.* World War I is most often left out of the literature. But cf. Reidegeld, *Staatliche Sozialpolitik.*

9. My view of politics is influenced by historians of everyday life and feminist theorists. Cf.

Lüdtke, "Historiography of Everyday Life," "Polymorphous Synchrony," and *Eigen-Sinn;* Lindenberger, *Straßenpolitik;* Medick, *Weben und Überleben;* James C. Scott, *Weapons of the Weak;* and see Certeau, *Practice of Everyday Life.* Compare Butler and Scott, *Feminists Theorize the Political;* Mouffe, *Dimensions;* Hirschmann and Di Stefano, *Revisioning the Political.*

10. Karen Hagemann suggests that Weimar officials actively so worried about the political valence of street activism that they sought to redefine "politics" in more formal terms. See Hagemann, *Frauenalltag;* cf. Rosenhaft, "Women, Gender." Alf Lüdtke is one of the few historians to treat the political significance of the wartime food protest, including early in the war; cf. "Hunger, Essens-'Genuß' und Politik bei Fabrikarbeitern und Arbeiterfrauen," in Lüdtke, *Eigen-Sinn,* 194–209, which is a model for the present study. There is a large literature on inflation and the "decade of unrest," 1914–23, though much of it concentrates on the postwar period. Exceptions are Feldman, *Great Disorder;* Martin Geyer, *Verkehrte Welt;* Tenfelde, "Riscoperta dell' 'Autodifesa Collettiva'"; Ay, *Entstehung;* Schwarz, *Weltkrieg und Revolution;* on Berlin, see Scholz, "Ein Unruhiges Jahrzehnt."

11. Drawing on the 1930s work of Eckert Kehr, Hamburg historian Fritz Fischer traced Germany's path to National Socialism through World War I. See Fritz Fischer, *Germany's Aims* and *War of Illusions.* On the Second Empire's authoritarian nature and truncated democratic potential, cf. Wehler, *German Empire,* and Stegmann, *Erben Bismarcks;* for a central critique of this characterization, see Eley, *From Unification to Nazism.* On the continuity question in social histories of the war, cf. Kocka, *Facing Total War.*

12. This work reflected the tumultuous era in which it was written, revisiting particularly the direct democratic forms of the council movement and offering a more positive valuation of the revolution than had their predecessors. Cf. Rürup, "Demokratische Revolution und 'Dritter Weg'"; Mommsen, "German Revolution"; Eberhard Kolb, *Weimar Republic.*

13. See, for Germany, the pioneering studies Kocka, *Facing Total War;* Feldman, *Army, Industry, and Labor;* Ay, *Entstehung;* as well as Wilhelm Deist's important articles, collected in his *Militär, Staat.* Compare, more recently, Faust, *Sozialer Burgfrieden;* Mai, *Kriegswirtschaft* and *Arbeiterschaft in Deutschland;* Ullrich, *Hamburger Arbeiterbewegung;* Niehuss, *Arbeiterschaft in Krieg;* Knoch, *Kriegsalltag;* Berliner Geschichtswerkstatt, *August 1914;* Michalka, *Der Erste Weltkrieg;* Roerkohl, *Hungerblockade;* on Berlin, Eifert, "Berliner 'Heimatfront' im Kriege." For recent comparative work, see Wall and Winter, *Upheaval of War;* Horne, *State, Society, and Mobilization;* Cecil and Liddle, *Facing Armageddon;* Winter and Robert, *Capital Cities at War;* Hirschfeld and Krumeich, *Keiner fühlt sich.* Other recent emphases include memory and memorialization and the social history of the trenches. Cf. George Mosse, *Fallen Soldiers;* Koselleck and Jeismann, *Der politische Totenkult;* Winter, *Sites of Memory;* Ulrich and Ziemann, *Krieg im Frieden;* Gregory, *Silence of Memory;* Ulrich, "Feldpostbriefe"; Ziemann, *Front und Heimat;* Audoin-Rouzeau, *Men at War.*

14. Cf. Kundrus, *Kriegerfrauen;* Higonnet, Jenson, Michel, and Weitz, *Behind the Lines;* Kent, *Making Peace;* Thébaud, *La Femme.* Cf. Seidel's early *Frauenarbeit,* which casts German women dubiously as war saboteurs.

15. Daniel, *Arbeiterfrauen.*

16. See Ay, *Entstehung;* Kocka, *Facing Total War;* Ullrich, *Kriegsalltag.* For work on the eve of war, see Evans, *Kneipengespräche* and *Proletarians and Politics.*

17. An exception is Scholz, "Ein Unruhiges Jahrzehnt."

18. Cf. Kocka, *Facing Total War.*

1. Cf. Eley, *Reshaping the German Right;* Chickering, *We Men Who Feel Most German.* Compare Davis, "L'Etat *Contre* la Société?"

2. See Wehler, *German Empire;* Stegmann, *Erben Bismarcks;* Puhle, *Agrarische Interessen;* Kaelble, *Industrielle Interessenpolitik;* Saul, *Staat, Industrie;* Ullmann, *Bund der Industriellen.*

3. Cf., on franchise campaigns, B. J. Warneken, "'Massentritt'-Zur Körpersprache von Demonstranten im Kaiserreich," and Andrea Erne, "'Mit einer Zigarre im Mund, die Frau oder Braut im Arme,'" in Assion, *Transformationen der Arbeiterkultur,* 64–79, 80–85. Women first gained the right to assemble politically in 1908.

4. See Fairbairn, *Democracy;* Suval, *Electoral Politics.*

5. On integration and reformism, see Conze and Groh, *Arbeiterbewegung;* Roth, *Social Democrats;* Schorske, *German Social Democracy.* On party culture and services, cf. Lidtke, *Alternative Culture;* Langewiesche and Schönhoven, *Arbeiter in Deutschland;* Gerhard A. Ritter, *Arbeiterkultur.*

6. See Glaeßner, *Arbeiterbewegung;* Nonn, *Verbraucherprotest;* Mathews, "German Social Democrats," on the SPD's national-level efforts on consumer issues. Cf. Ferguson, *Paper and Iron;* Prinz, *Brot und Dividende.*

7. Cf. Pulzer, *Political Anti-Semitism;* Rürup, *Jüdische Geschichte.* On anti-Slavic as well as anti-Semitic sentiment, see Hagen, *Germans, Poles, and Jews;* Chickering, *We Men Who Feel Most German.* Otto von Bismarck designated Catholics the original inner enemies.

8. On *Volksnation* before the war, see Chickering, *We Men Who Feel Most German;* cf. Davis, "Gendered Images."

9. See Brubaker, *Citizenship and Nationhood,* 61–72, 114–37, on the ambivalent effects of Wilhelmine Germany's "statist" nationalism. Cf. John, *Politics and the Law.*

10. See Fait, "Arbeiterfrauen"; cf. Tennstedt, *Sozialgeschichte der Sozialpolitik;* Küster, *Alte Armut.* Gerhard A. Ritter, *Der Sozialstaat,* and Steinmetz, *Regulating the Social,* insist on the "modernity" of social policy during the *Kaiserreich,* though not on the notion of entitlement.

11. See Lindenberger, "Fleischrevolte am Wedding"; Glatzer and Glatzer, *Berliner Leben, 1900–1914,* 2:406–12. Cf. Nonn, *Verbraucherprotest.*

12. On "social imperialism," cf. Wehler, *German Empire,* 171–76; Eley, *From Unification to Nazism,* 110–67.

13. On prewar imperialism, cf. Fritz Fischer, *War of Illusions;* Hallgarten, *Imperialismus vor 1914;* Woodruff D. Smith, *German Colonial Empire* and *Ideological Origins of Nazi Imperialism.*

14. On the contribution of intellectuals and artists to this view, see Mommsen and Müller-Lückner, *Kultur und Krieg.* On masculinity before the war, see Frevert, *"Mann und Weib";* Kühne, *Männergeschichte, Geschlechtergeschichte;* after the war, Theweleit, *Male Fantasies.*

15. See Berliner Geschichtswerkstatt, *August 1914;* Rürup, "Der 'Geist von 1914'"; Verhey, "'Spirit of 1914'"; Dülffer and Holl, *Bereit zum Krieg.* Cf. Horne, *State, Society, and Mobilization.*

16. The German population grew from 40 million in 1872 to 67 million in 1914, shifting from a two-thirds rural to two-thirds urban population. Cf. Quataert, "Demographic and Social Change."

17. See Fritz Fischer, *Germany's Aims,* 247–73. The campaign to make Germany self-sufficient in food production came from many sides, including the League of German Farmers and constituents of the Navy movement. See Burchardt, *Friedenswirtschaft,* 121. Cf. Rubner, "Ernährungswesen," 41.

18. Cf. Graf von Moltke, "Noch ein Wort"; Ballod, "Deutsche Volksernährung." On the failure to prepare adequately for military raw materials needs as well, cf. Feldman, *Great Disorder,* 56.

19. Lüdtke, introduction to *"Sicherheit" und "Wohlfahrt,"* 7–33; Saul, "Der Staat und die 'Mächte des Umsturzes.'"

20. On "citadel practice" and the heritage of the Prussian police, see Lüdtke, *Police and State in Prussia.*

21. On professionalization, cf. Funk, *Polizei und Rechtsstaat;* on reform after the 1889 Ruhr episode, see Jessen, *Polizei im Industrierevier.* See also Fricke, *Bismarcks Prätorianer;* Spencer, *Police and the Social Order;* more broadly, Peukert, *Grenzen der Sozialdisziplinierung;* Lüdtke, *"Sicherheit" und "Wohlfahrt."*

22. Funk, *Polizei und Rechtsstaat.*

23. See Lüdtke, *Police and State in Prussia* and *"Sicherheit" und "Wohlfahrt";* Lindenberger and Lüdtke, *Physische Gewalt.*

24. Materna and Schreckenbach, *Dokumente,* xii. There was a higher ratio of police to population in Berlin than anywhere else in Prussia; see Funk, *Polizei und Rechtsstaat,* 212–13.

25. See Funk, *Polizei und Rechtsstaat;* Fricke, *Bismarcks Prätorianer;* Hoheisel and Hoheisel, "Tätigkeit der Berliner politischen Polizei."

26. They also followed the activities of "known anarchists and Social Democrats," including members of the Reichstag. See Materna and Schreckenbach, *Dokumente,* xv–xvi. In Hamburg, political policemen spied in perceived Social Democratic pubs. Cf. Evans, *Kneipengespräche.*

27. Lindenberger, *Straßenpolitik,* 107–72.

28. Annemarie Lange, *Das Wilhelminische Berlin,* 331; Materna and Schreckenbach, *Dokumente,* xxvi.

29. Annemarie Lange, *Der Wilhelminische Berlin,* 329–30. On such police "schizophrenia," cf. Brewer, *Police, Public Order, and the State.*

30. Lüdtke, introduction to *"Sicherheit" und "Wohlfahrt,"* 7; Schulze, *Aus dem Notizbuch eines Berliner Schutzmannes;* Fricke, *Bismarcks Prätorianer.* Cf. Caplan, "Imaginary Universality of Particular Interests."

31. See *Innere Front;* Sachße and Tennstedt, *Soziale Sicherheit und Soziale Disziplinierung.*

32. Fritzsche, *Reading Berlin,* 78.

33. On Germans as "readers," see Fritzsche, *Reading Berlin;* Langewiesche and Schönhoven, "Arbeiterbibliotheken und Arbeiterlektüre."

34. See Habermas, *Strukturwandel.*

35. Authorities used these organizations moreover as policing forces. See Daniel, *Arbeiterfrauen,* 249–55. On intellectuals and propaganda, cf. Ungern-Steinberg and Ungern-Steinberg, *Aufruf an die Kulturwelt.*

36. Cf. Deist, *Militär, Staat,* 153–64, 117–26; Stegmann, "Deutsche Inlandspropandanda"; Kosyk, *Deutsche Pressepolitik;* Daniel and Siemann, *Propaganda, Meinungskampf;* Creutz, *Pressepolitik;* Nicolai, *Nachrichtendienst;* Thimme, *Weltkrieg ohne Waffen.*

37. Correspondence of the BDF and Evangelical Church Consistorium regularly attests to difficulty in getting promised reimbursements for expenditures. Cf. BLHA, PPB, Nr. 15806, pp. 68–71, Reichstag representative Oscar Cohn to Police Captain Henninger, 22 Aug. 1914; LAB, HLA, Nr. 42-186 (1), p. 13, Bäumer to Reichstag Budget Committee, 24 Nov. 1916.

38. Cf. Gertrud Bäumer's correspondence of the war era, as head of the BDF, e.g., LAB, HLA, Nr. 42-187 (2–3), Wartime Appeals, and Nr. 40-180 (3), letter, Bäumer to Bensheimer, 3 Dec. 1918. Cf. Boyd, "'Nationaler Frauendienst.'"

39. SPD representatives in the Reichstag unanimously voted for war credits in August 1914

—as did their counterparts among the other belligerents, except in Italy. On the state's ambivalence toward the SPD, cf. Feldman, *Army, Industry, and Labor;* Deist, *Militär, Staat,* 107–10.

40. Cf. Roerkohl, *Hungerblockade,* and Yaney, *World of the Manager,* on tensions over autonomy between communal and Prussian or imperial authorities.

41. Cf. Brunn and Reulecke, *Metropolis Berlin;* Mattern, "Creating the Modern Metropolis."

42. This study also helps fill a lacuna in the wartime history of the German capital city, outside Ernst Kaeber's contemporary *Berlin im Weltkriege,* which is limited to the war economy and domestic policy. Understanding the political cultural history of the city is all the more important now as Berlin becomes the German capital once more.

43. Wermuth, a social reformist fiscal conservative, lost his position in 1920 after attempting to limit deficit spending. See Wermuth, *Ein Beamtenleben;* Berghahn, *Germany and the Approach of War in 1914,* 109–11.

44. Cf. Yaney, *World of the Manager.*

45. The SPD received 48,801 of 56,573 votes in the 1913 city assembly election but won only 45 of 126 seats. See Materna and Schreckenbach, *Dokumente,* xxi.

46. Cf. Annemarie Lange, *Das Wilhelminische Berlin,* 465.

47. Cf. Dietrich, "Berlins Weg"; Homburg, *Rationalisierung und Industriearbeit.*

48. Cf. Erbe, "Berlin im Kaiserreich."

49. Cf. Orthmann, *Out of Necessity,* 34.

50. See Glatzer and Glatzer, *Berliner Leben, 1900–1914,* 2:153. The city proper held about 2.5 million.

51. Cf. Saldern, *Häuserleben;* C. Wischermann, "Wohnungsmarkt, Wohnungsversorgung, und Wohnmobilität," in Borscheid et al., *Stadtwachstum,* 101–34; Hegemann, *Das Steinerne Berlin;* D. Lehnert, "Zwischen Hinterhof und Siedlungshaus," in Glaeßner, Lehnert, and Sühl, *Studien,* 65–88. On urban policy and design, see Mattern, "Creating the Modern Metropolis"; Ladd, *Urban Planning and Civic Order;* Lees, *Cities Perceived.*

52. Cf. Wertheimer, *Unwelcome Strangers.*

53. Cf., within this enormous literature, see Glaeßner, Lehnert, and Sühl, *Studien;* Ritter and Tenfelde, *Arbeiter im Deutschen Kaiserreich;* Assion, *Transformationen der Arbeiterkultur;* Boll, *Arbeiterkulturen zwischen Alltag und Politik;* Homburg, *Rationalisierung und Industriearbeit;* Mai, *Arbeiterschaft in Deutschland;* Mühlberg et al., *Arbeiterleben um 1900;* Mooser, *Arbeiterleben in Deutschland.*

54. Cf. Gailus, *Pöbelexzesse;* Lehnert, "Das 'rote' Berlin." On the independent metalworkers, see Dirk Müller, *Gewerkschaftliche Versammlungsdemokratie.*

55. See Lehnert, "Das 'rote' Berlin," 36.

56. On street protest in Berlin, see Gailus, *Pöbelexzesse,* as well as his *Strasse und Brot;* Lindenberger, *Straßenpolitik.*

57. Compare Brandt and Rürup, *Volksbewegung,* 11, which identifies Berlin as "showplace of the great revolutionary mass movement and civil-war-like conflicts," while noting Baden's perhaps more typical physiognomy.

58. *Berliner Tageblatt,* 4 Aug. 1914, cited by Materna and Schreckenbach, *Dokumente,* x.

59. Cf. Wirz, *Moral auf dem Teller,* 9.

60. Within this enormous literature, cf., on prerevolutionary France, Lefebvre, *Great Fear;* Steven Kaplan, *Bread, Politics, and Political Economy;* Bouton, *Flour War;* on Britain, Thompson, "Moral Economy Revisited"; Bohstedt, *Riots and Community Politics;* comparatively, Gailus and Volkmann, *Kampf um das tägliche Brot;* Medick, "'Hungerkrisen' in der historischen Forschung"; Dreze, Sen, and Hussain, *Political Economy of Hunger;* Sen, *Poverty and Famines.*

61. See, as a sampling, Forster and Ranum, *Food and Drink in History;* Abelove "Colonialism and Philosophy"; Rudolph Bell, *Holy Anorexia.* Cf. historical anthropologists and sociologists Mintz, *Sweetness and Power;* Goody, *Cooking, Cuisine, and Class;* Rappaport, *Pigs for the Ancestors;* Appadurai, "How to Make a National Cuisine"; Bourdieu, *Distinction.*

62. See Teuteberg and Wiegelmann, *Wandel der Nahrungsgewohnheiten;* Teuteberg and Wiegelmann, *Unsere tägliche Kost,* including on the "revolution" ending cyclical famine. Cf., inter alia, Wierlacher, Neumann, and Teuteberg, *Kulturthema Essen;* Prinz, *Brot und Dividende;* Meyer-Renschhausen, "Von der Schwarzen zur weißen Küche"; Wirz, *Moral auf dem Teller;* Schivelbusch, *Tastes of Paradise;* Rath, *Reste der Tafelrunde;* Schaffner, *Brot, Brei, und was Dazugehört.* Cf. "Hunger" and "Hunger, Ernährung, und Politik." Alf Lüdtke challenges the notion of the food revolution; cf. "Hunger, Essens-'Genuß' und Politik bei Fabrikarbeitern und Arbeiterfrauen," in Lüdtke, *Eigen-Sinn,* 194–209.

63. Cf. Schmauderer, "Beziehungen zwischen Lebensmittelwissenschaft."

64. Dewey, "Nutrition and Living Standards in Wartime Britain," 197. Cf. Barnett, *British Food Policy;* Winter, *Great War and the British People;* Bonzon and Davis, "Feeding the Cities."

65. Dewey, "Nutrition and Living Standards in Wartime Britain," 203–4. Likewise, figures for consumption of grams of fats, carbohydrates, and proteins were all more than twice those of the average German.

66. Cf. Fridenson, "Impact of the War" and *French Home Front;* Jean-Jacques Becker, *Great War and the French People.*

67. Compare severe housing problems in wartime Scotland, in Melling, *Rent Strikes.* Bessel, *Germany after the First World War,* makes the case for the severity of the housing shortage and its impact in Germany after the war. Cf. Saldern, *Häuserleben;* Führer, *Mieter;* Martin Geyer, *Verkehrte Welt.*

68. See Fridenson, "Impact of the War"; Hatry, "Shop Stewards at Renault." On postwar corporatism, see Charles Maier, *Recasting Bourgeois Europe.*

69. On Russia, see Engel, "Not by Bread Alone"; Lih, *Bread and Authority;* McAuley, "Bread without the Bourgeoisie." On Austria, see Healy, "Divided Home."

70. Offer, *First World War;* Bessel, *Germany after the First World War.* My sources suggest that Offer's aggregate measures obscure real physical hunger and related illness and death, in cities, in certain regions, and among certain segments of the populace. Cf., too, Kuczynski, *Geschichte der Lage der Arbeiter;* Howard, "Social and Political Consequences." Compare Aeroboe, *Einfluss des Krieges;* Roerkohl, *Hungerblockade;* Vincent, *Politics of Hunger;* Siney, *Allied Blockade of Germany;* Triebel, "Consumption in Wartime Germany."

71. Cf. Eltzbacher, *Deutsche Volksernährung;* Eltzbacher et al., *Ernährung in der Kriegszeit;* F. E. von Braun, *Kann Deutschland durch Hunger besiegt Werden?*

72. Cf. General Groener's memoirs, cited in Burchardt, "Auswirkungen der Kriegswirtschaft," 72.

73. Offer, *First World War,* 62.

74. Vincent, *Politics of Hunger;* Offer, *First World War.*

75. Skalweit, *Kriegsernährungswirtschaft,* 34.

CHAPTER TWO

1. See Burchardt, *Friedenswirtschaft,* 108, on grain production and consumption.

2. See Rubner, "Ernährungswesen," 7. Farmers also routinely distilled their cereals and

potatoes into spirits, though this was first discussed as a serious problem in the second half of the war and later, especially outside Berlin. Cf. Ay, *Entstehung,* 124–25.

3. Spalding, *Historical Dictionary,* 404. Compare, in contemporary documents, BLHA, Pr. Br., Rep. 1a, Nr. 13023, p. 194, private letter (anon.) to deputy commander, 12 Mar. 1915.

4. Spalding, *Historical Dictionary,* 403.

5. Baier and Puls, *Arbeiterlieder,* 160.

6. Over 21 percent of unionized workers were unemployed in the first month of war; the figure was much higher for nonunionized laborers. By early 1915 unemployment had dropped, as men left for the front and war industries expanded. Cf. Umbreit, *Krieg und die Arbeitsverhältnisse,* 50.

7. Kaeber, *Beiträge,* 158.

8. *Der Interfraktionelle Ausschuß,* 1:xiii.

9. Cf. claims of Paul Eltzbacher's panel in August and December 1914 reports, despite the near-depletion of the 1914 harvest by December, in Eltzbacher, *Deutsche Volksernährung.*

10. *Vossische Zeitung,* 2 Feb. 1915, cited in Skalweit, *Kriegsernährungswirtschaft,* 28.

11. Schreiner, *Iron Ration,* 7.

12. BLHA, PPB, Nr. 15808, p. 231, report, Klonicki, 18 Dec. 1914.

13. "Aus den Feldpostbriefen eines Brandenburger Reservemannes," *Brandenburger Zeitung,* 12 Oct. 1914.

14. Skalweit, *Kriegsernährungswirtschaft,* 26.

15. *Berliner Tageblatt,* 17 Jan. 1915, cited in Skalweit, *Kriegsernährungswirtschaft,* 28.

16. Cf. Lüdtke, *Police and State in Prussia,* 49.

17. "Höchstpreise für Kartoffeln," *Berliner Tageblatt,* 22 Oct. 1914.

18. Cf. KAKI's regular newsletter, *Rundschau der Deutschen Verbraucherbewegung und Mitteilung für Preisprüfer,* and the more widely available *Verbraucherwirtschaft im Kriege.*

19. Skalweit, *Kriegsernährungswirtschaft,* 31. The text of all edicts at the imperial level concerning food is reprinted in the *Reichs-Gesetzblatt.* Largely for this reason the latter expanded to two volumes per year by 1916.

20. Skalweit, *Kriegsernährungswirtschaft,* 31.

21. Cf. Lüdtke, "Hunger, Essens-'Genuss' und Politik" and "Hunger in der grossen Depression." On food culture and German identity, cf. Rath, *Reste der Tafelrunde;* Reagin, "Comparing Apples and Oranges."

22. "Die Lebensmittelversorgung: Maßnahmen gegen die Teuerung," *Königsberger Volkszeitung,* 27 Oct. 1914.

23. GStAPK, 2.2.1, Rep. 197A, It Nr. 1a, p. 130, n.d. [ca. Feb. 1915].

24. Cf. Skalweit, *Kriegsernährungswirtschaft,* 33.

25. Creating municipal food stocks was unusual but not unprecedented. Cf. Lindenberger, "Fleischrevolte am Wedding."

26. Cf. in "Höchstpreise für Nahrungsmittel," *Norddeutsche Allgemeine Zeitung,* 29 Oct. 1914. Compare Kaeber, *Beiträge,* 158–73.

27. Skalweit, *Kriegsernährungswirtschaft,* 33.

28. Cf. Davis, "Geschlecht und Konsum."

29. Cf. "Das Brot auf dem Gastwirtstisch," *Vossische Zeitung,* 6 Nov. 1914.

30. See Luther, *Im Dienst des Städtetags,* 43. Members of the parliament of cities also heavily pressured high-level authorities to take these steps. German states had limitedly provided for their subjects during the subsistence crisis of *Vormärz.* Cf. Hans-Heinrich Bass, "Hungerkrisen

in Posen und im Rheinland, 1816/17 and 1847," in Gailus and Volkmann, *Kampf um das tägliche Brot,* 15–75.

31. GStAPK, 2.2.1, Rep. 197A, It Nr. 1a, pp. 6–46, (published) speech, Justizrat Eschbach, 12 Jan. 1915.

32. Ibid.; sentence heavily underscored by reader.

33. Skalweit, *Kriegsernährungswirtschaft,* 33.

34. In Grimm, *Berliner Geschichten,* 26.

> Det beste Leben hab ick doch
> Ick kann mir nich beklagen
> Pfeift ooch der Wind durch's Ärmelloch
> Det will ick schon vatragen.
>
> Det Morjens, wenn mir hunger hut
> Ess ick ne Butterstulle
> Dazu schmeckt mir der Kümmel jut
> Aus meine volle Pulle.

35. The female shopper was more universal in image than reality, however. This remained the case through the war years, insofar as men remained at home. See C. Lipp, "Frauenspezifische Partizipation an Hungerunruhen des 19. Jahrhunderts," in Gailus and Volkmann, *Kampf um das tägliche Brot,* 200–213; Davis, "Food Scarcity."

36. *Berliner Zeitung,* 17 Jan. 1915, cited in Skalweit, *Kriegsernährungswirtschaft,* 28; GStAPK, 2.2.1, Rep. 197A, It Nr. 1a, p. 171, memorandum, Loebell to Prussian doctors, 15 Apr. 1915. Cf. Schlegel-Matthies, *"Im Haus und am Herd";* Hartewig, *Das Unberechenbare Jahrzehnt,* 153–88.

37. GStAPK, 2.2.1, Rep. 197A, It Nr. 1a, p. 171, letter from Loebell to the Association of Prussian Doctors and Berlin officials, 15 Apr. 1915. Doctors had new prestige in this era as scientific experts.

38. GStAPK, 2.2.1, Rep. 197A, It ig, p. 66, memorandum of the minister for public works to Stieger, director of the railroads, 3 Apr. 1915. Cf. Wohltmann, *Unsere Volksernährung.*

39. Cf. LAB, HLA, Nr. 42-185 (3), 42-187 (2); Hering, *Kriegsgewinnlerinnen;* Reagin, *German Women's Movement,* 193.

40. GStAPK, 2.2.1, Rep. 197A, It 1a, p. 108, letter from mayor of Lüdenscheid to Loebell, 26 Jan. 15.

41. Ibid., pp. 47–51, memorandum, Loebell to Sering, Jan. 1915.

42. BLHA, PPB, Nr. 15807, p. 96, report, Schwarz, 10 Oct. 1914. Cf. p. 60, report, Starost, 4 Oct. 1914.

43. Officials also issued reminders in the press that "property owners were not relieved of their responsibility to pay their mortgages" (ibid., p. 99, report, Starost, 12 Oct. 1914). Officials barred landlords from evicting war dependents, though it is not clear how carefully this was enforced.

44. Ibid., Nr. 15810, pp. 112–13, report, Schwarz, 16 Apr. 1915. Cf. Nr. 15808, p. 199, mood report, Schwarz, 11 Dec. 1914, and p. 229, report, Diercks, 18 Dec. 1914; "Mitgliedsbuch legitimiert," *Vorwärts,* 20 Oct. 1914. Of course, this made no sense insofar as the city paid rent supplements directly to landlords.

45. BAL, 07.01, Nr. 2398/1, p. 183, 23 Jan. 1915.

46. BLHA, PPB, Nr. 15808, p. 199, report, Schwarz, 11 Dec. 1914. Cf. p. 141, mood report,

Jagow, 30 Nov. 1914; Nr. 15809, p. 17, report, Hartwig, 16 Feb. 1915. On negative images of soldiers' wives nationally, see Kundrus, *Kriegerfrauen,* 200–204.

47. BLHA, PPB, Nr. 15808, p. 229, report, Diercks, 18 Dec. 1914; cf. Nr. 15819, p. 281, report, Schrott, n.d. [23 Nov. 1916]. The process of emiseration is documented in Kocka, *Facing Total War;* Triebel, "Consumption in Wartime Germany."

48. Ibid., p. 199, report, Schwarz, 11 Dec. 1914.

49. Cf. "Eine Soldatenfrau sucht eine Wohnung," *Vorwärts,* 26 Jan. 1915.

50. BLHA, PPB, Nr. 15808, p. 213, mood report, Jagow, 12 Dec. 1914.

51. Ibid., Nr. 15809, p. 292, report, König, 26 Mar. 1915, and p. 293, report, Klonicki, 26 Mar. 1915.

52. Ibid., Nr. 15808, p. 229, report, Diercks, 18 Dec. 1914; cf. Nr. 15809, p. 236, report, König, 19 Mar. 1915.

53. Cf. "Zur Kuchenfrage," *Reichsbote,* 2 June 1915.

54. BLHA, PPB, Nr. 15810, p. 3, report, Schulz, 1 Apr. 1915.

55. The extra 3 marks were reckoned for the winter months. Cf. P. Hirsch, *Die Versorgung der Kriegsteilnehmer,* 46–49. Widows' supplements were not yet a burning public issue.

56. See Bry, *Wages in Germany,* 58. Zimmermann, "Veränderungen," 307, 310, puts the rate slightly higher. Except at the very beginning, for the vast majority of workers, wage increases never caught up to the cost of living.

57. "Zentralvorstand Sitzung von 23. Oktober 1914," *Mitteilungsblatt,* 11 Nov. 1914.

58. BLHA, PPB, Nr. 15814, pp. 29–30, report, Sauer, 16 Oct. 1915. Cf. Nr. 15809, p. 104, report, Kurtz, 28 Nov. 1914, and p. 141, mood report, Jagow, 30 Nov. 1914.

59. Those who could afford to eat were "objects of hate" and "foreign" (Ay, *Entstehung,* 126). On the axis of married versus unmarried women, see Heineman, *What Difference Does a Husband Make?*

60. Cf. BLHA, PPB, Nr. 15808, p. 199, report, Schwarz, 11 Dec. 1914, and p. 229, mood report, Diercks, 18 Dec. 1914.

61. These were not absolute distinctions but powerful general trends. *Hausfrau* described both the figure defeated in her efforts to procure bread, despite compliance with government mandates, and the pernicious *Hamster* (hoarder). Police Commissioner Jagow claimed that "the entire world of women" was energetically producing care packages for the troops. See BLHA, PPB, Nr. 15809, p. 141, mood report, Jagow, 30 Nov. 1914. Cf. Domansky, "Der Erste Weltkrieg."

62. Cf. pictorial images in *Ulk* and *Kladderadatsch. Berliner Illustrirte* tended to avoid such images of women, as did *Simplicissimus*—at least once the war started. This imagery appeared well before the story of Mata Hari (who was incidentally reported to have numbered Police Commissioner Jagow among her clients).

63. BLHA, PPB, Nr. 15808, p. 158, letter from Kendall, Navy Admiral Staff, News Dept., to Jagow, 3 Dec. 1914, reporting the claims of a staff member. Cf. reports on Social Democratic "women's reading evenings," which police increasingly feared as a wartime site of radical politics. See ibid., Nr. 15809, mood report, Jagow, 2 Nov. 1914, and entire file Nr. 15853. Compare Tramwitz, "Vom Umgang mit Helden."

64. Cauer, *Leben und Werk,* 184–85.

65. On state industrial and economic policy according to the distinction between war, peace, and "mixed industries," see Kocka, *Facing Total War,* 85.

66. BLHA, PPB, Nr. 15810, p. 61, report, Diercks, 9 Apr. 1915. Cf. Nr. 15809, p. 32, report, Schwarz, 19 Feb. 1915.

67. Ibid., Nr. 15820, p. 64, report, Starost, 15 Dec. 1916.

68. Ibid., Nr. 15809, p. 99, report, Kurtz, 25 Feb. 1915; cf. pp. 96–97, report, Schulz, 26 Feb. 1915.

69. BAL, 15.01, Rep. 177, Nr. 13023, pp. 160–61, letter from private citizen M. Schneider to Imperial Office of the Interior, 12 Dec. 1914.

70. Natality fell sharply throughout the war, a combination of likely disinclination, absent men, and after 1916, malnutrition, by some estimations. See Roesle, "Geburts- und Sterblichkeitsverhältnisse." On Britain, compare Winter, *Great War and the British People.* On infant mortality, cf. Winter and Cole, "Fluctuations in Infant Mortality"; Stöckel, "Bekämpfung der Säuglingssterblichkeit."

71. See, e.g., GStAPK, 2.2.1, Rep. 197A, Io Nr. 1, p. 12, 18 Oct. 1915.

72. BLHA, PPB, Nr. 15807, p. 60, report, Starost, 4 Oct. 1914.

73. See, e.g., "Ehebruchstragödie einer Soldatenfrau," *Niederbarnimer Kreisblatt,* 23 Oct. 1915. Cf. Daniel, *Arbeiterfrauen,* 144–47; in England, Pedersen, "Gender, Welfare, and Citizenship." In England evidence of unfaithfulness was grounds for termination of separation allowances.

74. BLHA, PPB, Nr. 15808, p. 199, report, Schwarz, 11 Dec. 1914.

75. Cited in Gutt, *Frauen in Berlin,* 61. Dietrich noted that many of the children feared their fathers' return. Cf. Kundrus, *Kriegerfrauen,* 207. Compare Eva Brücker's bleak portrait of gendered violence in Berlin tenements, both within and outside the family, "'Und ich bin heil da rausgekommen': Gewalt und Sexualität in einer Berliner Abeiternachbarschaft zwischen 1916–17 und 1958," in Lindenberger and Lüdtke, *Physische Gewalt,* 337–65.

76. See Davis, "Reconsidering Habermas." Cf. Kent, *Making Peace;* Mary Louise Roberts, *Civilization without Sexes.*

77. Compare Daniel, *Arbeiterfrauen,* 127–38, 183. Cf., for Weimar, Flemming, Saul, and Witt, *Familienleben;* for post–World War II, Moeller, *Protecting Motherhood;* Heineman, *What Difference Does a Husband Make?*

78. Cf. Weber-Kellermann, *Die Deutsche Familie,* 127–47; Mühlberg et al., *Arbeiterleben um 1900;* Mooser, *Arbeiterleben in Deutschland.*

79. Cf. Weber-Kellermann, *Die Deutsche Familie;* Joris and Witzig, *Brave Frauen;* Berghahn, *Imperial Germany,* 69–80. Compare Fischer-Eckert, *Wirtschaftliche und soziale Lage,* and Gerhard Hauptmann's description of his mother's life in Berlin, in Gutt, *Frauen in Berlin,* 54–55.

80. The National Women's League and other groups sponsored a program sending urban children indefinitely to the countryside (with dubious benefits to the children, who were often exploited as agricultural laborers) and abroad. See Lorenz, *Gewerbliche Frauenarbeit,* 372–73.

81. Cf., in prewar Berlin, Lindenberger, *Straßenpolitik.* This "porousness" was intensified by wartime circumstances.

82. BLHA, PPB, Nr. 15810, p. 69, report, Jagow, 17 Apr. 1915; cf. Nr. 15809, p. 236, report, König, 19 Mar. 1915. "Simple circles" implies the poor but intimates also "simple-minded"—like "of little means"—those who ought not perhaps to be trusted to handle prudently the cash that they received.

83. Ibid., Nr. 15807, p. 60, report, Starost, 4 Oct. 1914.

84. Ibid., Nr. 15810, p. 200, report, Klonicki, 30 Apr. 1915.

85. "Die Volksernährung während der Kriegszeit," *Mitteilungsblatt,* 10 Mar. 1915.

86. BLHA, PPB, Nr. 15809, p. 172, Loebell's notes accompanying his copy of Hirsch's brochure, 10 Mar. 1915. Compare Pedersen, "Gender, Welfare, and Citizenship," on means testing.

87. "Zur Kuchenfrage," *Reichsbote,* 2 June 1915.

88. BLHA, PPB, Nr. 15808, p. 199, report, Schwarz, 11 Dec. 1914.

89. On Bethmann's position between conflicting interests and his own ambivalence toward the war, cf. Bethmann Hollweg, *Betrachtungen;* Stern, "Bethmann Hollweg und der Krieg."

90. "Volksernährung in Kriegszeiten," *Deutsche Tageszeitung,* 9 Dec. 1914.

91. BLHA, PPB, Nr. 15808, p. 230, report, Schwarz, 18 Dec. 1914.

92. Ibid., p. 148, report, Görl, 4 Dec. 1914.

93. "Höchstpreise für Nahrungsmittel," *Norddeutsche Allgemeine Zeitung,* 29 Oct. 1914.

94. Ibid.

CHAPTER THREE

1. See Kaeber, *Berlin im Weltkriege,* 202, also on Germany as the "greatest potato land." Cf. Ottenjann and Ziessow, *Die Kartoffel.*

2. Skalweit, *Kriegsernährungswirtschaft,* 31.

3. See Arnoldt, *Kartoffelversorgung im Kriege;* Thiess, Wiedenfeld, and Batocki, *Die Preisbildung im Kriege.*

4. Skalweit, *Kriegsernährungswirtschaft,* 213. Cf. Rubner, "Ernährungswesen," 8.

5. Acreage grew 26 percent between 1878 and 1913. See Rubner, "Ernährungswesen," 8.

6. Cf. Weber-Kellermann, *Die Deutsche Familie,* 144.

7. Cf. Pennington and Church, *Food Values,* 154. Available potatoes actually grew less nutritious as the war continued, due to uncompensated exhaustion of the soil and to processing. The new science of nutrition placed great value on the potato.

8. The next cheapest food, rye, at 30 pfennig per kilo, cost over four times as much per measure. See Zimmermann, "Veränderungen," 320.

9. BLHA, PPB, Nr. 15809, p. 103, mood report, Jagow, 27 Feb. 1915.

10. Ibid., p. 165, report, Starost, 5 Mar. 1915. Cf. p. 99, report, Kurtz, 25 Jan. 1915, and p. 162, report, Kurtz, 4 Mar. 1915.

11. Ibid., p. 99, report, Kurtz, 25 Feb. 1915. Cf. pp. 154–55, report, Schwarz, 4 Mar. 1915.

12. Cf. Spalding, *Historical Dictionary,* 1441.

13. Contemporary studies concluded that of all classes, working families spent the largest percentage of their income on food. Cf. Triebel, "Consumption in Wartime Germany." This is logical in terms of income, as well as of workers' relative freedom from the accoutrements of status on which petty civil servants and other members of the lower *Mittelstand* spent much of their meager income.

14. BLHA, PPB, Nr. 15807, p. 129, report, Kurtz, 17 Oct. 1914.

15. See Puhle, *Agrarische Interessen.*

16. See BLHA, PPB, Nr. 15809, p. 5, report, Schulz, n.d. [ca. 12 Feb. 1915].

17. Ibid., p. 7, report, Kurtz, 12 Feb. 1915.

18. Ibid., p. 18, report, Rhein, 17 Feb. 1915. This report was passed on directly to Jagow. The German pound equals .5 kilograms, or about 1.1 American pounds.

19. Cf. "Städtischer Kartoffelverkauf: Erregte Szenen in Schöneberg," *Berliner Tageblatt,* 17 Feb. 1915.

20. Cf. BLHA, PPB, Nr. 15809, p. 41, mood report, Jagow, 20 Feb. 1915.

21. Cf. Gailus, introduction to *Pöbelexzesse,* iii.

22. Cf. Le Bon, *The Crowd* (as well as his *Psychology of the Great War*); Freud, *Group Psychology;* Sorel, *Reflections on Violence.* Cf. Chevalier, *Laboring Classes;* Barrows, *Distorting Mirrors.*

23. BLHA, PPB, Nr. 15820, p. 213, report, Diercks, 4 Apr. 1917. To be sure, in some instances, this physical proximity elicited a sense of competition and enmity.

24. Cf. ibid., Nr. 15806, p. 46, report, Klonicki, 22 Aug. 1914. On the "festival" quality of mass gatherings, cf. Friedemann and Munch, *Öffentliche Festkultur;* Warneken, *Massenmedium Strasse;* Ozouf, *Festivals;* Perrot, *Workers on Strike.*

25. See, e.g., BLHA, PPB, Nr. 15806, p. 44, report, König, 22 Aug. 1914. Naturally the "planned lack of planning" for the domestic food supply helped ensure the streets and marketplaces would be a site of unrest.

26. Cf. ibid., Nr. 15809, p. 20, memorandum, Jagow to Loebell, 18 Feb. 1915, on the "circumstances that police are unable to control."

27. Ibid., p.17, report, Hartwig, 16 Feb. 1915; p. 14, report, Dittmann, 15 Feb. 1915.

28. Ibid., p. 17, report, Hartwig, 16 Feb. 1915.

29. Cf. radical Social Democrats' flyer and call for demonstration in spring 1915, "Der Hauptfeind steht im eigenen Land!"

30. BLHA, PPB, Nr. 15809, p. 3, report, Diercks, 12 Feb. 1915.

31. Ibid., p. 6, report, Klonicki, 12 Feb. 1915.

32. Ibid., p. 32, report, Schwarz, 19 Feb. 1915. Cf. pp. 14–15, report, Dittmann, 14 Feb. 1915.

33. Ibid., p. 20, memorandum, Jagow to Loebell, 18 Feb. 1915.

34. "Städtischer Kartoffelverkauf: Erregte Szenen in Schöneberg," and "Kampf um die Kartoffel: Auf den Märkten und in den Hallen, *Berliner Tageblatt,* 17 Feb. 1915; "Kartoffel-'Schlachten,'" *Berliner Volkszeitung,* 23 Feb. 1915. Cf. "Um die Kartoffel," *Vorwärts,* 18 Feb. 1915; "Der Kartoffelverkauf," *Vossische Zeitung,* 18 Feb. 1915; "Der städtische Kartoffelverkauf," *Vorwärts,* 19 Feb. 1915; "Der heutige Kartoffelverkauf" and "Kartoffelhändler und Magistrat," *Vossische Zeitung,* 19 Feb. 1915.

35. Cf. BLHA, PPB, Nr. 15809, p. 4, report, König, 12 Feb. 1915.

36. Ibid., p. 103, mood report, Jagow, 27 Feb. 1915.

37. Ibid., p. 165, report, Starost, 5 Mar. 1915; p. 4, report, König, 12 Feb. 1915.

38. Ibid., pp. 154–55, report, Schwarz, 4 Mar. 1915. Compare p. 7, report, Kurtz, 12 Feb. 1915; p. 99, report, Kurtz, 25 Feb. 1915; "Wie die Arbeiter denken," *Berliner Volkszeitung,* 11 Mar. 1915.

39. In addition to the sources cited above, see BLHA, PPB, Nr. 15809, p. 166, report, Jagow, 6 Mar. 1915; p. 239, report, Klonicki, 19 Mar. 1915; p. 236, report, König, 19 Mar. 1915; p. 162, report, Kurtz, 4 Mar. 1915.

40. Ibid., p. 165, report, Starost, 5 Mar. 1915.

41. Ibid., p. 166, report, Jagow, 6 Mar. 1915. Accordingly, for the entirety of the war Berliners focused far less on industrial profiteers than on growers and commercial figures. Ute Daniel finds concern for profiteering industrialists elsewhere in the nation; see Daniel, *Arbeiterfrauen.* The French worried far more about industrial profiteers; see Thébaud, *La Femme,* 176.

42. BLHA, PPB, Nr. 15809, p. 18, report, Rhein, 17 Feb. 1915.

43. Ibid., p. 7, mood report, Kurtz, 12 Feb. 1915. Grocery stores relied more often on middlemen than did market stalls, rendering prices generally higher.

44. Cf. ibid., p. 17, report, Hartwig, 16 Feb. 1915, which refers repeatedly to "hundreds of women."

45. Ibid., p. 18, report, Rhein, 17 Feb. 1915.

46. Ibid., p. 32, report, Schwarz, 19 Feb. 1915.

47. Cf. Davis, "Gendered Images."

48. BLHA, PPB, Nr. 15809, p. 5, report, Schulz, n.d. [ca. 12 Feb. 1915].

49. Cf. Blücher, *English Wife,* 77; Triebel, "Consumption in Wartime Germany," 189.

50. *Vossische Zeitung,* 15 Mar. 1915.

51. BLHA, PPB, Nr. 15809, p. 18, report, Rhein, 17 Feb. 1915, Schwarz marginalia.

52. Ibid., p. 32, report, Schwarz, 19 Feb. 1915.

53. Ibid., p. 20, memorandum, Jagow to Loebell, 18 Feb. 1915.

54. On cleavages within the SPD over the civil peace, cf. Miller, *Burgfrieden;* Schorske, *German Social Democracy;* Groh, "'Unpatriotic Socialists'"; Faust, *Sozialer Burgfrieden.*

55. "Mußte es dahin Kommen?!," *Schwäbische Tagewacht,* 30 Mar. 1915.

56. "Zur Frage der Kartoffelversorgung," *Freisinnige Zeitung,* 22 Apr. 1915.

57. "Halbheiten ohne Ende!," *Welt am Montag,* 6 Mar. 1916; cf. "Menschen, Schweine, und Kartoffeln," ibid.

58. This was naturally a matter of perspective. Cf., on Bavarians' "Prussian-hate," Ay, *Entstehung,* 134–48. On Rhenish antipathy to Berlin, see Roerkohl, *Hungerblockade;* Faust, *Sozialer Burgfrieden;* Tobin, "Revolution in Düsseldorf." Generally, see BAL, 15.01, Nr. 12478–79, monthly reports of the deputy commanders. On rural antiurbanism, see Moeller, "Dimensions of Social Conflict" and *German Peasants.*

59. "Unerhörter Kriegswucher," *Berliner Morgenpost,* 8 June 1915. Cf. BLHA, PPB, Nr. 15811, p. 84, report, Kurtz, 11 June 1915, and p. 91, report, Starost, 11 June 1915.

60. "Zur Ernährungsfrage," *Reichsbote,* 17 Jan. 1916.

61. Cf. "Wie die Arbeiter denken," *Berliner Volkszeitung,* 11 Mar. 1915. Protesters began to employ such rights rhetoric in mid-nineteenth-century Berlin, but there is little evidence others supported them in such language. Cf. Gailus, *Straße und Brot.*

62. "Der Kaiser mobilisiert die Internationale," *Der Deutsche Kurier,* 17 Apr. 1915.

63. BLHA, PPB, Nr. 15809, p. 30, report, König, 19 Feb. 1915. Policemen's habit of reporting "it is said that" and "one hears everywhere" reinforced for officials the notion of generalized support for such measures.

64. "Mehr Verständnis für die Landwirtschaft," *Deutsche Tageszeitung,* 25 Feb. 1915.

65. "Die Kartoffelversorgung versichert," ibid., 20 Apr. 1915.

66. "Kartoffelnot in Schöneberg," *Berliner Börsen Kurier,* 8 Mar. 1915. Cf. "Der erste Tag der Kartoffelkarten-Ausgabe in Wilmersdorf," *Berliner Börsen Zeitung,* 23 Mar. 1915.

67. "Die Höchstpreise auf dem Kartoffelmarkt: Beseitigung der Kartoffelnot," *Berliner Tageblatt,* 18 Feb. 1915.

68. Jagow noted Berliners' support of war credits; see BLHA, PPB, Nr. 15809, mood report, Jagow, 20 Mar. 1915. Cf. Schreiner, *Iron Ration,* 59.

69. Cf. GStAPK, 2.2.1, Rep. 77, Tit. 332r, Nr. 26, 20 Feb. 1915.

70. See Kaeber, *Berlin im Weltkriege,* 199.

71. "Zur Frage der Kartoffelversorgung," *Freisinnige Zeitung,* 22 Apr. 1915.

72. "Zur Kartoffelnot," *Vorwärts,* 4 Mar. 1915.

73. Skalweit, *Kriegsernährungswirtschaft,* 33.

74. Cf. BLHA, PPB, Nr. 15809, p. 7, report, Kurtz, 12 Feb. 1915.

75. Cf. "Noch immer Kartoffelnot," *Tägliche Rundschau,* 27 Mar. 1915. Officials conceded in retrospect that millions of tons of potatoes had spoiled. Although the new Council on Potato Drying created the capacity to dry 3.75 million tons per year, this was useless if potatoes never reached the drying works. See Rubner, "Ernährungswesen," 23; Lautenbach, *Kartoffeltrocknung im Kriege.*

76. Cf. BLHA, PPB, Nr. 15809, p. 41, mood report, Jagow, 20 Feb. 1915; pp. 18–19, report, Rhein, 17 Feb. 1915; p. 32, report, Schwarz, 19 Feb. 1915; p. 37, report, Kurtz, 18 Feb. 1915.

77. "Wo bleibt die Beschlagnahme der Kartoffel?," *Berliner Tageblatt,* 24 Feb. 1915. Cf. "Kartoffelnot in Schöneberg," *Berliner Börsen Kurier,* 8 Mar. 1915.

78. Cf. "Die Stadtverordnetenversammlung," *Vorwärts,* 4 Mar. 1915; BLHA, PPB, Nr. 15809, pp. 157–60, report, Dittmann, 5 Mar. 1915; Kaeber, *Berlin im Weltkriege,* 203.

79. GStAPK, 2.2.1, Rep. 197a, It Nr. 1a, pp. 116–29, brochure "Ernährung im Kriege," issued February 1915 in millions. Cf. BLHA, PPB, Nr. 15809, pp. 18–19, report, Rhein, 17 Feb. 1915; p. 32, report, Schwarz, 19 Feb. 1915; p. 37, report, Kurtz, 18 Feb. 1915.

80. Many advisers believed that the slaughter would be more effective than confiscation. Ironically, the growth of the national swine stock in the years preceding the war was the product of one of the very few official economic planning efforts.

81. Cf. brochure included in GStAPK, 2.2.1, Rep. 197A, It Nr. 1g, pp. 1–8.

82. In this period Germans frequently played on the dual meaning of *Schlacht* as battle and slaughter.

83. BAL, 15.01, Rep. 77, Nr. 2416, p. 93, letter, Matthias Erzberger to Imperial Office of the Interior, 4 Feb. 1915.

84. Copy of Eltzbacher's speech, in ibid., p. 176, 17 Feb. 1915. Rubner claimed that a pig might eat at least 2,500 pounds of potatoes and 375 pounds of grain a year, while a person would eat about 312 pounds of potatoes and 170 of bread grains. By early 1917 experts sighed, "If we had no pigs, we'd have no food worries. Perhaps we'll learn at least from the war, that swine husbandry is for the politics of food an example of insanity" (Max Rubner, in *Klinische Wochenschrift,* 19 Mar. 1917). See also Rubner, "Ernährungswesen," 2; Skalweit and Klaas, *Das Schwein in der Kriegsernährungswirtschaft,* 10–16, 34–43.

85. Speech before city council, 4 Mar. 1915, included in BLHA, PPB, Nr. 15809, pp. 157–60, report, Dittmann, 5 Mar. 1915.

86. Cf. BAL, 15.01, Rep. 77, Nr. 12473, monthly report, 3 Feb. 1916.

87. Theodor Wolff, *Tagebücher,* 1:184.

88. "Menschen, Schweine, und Kartoffeln," *Welt am Montag,* 6 Apr. 1915.

89. Cf. "Die Ursache der wahnsinnigen Kartoffelpreise," *Dortmunder Arbeiter Zeitung,* 18 Feb. 1915.

90. Cf. *Schweinehund, Schweinemässig, Schweinerei, schweinigeln, Schweinetreiber, Schweinewirtschaft, Schweinefrass* and *Schweinegeld,* and *Schwein* (pig) itself. The pig's association with good luck, as in the signs marking lottery stands, must have provoked a cynical response. These expressions were not necessarily in far greater use during the period, but they were the contemporary cultural associations of an animal that was on every Berliner's lips. Cf. BLHA, PPB, Nr. 15811, pp. 95–96, report, Sauer, 10 June 1915; Wellmann, *Meine Mutter,* 92–103; *Unter der roten Fahne,* 97.

91. *1918: Erinnerungen von Veteranen,* 315; Annemarie Lange, *Das Wilhelminische Berlin,* 332.

92. BAL, 07.01, Nr. 2416, p. 323, letter, Eltzbacher, Kuczynski, Lehmann, Rümcker, and Zuntz to Reichstag, 8 Mar. 1915. The commission's report, dated 13 Mar. 1915, still suggested that Germany should cover its own potato supply for the duration of the war.

93. Ballod, "Die Volksernährung in Krieg und Frieden," 78.

94. Cf. "Beschlagnahme der Kartoffeln," *Vorwärts,* 25 Feb. 1915; "Volksernährung im Kriege," *Königsberger Volkszeitung,* 10 Mar. 1915; "Die Volksernährung im Kriege," *Mitteilungsblatt,* 3 Oct. 1915; "Wenn der Reichstag Energie Hat," *Das Neumärkische Volksblatt,* 12 Mar.

1915. Cf., on the SPD's new prestige, "Spaltet sich die Sozialdemokraten?," in *Welt am Montag,* 8 Mar. 1915; BLHA, PPB, Nr. 15809, p. 41, mood report, Jagow, 20 Feb. 1915.

95. Skalweit, *Kriegsernährungswirtschaft,* 97. The slaughter still represented only 900,000 more swine than in the same quarter the year before. See Kaeber, *Berlin im Weltkriege,* 182.

96. Cf. "Schorlemer und Kartoffeln," *Das Neumärkische Volksblatt,* 22 Mar. 1915. This price was scarcely above the previous November's wholesale ceiling; in any case, no average person could find that many potatoes, no one was legally permitted to buy that many retail, and many workers could not (or could no longer) afford to buy by the *Zentner,* either cost- or spacewise.

97. "Phantasiepreise für Schweine," *Berliner Lokal Anzeiger,* 21 Apr. 1915.

98. Kaeber, *Berlin im Weltkriege,* 181. See, too, Nonn, *Verbraucherprotest,* 26. The Berlin meat riots of 1912 exemplified this point. Kaeber notes this was the city's first intervention in food provision on an international basis; as with each of these measures, authorities conceived of it as a one-time act.

99. Rubner, "Ernährungswesen," 2; Teuteberg, "Wie Ernähren sich Arbeiter," 60.

100. Teuteberg, "Wie Ernähren sich Arbeiter," 60.

101. For Germans, beef was no substitute for pork; see Rubner, "Ernährungswesen," 5. Moreover, promoting consumption of beef over pork would have made no sense. Cattle must be older than swine before they can be slaughtered, and calves required scarce milk to grow old enough for meat slaughter.

102. "Phantasiepreise für Schweine," *Berliner Lokal Anzeiger,* 21 Apr. 1915; "Wucherische Steigerung der Schweinepreise," *Vorwärts,* 30 Apr. 1915.

103. Kaeber, *Berlin im Weltkriege,* 180.

104. BLHA, PPB, Nr. 15809, p. 11, report, Starost, 12 Feb. 1915.

105. Kaeber, *Berlin im Weltkriege,* 180.

106. BLHA, PPB, Nr. 15809, p. 5, report, Schulz, n.d. [ca. 12 Feb. 1915].

107. Ibid., Nr. 15810, p. 284, mood report, Jagow, 15 May 1915.

108. BAL, 07.01, Nr. 2416, p. 323, letter, Eltzbacher commission to Reichstag, 8 Mar. 1915.

109. Kaeber, *Berlin im Weltkriege,* 183.

110. BLHA, PPB, Nr. 15810, p. 208, mood report, Jagow, 1 May 1915. There is no mention of May Day activities in this report. In later war years Berliners used May Day to express demands for government aid in providing food. Cf. ibid., Nr. 15894, 1 May 1917 and 1 May 1918.

111. Ibid., Nr. 15811, p. 81, report, Diercks, 11 June 1915, and p. 84, report, Kurtz, 11 June 1915. Cf. "Gegen die Teuerung," *Volksstimme Frankfurt,* 7 May 1915.

112. On the increase in expenditures, cf. Materna, Demps, et al., *Geschichte Berlins,* 532.

113. BLHA, PPB, Nr. 15810, p. 284, mood report, Jagow, 15 May 1915.

114. Cf. "Die Kartoffelversorgung versichert," *Deutsche Tageszeitung,* 20 Apr. 1915. See also BLHA, PPB, Nr. 15809, report, Starost, 19 Mar. 1915.

115. BLHA, PPB, Nr. 15809, p. 166, mood report, Jagow, 6 Mar. 1915.

116. "Kriegspreise," *Grundstein,* 1 May 1915. This theme dominated the SPD steering committee discussion, June 1915. In this period the Social Democratic press attended primarily to internal party conflicts. At the same time, shoring up support, majority Social Democrats exhibited special attention to the needs of its rank-and-file members, which at this moment meant concern for food.

117. "Die Politische Schicksalsfrage Preussens und Deutschlands," *Volksfreund Karlsruhe,* 4 June 1915.

118. Cf. "Die Händler und Wechsler," ibid., 5 May 1915. The article reviewed like sentiments across the German population.

119. Cf. Thompson, "Moral Economy Revisited"; Martin Geyer, "Konsumentenpolitik."

120. Cf. e.g. "Wucherpreise im Kleinhandel," *Tägliche Rundschau,* 30 Apr. 1915; "Ein Bild vom Gemüsemarkt," *Berliner Volkszeitung,* 3 Aug. 1915; BLHA, PPB, Nr. 15809, p. 166, mood report, Jagow, 6 Mar. 1915; Nr. 15810, p. 274, report, Schwarz, 14 May 1915; Nr. 15811, pp. 139–40, report, Rhein, 16 June 1915.

121. See, e.g., BLHA, PPB, Nr. 15809, p. 243, report, König, 19 Mar. 1915; Nr. 15811, p. 205, report, Klonicki, 24 June 1915; "Der Erste Tag der Kartoffelkarten-Ausgabe in Wilmersdorf," *Berliner Börsen Zeitung,* 23 Mar. 1915.

122. BLHA, PPB, Nr. 15809, p. 5, report, Schulz, 12 Feb. 1915. Schulz speaks of the incident as true.

123. Luther, *Im Dienst des Städtetags.*

124. Sombart, *Händler und Helden.*

125. "'Ein Unsagbarer Ekel Überkommt Uns,'" *Offenbacher Abendblatt,* 4 June 1916. Cf. "Der Kaiser mobilisiert die Internationale," *Der Deutsche Kurier,* 17 Apr. 1915. Poorer Berliners cast rural producers as outside the country, conflating the interests of Berlin and Germany. Cf. "Die teuere Butter," *Berliner Volkszeitung,* 22 July 1915; "Ein lehrreiches Beispiel für das Zustandekommen der hohen Gemüsepreise," *Tägliche Rundschau,* 7 Sept. 1915.

126. "Das tägliche Brot," *Vorwärts,* 14 Aug. 1915.

127. BLHA, PPB, Nr. 15820, p. 46, report, Schade, 18 Dec. 1916. At the same time, officials tended to name the enemy "profiteering" rather than "the profiteer," contributing to the sense that the urban population spoke in a common voice.

128. See, e.g., Rubner, "Ernährungswesen," 41.

129. BLHA, PPB, Nr. 15810, p. 43, report, Hartwig, 4 June 1915; Nr. 18513, p. 121, mood report, Diercks, 17 Sept. 1915.

130. Cf. "Lebensmittelteuerung," *Berliner Tageblatt,* 13 Sept. 1915; "Hier stehe ich, ich kann nicht Anders!," *Schwäbische Tagewacht,* 23 June 1915; "Die politische Schicksalsfrage Preußens und Deutschlands," *Volksfreund Karlsruhe,* 4 June 1915; Helfferich, *Der Weltkrieg,* 76.

131. On some Germans' vision of the nation's war aims, cf. Fritz Fischer, *War of Illusions;* Eley, *Reshaping the German Right;* Chickering, *We Men Who Feel Most German;* Shevin-Coetzee, *German Army League;* Woodruff D. Smith, *Ideological Origins of Nazi Imperialism;* Burleigh, *Germany Looks Eastward.*

132. BLHA, PPB, Nr. 15812, p. 180, mood report, Jagow, 24 July 1915. In this period urban newspapers appealed to authorities at all levels. Protesters still assumed that the burden of support measures might come from lower levels of government. But Lord Mayor Wermuth, leader of the Council of Cities, claimed only the central authorities could adequately control distribution and pricing. Municipal officials, too, cast themselves as allies of the public.

133. The Social Democratic *Dortmunder Arbeiter Zeitung* triumphantly reproduced this statement; see "Die Ursache der wahnsinnigen Kartoffelpreise," ibid., 18 Feb. 1915.

134. BLHA, PPB, Nr. 15813, p. 9, report, Gerhardt, 3 Sept. 1915.

CHAPTER FOUR

1. The crisis spurred the initiation of monthly reports to the War Ministry and elsewhere on domestic unrest around the country. Cf. Deist, *Militär- und Innenpolitik,* 1:154.

2. Ruge, *Deutschlands Milch- und Speisefettversorgung,* 3.

3. Ibid., 3.

4. Kaeber, *Beiträge,* 235.

5. See Ruge, *Deutschlands Milch- und Speisefettversorgung,* 2. Cf. Flemming, *Landwirtschaftliche Interessen.*

6. Cf. Skalweit, *Kriegsernährungswirtschaft,* 12.

7. From *Meyers Lexikon,* as cited in Lüdtke, "Hunger, Essens-'Genuss' und Politik," 123.

8. Ibid., 125.

9. Kaeber, *Beiträge,* 235.

10. Cf. Scholz, "Ein Unruhiges Jahrzehnt," 82.

11. Cf. *Der richtige Berliner,* 30.

12. Lüdtke, "Hunger, Essens-'Genuss' und Politik," 125.

13. Ibid., 123.

14. BLHA, PPB, Nr. 15821, p. 251, mood report, Oppen, 24 Aug. 1917.

15. See "Nationaler Frauendienst über Deutsche Volksernährung," *Königsberger Volkszeitung,* 1 Mar. 1915, which spoofs the use of such platitudes in the organization's propaganda.

16. Kaeber, *Beiträge,* 235. Cf., by contrast for Germany overall, Triebel, "Consumption in Wartime Germany." In the Rhineland, workers found butter to "'scratch [their] throats'" (Lüdtke, "Hunger, Essens-'Genuss' und Politik," 120). For Bavaria, cf. Ay, *Entstehung,* 111.

17. Cf. "Wer Verteuert die Butterpreise?," *Vossische Zeitung,* 16 Oct. 1915.

18. Cf. *Der richtige Berliner,* 82; *Duden,* 297; and Spalding, *Historical Dictionary,* 433–35.

19. Cf. Triebel, "Consumption in Wartime Germany," 179–81.

20. Lüdtke, "Hunger, Essens-'Genuss' und Politik," 123.

21. Kaeber, *Beiträge,* 237.

22. BLHA, PPB, Nr. 15811, p. 241, mood report, Jagow, 29 June 1915.

23. Ibid. Cf. Ruge, *Deutschlands Milch- und Speisefettversorgung,* 1; Skalweit and Klaas, *Das Schwein in der Kriegsernährungspolitik.*

24. On wartime restrictions on the butter exports of neutral countries, see Ruge, *Deutschlands Milch- und Speisefettversorgung,* 9.

25. Kaeber, *Beiträge,* 235. See also on "the butter period," from October 1915 to July 1916, Ruge, *Deutschlands Milch- und Speisefettversorgung,"* 5.

26. "Abhandlung des Preussischen Ministeriums des Innern," 39.

27. The number of riots is approximate because of the ambiguity created when certain small outbreaks that merged into larger conflagrations are counted.

28. On Wedding and Spandau Quarter, compare Lindenberger, *Straßenpolitik;* cf. Glaeßner, Lehnert, and Sühl, *Studien.*

29. Cf. the 16 Oct. 1915 ordinance on butter prices, reprinted in "Das Pfund Butter: 2,80M," *Vossische Zeitung,* 17 Oct. 1915.

30. Meat shops now demanded customers present a special card, available from the Municipal Bread Commission. Access to this card was based on income, though *Berliner Tageblatt* complained that wealthier customers were using them. See "Nachtlager in der Thaerstraße," *Berliner Tageblatt,* 16 Oct. 1915. The other stipulations only reinforced this contraindicated use. Although shoppers could come only once a week, they had to buy between four and six pounds at a time. This amount was prohibitive for most poorer consumers.

31. In many of the instances before Assmann, police explicitly named excessive prices as cause. However, Bolle's prices were higher, and consumers also thought that Bolle was chain

trading. See BLHA, PPB, Nr. 15814, p. 28, report, Lewald, 16 Oct. 1915. There may have been some organized strategy; consumers may also have perceived Assmann to be a Jewish-owned firm. There were no reported attacks on the familiar horse-drawn Bolle wagons selling dairy products. On chain trading, see Hirsch and Falck, *Der Kettenhandel.*

32. BLHA, PPB, Nr. 15813, pp. 226–27, report, Dittmann, 11 Oct. 1915.

33. Ibid., Nr. 15808, p. 17, report, Hartwig, 16 Feb. 1915; Nr. 15809, p. 41, mood report, Jagow, 20 Feb. 1915.

34. Cf. Nr. 15814, p. 97, report, Hanff, 18 Oct. 1915.

35. BLHA, PPB, Nr. 15814, pp. 25–28, report, Lewald, 16 Oct. 1915; cf. Steven Kaplan, *Bread, Politics;* Gailus, *Straße und Brot.*

36. BLHA, PPB, Nr. 15814, pp. 25–28, report, Lewald, 16 Oct. 1915.

37. Of course this rapid transformation was not without exception. Cf. GStAPK, 2.2.1, Rep. 197A, Io Nr. 1, pp. 6–11, memo, Lewald to Loebell, 21 Oct. 1915. Had police caught them, they would not have charged very young boys, while they would likely have charged women.

38. BLHA, PPB, Nr. 15814, pp. 16–17, report, Marschke, 15 Oct. 1915. This officer's name does not appear again among police reports. Whether superiors found his reports too threatening or whether Marschke felt he was not up to the task is unknown. Shops now regularly stayed open an extra two hours, until 8:00 P.M. This should have benefited factory workers, but laborers complained the open shops without goods only increased frustration. The Bundesrat responded by prohibiting extra hours.

39. Ibid., pp. 110–11, report, Schwarz, 19 Oct. 1915. One might have thought of the expression, "to spread something on the bread" for someone, implying the repetition of some particularly aggravating action or word.

40. Ibid., pp. 29–30, report, Sauer, 16 Oct. 1915. See also "Wer Verteuert die Butterpreise?," *Vossische Zeitung,* 16 Oct. 1915 (evening edition).

41. BLHA, PPB, Nr. 15813, p. 258, report, Schwarz, 14 Oct. 1915.

42. Ibid., Nr. 15814, p. 101, report, Hanff, 18 Oct. 1915. Cf., e.g., p. 358, report, Schwarz, 11 Nov. 1915, and Nr. 15810, p. 112, telegram, Kaiser Wilhelm to Jagow. The implicated children were often quite young, between ten and twelve years old. On the youth question in war, cf. Daniel, *Arbeiterfrauen,* 159–63; Scholz, "Ein Unruhiges Jahrzehnt." For early Weimar, cf. Peukert, *Jugend zwischen Krieg und Krise;* Harvey, *Youth and the Welfare State.*

43. In Bavaria it was already difficult to muster sufficient police forces due to conscription. The Bavarian government's call for a volunteer security force met with a zealous and, to officials, frightening response. See Ay, *Entstehung,* 32.

44. Cf. BLHA, PPB, Nr. 15814, p. 357, report, Diercks, 11 Nov. 1915; p. 360, report, Kurtz, 11 Nov. 1915; p. 248, report, Klonicki, 28 Oct. 1915.

45. Ibid., p. 179, memorandum, Saefft, 23 Oct. 1915.

46. Cf. ibid., p. 65, response, Jagow to Berge, 16 Oct. 1915.

47. *Vossische Zeitung,* 15 Oct. 1915. Police clipped and heavily underscored the piece, as they did many items in these weeks, though it had escaped censors. Cf. BLHA, PPB, Nr. 15813, p. 272, containing the marked clipping. Officials issued new censorship guidelines yet again in December and stepped up enforcement.

48. See, e.g., BLHA, PPB, Nr. 15813, p. 257, report, Diercks, 15 Oct. 1915.

49. Ibid., Nr. 15814, pp. 29–30, report, Sauer, 16 Oct. 1915. Sergeant Schwarz struck the clause concerning "exploitations."

50. Ibid., Nr. 15813, p. 257, report, Diercks, 15 Oct. 1915.

51. Ibid., p. 265, mood report, Jagow, 16 Oct. 1915.

52. Ibid.

53. See, e.g., "Der Einfluß der Prüfungsstellen," *Vossische Zeitung,* 16 Oct. 1915.

54. See "Maßnahmen gegen die Butterteuerung," *Vossische Zeitung,* 19 Oct. 1915. Cf. "Keine Butterkarte in Sicht," *Berliner Börsen Zeitung,* 16 Oct. 1915, hoping to soothe merchants' fears.

55. Cf. BLHA, PPB, Nr. 15814, pp. 132–33, memorandum, Baerecke to Jagow, 21 Oct. 1915.

56. See, e.g., "Höchstpreise für Butter: Bevorstehendes Verbot gewerblicher Milchverwertung," *Berliner Morgenpost,* 17 Oct. 1915; "Butterhöchstpreise," *Vorwärts,* 17 Oct. 1915; "Das Pfund Butter: 2,80M," *Vossische Zeitung,* 17 Oct. 1915.

57. BLHA, PPB, Nr. 15814, p. 95, Schwarz marginalia on press clipping, 18 Oct. 1915. Some shops now opened on Sunday afternoons. There is some confusion in reports over how quiet the day actually was, despite Schwarz's unequivocal claim to his superiors. If there were activity, Schwarz's claim is all the more interesting.

58. The anniversary was to be celebrated on 21 October, a day on which public celebration was not a prominent feature.

59. BLHA, PPB, Nr. 15814, p. 95, Schwarz marginalia on press clipping, 18 Oct. 1915. Jagow struck the implied causality in ibid., pp. 112–13, 19 Oct. 1915.

60. Cf. "Das Pfund Butter: 2,80M," *Vossische Zeitung,* 17 Oct. 1915.

61. "Der Einfluß der Prüfungsstellen," ibid., 16 Oct. 1915.

62. "Kampf um Fleisch und Fett," *Vorwärts,* 15 Oct. 1915; "Kampf um Fleisch und Fett," ibid., 16 Oct. 1915. Cf. "In der Wedding Halle," ibid., 15 Oct. 1915, on "life-threateningly" large crowds.

63. BLHA, PPB, Nr. 15814, p. 97, report, Hanff, 18 Oct. 1915; p. 125, report, Starost, 20 Oct. 1915.

64. Ibid., pp. 101, 103, report, Hanff, 18 Oct. 1915; p. 100a, transcript, telephone report, Schneider, n.d. [18 Oct. 1915]. Working women and shopkeepers normally used the formal "you" to address one another, marking class differences. The last version included the shopkeeper's retort, "You [*Ihr*] all will eat shit yet!" Cf. Scholz, "Ein Unruhiges Jahrzehnt," for other similar incidents.

65. BLHA, PPB, Nr. 15814, transcript, telephone report, Schneider, n.d. [18 Oct. 1915].

66. Ibid., pp. 129–30, memorandum, Jagow to Berge, 20 Oct. 1915.

67. Ibid., pp. 25–28, report, Lewald, 16 Oct. 1915.

68. Ibid., p. 111, report, Schwarz, 19 Oct. 1915.

69. Cf. ibid., pp. 25–28, report, Lewald, 16 Oct. 1915.

70. Reprinted in "Höchstpreise für Butter," *Vorwärts,* 19 Oct. 1915.

71. See, e.g., "Butterangstkäufe," *Vossische Zeitung,* 14 Dec. 1915; "Fett- und Fleischarme Kost," ibid., 16 Oct. 1915. On the precarious conditions of some working-class women even before the war, cf. Fischer-Eckert, *Wirtschaftliche und soziale Lage,* cited in Lucas, *Zwei Formen,* 57–61. When asked what they would like their later years to bring, these Hamborn women agreed: "To eat until satisfied."

72. Across Germany leases were renegotiated in quarterly periods. In Berlin, landlords gave tenants notice on 1 July if they planned to raise rents; the new contract went into effect 1 October. For many Berliners and other Germans, especially those living in centers of war industry, rents had substantially increased, while the portion of income tenants were able to devote to rent diminished considerably between July and October 1915.

73. On the constant dread of the telegram, cf. Blücher, *English Wife,* 92; Gläser, *Class of 1902,* 262–63. Approximately one-half million German soldiers died each year because of the war; see Weldon, *Bitter Wounds,* 40. Weldon cites Leonard Frank's comment that, by the end of war, there could be 2 million German women thinking about their dead husbands. Cf. Annette Becker, *La guerre et la foi;* Winter, *Sites of Memory.*

74. Cf., in Austria-Hungary, Hammerle, *Kindheit im ersten Weltkrieg,* 33–42, 210–25.

75. BLHA, PPB, Nr. 15814, p. 137, memorandum, Jagow to police captains of Greater Berlin, 21 Oct. 1915.

76. Ibid., p. 247, report, Schwarz, 28 Oct. 1915.

77. Cf. discussion of a curfew for women and children in these districts, in the end limited only to children, in ibid., pp. 132–33, meeting minutes, Geheimrat Baerecke, 21 Oct. 1915.

78. Ibid. See also Berge's emphasis on swift punishment in a memo to Prussian authorities, GStAPK, 2.2.1, Rep. 77A, Io Nr. 1, p. 26, 20 Oct. 1915. Officials ordered police to hang and maintain huge copies of the proclamation, which banned inciting unrest by pain of death. See BLHA, PPB, Nr. 15814, p. 161, memorandum, Officer Lindig to Jagow, 22 Oct. 1915.

79. BLHA, PPB, Nr. 15814, pp. 132–33, meeting minutes, Geheimrat Baerecke, 21 Oct. 1915.

80. Interior Ministry files are rife with conflicts, particularly between Bethmann and Prussian agricultural minister Klemens von Schorlemer, over how and on whose behalf the government should intervene on the food question. See also Burchardt, *Friedenswirtschaft;* Schumacher, *Land und Politik;* Flemming, *Landwirtschaftliche Interessen.*

81. Cf. "Die Angst vor der Fleischkarte," *Berliner Börsen Zeitung am Montag,* 16 Nov. 1915.

CHAPTER FIVE

1. An early exception is Ay, *Entstehung.* Friedhelm Boll, too, includes food protests as a part of the "mass movement," which he names as political from 1916; see Boll, *Massenbewegung.* See also Ullrich, *Kriegsalltag;* Martin Geyer, *Verkehrte Welt;* Daniel, *Arbeiterfrauen;* Scholz, "Ein Unruhiges Jahrzehnt."

2. Jagow cites from "Not kennt kein Gebot," *Volksfreund Braunschweig,* 3 Nov. 1915, which in turn cites a party resolution. See BLHA, PPB, Nr. 15814, p. 298, mood report, Jagow, 5 Nov. 1915.

3. See Feldman, *Army, Industry, and Labor,* esp. 407–58, and Kocka, *Facing Total War.*

4. On the state's potential for and realization of reform, viewed predominantly with reference to parliamentarism, cf. Rauh, *Parlamentarisierung;* Gerhard A. Ritter, *Deutsche Parteien;* Stürmer, *Regierung und Reichstag;* Wehler, *German Empire;* Struve, *Elites against Democracy;* Witt, *Finanzpolitik;* Fairbairn, *Democracy.* On the war years, cf. Kocka, *Facing Total War,* 47–48. This is not to suggest equivalence between parliamentary structures of influence and popular pressures. See Davis, "Reconsidering Habermas, Politics, and Gender."

5. Cf. *Der Interfraktionelle Ausschuß,* 1:xv; Bethmann Hollweg, *Betrachtungen,* 2:35–36.

6. Cf. German concern, BLHA, PPB, Nr. 15816, pp. 46–47, clippings, foreign socialist press, Jan. 1916; LAB ADF 4-20(2), letter, A. Edinger to H. Lange, 22 June 1915. Compare Horne and Kramer, "German 'Atrocities.'"

7. Cf. Mathews, "German Social Democrats."

8. Blücher, *English Wife,* 90.

9. Ibid., 86–90.

10. Cf. BLHA, PPB, Nr. 15815, p. 203, memorandum, High Court Market Hall Office of

the kaiser, 18 Dec. 1915; Blücher, *English Wife,* 154; Theodor Wolff, *Tagebücher,* 1:315–16. See Deist, *Militär- und Innenpolitik,* 1:388, on concerns to avoid violent police response. Authorities appointed Jagow *Regierungspräsident* in Breslau; he was succeeded in Berlin by Heinrich von Oppen. Jagow's frustration with his superiors' management style apparently continued into Weimar; he was a leading figure in the 1920 Kapp Putsch.

11. Cf. BLHA, PPB, Nr. 15814, report, König, 11 Nov. 1915.

12. GStAPK, 2.2.1, Rep. 77A, Io Nr. 1, p. 1, anonymous private letter to Loebell, 13 Oct. 1915.

13. Cf. the Willy Röhmer photograph bearing this message. On letters of lament, cf. Ulrich, "Feldpostbriefe"; Daniel, *Arbeiterfrauen.*

14. BLHA, PPB, Nr. 15813, p. 261, report, Starost, 14 Oct. 1915.

15. Ibid., p. 257, report, Diercks, 15 Oct. 1915. Cf. Nr. 15814, p. 356, report, Schiller, 11 Nov. 1915, on conflicting military and civilian needs. This anticipates Hermann Göring's sentiment, "Guns will make us powerful; butter will only make us fat," cited in Lockhart, *Guns or Butter,* title page. It is well known that Hitler attempted at least in principle to prevent competition between domestic and military resources in preparation for World War II, as a consequence of the World War I experience.

16. BLHA, PPB, Nr. 15814, p. 366, mood report, Jagow, 13 Nov. 1915.

17. Blücher, *English Wife,* 79–80.

18. Cf. David, *Kriegstagebuch,* 147.

19. See Deist, *Militär- und Innenpolitik,* 1:271–76.

20. See Theodor Wolff, *Tagebücher,* 1:314–15.

21. BLHA, PPB, Nr. 15817, p. 130, letter, machinist Karl Sachs to Jagow, 20 Mar. 1916.

22. Ibid., Nr. 15819, memorandum, Privy Councillor Mekergen, 17 Mar. 1916. Privy Councillor Baerecke worried for "the mood in my own circles," related also to the controversy over the new submarine campaign and Admiral Alfred von Tirpitz's resignation. While positive news from the front no longer seemed to revive the spirits of the broader population, negative news had the ability to reinforce the depression.

23. Blücher, *English Wife,* 94–95.

24. Ay, *Entstehung,* 47. Discussion at the International Women's Congress after the Berlin unrest of February 1915 also reflected this sentiment.

25. Zimmerwald was the international (radical) Social Democratic peace conference, held in the first week of September 1915 in Zimmerwald, Switzerland, and followed by a spring 1916 conference in Kienthal. By the end of 1915, as SPD Reichstag representatives split rancorously over the support of new war credits, tensions within the party deepened considerably.

26. Cf. BLHA, PPB, Nr. 15814, pp. 29–30, report, Sauer, 16 Oct. 1915. Reports of the political police traveled from the original author to the various sergeants and then from all six commissariats to the police director, Eugen Henninger, who compiled reports into a draft communication for the police commissioner. The police commissioner passed the communications, including his own revisions, to the high commander, the Prussian interior minister, and as the war went on, fifty other officials and the kaiser. Higher-ups were aware of often doctored representations but did little to correct this tendency. Cf. Friedrich Freund, minister director in the Interior Ministry, cited by Materna and Schreckenbach, *Dokumente,* xxvi.

27. BLHA, PPB, Nr. 15814, p. 3, report, Lilsen, 14 Oct. 1915.

28. While Richard Evans reports Hamburg police informers themselves often came from the ranks of the working class, political policemen in Berlin and Prussia generally came from

lower middle-class backgrounds. Cf. Evans, *Proletarians and Politics,* 125; Materna and Schreckenbach, *Dokumente,* 12.

29. Contrast Cobb, *People and the Police;* Darnton, "Police Inspector Sorts His Files."

30. See, e.g., BLHA, PPB, Nr. 15814, 29–30, report, Sauer, 16 Oct. 1915.

31. Between 1915 and 1916, charges against women increased 70 percent to 128,000 offenses, primarily on property matters, and well over the actual amount carried out by youth; see Preller, *Sozialpolitik,* 11. Cf. Liepmann, *Krieg und Kriminalität.*

32. Cf. Lindenberger, *Straßenpolitik.*

33. Mihaly, . . . *da gibt's ein Wiedersehn!,* 208. Cf. BLHA, PPB, Nr. 15814, p. 67, report, Krupphausen, 17 Oct. 1915, and p. 101, report, Hanff, 18 Oct. 1915.

34. BLHA, PPB, Nr. 15814, pp. 6, 8, report, Sauer, 15 Oct. 1915.

35. Cf. ibid., pp. 25–28, report, Lewald, 16 Oct. 1915.

36. Ibid., Nr. 15815, pp. 128–29, report, Ludwig, 6 Dec. 1915. Ludwig had a propensity for more dramatic reports than most of his colleagues; this is not to say that his views are less valid.

37. Blücher, *English Wife,* 91. In earlier times police were far less concerned to distinguish between women and men in exercising violence, which reached new peaks in the prewar years, as in the Moabit unrest of 1910 and the 1912 Ruhr miners' strike. Physical violence in the streets increased exponentially in wartime, all the more among women, contributing to the tension of everyday life.

38. BLHA, PPB, Nr. 15814, p. 131, marginalia, Jagow to Schwarz, 20 Oct. 1915. Officer Saefft offered the common excuses that the perpetrator disappeared into the crowd and that she or he was a child, whom the police would not have arrested in any case. Cf. ibid., pp. 129–30, memorandum, Jagow to Berge, 20 Oct. 1915.

39. Cf. BLHA, Pr. Br., Rep. 30, Berlin C, Titel 133, Nr. 18717, p. 9, letter, landlord P. Gerlach to Police Division of Streets, 4 Feb. 1916.

40. Cf. BLHA, PPB, Nr. 15814, pp. 25–28, report, Lewald, 16 Oct. 1915.

41. Ibid., Nr. 15813, p. 262, report, Kurtz, 14 Oct. 1915.

42. Ibid., Nr. 15815, pp. 122–23, report, Schrott, 6 Dec. 1915. The women to whom Schrott refers in this particular incident may have been radical Social Democratic women rather than working-class shopping women (naturally the same women could play both roles); Schrott fails to make the distinction. *Trupp* can also mean simply group or band, but in these instances the military resonance seems clear.

43. GStAPK, 2.2.1, Rep. 197A, Io Nr. I, p. 236, special report, Lewald, 17 Oct. 1916.

44. BLHA, PPB, Nr. 15814, pp. 31–32, mood report, Jagow, 16 Oct. 1915.

45. Ibid., pp. 29–30, report, Sauer, 16 Oct. 1915.

46. Ibid., p. 293, report, Schiller, 17 Feb. 1916.

47. Ibid., Nr. 15816, p. 36, report, Dittmann, 4 Jan. 1916.

48. Ibid., Nr. 15815, p. 154, mood report, Jagow, 11 Dec. 1915; Nr. 15813, p. 275, marginalia, report, Schwarz, 12 Oct. 1915.

49. "Höchstpreise und Pfennige," *Berliner Volkszeitung,* 6 Dec. 1915. Cf. *Vossische Zeitung,* 18 Oct. 1915, citing the views of the Hansa Bund subcommittee on German retail, which cast off any blame on retailers. The net effect was that virtually all were in unison—except the state. Women's voices in the press, such as they were, and such representations, offer a contrast to the otherwise long-standing "masculinist" voice that the press represented. Cf. Fritzsche, *Reading Berlin.*

50. Cf. Theodor Wolff, *Tagebücher,* 1 : 300–301, in which Wolff also remarks on Bethmann's plea to the press not to give evidence to Germany's enemies that "'dire hunger reigns.'"

51. "Not Kennt Kein Gebot," *Volksfreund Braunschweig,* 2 Nov. 1915.

52. Cauer, *Leben und Werk,* 189–91. Compare Ay, *Entstehung,* 47–48.

53. Cf. BLHA, PPB, Nr. 15814, p. 97, report, Hanff, 18 Oct. 1915; see p. 357, report, Schwarz, 11 Nov. 1915.

54. "Kampf um Fleisch und Fett," *Vorwärts,* 15 Oct. 1915. Cf. Reichstag representative Eduard David's comment that the domestic political upheaval was "too much. It takes almost all my strength, but hold out, hold out, like those outside" (David, *Kriegstagebuch,* 144).

55. *Berliner Tageblatt,* 16 Oct. 1915.

56. "Die Teuerung und ihre Folgen: Hilfe für die Bedrängten," *Der Deutsche Kurier,* 15 Oct. 1915.

57. "Kampf um Fleisch und Fett," *Vorwärts,* 15 Oct. 1915.

58. "Die Teuerung und ihre Folgen," *Der Deutsche Kurier,* 15 Oct. 1915. Claiming "pretty words don't help," the author must certainly have been thinking of the phrase, "Fine words butter no parsnips" (*schöne Wörter machen den Kohl nicht fett*).

59. Deist, *Militär- und Innenpolitik,* 1 : 362.

60. See, respectively, *Vossische Zeitung,* 14 Oct. 1915; *Berliner Lokal Anzeiger,* 15 Oct. 1915; *Berliner Tageblatt,* 14 Oct. 1915.

61. The birthdays were muted events in order to respect the "seriousness of the moment"; the imperial couple and the wider public may have had slightly different ideas in mind. The Patriotic Women's League designated the kaiserin's birthday in 1915 as "Jam Day," during which "housewives" around the city were to produce marmalade for soldiers in the field and in lazarettos. See "Der Marmeladentag: Die Geburtstagsgabe für die Kaiserin," *Berliner Tageblatt,* 19 Oct. 1915, evening edition.

62. "Das tägliche Brot: Die Regelung der Butterpreise," *Vorwärts,* 22 Oct. 1915; cf. "Das tägliche Brot: Die Butter," ibid., 23 Oct. 1915; "Maßnahmen gegen die Butterteuerung," *Vossische Zeitung,* 19 Oct. 1915. The use of the rhetoric "the butter card again!" also emphasized the need of the public to make its demands multiple times before officials responded.

63. See, e.g., "Die Butterfrage," *Vorwärts,* 19 Oct. 1915; "Das tägliche Brot," ibid., 20 Oct. 1915.

64. "Unvermeidlich?," ibid., 11 Oct. 1915.

65. See "Butter," ibid., 23 Oct. 1915; "Teuerungsfragen," ibid., 25 Oct. 1915; "Teuerung der Butterpreise," ibid., 14 Oct. 1915; "Der Einfluß der Prüfungsstellen," *Vossische Zeitung,* 16 Oct. 1915, and in the evening edition, "Wer verteuert die Butterpreise?" Jagow agreed with the characterization of the bourgeois and Social Democratic press working together against the government. See BLHA, PPB, Nr. 15815, p. 265, mood report, Jagow, 30 Oct. 1915.

66. Cf. "Fleischteuerung und Fleischkarten," *Vorwärts,* 27 Oct. 1915, and the trenchant "Sieg über Konsumenten," ibid., 8 Oct. 1915.

67. "Fleischteuerung und Fleischkarten," ibid., 27 Oct. 1915. By 1916 attacks on the government and the inner war had become increasingly vitriolic. Though an extreme example, one small Social Democratic paper remarked, "The British, Russians, and even the Hottentots are angels compared to the miserable, disgusting behavior of agents of the state toward the poor *People.* . . . The state is the speculator's hero."

68. "Die Lebensmittelpolitik der Reichsregierung," *Berliner Tageblatt,* 14 Oct. 1915, evening edition.

69. *Offenbacher Abendblatt,* 24 Nov. 1915.

70. "Die Butterfrage," *Vorwärts,* 19 Oct. 1915.

71. "Das tägliche Brot," ibid., 20 Oct. 1915.

72. Cf., e.g., *Vossische Zeitung,* 18 Oct. 1915; "Die neue Speisekarte," *8 Uhr Abendblatt,* 30 Oct. 1915; "Keine großen Butterankäufe," *Berliner Morgenpost,* 26 Nov. 1915; "Der Mangel an Schweinefleisch," *Berliner Lokal Anzeiger,* 8 Dec. 1915; "Wirrwarr auf dem Gemüsemarkt," *Berliner Tageblatt,* 13 Dec. 1915; "Halbheiten ohne Ende!," *Welt am Montag,* 3 June 1916.

73. Cited in BLHA, PPB, Nr. 15815, 20 Nov. 1915. Cf. August Winnig's column in the Social Democratic *Münchener Post,* 25 Oct. 1915, in which he depicts speculators as violating women and children through high food prices.

74. BLHA, PPB, Nr. 15814, p. 246, report, Diercks, 28 Oct. 1915.

75. "Demonstrierende Kriegerfrauen," *Schwäbische Tagewacht,* 19 Oct. 1915. Cf. BLHA, PPB, Nr. 15813, p. 258, report, Schwarz, 14 Oct. 1915.

76. "Politische Übersicht," *Vorwärts,* 25 Oct. 1915.

77. LAB, Rep. 142, Städtetag memo, 23 Oct. 1915.

78. BAL, 07.01, Nr. 2436/1, pp. 1, 13, meetings on food distribution, 19 Nov., 13 Dec. 1915. On the transformation of the role of the ZEG, see Michaelis, *Für Staat und Volk,* 269–73.

79. BLHA, PPB, Nr. 15814, p. 246, report, Diercks, 28 Oct. 1915.

80. See, e.g., ibid., p. 11, report, Neugebauer, 15 Oct. 1915, who noted that it had taken two hours to disperse the crowds, while Sergeant Schwarz labeled the protest "defensible." Cf. ibid., pp. 29–30, report, Sauer, 16 Oct. 1915, and pp. 107–9, report, Lewald, 19 Oct. 1915. Police did arrest some adult women; cf. ibid., pp. 31–33, mood report, Jagow, 16 Oct. 1915.

81. Cf. "Kampf um Fleisch und Fett," *Vorwärts,* 15 Oct. 1915. On the importance of fair lines, cf. Wermuth, *Ein Beamtenleben,* 364; BLHA, PPB, Nr. 15815, pp. 130–32, mood report, Rhein, 7 Dec. 1915.

CHAPTER SIX

1. Theodor Wolff, *Tagebücher,* 1:377, 9 May 1916.

2. Cf. Hesse, *Freie Wirtschaft.*

3. See Roerkohl, *Hungerblockade,* 70–77; Feldman, *Army, Industry, and Labor,* 109–15, on formation of the KEA.

4. Military requisitioning of means of transportation also hindered domestic delivery. Soldiers and especially sailors did not fare well themselves, particularly relative to their superiors, a factor in the sailors' mutinies of 1918. But they did receive basic rations including special meat reserves. Cf. Reinhold Maier, *Feldpostbriefe;* Carsten, *War against War,* 112–15; Horn, *German Naval Mutinies,* 42–44.

5. Compare discussions in Theodor Wolff's "Club," in Wolff, *Tagebücher,* 1:380–83.

6. Groener, *Lebenserinnerungen,* 335. Cf. BAL, 07.01, Nr. 2421, p. 273, letter, Bethmann to Falkenhayn, 15 May 1916.

7. Lüders, *Das Unbekannte Heer,* 51. Cf. Deist, *Militär- und Innenpolitik,* 1:397.

8. See BAL, Nr. 2421, p. 79. This entire file exposes infighting over the extent of KEA powers, e.g., pitting Bethmann and General Adolf Wild against Falkenhayn and Groener. Compare Feldman, *Army, Industry, and Labor,* 111; Roerkohl, *Hungerblockade,* 93.

9. Wermuth, *Ein Beamtenleben,* 375.

10. Groener, *Lebenserinnerungen,* 550, cf. 551.

11. See BLHA, PPB, Nr. 15818, p. 131, report, Schiller, 25 May 1916; Cf. Nr. 15819, p. 125, mood report, Oppen, 2 Sept. 1916.

12. Rubner, "Ernährungswesen," 14–16; Kaeber, *Berlin im Weltkriege*, 96. Cf. Offer, *First World War*, 43–46.

13. Dr. Alfred Grotjahn, cited in Glatzer and Glatzer, *Berliner Leben, 1914–1918*, 335.

14. BLHA, PPB, Nr. 15819, p. 4, report, Görl, 19 July 1916; Nr. 15851, p. 54, report, Schwarz, 6 July 1916.

15. Ibid., Nr. 15823, p. 17, memorandum, Lettow to Oppen, 26 July 1916.

16. Cf. ibid., Nr. 15818, pp. 24, 27, 32, reports of Charlottenburg police chief, 7, 8 May 1916.

17. Ibid., Nr. 15819, p. 59, report, Schade, 17 Aug. 1916.

18. Cf. Deist, *Militär- und Innenpolitik*, 1:409, 420–21. On Bethmann and a new orientation, cf. ibid., 649–802.

19. Ibid., 380, 384–85, 399.

20. Cf. BAL, 07.01, Nr. 2421, p. 277, memorandum, Privy Councillor Klitzing, 11 May 1916.

21. "Das tägliche Brot: Vom Kriegsernährungsamt," *Vorwärts*, 15 July 1916.

22. See Feldman, *Army, Industry, and Labor*, 108. Cf., however, Oppen's comment that "the renewed feeling of security arising from the naming of Hindenburg as chief of staff of the army is strongly compromised only by concerns for the provisioning difficulties" (BLHA, PPB, Nr. 15819, p. 125, mood report, Oppen, 2 Sept. 1916).

23. Cf. Deist, *Militär- und Innenpolitik*, 1:386, 408, 421.

24. For a fuller discussion, see Feldman, *Army, Industry, and Labor*, 190–96.

25. See OHL communications, e.g., in Deist, *Militär- und Innenpolitik*, 1:421, in which Max Bauer asserts the "necessity of the drastic intervention of the highest military authorities."

26. Cf. ibid., 429–36.

27. See *Schulthess' Europäischer Geschichtskalender*, vol. 57, pt. 1, 11 Oct. 1916.

28. BLHA, PPB, Nr. 15819, p. 251, report, Dittmann, 12 Oct. 1916.

29. Cf. ibid., p. 286, report, König, 23 Nov. 1916; p. 282, report, Faßhauer, n.d. [ca. 23 Nov. 1916].

30. "Unzulänglichkeiten," *Tägliche Rundschau*, 19 Dec. 1916; cf. "Ganswucher," ibid., 20 Dec. 1916.

31. BLHA, PPB, Nr. 15818, p. 264, report, Görl, 22 June 1916.

32. See BAL, 15.01, Nr. 12478, pp. 7, 10, 24–28, monthly report, 3 Jan. 1917. Cf. accounts of peace protesters joining bread rioters in Hamburg, in Ullrich, *Kriegsalltag*, 48–62.

33. Cf. *Der Interfraktionelle Ausschuß*, 1:xi–xiii; Deist, *Militär- und Innenpolitik*, 1:248–89; LAB, HLA, Nr. 42-187(2), memorandum, n.d. [early 1917], in which the goals of the League of German Women's Groups are also spelled out in terms of the new orientation. Cf. Feldman, *Army, Industry, and Labor*, 19–22.

34. See Winnig, *Neuorientierung*, and the SPD appeal of July 1916, reprinted in *Schulthess' Europäischer Geschichtskalender*, vol. 57, pt. 1 (1916). Cf. Miller, *Burgfrieden*, 284–87.

35. Cf. Gutsche, "Bethmann Hollweg"; Miller, *Burgfrieden*, 284–87. By 1917 even the military leadership assumed this language, though not unselfconsciously. Cf. Deist, *Militär, Staat*, 94.

36. See Nolan, *Visions of Modernity*, on Germans' ambivalence toward rationalization and close government direction of the economy. Cf. Hatry, "Shop Stewards at Renault."

37. "Das Sozialdemokratische Steuerideal," *Germania*, 19 Mar. 1916.

38. Center Party leader Dr. Julius Bachem, printed in *Der Tag*, reprinted in "Zentrum und Neuorientierung," *Vorwärts*, 13 July 1916.

39. Cited in Feldman, *Army, Industry, and Labor,* 104–5.

40. Cf. Bethmann Hollweg, *Betrachtungen,* 215.

41. See also Fuchs, *Deutsche Volkswirtschaft im Kriege;* Köppe, *Kriegswirtschaft und Sozialismus;* Heuss, *Kriegssozialismus;* Rubner, *Deutschlands Volksernährung;* and the KEA defense, Hesse, *Freie Wirtschaft.* Cf., before the war, Dawson, *Bismarck and State Socialism.*

42. Cf. Zunkel, *Industrie und Staatssozialismus.*

43. Hesse, *Freie Wirtschaft,* 36.

44. Groener, *Lebenserinnerungen,* 551.

45. Merton, *Erinnernswertes,* 20.

46. Ibid., 12–13.

47. "Sozialismus von Heute," *Deutsche Tageszeitung,* 9 Dec. 1916.

48. Reichstag proceedings, 28 Oct. 1916, reprinted in *Vorwärts,* 29 Oct. 1916. Cf. Helfferich, *Der Weltkrieg,* 76, 85–92. Helfferich claimed his predecessor Delbrück enacted reforms too quickly.

49. GStAPK, 2.2.1, Rep. 72, p. 67, report, Berlepsch, 11 Dec. 1916.

50. Ibid., p. 170, report, Berlepsch, 9 Oct. 1916.

51. Ibid., p. 115, 21 Nov. 1916. Cf. "Vorgeplänkel zur Neuorientierung," *Vorwärts,* 26 Oct. 1916.

52. *Breslauer Tagewacht,* 9 Dec. 1916.

53. Rathenau, *Rathenau,* 218–22.

54. Cf., on Conservatives' reluctant adoption of other popular views, Planert, "Antifeminismus im Kaiserreich." On adoption of a "forced economy" in housing in late 1917, cf. Führer, *Mieter,* 15.

55. BLHA, PPB, Nr. 15818, p. 131, report, Schiller, 25 May 1916. Wilhelmine officials were not on the whole champions of a free market before the war, but this apparent widespread philosophical conviction was something new.

56. "'Laß das Fleisch die Berliner ruhig fressen!,'" *Berliner Volkszeitung,* 27 May 1916.

57. GStAPK, 2.2.1, Rep. 72, p. 187, report, Berlepsch, 9 Oct. 1916.

58. See also "Der Mangel der Kohlenzufuhr," *Berliner Tageblatt,* 21 Jan. 1917.

59. *Vorwärts* and other newspapers provocatively voiced popular concern regarding the "disappearance from the scene" of different foods. Cf., in *Vorwärts,* "Wo bleibt die Magermilch?," 22, 25 Nov. 1916; "Wo bleibt der Sauerkohl?," 2, 12 Dec. 1916; "Wo ist die Soda geblieben?," 12 Dec. 1915. Cf., in *Berliner Volkszeitung,* "Wo bleibt die Marmelade? Ein Notschrei," 22 Nov. 1916; "Die verkrümelte Marmelade," 25 Nov. 1916.

60. BLHA, PPB, Nr. 15819, pp. 258–59, report, Klonicki, 7 Nov. 1916.

61. Ibid., p. 257, report, Rüschel, 4 Nov. 1916. Cf. pp. 242–43, memorandum, Privy Councillor Schlieben to Oppen, 26 Oct. 1916.

62. "Kuchen: Ein Stein im Weg der Brotversorgung," *Berliner Volkszeitung,* 4 Dec. 1916.

63. Cf. GStAPK, 2.2.1, Rep. 72, p. 19, report, Berlepsch, 21 Dec. 1916.

64. "Wer kauft die goldene Gans?," *Berliner Volkszeitung,* 7 Dec. 1916.

65. Cf. LAB, Rep. 142, Nr. 318, Council Committee on the Egg Question, 20 July 1916; GStAPK, 2.2.1, Rep. 197A, Nr. II K 5, p. 48.

66. Cf. "Aus Gross-Berlin: Über die Nahrungsmittelversorgung," *Vorwärts,* 15 Sept. 1916.

67. Ibid.

68. See, e.g., "Fleischlose Tage: Eine unzeitmässige Beschränkung," *Vossische Zeitung,* 4 Oct.

1916; "Zwei Wursttage in Berlin," *Berliner Tageblatt,* 2 Nov. 1916; BLHA, PPB, Nr. 15819, p. 147, mood report, Oppen, 16 Sept. 1916; Theodor Wolff, *Tagebücher,* 1:316–17.

69. "'Jedermann ein Ei,'" *Vorwärts,* 24 Dec. 1916.

70. GStAPK, 2.2.1, Rep. 197A, Nr. II K 5, p. 37, n.d. [ca. October 1916]; "Die verkrümelte Marmelade," *Berliner Volkszeitung,* 25 Nov. 1916.

71. "In der Reichshauptstadt: Ein Erfolg der Butterkarte," *Norddeutsche Allgemeine Zeitung,* 3 Apr. 1916.

72. Cf. "Die verkrümelte Marmelade," *Berliner Volkszeitung,* 25 Nov. 1916.

73. See "Die ersten Konserven: Eine Prämie auf die Hamsterei," *Berliner Volkszeitung,* 22 Mar. 1917. Cf. "Freie Bahn den Hamstern!," *Vorwärts,* 14 Dec. 1916, and "Mehr Ergebenheit," *Berliner Lokal Anzeiger,* 5 July 1916. Compare GStAPK, 2.2.1, Rep. 72, p. 109, report, Berlepsch, 11 Nov. 1916, and p. 187, 9 Oct. 1916; "Die Verteilung der Lebensmittel in Groß-Berlin," *Berliner Tageblatt,* 9 Nov. 1916.

74. Deist, *Militär- und Innenpolitik,* 1:402. Cf. BAL, 15.01, Nr. 12478, 3 July 1916.

75. "Milchpolonaisen," *Berliner Tageblatt,* 17 Nov. 1916. Cf., in Weimar, "Bei mir, nee, da hungert keena—Eine Berliner Arbeiterfrau kauft ein," in Flemming, Saul, and Witt, *Familienleben,* 78–79.

76. "Mangel an Brot: Überfluss des teueren Kuchen," *Berliner Morgenpost,* 3 Nov. 1916.

77. BLHA, PPB, Nr. 15820, p. 47, report, Schrott, 18 Dec. 1916. Cf. Nr. 15819, p. 244, report, Schrott, 11 Oct. 1916, and p. 282, report, Faßhauer, n.d. [ca. 23 Nov. 1916].

78. See, e.g., LAB, HLA, 42-187(2), p. 109, 26 Nov. 1916.

79. Cf. "Was werden wir Essen?," *Tägliche Rundschau,* 10 Dec. 1916; Robert Schmidt, "Ungleichheit in der Volksernährung," *Vorwärts,* 14 Dec. 1916; BLHA, PPB, Nr. 15819, pp. 251–52, mood report, Dittmann, 12 Oct. 1916, and Nr. 15820, p. 46, mood report, Schade, 18 Dec. 1916; "Unzulänglichkeiten," *Tägliche Rundschau,* 19 Dec. 1916.

80. See discussion in *Die Gleichheit* in the weeks following the conference, including "Frauenarbeit und ihre Konsequenzen," 1 Nov. 1916, and Berlepsch's observation of widespread debate, GStAPK, 2.2.1, Rep. 72, p. 102, report, Berlepsch, 1 Nov. 1916. Cf., in advance of the conference, BLHA, PPB, Nr. 15851, p. 84, report, Linde to Loebell, 29 Oct. 1916.

81. Cf. "Rübner über die Volksernährung," *Deutsche Tageszeitung,* 2 Nov. 1916.

82. "Was werden wir Essen?," *Tägliche Rundschau,* 10 Dec. 1916.

83. "Die Verteilung der Lebensmittel in Groß-Berlin," *Berliner Tageblatt,* 9 Nov. 1916.

84. Merton, *Erinnernswertes,* 16, cf. 21; Michaelis, *Für Staat und Volk,* 287. The *Mittelstand,* composed of urban and rural members, was thereby torn apart in war. Compare Kocka, *Facing Total War,* 84; Moeller, *German Peasants.*

85. BLHA, PPB, Nr. 15819, p. 83, mood report, Oppen, 19 Aug. 1916. Oppen notes the influence of those traveling for vacation to the east in bringing back this news to the city. Cf. Jo Mihaly, . . . *da gibt's ein Wiedersehn!;* the author's mother travels regularly between Berlin and Schneidemühl, observing the far better provisioning possibilities in the latter.

86. Wermuth, *Ein Beamtenleben,* 373.

87. Skalweit, *Kriegsernährungswirtschaft,* 45.

88. See "Batocki über Nahrungsmittelversorgung," *Vorwärts,* 13 Dec. 1915. Cf. Skalweit, *Kriegsernährungswirtschaft,* 41.

89. Municipal assembly meeting, 6 July 1916, recorded in "Massenspeisung," *Vorwärts,* 7 July 1916. Liberal representative Mommsen responded, "This is a matter of a necessity of the

war, which must be taken care of. Oppositions between the populations of means and those without means must not be played out here. No one has as yet succumbed to hunger in Berlin." To this statement he heard "much opposition."

90. Beginning in January, urban dwellers' normal ration was three-quarters of a pound of potatoes per week, compared with one pound for rural dwellers. This was especially egregious, as the cold season marked a time of particular strain for urban dwellers, who had to stand in lines for hours on end, while farmers actually required less caloric intake than in seasons of planting or harvesting.

91. Michaelis, *Für Staat und Volk*, 283.

92. Officials also responded by planting bad press about the cities. Wermuth retorted, "It is . . . completely wrong to regard the cities as a flaming champion of the forced economy." Wermuth, *Ein Beamtenleben*, 375. Cf. Lenz, *Lebensmittel-Zulagen*.

93. BLHA, PPB, Nr. 15820, pp. 55–56, report, Klonicki, 20 Dec. 1916.

94. Ibid., p. 46, report, Schade, 18 Dec. 1916. Cf. Sichler and Tibertius's discussion of "fatherlandless industrialists," cited in Feldman, *Army, Industry, and Labor*, 164.

95. Robert Schmidt, "Ungleichheit in der Volksernährung," *Vorwärts*, 14 Dec. 1916. Cf. Michaelis, *Für Staat und Volk*, 287; GStAPK, 2.2.1, Rep. 72, p. 19, report, Berlepsch, 21 Dec. 1916.

96. Cited in Roerkohl, *Hungerblockade*, 61.

97. GStAPK, 2.2.1, Rep. 72, p. 19, report, Berlepsch, 21 Dec. 1916.

98. Bavarians naturally saw the situation differently. See, on "Prussian-hate," Ay, *Entstehung*, 134–48; on anti-Berlin sentiment, see Martin Geyer, *Verkehrte Welt*, 115. A Hamburger army reservist commented, "We wouldn't have been worse off under the Russians or French" (Ullrich, *Kriegsalltag*, 100). Anti-Berlin sentiments only grew as officials began setting rations by city size, according slightly less to cities of populations under 10,000.

99. "Die Verteilung der Lebensmittel in Groß-Berlin," *Berliner Tageblatt*, 9 Nov. 1916. Cf. "Der Fettganspreis," ibid., 15 Nov. 1916.

100. "Ungenügende Lebensmittel-Versorgung in Berlin," *Berliner Morgenpost*, 10 Dec. 1916. On the Rhenish provisioning crisis, cf. Roerkohl, *Hungerblockade;* Tobin, "War and the Working Class"; Faust, *Sozialer Burgfrieden*.

101. See, e.g., "Rübner über die Volksernährung," *Deutsche Tageszeitung*, 2 Nov. 1916; GStAPK, 2.2.1, Rep. 72, pp. 19, report, Berlepsch, 21 Dec. 1916; BLHA, PPB, Nr. 15820, pp. 55–56, report, Klonicki, 20 Dec. 1916. On Jewish Germans and anti-Semitism in World War I, see Egmont Zechlin, *Juden und Antisemitismus in Weltkrieg;* Werner E. Mosse, *Deutsches Judentum;* C. Picht, "Zwischen Vaterland und Volk," in Michalka, *Der Erste Weltkrieg*, 736–55.

102. See Zechlin, *Juden und Antisemitismus in Weltkrieg*, 521.

103. Reichs-Hammer-Bund pamphlet, in EVK, Rep. 7, Nr. 2950, p. 24, Mar. 1916.

104. Cf. BLHA, PPB, Nr. 15810, p. 351, report, Schwarz, 27 June 1915; p. 208, mood report, Jagow, 1 May 1915. Raymond Wolff, "Zwischen formaler Gleichberechtigung," avers that Berlin was the center of the "Jewish Question" before the war. Cf. Boehlich, *Antisemitismusstreit;* Rürup, *Jüdische Geschichte;* Geisel, *Im Scheunenviertel*.

105. BLHA, PPB, Nr. 15819, p. 83, mood report, Oppen, 19 Aug. 1916. "Predominantly Jews" refers to middlemen, not Prussian producers, but the comment points up how in this period the description "Jewish" came to refer to a type of behavior. The author's use of the passive and other stylistic devices give the sense that "all" feel this way. Cf. Medick, *Weben und Überleben*, 561–79. The deputy commanders' monthly reports and contemporary memoirs indicate significant nationwide anti-Semitism in this period.

106. BLHA, PPB, Nr. 15818, p. 174, mood report, Oppen, 10 June 1916.

107. Cf., on the association of Jews and pigs, Wellmann, *Meine Mutter,* 92–103, 158.

108. Cf. BLHA, PPB, Nr. 15817, p. 118, postcard, private citizen to Jagow, 20 Mar. 1916, also identifying tight connections between rich Jewish merchants in Germany and other "outsiders."

109. Ibid., Nr. 15820, p. 45, mood report, Oppen, 25 Nov. 1916.

110. "Die Judenzählung von 1916: Ein Protest von Philipp Scheidemann," *Vorwärts,* 21 Oct. 1916. Authorities in turn hinted at the prominence of Jews among SPD leaders; GStAPK, 2.2.1, Rep. 72, p. 102, report, Berlepsch, 1 Nov. 1916.

111. The population of Jews in Greater Berlin rose from 36,326 in 1871 to 142,289 in 1910, still less than .5 percent. Berlin was home to 26.9 percent of all Jewish Germans in wartime. Cf. Wertheimer, *Unwelcome Strangers;* Raymond Wolff, "Zwischen formaler Gleichberechtigung," 127–28. Politically, Jews were most strongly associated with leftist liberalism.

112. EVK, Rep. 7, Nr. 2950, p. 43, letter from a member of the Reichs-Hammer-Bund to Evangelical Consistorium, 17 Nov. 1916.

113. BLHA, PPB, Nr. 15817, report, Berthefel, 28 Aug. 1916.

114. "Die Judenzählung von 1916: Ein Protest von Philipp Scheidemann," *Vorwärts,* 21 Oct. 1916.

115. See Zechlin, *Juden und Antisemitismus,* 518.

116. BLHA, PPB, Nr. 15819, p. 55, mood report, Oppen, 5 Aug. 1916. The ban lasted from 2 through 6 August.

117. "Die Judenzählung von 1916: Ein Protest von Philipp Scheidemann," *Vorwärts,* 21 Oct. 1916; "Zur Judenzählung von 1916," ibid., 25 Oct. 1916. Cf. Angress, "Das Deutsche Militär." On Bauer's anti-Semitism, see Feldman, *Army, Industry, and Labor,* 151. Religious orientation was always indicated in German censuses. Authorities released the survey as Hindenburg attempted to draft all available manpower and to put the remaining population in war-industry factories. Many Jews hoped that the war would provide an opportunity for them to prove definitely their place as "real Germans." See Gläser, *Class of 1902,* 9–16; *Kriegsbriefe.*

118. "Die Judenzählung von 1916: Ein Protest von Philipp Scheidemann," *Vorwärts,* 21 Oct. 1916.

119. See, e.g., BLHA, PPB, Nr. 15819, pp. 253–54, report, Lobiecki, n.d. [ca. 12 Oct. 1916].

120. See Chickering, *We Men Who Feel Most German,* 38.

121. Cynical suggestions ranged from *Vossische Zeitung*'s "to the German army" (*dem deutschen Heere*) to "entry only for lords" (*Eingang nur für Herrschaften*), with the double entendre of feudal lords and sovereign authority. See Cullen, *Reichstag,* 313–25; cf. Cullen's columns in the *Süddeutsche Zeitung,* 28, 29 Aug. 1981, and in the *Tagesspiegel,* 26 July 1981.

122. *Vorwärts,* 7 Dec. 1894, from Cullen, *Reichstag,* 313.

123. *Der Interfraktionelle Ausschuß,* 1:157.

CHAPTER SEVEN

1. See Krüger, *Die Massenspeisung,* 3. Cf. on early war, e.g., Abraham, *Drei Kriegsjahre;* Simon, *Das Kriegs-Ernährungsproblem;* Phillip Stein, *Kriegshilfsmaßnahmen deutscher Städte;* Harnack, *Krieg und die Frauen;* Roerkohl, *Hungerblockade,* 230–60. Compare LAB, Rep. 142, Nr. 316, p. 20, Städtetag report, n.d. [ca. 1 June 1916]; Gottstein, "Volksspeisung, Schulkinderspeisung, Notstandsspeisung, Massenspeisung"; Harald Dehne, "Hauptsache: Ordnung. Hungrige Kinder, Schul-

speisung und der Berliner Rektorenprotest von 1895," in Gailus and Volkmann, *Kampf um das tägliche Brot,* 258–81, on the prewar system.

2. Cf. Kaeber, *Berlin im Weltkriege,* 148.

3. Cf. BLHA, PPB, Nr. 15819, p. 92, report, Chief of Staff Lettow, High Command, to the War Ministry, 3 Aug. 1916; p. 278, mood report, Oppen, 28 Oct. 1916; BAL, 15.01, Nrs. 12478–79, special reports on mass dining from December 1916 on.

4. Cf. Wermuth, *Ein Beamtenleben,* 380.

5. See LAB, Rep. 142, Nr. 316, p. 20, Städtetag report, n.d. [ca. 1 June 1916]; Kaeber, *Berlin im Weltkriege,* 144.

6. Berlin city representative Hintze, municipal meeting, 6 July 1916, in "Massenspeisung," *Vorwärts,* 7 July 1916. On Hamburg's relative success, cf. Zodtke-Heyde, *Ausbildung von Leiterinnen;* Thomas, *Die Massenspeisung.*

7. See proceedings of the groups' expansive July conference in Berlin, *Praktische Durchführung.*

8. Luther, "Das Problem der Massenspeisung," 3.

9. Kaeber, *Berlin im Weltkriege,* 144.

10. LAB, Rep. 142, Nr. 316, p. 20, Städtetag discussion, n.d. [ca. 1 June 1916].

11. Theodor Wolff, *Tagebücher,* 1:377, 9 May 1916.

12. Cf., for sites, "Andrang zur Volksspeisung," *Vorwärts,* 10 Dec. 1916.

13. See Heyl, *Drei Monate Volksspeisung.* The system developed in 1853 Elberfeld negatively marked most prewar institutions for the distribution of food to the needy. Born of the experience of the famine of 1847, the Elberfeld system symbolized Prussian attitudes toward public welfare that spanned the second half of the century.

14. "Das tägliche Brot," *Vorwärts,* 1 June 1916.

15. Cf. report on the municipal assembly of 6 July 1916, *Vorwärts,* 7 July 1916. Clients had to give up two-thirds of their potato rations and seven-tenths of their meat coupons for the week. The Social Democratic faction had pressed for a lesser amount.

16. Batocki planned to allocate remaining reserves of food to the public kitchens; see BAL, 07.01, Nr. 2324, pp. 16–16a, memorandum, Batocki to Bethmann, 2 June 1916. These supplies were, however, rapidly exhausted.

17. Cf. "Massenspeisung," *Vorwärts,* 7 July 1916.

18. Skalweit, *Kriegsernährungswirtschaft,* 47. Cf. Daniel, *Arbeiterfrauen,* 203.

19. Harnack, *Krieg und die Frauen,* reprinted in BAL, 15.01, Nr. 12478, p. 29, 3 Jan. 1917. In the fall of 1916 Harnack, along with Marie-Elisabeth Lüders, headed the effort to bring women into war factories.

20. Krüger, *Die Massenspeisung,* 1.

21. "Aus Gross-Berlin: Die Eröffnung der Massenspeiseanstalt," *Vorwärts,* 9 July 1916; cf. "Die Küche der Sechstausend," ibid., 10 July 1916; "Die Massenspeisung erster Tag," ibid., 11 July 1916.

22. Cf. "Massenspeisung: Das erste Mittagsessen in der Tresckowstrasse," *Berliner Tageblatt,* 10 July 1916, evening edition; Skalweit, *Kriegsernährungswirtschaft,* 48. Cf. Daniel, *Arbeiterfrauen,* 203.

23. Cf. Dehne, "Dem Alltag ein Stück Näher?," 157, 160. Compare to *Tischgesellschaft,* dinner company from outside.

24. Zodtke-Heyde, introduction to *Ausbildung von Leiterinnen,* 5.

25. Kaeber, *Berlin im Weltkriege,* 150. See Theodor Thomas's frank embrace of a "dual system," in Thomas, *Die Massenspeisung,* 8.

26. See, e.g., BLHA, PPB Nr. 15818, p. 278, report, Dittmann, 6 June 1916; Nr. 15819, p. 3, report, Stolle, 8 July 1916, and p. 11, report, König, 18 July 1916.

27. See ibid., Nr. 15819, p. 249, report, Görl, 12 Oct. 1916.

28. Kaeber, *Berlin im Weltkriege,* 147–48. Cf. BLHA, PPB, Nr. 15819, p. 249, report, Görl, 12 Oct. 1916.

29. Luther, "Das Problem der Massenspeisung," 3, 8.

30. See "Städtische Massenspeisung," *Berliner Tageblatt,* 7 July 1916; "Massenspeisung," *Vorwärts,* 7 July 1916.

31. Compare Thomas, *Die Massenspeisung,* 3.

32. Cited in "Massenspeisung," *Vorwärts,* 7 July 1916. Cf. Thomas, *Die Massenspeisung,* 8, describing potential users as "free, upstanding citizens."

33. These statements appeared in the press throughout July; compare minutes of KAKI, included in BLHA, Pr. Br., Rep. 30, Berlin C, Titel 133, Nr. 18719, pp. 163–94, July 1916.

34. Kaeber claims that, except at one point in December, Berlin authorities made good on this promise; see Kaeber, *Berlin im Weltkriege,* 149. Skalweit offers a slightly less sanguine picture; see Skalweit, *Kriegsernährungswirtschaft,* 48.

35. Wermuth, at municipal assembly, 6 July 1916, reprinted in "Massenspeisung," *Vorwärts,* 7 July 1916.

36. "Die Massenspeisung in der Tresckowstrasse," *Berliner Tageblatt,* 13 July 1916.

37. Ibid.

38. See "Massenspeisung: Das erste Mittagsessen in der Tresckowstrasse," *Berliner Tageblatt,* 10 July 1916; "Aus Gross-Berlin: Die Eröffnung der Massenspeiseanstalt," *Vorwärts,* 9 July 1916.

39. Cf. Wittig, *Die 64. Kriegs-Volksküche,* 22–23, which also exemplifies the resurgence of the notion of the sacrificing consumer after the war.

40. Wiernik, *Die Arbeiterernährung,* 72. Cf. Thomas, *Die Massenspeisung.*

41. *Deutsche Tageszeitung,* 14 Aug. 1916, cited in Kaeber, *Berlin im Weltkriege,* 42; "Aus Gross-Berlin: Die Eröffnung der Massenspeiseanstalt," *Vorwärts,* 9 July 1916.

42. *Deutsche Tageszeitung,* 14 Aug. 1916, cited in Kaeber, *Berlin im Weltkriege,* 42.

43. *Deutsche Tageszeitung,* 14 Aug. 1916; "Aus Gross-Berlin: Die Eröffnung der Massenspeiseanstalt," *Vorwärts,* 9 July 1916; "Massenspeisung: Das erste Mittagsessen in der Tresckowstrasse," *Berliner Tageblatt,* 10 July 1916. The common themes in these three articles suggest they reflected official press releases.

44. "Aus Gross-Berlin: Die Eröffnung der Massenspeiseanstalt," *Vorwärts,* 9 July 1916. *Vorwärts* also emphasized growing numbers of participants. Cf., in *Vorwärts,* "Die Küche der Sechstausend," 10 July 1916; "Wachsende Beteiligung an der Massenspeisung," 12 Aug. 1916; "Mehr Zudrang zu den Massenspeisungen," 18 Aug. 1916; "Ausdehnung der Massenspeisung," 18 Nov. 1916; "Andrang zur Volksspeisung," 10 Dec. 1916.

45. Cf. also "Die Frage der Massenspeisungen," *Berliner Tageblatt,* 12 Dec. 1916. Such descriptions differentiated between "women" and "working women," and between "ladies" and "women." See "Massenspeisung: Das erste Mittagsessen in der Tresckowstrasse," *Berliner Tageblatt,* 10 July 1916; Kaeber, *Berlin im Weltkriege,* 146; Skalweit, *Kriegsernährungswirtschaft,* 47, on the zealous "dilettantism" of the program's coordinators.

46. GStAPK, 2.2.1, Rep. 72, p. 109, report, Berlepsch, 11 Nov. 1916.

47. See Krüger, *Die Massenspeisung,* 5–10.

48. Cf. Skalweit, *Kriegsernährungswirtschaft,* 43–45.

49. See SPD flyers, IML, V DF viii/132, ü, e.g., p. 82. August Bebel, who died in 1913, had long championed public dining halls to "free women up from the chains of the home" (Bebel, *Women under Socialism,* 185). Compare Vladimir Lenin's 1919 statement, "Public eating halls, day cares, kindergartens . . . are . . . the simplest, everyday means . . . appropriate *to emancipate women*" (cited in Dehne, "Dem Alltag ein Stück Näher?," 159).

50. See Calwer, *Ernährung* and *Zerfall der deutschen Volkswirtschaft.*

51. Minutes, meeting of the state presidents in Berlin, 11 Oct. 1916, cited in Daniel, *Arbeiterfrauen,* 202.

52. Merton, *Erinnernswertes,* 13–14.

53. GStAPK, 2.2.1, Rep. 197A, pp. 105–7, Minutes of discussion between representatives of the KEA and Städtetag, 31 Oct. 1916.

54. "Aus Gross-Berlin: Keine zwangsmässige Massenspeisung," *Vorwärts,* 12 Dec. 1916. See also in *Vorwärts,* "Kommt die Zwangsmassenspeisung?," 12 Dec. 1916, and Robert Schmidt, "Ungleichheit in der Volksernährung," 14 Dec. 1916.

55. Kaeber, *Berlin im Weltkriege,* 145. See, again, Skalweit's more dubious characterization, in Skalweit, *Kriegsernährungswirtschaft,* 40, 50.

56. Kaeber, *Berlin im Weltkriege,* 150.

57. Ibid., 146. The price may be misleading; adults may have required more than one portion. Cf. Daniel, *Arbeiterfrauen,* 204.

58. Kaeber, *Berlin im Weltkriege,* 150.

59. See "Ungenügende Lebensmittelversorgung in Berlin," *Berliner Morgenpost,* 10 Dec. 1916; BLHA, PPB, Nr. 15819, p. 147, mood report, Oppen, 16 Sept. 1916; p. 197, mood report, Oppen, 14 Oct. 1916; p. 278, mood report, Oppen, 28 Oct. 1916; p. 92, report, Chief of Staff Lettow, High Command, to the War Ministry, 3 Aug. 1916.

60. See "Ungenügende Lebensmittelversorgung in Berlin," *Berliner Morgenpost,* 10 Dec. 1916; "Andrang zur Volksspeisung," *Vorwärts,* 10 Dec. 1916. Most cities averaged 5 to 7 percent participation, above 10 percent only in the first months of 1917. See Skalweit, *Kriegsernährungswirtschaft,* 49–51. Cf. Roerkohl, *Hungerblockade,* 246–47.

61. BAL, 15.01, Nr. 12478, p. 38, 3 Dec. 1916.

62. BLHA, PPB, Nr. 15819, p. 59, Schade report, 17 Aug. 1916.

63. Cf., from spring 1916, BLHA, PPB, Nr. 15818, p. 147, letter, Paul Scholz to the Berlin Police Commission, 27 May 1916; Nr. 15819, p. 3, report, Stolle, 8 July 1916; Nr. 15851, reports on "women's reading evenings," e.g., p. 54, 6 July 1917; p. 76, 19 Sept. 1916; p. 87, 24 Sept. 1916.

64. See Daniel, *Arbeiterfrauen,* 227.

65. Cf. Robert Schmidt, "Ungleichheit in der Volksernährung," *Vorwärts,* 14 Dec. 1916; "Aus Gross-Berlin: Die Vieh- und Fleischverteilung in Berlin," ibid., 19 Oct. 1916.

66. See, e.g., BAL, 15.01, Nr. 12478, pp. 7–8, 3 Jan. 1917; pp. 8–9, 3 Feb. 1917.

67. Cf. Groener, *Lebenserinnerungen,* 552–55.

68. Skalweit, *Kriegsernährungswirtschaft,* 45.

69. Ibid.

70. See Roerkohl, *Hungerblockade,* 237.

71. Cf. speech of Professor Thiess, KEA, reprinted in *Berliner Lokal Anzeiger,* 8 Nov. 1916. The speech offers indications of the great schisms among the upper echelons of government.

72. "Was werden wir Essen?," *Tägliche Rundschau,* 10 Dec. 1916.

73. See Robert Schmidt, "Ungleichheit in der Volksernährung," *Vorwärts,* 14 Dec. 1916. It is possible, in the transformations of the war years, that Schmidt was also author of the regular column in the National Liberal *Tägliche Rundschau* signed "R. Sch.," the author of which also pleaded for heavy intervention.

74. "Die Massenspeisungen in den Großstädten," *Deutsche Tageszeitung,* 23 Dec. 1916. The author cites as his authority (male) mayor Dr. Fromhold of Stade, writing in the *Korrespondenz für Kriegswohlfahrtspflege.* See Fromhold's position also in *Praktische Durchführung.*

75. See ADW, CA 734, 3 Jan. 1917, memorandum of the Evangelical Women's Organization, citing the role of (bourgeois) women in the Frauenarbeitszentrale and in the Fürsorgever-mittelungsstellen.

76. Merton, *Erinnernswertes,* 13–14.

77. Skalweit, *Kriegsernährungswirtschaft,* 46–7.

78. Thomas, *Die Massenspeisung,* 10.

79. Harnack, cited in Daniel, *Arbeiterfrauen,* 203.

80. Cited by Skalweit, *Kriegsernährungswirtschaft,* 44. See also IML, V DF viii/132, ü, p. 82, SPD flyers bearing claims to champion the cause of "what women want."

81. "Aus Gross-Berlin: Keine Zwangsmässige Massenspeisung," *Vorwärts,* 12 Dec. 1916.

82. Cf. BLHA, PPB, Nr. 15819, p. 200, report, Schade, 25 Oct. 1916; p. 208, report, König, 25 Oct. 1916; p. 250, report, König, 12 Oct. 1916.

83. Municipal and Prussian officials discussed the possibility of instituting public kitchens for war dependents alone in Berlin, as existed in other German cities, but they quickly voted this notion down. See BLHA, Pr. Br., Rep. 30, Berlin C, Titel 133, Nr. 18719, minutes of KAKI. Cf. report on the municipal assembly, *Vorwärts,* 7 July 1916, and "Die Erwerbsarbeit der Frauen im Kriege," *Vorwärts,* 5 Nov. 1916.

84. See Calwer, *Ernährung;* Engelhardt, *Zentralisation.* Cf. Roerkohl, *Hungerblockade,* 235.

85. See, e.g., GStAPK, 2.2.1, Rep. 72, p. 109, report, Berlepsch, 11 Nov. 1916.

86. Cf. Calwer, *Zerfall der deutschen Volkswirtschaft;* Skalweit, *Kriegsernährungswirtschaft,* 45–47. In many areas dining programs remained an anarchic tangle of public and private facilities.

87. "Volksernährung und Massenspeisung," *Berliner Allgemeine Zeitung,* 8 Mar. 1917.

88. Cf. Theodor Wolff, *Tagebücher,* 1:479. Other schools were turned into lazarettos.

89. Cf. Robert Schmidt, "Ungleichheit in der Volksernährung," *Vorwärts,* 14 Dec. 1916.

90. BAL 15.01, Nr. 12478, p. 39, 3 Dec. 1917.

91. Skalweit, *Kriegsernährungswirtschaft,* 51.

92. See, e.g., Thomas, *Die Massenspeisung;* Zodtke-Heyde, introduction to *Ausbildung von Leiterinnen.*

93. Kaeber, *Berlin im Weltkriege,* 151. Cf. Skalweit, *Kriegsernährungswirtschaft,* 48; Phillip Stein, "Der Besuch der Massenspeisung."

94. Cf. "Volksernährung und Massenspeisung," *Berliner Allgemeine Zeitung,* 8 Mar. 1917.

95. Some facilities reopened after the war, in light of both food scarcity and a more positive valuation of such facilities. Cf. Kaeber, *Berlin im Weltkriege,* 151.

96. "Ungenügende Lebensmittelversorgung in Berlin," *Berliner Morgenpost,* 10 Dec. 1916.

97. "Volksernährung und Massenspeisung," *Berliner Allgemeine Zeitung,* 8 Mar. 1917.

98. Ibid.; BAL 15.01, Nr. 12478, p. 38, 12 Jan. 1916. See also LAB, Rep. 142, Nr. 316, Städtetag survey of cities to Batocki, 2 June 1916.

99. Michaelis, *Für Staat und Volk,* 286–87. Cf. BLHA, PPB, Nr. 15820, pp. 143–45, mood report, Oppen, 23 Dec. 1916. One hundred grams of the turnips humans normally consume pro-

vide 23 calories, 0.8 grams of protein, 0.2 grams of fat, 4.9 grams of carbohydrates, and 188 milligrams of potassium (Pennington and Church, *Food Values,* 160). Swede turnips are inferior as a source of these nutrients, as they contain far more indigestible fiber. But even considering figures for the more commonly consumed turnip, one would have to ingest over nine pounds of the root a day to receive 1,000 calories.

100. *Kölnische Zeitung,* 20 Sept. 1916, as cited by Skalweit, *Kriegsernährungswirtschaft,* 47.

101. "Was werden wir Essen?," *Tägliche Rundschau,* 10 Dec. 1916. Cf. Skalweit, *Kriegsernährungswirtschaft,* 7.

102. "Das tägliche Brot," *Vorwärts,* 1 June 1916.

103. See Yaney, *World of the Manager,* 205.

104. BLHA, PPB, Nr. 15819, p. 278, mood report, Oppen, 28 Oct. 1916.

105. Ibid., p. 207, report, Meier, 26 Oct. 1916. Compare postwar workers at Krupp, Essen, of whom about 25 percent used the firm's canteen. See Lüdtke, "Hunger, Essens-'Genuß' und Politik bei Fabrikarbeitern und Arbeiterfrauen," in Lüdtke, *Eigen-Sinn,* 205.

106. Cf. GStAPK, 2.2.1, Rep. 77, p. 61, Interior Ministry report, 1 Dec. 1916.

107. BLHA, PPB, Nr. 15819, p. 207, report, Meier, 26 Oct. 1916.

108. Ibid.

109. Ibid. See "Die Frage der Massenspeisung," *Berliner Tageblatt,* 12 Dec. 1916.

110. Cf. Kaeber, *Berlin im Weltkriege,* 150.

111. See, e.g., BLHA, PPB, Nr. 15820, pp. 43–45, mood report, Oppen, 25 Nov. 1916.

112. Cited in "Ein bedenklicher Schritt," *Deutsche Tageszeitung,* 7 Dec. 1916.

CHAPTER EIGHT

1. BAL, Rep. 15.01, Nr. 12478, p. 18, monthly report, 3 July 1917. Cf. Lüdtke, "Ihr könnt nun wissen, wie die Glocken eigentlich leuten sollen," in Lüdtke, *Eigen-Sinn,* 210–19.

2. LAB, Rep. 142, Nr. 1238, memorandum, Luther to the Steering Committee of the Städtetag, 14 Sept. 1916.

3. Cf. Stegerwald, *Zur Schwer- und Schwerstarbeiterversorgung,* 2.

4. Cf. BLHA, PPB, Nr. 15817, p. 94, report, Klonicki, 16 Mar. 1916.

5. Cf. "Bevorzugung schwächlicher Personen beim Lebensmitteleinkauf," *Berliner Lokal Anzeiger,* 30 Sept. 1916; "Ab 1. September neue Milchkarten: Eine bedenkliche Verordnung — unterschiedliche Behandlung der Kinder nach dem Alter," *Berliner Morgenpost,* 17 Aug. 1916.

6. Compare Kundrus, *Kriegerfrauen,* 51–62.

7. Cf. religious sources, such as "the milk of godly thinking." Compare Spalding, *Historical Dictionary,* 1692–93; *Duden,* 1015.

8. Spalding, *Historical Dictionary,* 1692.

9. Cf. "Bravo, Weimar," *Welt am Montag,* 18 Oct. 1915, and from *Vorwärts,* "Zur Milchversorgung," 16 Dec. 1915, and "Aus Groß-Berlin: Zur Sicherung der Milchversorgung" and "Das tägliche Brot: Milch und Butter," 21 Oct. 1915.

10. Kaeber, *Berlin im Weltkriege,* 217.

11. Cf. BLHA, PPB, Nr. 15813, p. 129, report, Jagow, 18 Sept. 1915; "Höchstpreise für Butter: Bevorstehendes Verbot gewerblicher Milchverwertung," *Berliner Morgenpost,* 17 Oct. 1915; "40 Pf. für einen Liter Milch," *Vorwärts,* 19 Oct. 1915; "Kindermilch — 8,00M," *Tägliche Rundschau,* 27 Oct. 1915; "Die Teuerung und ihre Folgen: Hilfe für die Bedrängten," *Der Deutsche*

Kurier, 15 Oct. 1915; "Das tägliche Brot: Regelung der Milch- und Schweinefleischpreise," *Vorwärts,* 5 Nov. 1915.

12. Rubner, "Ernährungswesen," 9; cf. "Halbheiten ohne Ende!," *Welt am Montag,* 6 Mar. 1916.

13. Wermuth, *Ein Beamtenleben,* 373. Aeroboe claims that milk delivery to Berlin was still at over half its prewar levels in 1916, or 486,000 liters per day versus approximately 900,000. See Aeroboe, *Einfluss des Krieges,* 90; cf. chart 8.1. Butter production in the city accounts for most of the discrepancy.

14. Cf. BLHA, PPB, Nr. 15817, p. 94, report, Klonicki, 16 Mar. 1916; Nr. 15818, pp. 264–65, report, Görl, 26 June 1916, and p. 257, mood report, Oppen, 24 June 1916; Nr. 15819, p. 51, report, König, 3 Aug. 1916.

15. See "Halbheiten ohne Ende!," *Welt am Montag,* 6 Mar. 1916; "Stallpreise und Kriegswürste," *Berliner Volkszeitung,* 18 Feb. 1916. Cf. "17 Landwirtsfrauen als Milchpanscherinnen," *Königsberger Volkszeitung,* 29 Feb. 1916.

16. Cf. Wermuth, *Ein Beamtenleben,* 373; Kaeber, *Berlin im Weltkriege,* 217, 220.

17. Until the war the last had constituted less than 10 percent of new mothers. In this era the numbers of women attempting to nurse for lack of alternatives rose, but their ability to nurse successfully fell sharply. See Rubner, "Der Gesundheitszustand im allgemeinen," 90–91.

18. LAB, Rep. 142, Nr. 318, secret meeting of Council Committee on Butter and Fat, 20 July 1916.

19. See "Nachahmenswert!," *Tägliche Rundschau,* 31 July 1916; the ordinance first appeared in *Gemeindeblatt* 31 (25 July 1916): 328.

20. BLHA, PPB, Nr. 15819, p. 51, report, König, 3 Aug. 1916.

21. See "Ab 1. September neue Milchkarten: Eine bedenkliche Verordnung—unterschiedliche Behandlung der Kinder nach dem Alter," *Berliner Morgenpost,* 17 Aug. 1916; Kaeber, *Berlin im Weltkriege,* 219. Nursing mothers could presumably drink their infants' rations themselves.

22. See, e.g., BLHA, PPB, Nr. 15819, pp. 127, 129, report, Büchel, 14 Sept. 1916; pp. 251–52, report, Dittmann, 12 Oct. 1916; "Milchpolonaisen," *Berliner Tageblatt,* 17 Nov. 1916. Cf. BAL, 15.01, Nr. 12478, p. 15, report from Hanover, 3 Sept. 1916.

23. See "Milchpolonaisen," *Berliner Tageblatt,* 17 Nov. 1916; BLHA, PPB, Nr. 15819, pp. 202, 206, mood report, Münn, 26 Oct. 1916; articles throughout October in *Vorwärts, Tägliche Rundschau,* and *Berliner Lokal Anzeiger;* still later, "Milchklagen," *Berliner Börsen Courier,* 2 Dec. 1916.

24. BLHA, PPB, Nr. 18717, n.p., memorandum, Berge to area police commissioners, 31 Oct. 1916. Outside Berlin, see BAL, Rep. 15.01, Nr. 12478, p. 35, 3 Dec. 1916; Roerkohl, *Hungerblockade,* 303–4.

25. See LAB, Rep. 142, Nr. 318, Städtetag memo, 28 Aug. 1916.

26. Cf. BLHA, PPB, Nr. 15819, p. 244, report, Schrott, 11 Oct. 1916.

27. See Skalweit, *Kriegsernährungswirtschaft,* 208–9.

28. "Milchpolonaisen," *Berliner Tageblatt,* 17 Nov. 1916.

29. Cf. LAB, Rep. 142, Nr. 318, Städtetag memo, 28 Aug. 1916.

30. See Skalweit, *Kriegsernährungswirtschaft,* 217; cf. GStAPK, 2.2.1, Rep. 72, p. 182, report, Berlepsch, 21 Oct. 1916, for a perplexing discussion of supplemental rations for schoolchildren, soldiers on leave, POWs, and domestic prisoners.

31. BLHA, PPB, Nr. 15819, pp. 202, 206, report, Münn, 26 Oct. 1916.

32. Cf. Martin Hahn, "Influenza, Genickstarre, Tetanus, Weilsche Krankheit," and Bern-

hard Möllers, "Tuberkulose," both in Bumm, *Deutschlands Gesundheitsverhältnisse,* 1:191–222, 327–52. In 1917 in Prussia overall, cases of tuberculosis rose almost 50 percent over the preceding year, to over 54,000 reported cases. Cf. BLHA, PPB, Nr. 15819, p. 208, report, König, 25 Oct. 1916. Compare C. Rollet, "The 'Other War' II," and J. Winter, "Surviving the War," both in Winter and Robert, *Capital Cities at War,* 456–86, 487–523.

33. See LAB, Rep. 142/2, Nr. 1238, 14 Sept. 1916.

34. BLHA, PPB, Nr. 18717, Price Monitoring Authority, Greater Berlin, to Greater Berlin police commissioners (political division), 24 Nov. 1916. Among early discussions, see LAB, Rep. 142, Nr. 318, secret meeting of Council Committee on Butter and Fat, 20 July 1916.

35. Some historians have emphasized the profusion of pronatalist rhetoric from certain quarters, pertaining especially to women's presumed duties after the war to compensate for the lost generation. See Usborne, "Pregnancy Is a Woman's Active Service"; Domansky, "Militarization and Reproduction." But there was little popular regard for pronatalist campaigns during the war and notably little official response to these efforts, above all after the accession of the Third Supreme Army Command to power. Compare, e.g., BAL, 15.01, Rep. 77, Nr. 9342, Ministerium des Innern, Maßregeln gegen den Geburtenrückgang, 4 Aug. 1915–30 June 1916; LAB, HLA, 40-179(3), letter, Bäumer to Bensheimer, 13 June 1916; E. E. Roesle, "Der Enfluß des Weltkrieges auf die Natalität," in Bumm, *Deutschlands Gesundheitsverhältnisse,* 1:9–21. On Austria, cf. Healy, "Divided Home."

36. Cf. "Mutter und Kind: Delegiertenversammlung des Deutschen Bundes für Mutterschutz," *Vorwärts,* 7 Nov. 1916.

37. Cf. LAB, HLA, 40-179(3), BDF policy on birthrate, 13 June 1916. See also Social Democratic warnings, "Frauenerwerbsarbeit und Arbeiterinnenschutz," *Vorwärts,* 26 Oct. 1916, and "Mutter und Kind: Delegiertenversammlung des Deutschen Bundes für Mutterschutz," *Vorwärts,* 7 Nov. 1916.

38. Compare BAL, 15.01, Rep. 77, Nr. 9342, Ministerium des Innern, Maßregeln gegen den Geburtenrückgang, 4 Aug. 1915–30 June 1916, on the "desired diminution" of births, particularly among working-class women. In Berlin, women terminated approximately one-quarter of all pregnancies, even before the war. See Berghahn, *Imperial Germany,* 73. Cf. Anna Bergmann, *Verhütete Sexualität;* Woyke, *Birth Control in Germany.* Reformers had already condemned the birthrate in 1913 as representing a birth strike. There is good evidence of amenorrhea in this period, at least among some segments of the population. Cf. Hugo Sellheim, "Frauenkrankheiten und Geburtshilfe," in Bumm, *Deutschlands Gesundheitsverhältnisse,* 291–317.

39. Recent work has focused on maternalist images of women as recipients (and distributors) of government aid and on women's political claims as mothers in modern Germany and Europe. Cf. Koven and Michel, *Mothers of a New World;* Bock and Thane, *Maternity;* Sachße, *Mütterlichkeit als Beruf;* Stoehr "Organisierte Mütterlichkeit"; A. T. Allen, *Feminism and Motherhood.* Contrast Canning, *Languages of Labor and Gender,* 170–217.

40. See, e.g., LAB, HLA, 40-179(3), Bäumer to Bensheimer, 18 Aug., 23 Dec. 1916. Compare Daniel, *Arbeiterfrauen,* 143–46; for Britain, see Pedersen, "Gender, Welfare, and Citizenship."

41. Compare Beck, *Frau und der Kriegsgefangene;* GStAPK, 2.2.1, Rep. 72, pp. 61–66, report, Berlepsch, 1 Dec. 1916, including concerns for black POWs. By late 1916 this image was largely displaced by a more positive image of women working in war factories.

42. Cf. "Kindermilch: 8.00M," *Tägliche Rundschau,* 27 Oct. 1915.

43. Compare Grossmann, *Reforming Sex.*

44. Cf. BLHA, PPB, Nr. 15819, p. 244, report, Schrott, 11 Oct. 1916.

45. Cf. ibid., Nr. 15817, p. 94, report, Klonicki, 16 Mar. 1916; pp. 121–23, mood report, Ludwig, 21 Mar. 1916; "Die Vorräte an Mehl und Kartoffeln in Groß-Berlin: Die Butterkarte für Groß-Berlin," *Berliner Tageblatt,* 10 Mar. 1916.

46. Cf. GStAPK-M, 2.2.1, Rep. 197A, Nr. II K, p. 106, letter, homeowner N. N. to Michaelis, 7 Mar. 1917.

47. Working-class women got married later and had fewer children on the eve of war than they had even a few decades earlier; prewar public discourse vacillated between condemning such women for having too many children and too few. Cf. Beier, *Frauenarbeit und Frauenalltag,* 72–73, which also indicates the need to distinguish between present children and those cared for and/or working elsewhere.

48. Cf. "Die Lebensmittelversorgung Groß-Berlins: Ein Vortrag," *Berliner Tageblatt,* 2 Sept. 1916; BLHA, PPB, Nr. 18719, p. 61, report, Dittmann, 17 Aug. 1916, and pp. 251–52, mood report, Dittmann, 12 Oct. 1916.

49. BLHA, PPB, Nr. 15816, p. 295, report, Dittmann, 16 Feb. 1916; Nr. 15819, p. 61, report, Dittmann, 17 Aug. 1916.

50. Cf. "Milchpolonaisen," *Berliner Tageblatt,* 17 Nov. 1916; "Milchklagen," *Berliner Börsen Courier,* 2 Dec. 1916. See also BLHA, PPB, Nr. 18717, PPS, Greater Berlin, to Greater Berlin police commissioners, 24 Nov. 1916.

51. Cf. "Hamburg: Neben der Lebensmittelversorgung des deutschen Volkes," *Hamburger Echo,* 12 Aug. 1916.

52. Compare BAL, 15.01, Nr. 12478, p. 39, 3 Dec. 1916.

53. Cf. BLHA, PPB, Nr. 15816, report, Dittmann, 12 Oct. 1916; Dr. Stephani, "Der Gesundheitszustand unter den Schulkindern," in Bumm, *Deutschlands Gesundheitsverhältnisse,* 1:115–30; Roerkohl, *Hungerblockade,* 305–12.

54. Compare UBD, File 215 320 72 02, Lebensmittelknappheit, 1918–20.

55. Cf. Kundrus, *Kriegerfrauen,* 203.

56. Ibid., 52.

57. See, e.g., BLHA, PPB, Nr. 15819, p. 147, report, Oppen, 16 Sept. 1916; pp. 247–48, report, Klonicki, 12 Oct. 1916; BAL, 15.01, Nr. 12478, p. 20, 3 Dec. 1916. Compare reports of great milk scarcity from Hanover, e.g., in BAL, 15.01, Nr. 12478, p. 15, 3 Sept. 1916.

58. See "Milchklagen," *Berliner Börsen Kurier,* 2 Dec. 1916. Cf. BAL, Rep. 15.01, Nr. 12478, p. 20, 3 Dec. 1916.

59. See "Neuregelung der Milchversorgung" and "Milch, Butter, und Eier," *Vorwärts,* 20 Oct. 1916. This strategy was nothing new for industrial cartels in wartime. Cf. Feldman, *Great Disorder,* 56.

60. "Misere in der Milch- und Fettversorgung," ibid., 14 Dec. 1916. See also the juxtaposition of "Vieh- und Fleischfragen" and "Milch, Butter, und Eier," under the Reichstag Budget Committee discussion, in *Vorwärts,* 29 Oct. 1916.

61. See the often-cited memo from Hindenburg to Bethmann, 13 Sept. 1916, included in Sichler and Tibertius, *Arbeiterfrage,* 106–7. See also the rise of "race hygiene" rhetoric in the war, in Daniel, *Arbeiterfrauen,* 154–55.

62. LAB, Rep. 142, Nr. 318, Meat and Fat Committee Meeting, 18 Jan. 1917.

63. See "Kriegsamt und Kriegsernährungsamt," *Vorwärts,* 7 Nov. 1916.

64. Spalding, *Historical Dictionary,* 1692.

65. This is clear in G. W. Pabst's 1925 film *Die freudlose Gasse,* in which a woman trades sex-

ual favors for a piece of meat—flesh for flesh—for her family. This film played over a year in Berlin cinemas.

66. Cf. Spalding, *Historical Dictionary,* 814–15.

67. See "Die Erzeugung," *Der Deutsche Kurier,* 11 Sept. 1916.

68. Cf. Lüders, *Das Unbekannte Heer,* 84. Popular suspicion of men who did not join military service contributed to this transformation.

69. Stegerwald, *Zur Schwer- und Schwerstarbeiterversorgung,* 43.

70. Groener, *Lebenserinnerungen,* 335.

71. Cf. BLHA, PPB, Nr. 15818, p. 174, report, Oppen, 10 June 1916.

72. Hindenburg took control on 28 August; Ludendorff and Bauer drafted the eponymous weapons program by 31 August. By 13 September the OHL had breached the customary jurisprudence of military territory. See Feldman, *Army, Industry, and Labor,* 176. In actuality Hindenburg's plan did not depart radically from Wild's expansive plan.

73. See Kocka, *Facing Total War,* 26–38; Lüders, *Das Unbekannte Heer,* 86. Cf. Annemarie Lange, *Das Wilhelminische Berlin,* 655–60; Homburg, *Rationalisierung und Industriearbeit.*

74. Cf. memorandum, Groener, 12 Dec. 1916, in Gersdorff, *Frauen im Kriegsdienst,* 119; Zietz, *Zur Frage der Frauenerwerbsarbeit;* Rathenau, *Rathenau,* 216. Compare Daniel, *Arbeiterfrauen,* 51, 74; Mai, *Kriegswirtschaft,* 190.

75. See Lorenz, *Gewerbliche Frauenarbeit,* 329.

76. Cf. Helene Lange, *Das "Weibliche Dienstjahr";* Bäumer, "Phantasien und Tatsachen"; Dammer, *Mütterlichkeit und Frauendienstpflicht;* Quataert, "German Patriotic Women's Work"; Boyd, "'Nationaler Frauendienst.'"

77. See Lüders, *Das Unbekannte Heer,* 86–87; Feldman, *Army, Industry, and Labor,* 182–83. Bethmann objected on "economic, moral, and social" grounds; see Gersdorff, *Frauen im Kriegsdienst,* 21.

78. Cf. "Die Erwerbstätigkeit der Frauen im Kriege," *Vorwärts,* 3 Nov. 1916; Lüders, *Das Unbekannte Heer,* 87.

79. Cf. BLHA, PPB, Nr. 15819, p. 158, mood report, Klonicki, 28 Sept. 1916; Nr. 15820, pp. 43–45, report, Oppen, 25 Nov. 1916; outside Berlin, see BAL, Nr. 12478, 3 Oct., 3 Nov. 1916.

80. Cf. Kitchen, *Silent Dictatorship,* 70. In Berlin at least, employers posted many more unfilled jobs for women than for men in this era. See, e.g., BLHA, PPB, Nr. 15819, p. 67, report, Görl, 17 Aug. 1916, which lists 5,085 current open jobs for women, versus 2,859 for men.

81. Groener, *Lebenserinnerungen,* 122, 340; compare ADW CA 734, Groener to Central Committee, Innere Mission, 12 Dec. 1916.

82. Lüders, *Das Unbekannte Heer,* 92, 96, reflecting a policy statement issued in late fall, before enactment of the VHDG.

83. See Levy-Rathenau, "Eingliederung."

84. See Lorenz, *Gewerbliche Frauenarbeit,* 336; Lüders, *Das Unbekannte Heer,* 85–90; H. Cunow, "Die Erwerbsarbeit der Frauen im Kriege," *Vorwärts,* 3 Nov. 1916. "Hard" labor does not signify skilled labor. Often the jobs requiring the most brute strength or entailing the least appealing conditions were unskilled or semiskilled. Officials did, however, take skill level into account.

85. LAB, HLA, Nr. 42-186 (1), p. c13, Bäumer to Reichstag Budget Committee, 24 Nov. 1916.

86. See Lüders, *Das Unbekannte Heer,* 86.

87. See LAB, HLA, 42-185 (3), G. Bäumer and A. Bensheimer to BDF organizations con-

cerning preliminary confidential arrangements with the War Office. Cf. Eifert, "Berliner 'Heimatfront' im Kriege."

88. See Daniel, *Arbeiterfrauen,* 81–8.

89. See ADW CA 734, Groener to Central Committee, Innere Mission, 12 Dec. 1916. Memoranda between December and February emphasize ever growing pressure, as the OHL became less and less willing to pull forces from the front. See documents, including War Office sanction for women to work at night in war factories, 4 Jan., 6 Feb. 1917; statement of the duties of the Women's Employment Bureau, 29 Jan. 1917; and memo permitting the "intensification of women's work in the munitions industry," 5 Feb. 1917, all in Gersdorff, *Frauen im Kriegsdienst,* 127–54.

90. See Groener, *Lebenserinnerungen,* 355; Merton, *Erinnernswertes,* 25; guidelines for organization of the Frauenreferat, 3 Jan. 1917, in Gersdorff, *Frauen im Kriegsdienst,* 125–26.

91. See Lüders, *Das Unbekannte Heer;* Boyd, "'Nationaler Frauendienst'"; Daniel, *Arbeiterfrauen,* 93–105, on the range of services offered through the Women's Bureau and through semiprivate bodies such as the Standing Committee for the Advancement of the Interests of Women Workers.

92. See LAB, HLA, Nr. 42-186 (1), BDF petition on the "protection of women workers"; Lüders, *Das Unbekannte Heer.* Cf. Daniel, *Arbeiterfrauen,* 81–88; Reagin, *German Women's Movement,* 187–202; Hausen, "German Nation's Obligations," 137. Compare Downs, *Manufacturing Inequality.*

93. See Lüders, *Das Unbekannte Heer,* 83. Compare Feldman, *Army, Industry, and Labor,* 222.

94. See Lüders, *Das Unbekannte Heer,* 92; cf. LAB, HLA, Nr. 42-186, pp. C8–9, BDF petition, 4 June 1917; ADW CA 734, meeting of NAFFIK, 3 Jan. 1917.

95. Lüders, *Das Unbekannte Heer,* 92. In light of the terrible harvest, producing food itself became a primary focus of the War Office; see Lorenz, *Gewerbliche Frauenarbeit,* 366.

96. These protections had been lifted "temporarily" on 4 Aug. 1914; cf. the debate on this in *Die Gleichheit* in the subsequent weeks, including "Frauenarbeit und ihre Konsequenzen," 1 Nov. 1916. The BDF brought a petition on the "protection of women workers" to the Reichstag in late 1916 to ensure physical and moral "regeneration" (from LAB, HLA, Nr. 42-186 [1]; n.d. [draft copy]). The petition suggested the BDF's concern that military authorities and industrialists conspired to single out women for dangerous and injurious jobs.

97. See Lüders, *Das Unbekannte Heer;* Stegerwald, *Zur Schwer- und Schwerstarbeiterversorgung,* 30. Compare the reprint from one year later, included in Stegerwald, 36–37.

98. BLHA, PPB, Nr. 15819, p. 92, report, Chief of Staff Lettow, Oberkommando, to War Ministry, 3 Aug. 1916.

99. GStAPK-M, 2.2.1, Rep. 77, p. 61, report, interior minister, 1 Dec. 1916.

100. *Correspondenzblatt,* 1 Jan. 1916. Cf. Feldman, *Army, Industry, and Labor,* 273.

101. See BLHA, PPB, Nr. 15820, pp. 43–45, mood report, Oppen, 25 Nov. 1916. It is not clear whether the women who felt slighted were the same as those who ultimately entered the factories.

102. See Lüders, *Das Unbekannte Heer,* 92.

103. Within Prussia, 101,178 servicemen were relieved by the entry of other populations into the war-industry workforce: 31,244 by men brought in by the VHDG; 2,878 by youths; 2,914 by men above the VHDG age limit; and 64,142 by women. See Lorenz, *Gewerbliche Frauenarbeit,* 329.

104. Wiernik, *Die Arbeiterernährung*, 44.

105. Lüders, *Das Unbekannte Heer*, 89.

106. Cf. ibid., 104–6; "Die Erwerbstätigkeit der Frauen im Kriege," *Vorwärts*, 3 Nov. 1916.

107. Stegerwald, *Zur Schwer- und Schwerstarbeiterversorgung*, 2; Wiernik, *Die Arbeiterernährung*, 53.

108. Stegerwald, *Zur Schwer- und Schwerstarbeiterversorgung*, 4. Cf. Skalweit, *Kriegsernährungswirtschaft*, 203.

109. See Stegerwald, *Zur Schwer- und Schwerstarbeiterversorgung*, 39.

110. Ibid., 43; Skalweit, *Kriegsernährungswirtschaft*, 213.

111. See Stegerwald, *Zur Schwer- und Schwerstarbeiterversorgung*, 43. It is unclear why authorities so little in control of actual supplies issued rations in amounts specific to tenths of a gram.

112. Cf. Dirk Müller, "Gewerkschaften Arbeiterausschüße und Arbeiterräte," in Mai, *Arbeiterschaft in Deutschland*, 155–78, German Metalworkers Union figures for December 1917. Compare Eifert, "Frauenarbeit im Krieg," 283, who sets the percentage of women in industry overall in Berlin at 65 in September 1916. Lorenz argues for a figure of just over one-third women in the armaments industries across the country. But if one subtracts the specially privileged categories as indicated above, the figure still climbs above 50 percent. See Lorenz, *Gewerbliche Frauenarbeit*, 329. Women's participation in these industries climbed to over 500 percent of that of the prewar era. See Lüders, *Das Unbekannte Heer*, 86. Women now filled up to 98 percent of many jobs within the war industries. See Gersdorff, *Frauen im Kriegsdienst*, 26; Daniel, *Arbeiterfrauen*, 88–97.

113. Cf. Lüders, *Das Unbekannte Heer*, 85, 92.

114. Ibid., 86–87. Among the regions obligated to report, Greater Berlin constituted the single industrial region in the country where the number of female workers was greater than that of all males in 1918, at a rate of 201,379 women to 176,841 men. See Lorenz, *Gewerbliche Frauenarbeit*, 349. The number of women working in Berlin in metal alone rose from 30,000 to 100,000 by mid-December 1916; women's membership in the Free Trade Unions spiraled in Berlin. Cf. "Die Frauenarbeit in der Berliner Metallindustrie," *Vorwärts*, 12 Dec. 1916; Heidrun Homburg, "Arbeiter, Gewerkschaften," in Glaeßner, Lehnert, and Sühl, *Studien*, 44–45. The continued rise in numbers after the end of the war did not correspond to women's much greater integration into the unions.

115. See Wiernik, *Die Arbeiterernährung*, 53.

116. Lenz, *Lebensmittel-Zulagen*, 26.

117. Cf. Stegerwald, *Zur Schwer- und Schwerstarbeiterversorgung*, 28.

118. See, e.g., Wiernik, *Die Arbeiterernährung*, 42–44; BAL, 15.01, Nr. 12478, p. 39, 3 Dec. 1916.

119. Wiernik, *Die Arbeiterernährung*, 43–44.

120. Cf. Umbreit, *Krieg und die Arbeitsverhältnisse*, 25; "Die Arbeiter und die Volksernährung," *Berliner Lokal Anzeiger*, 14 Apr. 1917.

121. See Zimmermann, "Veränderungen," 373; Lorenz, *Gewerbliche Frauenarbeit*, 332–33; Lüders, *Das Unbekannte Heer*, 90. In metal industries the wages of women rose sharply, from 28.9 to 51.4 percent of men's wages. See "Die Frauenarbeit in der Metallindustrie," *Vorwärts*, 12 Dec. 1916. Women's wages rose more modestly relative to men's in war industry across the country and across skill levels. See Daniel, *Arbeiterfrauen*, 111–17.

122. See, e.g., "Die Frauenarbeit in der Metallindustrie," *Vorwärts*, 12 Dec. 1916.

123. Cf. Max Bauer's negative view of women, including his theory of "pangynism," in Bauer, *Der Große Krieg*, e.g., 223.

124. See, e.g., Feldman, *Army, Industry, and Labor*, 149–50.

125. See, e.g., Hagemann, "'Heran, heran, zu Sieg oder Tod,'" which discusses this dilemma for women in the early nineteenth century.

126. On this retreat, see Daniel, *Arbeiterfrauen,* 259–65; Rouette, *Sozialpolitik;* Bessel, *Germany after the First World War.* Daniel marks this as one important sign that the war did not improve conditions for women.

127. Cf. "Die Erwerbstätigkeit der Frauen im Kriege," *Vorwärts,* 3 Nov. 1916; "Mehr Fett für die Industriearbeiter!," *Berliner Volkszeitung,* 17 Nov. 1916; "Die Frauenarbeit in der Berliner Metallindustrie," *Vorwärts,* 12 Dec. 1916; "Die Frage der Massenspeisung," *Berliner Tageblatt,* 12 Dec. 1916.

128. Stegerwald, *Zur Schwer- und Schwerstarbeiterversorgung,* 2. Stegerwald was the leader of the League of Christian Trade Unions.

129. Ibid., 4.

130. Groener saw this as a somewhat obsessive plan; see *Lebenserinnerungen,* 340. The law was the brainchild of Bauer; cf. *Der Große Krieg,* 153–55. The general notion predated the law.

131. Memo from Hindenburg to Bethmann, 13 Sept. 1916, cited in Sichler and Tibertius, *Arbeiterfrage,* 106–7. Hindenburg pushed unsuccessfully to apply this principle to war dependents as a condition of their separation allowances, as he did not consider their sacrifices "through their men" meaningful. In early discussions of an auxiliary service law, officials circulated the idea that "compulsory labor will be introduced for the entire population, perhaps in connection with the distribution of food." Cf. letter of 5 Sept. 1916, Moellendorf, technical adviser to the Weapons and Munitions Procurement Agency, to Fritz Haber, leader of the German chemical industry (and the future head of IG Farben), cited in Feldman, *Army, Industry, and Labor,* 171.

132. Rubner, "Ernährungswesen," 15–16. Offer concedes the dangerously inadequate level of nutrition during this winter. See Offer, *First World War,* 48–50.

133. Cf. BAL, 15.01, Nr. 12478, 3 Dec. 1916, "Allgemeine Stimmung." On rations, see Stegerwald, *Zur Schwer- und Schwerstarbeiterversorgung,* 40–41.

134. Theodor Wolff, *Tagebücher,* 1:492; H. Sivkovich in "Pflichten der Stunde," *Berliner Tageblatt,* 16 Feb. 1917; in Leipzig, Cooper, *Behind the Lines,* 182, 189.

135. Asta Nielsen, *Die schweigende Muse,* cited in Glatzer and Glatzer, *Berliner Leben, 1914–1918,* 265–66.

136. Cf. BAL, 15.01, Nr. 12478, p. 5, 3 Jan. 1917.

137. See Theodor Wolff, *Tagebücher,* 1:479n.

138. Cf. Schreiner, *Iron Ration,* 247–48.

139. See BLHA, PPB, Nr. 15819, p. 195, report, Büchel, 12 Oct. 1916; "Milchpolonaisen," *Berliner Tageblatt,* 17 Nov. 1916.

140. Cf. Asta Nielsen, *Die schweigende Muse,* cited in Glatzer and Glatzer, *Berliner Leben, 1914–1918,* 265; Kocka, *Facing Total War,* 26; BAPK, Nr. 1578, "Woman Collapsing."

141. See, e.g., BLHA, PPB, Nr. 15819, pp. 283–84, report, Dittmann, 23 Nov. 1916; Nr. 15820, p. 49, report, Dittmann, 19 Dec. 1916; p. 58, report, König, 20 Dec. 1916; pp. 143–45, report, Oppen, 23 Dec. 1916. The middle class used primarily gas to heat their homes.

142. *Berliner Tageblatt,* 6 Feb. 1917, cited in Theodor Wolff, *Tagebücher,* 1:479.

143. *Berliner Tageblatt,* 4 Jan. 1917, cited in Glatzer and Glatzer, *Berliner Leben, 1914–1918,* 301.

144. Cited in Glatzer and Glatzer, *Berliner Leben, 1914–1918,* 299.

145. See, e.g., BLHA, PPB, Nr. 15819, p. 208, report, König, 25 Oct. 1916; p. 250, mood report, König, 1 Dec. 1916.

146. See Bumm, *Deutschlands Gesundheitsverhältnisse;* Grotjahn, *Erlebtes und Erstrebtes;* Rubmann, *Hunger!*

147. Cf. E. E. Roesle, "Der Einfluß des Weltkrieges auf die Mortalität," in Bumm, *Deutschlands Gesundheitsverhältnisse,* 1:3–61.

148. Asta Nielsen, *Die schweigende Muse,* cited in Glatzer and Glatzer, *Berliner Leben, 1914–1918,* 265. Cf. Domansky, "Militarization and Reproduction."

149. See, e.g., BLHA, PPB, Nr. 15820, p. 46, report, Schade, 18 Dec. 1916; pp. 143–45, report, Oppen, 23 Dec. 1916; p. 198, report, Schrott/Büchel, 14 Feb. 1917. Cf., nationwide, BAL, 15.01, Nr. 12478, p. 11, 3 Dec. 1916, and pp. 4, 5, 3 Jan. 1917.

150. Ludendorff, *My War Memories,* 331.

151. BAL, 15.01, Nr. 12478, p. 39, 3 Dec. 1916; Stegerwald, *Zur Schwer- und Schwerstarbeiterversorgung,* 29.

152. See Michaelis, *Für Staat und Volk,* 276–7; Stegerwald, *Zur Schwer- und Schwerstarbeiterversorgung,* 28; Skalweit, *Kriegsernährungswirtschaft,* 47.

153. See Stegerwald, *Zur Schwer- und Schwerstarbeiterversorgung,* 34, 41; Wiernik, *Die Arbeiterernährung,* 78.

154. "Erhöhte Rationen für Beamte: Eine Abordnung bei Herrn von Batocki," *Berliner Tageblatt,* 7 Dec. 1916. Citing the *Beamten-Korrespondenz,* the article noted no response regarding the request to increase rations of bread, potatoes, and fat but cited Batocki's promise to raise for discussion at a KEA advisory board meeting the idea that civil servants' unions (like trade unions) should have representation on this body. Cf. BLHA, PPB, Nr. 15819, p. 282, report, Faßhauer, n.d. [ca. 23 Nov. 1916].

155. See Rubner, "Der Gesundheitszustand im allgemeinen"; Roerkohl, *Hungerblockade,* 307; Proctor, *Racial Hygiene,* 178.

156. Cf. BLHA, PPB, Nr. 15821, pp. 279–80, report, Schneider, 22 July 1917.

157. The BDF expressed great frustration at the lack of government support for such facilities relative to what they had expected; SPD efforts also fell far below expectation. See LAB, HLA, Nr. 42-186 (1), p. c13, Bäumer to Reichstag Budget Committee, 24 Nov. 1916. Before the war parents often felt forced to leave children alone while working, but not commonly under such particularly bad conditions.

158. See Rubner's vivid description, "Ernährungswesen," 14–30.

159. See, e.g., Kaeber, *Berlin im Weltkriege,* 144; report on the municipal assembly of 6 July 1916, *Vorwärts,* 7 July 1916.

160. Cf. BLHA, Pr. Br., Rep. 1A, Nr. 255, p. 91, SVS to Magistrat Berlin, 23 July 1917. Food was also especially scarce in the Ruhr region—another key center of the war industry.

161. See a representation of this idea in the Jean Renoir film *La Grande Illusion.*

162. Stegerwald, *Zur Schwer- und Schwerstarbeiterversorgung,* 7–8.

163. Cf. "Steglitzer Hausfrauen," *Die Post,* 4 November 1916; BLHA, PPB, Nr. 15820, pp. 143–45, report, Oppen, 23 Dec. 1916; Nr. 15819, p. 280, report, Büchel, 23 Nov. 1916.

164. "*Die Armen liefern die Leichen, der Mittelstand muß weichen, den Krieg gewinnen die Reichen,*" cited in Glatzer and Glatzer, *Berliner Leben, 1914–1918,* 265.

165. See "Die Vergeudung von Lebensmitteln," *Die Post,* 15 Nov. 1916; GStAPK, 2.2.1, Rep. 72, pp. 61–66, report, Berlepsch, 1 Dec. 1916; Lenz, *Lebensmittel-Zulagen,* 21; "Alles mogelt," *Welt am Montag,* 24 Dec. 1917. Cf. the startling suggestion that POWs be executed rather than take food from the mouths of "women" and "the cities," displacing the blame for food shortages back on the "outer enemy," in "Unverschämt wuchern und wucherische Händler,"

Reichsbote, 10 Apr. 1917. Authorities also took special status and supplements away from some categories of "hard laborers" outside the war industries.

166. "Mehr Fett für die Industriearbeiter!," *Berliner Volkszeitung,* 17 Nov. 1916.

167. Cf. economist Franz Eulenberg, cited in Roerkohl, *Hungerblockade,* 113; Annemarie Lange, *Das Wilhelminische Berlin,* 668.

168. "Wer kauft die goldene Kriegsgans?," *Berliner Volkszeitung,* 7 Dec. 1916; BLHA, PPB, Nr. 15819, p. 281, mood report, Schrott, 23 Nov. 1916, and Nr. 15820, pp. 143–45, report, Oppen, 23 Dec. 1916; "Soziales: Arbeitszwang für Kriegerfrauen," *Vorwärts,* 21 Oct. 1916; "Erhöhung der Kriegsunterstützung," *Vorwärts,* 12 Nov. 1916. Cf. BAL, 15.01, Nr. 12478, 3 Mar. 1917, "Allgemeine Stimmung," AK IX; Umbreit, *Krieg und die Arbeitsverhältnisse,* 69.

169. See, e.g., BLHA, PPB, Nr. 15820, p. 45, report, Oppen, 25 Dec. 1916; p. 188, report, Oppen, 22 Jan. 1917; p. 199, report, Gerhardt, 15 Feb. 1917; p. 232, report, Oppen, 19 Feb. 1917.

170. Prussian War Ministry, 21 Jan. 1917, to War Agency Offices, with appendix, Batocki, 29 Jan. 1917, to the state governments, cited in Daniel, *Arbeiterfrauen,* 195.

171. Lenz, *Lebensmittel-Zulagen,* 26.

172. Wiernik, *Die Arbeiterernährung,* 47.

173. Ibid., 48; cf. 53–54.

174. Compare figures on the attrition of women with children in Bavaria, cited in Ute Daniel, "Fiktionen, Friktionen, und Fakten," in Mai, *Arbeiterschaft in Deutschland,* 286–87.

175. BAL, 15.01, Nr. 12478, 3 Feb. 1917.

CHAPTER NINE

1. See "Aus der Reichshauptstadt: Der 'wünschenswerte Gleichmut' in der Krankenernährung," *Der Tag,* 22 Apr. 1917; "Die Milchversorgung Groß-Berlins," *Berliner Tageblatt,* 2 Feb. 1917; BLHA, Pr. Br., Rep. 1A, Nr. 2, p. 38, Health Minister Bumm's draft guidelines, 10 June 1917. Cf., outside Berlin, BAL, 15.01., Rep. 77, Nr. 12478, 3 Mar. 1917.

2. Cf. BLHA, PPB, Nr. 15820, p. 232, report, Oppen, 19 Feb. 1917; pp. 200–202, mood report, Meier, 19 Feb. 1917; p. 244, mood report, Schwarz, 14 Mar. 1917. Compare, e.g., BAL, 15.01, Rep. 77, Nr. 12478, p. 75, 3 Mar. 1917.

3. BAL, 15.01, Rep. 77, Nr. 12478, pp. 74–75, 3 Mar. 1917.

4. Compare BLHA, PPB, Nr. 15820, p. 240, mood report, Schrott/Büchel, 15 Mar. 1917; p. 247, mood report, König, 15 Mar. 1917. Cf. BAL, 15.01, Rep. 77, Nr. 12478, pp. 10–11, 3 Jan. 1917.

5. See BLHA, PPB, Nr. 15820, p. 240, mood report, Schrott/Büchel, 15 Mar. 1917. Cf., e.g., "Groß-Berlin: Heraus mit den landwirtschaftlichen Vorräten! Zur Ernährungsfrage der Städte," *Berliner Volkszeitung,* 17 Feb. 1917; "Hintenherum," *Große Glocke,* 14 Mar. 1917; "Wo es Konserven gibt: Die sonntäglichen Hamsterreisen," *Berliner Volkszeitung,* 22 Mar. 1917; "Der Handel, der mit den Dingen umzugehen versteht," *Vorwärts,* 24 Mar. 1917.

6. Michaelis, *Für Staat und Volk,* 286–87. Cf., e.g., Blücher, *English Wife,* 146, 155; Cooper, *Behind the Lines,* 175, 181; Käte Duncker's correspondence of this period, AFDG, Nachlässe Duncker, 45/247.

7. Carsten, *War against War,* 113.

8. Blücher, *English Wife,* 122. On the response of poorer Germans, see BLHA, PPB, Nr. 15820, p. 240, mood report, Schrott/Büchel, 15 Mar. 1917, and Nr. 15821, pp. 233–34, mood report, Kurtz, 13 July 1917; BAL, 15.01, Nr. 12478, 3 May 1917, "Allgemeine Stimmung."

9. Cf. Offer, *First World War,* 52–53.

10. "Die Klagen über ungleiche Lebensmittelversorgung in Groß-Berlin," *Tägliche Rundschau,* 14 Apr. 1917. Cf., e.g., "Die Lebensmittelverteilung: Ungleichheit in Gross-Berlin," *Der Tag,* 22 Apr. 1917; "Versorgungsnöte in den Vororten," *Der Tag,* 11 May 1917; BLHA, Pr. Br., Rep. 1A, Nr. 2, pp. 34–35; among war-industry workers, see BLHA, PPB, Nr. 15838/1, p. 23, communiqué, Loebell to Oppen, 30 Mar. 1917. Cf. BAPK, Nr. 1573, on the holdings of the Teltower Kriegswirtschaft-Gesellschaft, as women load and unload barrels of precious food.

11. Cf. "Die Klagen über ungleiche Lebensmittelversorgung in Groß-Berlin," *Tägliche Rundschau,* 14 Apr. 1917.

12. Cf., e.g., "Die hohen Verkaufspreise im Kleinhandel," *Berliner Tageblatt,* 11 Jan. 1917; "Der Hoteldirektor als Butterhändler," *Berliner Lokal Anzeiger,* 25 Jan. 1917; "Eine Mahnung an die Bäcker," *Vossische Zeitung,* 15 Feb. 1917; "Aufrufe an die Landwirte," *Vorwärts,* 12 Mar. 1917; "Lebensmittelvergeudung aus Profitsucht," *Vorwärts,* 9 June 1917.

13. "Wir füttern lieber die Schweine damit," *Vorwärts,* 7 June 1917.

14. BLHA, PPB, Nr. 15820, p. 154, mood report, Dittmann, 18 Jan. 1917.

15. From 1916 the War Committee for Consumers' Interests investigated ads for sources of food in Berlin newspapers, until the War Profiteering Office took over the task in 1917. See KWA director Falck's directive, in BLHA, PPB, Nr. 15821, pp. 19–21, mood report, Mercier, 4 Apr. 1917. Cf. Roerkohl, *Hungerblockade,* 262–63.

16. See communiqués of the High Censor Office to subordinate offices on discussion of food provisioning and the general mood in the press, in Deist, *Militär- und Innenpolitik,* 1 : 362, 437–38. Compare "Aufklärung erwünscht!," *Berliner Neueste Nachrichten,* 8 Dec. 1916.

17. "Ernährungsorgen," *Reichsbote,* 10 Apr. 1917. Cf., e.g., "Aufklärung erwünscht!," *Berliner Neueste Nachrichten,* 8 Dec. 1916; "Die Milchversorgung Groß-Berlins," *Berliner Tageblatt,* 2 Feb. 1917; "Zu wenig Fleisch," *Berliner Morgenpost,* 17 Mar. 1917; BLHA, PPB, Nr. 15821, p. 41, draft report, Oppen, 17 Mar. 1917. Compare "Ernährungsfragen," *Königsberger Volkszeitung,* 16 Feb. 1917.

18. "Pflichten der Stunde," *Berliner Tageblatt,* 16 Feb. 1917.

19. Cf. BLHA, PPB, Nr. 15820, p. 188, report, Oppen, 22 Jan. 1917; p. 199, mood report, Gerhardt, 15 Feb. 1917; p. 201, mood report, Eitner, 15 Feb. 1917; BAL, 15.01, Nr. 12478, p. 6, 3 Mar. 1917.

20. BLHA, PPB, Nr. 15820, pp. 153–54, mood report, Dittmann, 18 Jan. 1917; cf. p. 198, mood report, Schrott/Büchel, 14 Feb. 1917; pp. 240, mood report, Schrott/Büchel, 15 Mar. 1917.

21. Ibid., p. 244, mood report, Schwarz, 14 Mar. 1917; Nr. 15821, p. 41, report, Oppen, 17 Mar. 1917. In Halle likewise, the food situation was "the Achilles' heel of the popular morale." See BAL, 15.01, Rep. 77, Nr. 12478, p. 10, 3 Mar. 1917.

22. Compare, e.g., BLHA, PPB, Nr. 15820, p. 199, report, Gerhardt, 15 Feb. 1917; p. 200, report, Dittmann, 15 Feb. 1917; GStAPK, 2.2.1., Rep. 197A, Teil 10, Nr. 2, p. 200, report, Oppen to Oberkommando, 23 Feb. 1917.

23. BLHA, PPB, Nr. 15902, Märzfeier, 1917.

24. Cf. "'Auch'! Die erzwungenen Doppelkäufe," *Vossische Zeitung;* BLHA, PPB, Nr. 15820, pp. 143–45, report, Oppen, 23 Dec. 1916; p. 147, mood report, 9 Jan. 1917; p. 191, mood report, Kartmann, 7 Feb. 1917; p. 193, mood report, Kartmann, 14 Feb. 1917. Compare "Pfeffer und Salz," *Volksfreund Braunschweig,* 6 Feb. 1917.

25. BLHA, PPB, Nr. 15821, pp. 41–42, report, Oppen, 17 Mar. 1917.

26. Cf. Kiessig, *Berliner Sagen*, 46–47.

27. Martha Balzer, in Glatzer and Glatzer, *Berliner Leben, 1914–1918*, 307–8.

28. GStAPK, 2.2.1, Rep. 197A, Teil 10, Nr. 2, pp. 200–202, report, "Off Duty," Meier to Oppen, 19 Feb. 1917. Cf. BLHA, PPB, Nr. 15820, p. 202, mood report, Kurtz, 15 Feb. 1917.

29. Cf. BLHA, PPB, Nr. 15821, p. 45, report, Dittmann, 12 Apr. 1917; BAL, 15.01. Rep. 77, Nr. 12478, 3 Mar. 1917, and 3 Apr. 1917, "Verteilung."

30. Feldman, *Army, Industry, and Labor*, 149.

31. Cf. BAL, 15.01, Rep. 77, Nr. 12478, p. 18, 3 June 1917, on the new supplement regulations of 14 May 1917.

32. Cf. ibid., p. 10.

33. Cf. "Die Kohlenversorgung in Berlin," *Berliner Tageblatt*, 21 Feb. 1917; "Das Kriegswucheramt," *Berliner Neueste Nachrichten*, 29 Mar. 1917. The KWA was founded in August 1916, subsidiary to the Berlin police presidium.

34. Cf. "Ein Preußisches Landeskartoffelamt: Eine Aufsichtsbehörde," *Berliner Tageblatt*, 24 Feb. 1917.

35. Cf. Roerkohl, *Hungerblockade*, 91–94.

36. See "Änderung in der Lebensmittelverteilung," *Berliner Lokal Anzeiger*, 22 Mar. 1917.

37. Cf. BAL, 15.01, Rep. 77, Nr. 12478, 4 Apr. 1917.

38. Michaelis, *Für Staat und Volk*, 287–88.

39. Cf. BAL, 15.01, Rep. 77, Nr. 12478, 4 Apr. 1917.

40. LAB, Rep. 142, reports from Mar. 1917.

41. Cited in Feldman, *Army, Industry, and Labor*, 289. Cf. "Gesprächsstoff: Die ZEG in der Defensive," *Die Glocke*, 21 Mar. 1917; "Wo sind die Fische Geblieben?," *Berliner Tageblatt*, 22 Feb. 1917.

42. BLHA, PPB, Nr. 15838/1, communiqué, Loebell to Oppen, 30 Mar. 1917. See also "Ernährungsforderungen der Gewerkschaften. Batockis Garantien. Die Mitarbeit der Landwirtschaft. Durchführung der Beschlagnahmen," *Berliner Morgenpost*, 14 Apr. 1917.

43. See, e.g., "Aus Gross Berlin: Das Ende der Hamsterfahrten," *Vorwärts*, 31 Mar. 1917; "Aus der Reichshauptstadt: Die verbotenen Hamsterfahrten," *Tägliche Rundschau*, 1 Apr. 1917; "Die Hamsterjagd," *Vorwärts*, 22 Aug. 1917.

44. Cf. "Durch die Dörfer mit der Nachprüfungskommission," *Vorwärts*, 16 Apr. 1917.

45. Cf. EVK, Nr. 2950, communications to church personnel in both rural and urban districts to preach adherence to government rations.

46. Cf. "Das Kriegswucheramt," *Berliner Neueste Nachrichten*, 29 Mar. 1917.

47. On revolutionary activity, see BLHA, PPB, Nr. 15838/1, p. 23, communiqué, Loebell to Oppen, 30 Mar. 1917.

48. Cf., on the simultaneous political influence of women food protesters in Russia, Engel, "Not by Bread Alone."

49. "Das Hamstern hat abgenommen," *Die Post*, 8 Apr. 1917.

50. BLHA, PPB, Nr. 15821, p. 27, mood report, Felleg, 10 Apr. 1917.

51. BAL, 15.01, Rep. 77, Nr. 12478, p. 10, 9 Aug. 1916 and 3 Feb., 3 Mar., 4 Apr. 1917.

52. Moeller, "Dimensions of Social Conflict"; Ay, *Entstehung*, 24–30.

53. Cf. "Die Folgen der Gepäckrevisionen," *Berliner Abendblatt*, 4 Apr. 1917; "Eine Folge der Hamsterfahrten," *Tägliche Rundschau*, 4 Apr. 1917; "Unverschämt hamstern und wucherische Händlern," *Reichsbote*, 10 Apr. 1917; BLHA, PPB, Nr. 15821, pp. 19, 21, mood report, Mercier, 4 Apr. 1917. Cf. BAL, 15.01, Rep. 77, Nr. 12478, monthly report, p. 193, 2 July 1917.

54. BAL, 15.01, Rep. 77, Nr. 12478, p. 6, 3 May 1917; see also 3 Apr. 1917. Cf. BLHA, PPB, Nr. 15821, p. 44, mood report, Faßhauer, 12 Apr. 1917.

55. BLHA, PPB, Nr. 15821, p. 49, mood report, Kurtz, 12 Apr. 1917.

56. Ibid., p. 43, mood report, Büchel/Kamenz, 12 Apr. 1917.

57. "Die Defensive des Magens," *Münchener Post,* 29 Mar. 1917.

58. Cf. BLHA, PPB, Nr. 15838/1, pp. 24–26, report, Oppen to Loebell, 4 Apr. 1917; p. 3, report, Stolle to Oberkommando, 5 Apr. 1917; p. 90, Oppen to Deputy Commando, 14 Apr. 1917; Nr. 15821, p. 43, mood report, Büchel/Kamenz, 12 Apr. 1917; Nr. 15902, Märzfeier, 1917.

59. Cf. "Ernährungsforderungen der Gewerkschaften," *Berliner Morgenpost,* 14 Apr. 1917.

60. Cf. BLHA, PPB, Nr. 15821, p. 45, mood report, Dittmann, 12 Apr. 1917.

61. Ibid., p. 2, memorandum, Michaelis to local heads of government and police commissioners, 8 Mar. 1917.

62. Cf. "Die Arbeiter und die Volksernährung," *Berliner Lokal Anzeiger,* 14 Apr. 1917.

63. BLHA, PPB, Nr. 15838/1, p. 91, report, Oppen to Oberkommando, 14 Apr. 1917. Cf. "Die zukünftige Lebensmittelversorgung Groß-Berlins: Besprechung von Regierungs- und Arbeitervertretern im Rathaus," *Vorwärts,* 15 Apr. 1917.

64. Cf. BLHA, PPB, Nr. 15838/1, p. 169, report, Oppen to Roedenbeck in Interior Ministry, 16 Apr. 1917. GStAPK, 2.2.1, Rep. 77, Tit. 500, Nr. 52, p. 144, report, Berge to War Ministry, 19 Apr. 1917, names 148,903 strikers, against the shop stewards' claim of 206,000. Cf. BLHA, PPB, Nr. 15839, p. 330, report, Schwarz to Oppen, 17 Apr. 1917, and Nr. 15838/1, p. 431, report, Wodtke, 18 Apr. 1917.

65. BLHA, PPB, Nr. 15839, p. 330, report, Schwarz, 17 Apr. 1917. Police reports offer higher estimates of participants in the formal demonstration than do Social Democratic newspapers.

66. Ibid., Nr. 15838/1, pp. 169–70, report, Oppen to Roedenbeck, Interior Ministry, 16 Apr. 1917; p. 171, report, Oppen to Oberkommando, 16 Apr. 1917.

67. See ibid., p. 169, report, Oppen to Roedenbeck in Interior Ministry, 16 Apr. 1917; p. 171, report, Oppen to Oberkommando, 16 Apr. 1917; Nr. 15839, p. 70, press release, Oppen, 16 Apr. 1917.

68. Cf. "Streikgelüste," *Berliner Tageblatt,* 25 Apr. 1917.

69. "Zur Streikbewegung," *Vorwärts,* 17 Apr. 1917.

70. BLHA, PPB, Nr. 15838/1, p. 431, marginalia, Schwarz, 18 Apr. 1917.

71. BAL, 15.01, Rep. 77, Nr. 12478, 3 May 1917.

72. BLHA, PPB, Nr. 15821, p. 121, mood report, Faßhauer, n.d. [ca. 10 May 1917]. Cf. Nr. 15838/1, p. 120, report, Jastrow to Oppen, 15 Apr. 1917; "Ernährungsforderungen der Gewerkschaften," *Berliner Morgenpost,* 14 Apr. 1917; Annemarie Lange, *Das Wilhelminische Berlin,* 757.

73. BLHA, PPB, Nr. 15821, p. 44, mood report, Faßhauer, 12 Apr. 1917.

74. Cf. ibid., Nr. 15821, p. 121, mood report, Faßhauer, n.d. [ca. 10 May 1917]. Compare one year later, "Zwei Arten Streikender," *Simplicissimus,* 2 Apr. 1918.

75. BLHA, PPB, Nr. 15821, p. 116, report, Oppen, 18 Apr. 1917.

76. See "Ein Lebensmittelverteilungsamt für Gross-Berlin: Maßnahmen gegen die ungleiche Versorgung," *Berliner Tageblatt,* 8 May 1917.

77. BLHA, Pr. Br., Rep. 1A, Nr. 2, p. 34, memo, SVS president to war minister through the high commander, 22 May 1917. Cf. "Die Bedeutung der Staatlichen Verteilungsstelle für die Lebensmittelversorgung Gross-Berlins," *Deutsche Tageszeitung,* 22 May 1917.

78. "Die Arbeiter und die Volksernährung," *Berliner Lokal Anzeiger,* 14 Apr. 1917.

79. "Aus Gross-Berlin: Die Erste Woche der 'Umgruppierte' Nahrungsmittelversorgung Gross Berlins," *Reichsbote,* 22 Apr. 1917. Officials also put some effort into refurbishing the system of public kitchens, though in Berlin at least, this met with little interest.

80. BLHA, PPB, Nr. 15821, p. 118, mood report, Büchel/Schrott, 9 May 1917.

81. Ibid., p. 139, letter, Mayor Schulz to Charlottenburg Police Chief Hertzberg, 28 June 1917.

82. BAL, 15.01, Nr. 12478, p. 3, 3 May 1917.

83. See the flurry of correspondence on the subject in BLHA, Pr. Br., Rep. 1A, Nr. 255, pp. 1–32, June, July 1917, and Nr. 89, pp. 7–10, 22 May 1917.

84. BAL, 15.01, Rep. 77, Nr. 12478, 3 June 1917, p. 12. Cf. ibid., 2 July 1917; BLHA, PPB, Nr. 15821, p. 261, mood report, Feeger, 17 Aug. 1917, and Nr. 15822, p. 11, mood report, Büchel, 15 Nov. 1917.

85. BAL, 15.01, Rep. 77, Nr. 12478, 3 June 1917.

86. Cf. "Rückgang des Arbeitermangels," *Berliner Morgenpost,* 7 Aug. 1918.

87. Cf. "Aus Groß-Berlin: Das tägliche Wucher," *Vorwärts,* 25 Mar. 1917; "Groß-Berlin: Zu der neuen Ernährungsregelung," *Vorwärts,* 5 Apr. 1917; "Eine unbeabsichtigte Wirkung," *Deutsche Tageszeitung,* 15 Apr. 1917.

88. Cf. BLHA, PPB, p. 45, report, Dittmann, 12 Apr. 1917.

89. Cooper, *Behind the Lines,* 189.

90. Cf. BLHA, PPB, Nr. 15821, report, Oppen, 17 Mar. 1917; pp. 47–48, mood report, Klonicki, 12 Apr. 1917; p. 49, mood report, Kurtz, 12 Apr. 1917.

91. BAL, 15.01, Nr. 12478, p. 9, 8 Sept. 1916.

92. Cf. *Ulk,* 15 May 1918; "Pferdefleisch als Speise des Volkes," *Kleines Journal,* 3 Sept. 1918. Horsemeat was not customarily eaten in Germany as it was in France.

93. Cf. Anna Kunze, in *Das große Beispiel,* 26–27.

94. On state-run experiments, cf. KEA *Mitteilungsblatt,* 17 Apr. 1916; Glatzer and Glatzer, *Berliner Leben, 1914–1918,* 309.

95. See Skalweit, *Kriegsernährungswirtschaft,* 57.

96. Ibid.

97. Ibid., 55. Cf. Stadthagen, *Ersatzlebensmittel.*

98. See the list from 15 July 1919, in Skalweit, *Kriegsernährungswirtschaft,* 61.

99. Ibid., 57.

100. "Kaffeepolonäse!," *Berliner Volkszeitung,* 10 Mar. 1917. Cf. "Kaffee-Ersatz! Eine 'zeitgemässige' Betrachtung!," ibid.; BLHA, PPB, Nr. 15821, p. 120, mood report, Kurtz, 10 May 1917.

101. Skalweit, *Kriegsernährungswirtschaft,* 58–9.

102. Blücher, *English Wife,* 111.

103. BLHA, PPB, Nr. 15821, pp. 251–52, mood report, Oppen, 24 Aug. 1917.

104. See GStAPK, 2.2.1, Rep. 197A, II K 5, letters from Greater Berlin residents to the KEA, pp. 137–47, August 1917, requesting that bread be tested for edibility. One submission contained a sample of the flour being sold that remains to date in the file. It looks like sawdust and is tasteless, though naturally it is impossible on this basis to judge its edibility. Cf. "Ungeniessbares Brot," *Vossische Zeitung,* 11 Aug. 1917.

105. BAL, 15.01, Rep. 77, Nr. 12478, 2 Aug. 1917, "Allgemeine Stimmung."

106. Spalding, *Historical Dictionary,* 687.

107. Cf. BLHA, PPB, Nr. 15821, p. 297, mood report, Görl, 15 Sept. 1917.

108. See "Die Arbeiter und die Volksernährung," *Berliner Lokal Anzeiger,* 14 Apr. 1917.

109. See Lüders, *Das Unbekannte Heer,* 87; Feldman, *Army, Industry, and Labor,* 206. As layoffs of women increased, so too did this sense. Cf. "Rückgang des Arbeitermangels," *Berliner Morgenpost,* 7 Aug. 1918.

110. Cf. Roerkohl, *Hungerblockade,* 202.

111. See also discussion around the "ersatz election" to replace the Reichstag leader, who had died in office in May 1918, which bore these overtones. Cf. BAL, 15.01, Rep. 77, Reichskanzlei, Nr. 2398/12, p. 97, report, Oppen, 24 Sept. 1918.

112. Spalding, *Historical Dictionary,* 687.

113. Mihaly, . . . *da gibt's ein Wiedersehn!,* 221.

114. Oppen expressed in April his hope that the pressure on the food supply would be relieved with the onset of warm weather, among other things, as some workers sowed small garden plots (*Schrebergärten* and *Laubenkolonien,* the latter formally established in Berlin first in 1913). See BLHA, PPB, Nr. 15838/1, pp. 24–26, report, Oppen, 4 Apr. 1917. Cf. Hartwig Stein, *"Inseln im Häusermeer."*

115. BAL, 15.01, Rep. 77, Nr. 12478, monthly report, 2 July 1917, p. 32; cf. 3 Sept. 1917, "Allgemeine Stimmung."

116. See BLHA, PPB, Nr. 15821, p. 77, mood report, Cortemme, 19 June 1917.

117. Ibid.

118. Cf. Schreiner, *Iron Ration,* 215–16, 257–58.

119. Cf. "Die Kohlenpolonaisen kommen wieder: Was tut der Kohlenverband 'Gross-Berlin' dagegen?," *Berliner Volkszeitung,* 24 Oct. 1917, constituted by a letter from a working woman with a brother on the front lines and an elderly mother; "Wie bekomme ich Kohlen?," *Berliner Lokal Anzeiger,* 8 Nov. 1917.

120. Cf. "Infolge ganz erheblicher Steigerung der Hypothekszinsen von Seiten der Stadt Berlin," *Vorwärts,* 26 June 1917.

121. See, e.g., "Kein Verbot der Mietssteigerung: Der Oberbürgermeister beim Oberkommandierenden," *Berliner Morgenpost,* 28 June 1917.

122. "Mietssteigerungen, Kündigungen, und Wohnungsboykott," *Berliner Volkszeitung,* 4 July 1917.

123. BLHA, PPB, Nr. 15821, pp. 298–99, mood report, Klonicki, 15 Sept. 1917.

124. There was still resentment against soldiers' wives. Cf. BAL, 15.01, Rep. 77, Nr. 12478, report, 3 July 1917, "Allgemeine Stimmung," AK XX.

125. BLHA, PPB, Nr. 15821, p. 128, report, Schrott/Kamenz, 7 June 1917.

126. Ibid., p. 184, mood report, Schrott, 14 July 1917.

127. Ibid., p. 128, report, Schrott/Kamens, 7 June 1917; p. 224, mood report, Hannig, 30 June 1917; p. 245, telegram, 17 July 1917; p. 247, mood report, Sacktchewski, 14 July 1917.

128. See, e.g., ibid., pp. 233–34, mood report, Kurtz, 13 July 1917.

129. Ibid., pp. 229–30, mood report, Schneider, 28 June 1917.

130. Ibid., pp. 233–34, report, Kurtz, 13 July 1917. Cf. Annemarie Lange, *Das Wilhelminische Berlin,* 750.

131. From BLHA, PPB, Nr. 15821, p. 199, report, Kuhlmann to Oppen, 4 July 1917.

132. Cf. Lefebvre, *Great Fear;* under Louis XV, Steven Kaplan, *Famine Plot.*

133. BLHA, PPB, Nr. 15821, pp. 151–52, mood report, Borchert, 27 June 1917. Cf. "for the first time" in Teltow, ibid., p. 153, report, Landrat Teltow to Oppen, 3 July 1917.

134. Ibid., p. 186, mood report, Ferger, 14 July 1917; p. 128, report, Schrott/Kamenz, 7 June 1917. Cf. pp. 180–81, report, Görl, 14 July 1917; p. 187, mood report, Klonicki, 15 July 1917.

135. See Theodor Wolff, *Tagebücher,* 1:534–55.

136. Cf. BLHA, PPB, Nr. 15821, pp. 140–41, report, Kuhlmann to Oppen, 30 June 1917; p. 199, report, Kuhlmann to Oppen, 4 July 1917.

137. From ibid., p. 199, report, Kuhlmann, 4 July 1917. Cf. p. 187, report, Klonicki, 15 July 1917; p. 228, mood report, Oppen, 21 July 1917; pp. 279–80, report, Schneider, 22 July 1917.

138. Ibid., p. 173, Oppen, 3 July 1917.

139. "Lebensmittelunruhen," *Bremer Bürger Zeitung,* 7 July 1917. Cf. "Die Kohlenverteilung in Gross-Berlin," *Vorwärts,* 10 July 1917; "Überverteilung des Publikums," *Der Deutsche Kurier,* 10 July 1917.

140. Cf. BLHA, PPB, Nr. 15821, pp. 279–80, mood report, Schneider, 22 July 1917; p. 173, Oppen, 3 July 1917; BAL, 15.01, Rep. 77, Nr. 12478, p. 8, 3 Aug. 1917.

141. BLHA, PPB, Nr. 15821, p. 199, report, Kuhlmann, 4 July 1917.

142. Ibid.; pp. 222–23, mood report, Schwarz, 5 July 1917.

143. "Gross-Berliner Ernährungsfragen: Marktbilder," *Der Deutsche Kurier,* 4 July 1917. See also "Andauernder Obst- und Gemüsemangel," ibid., 12 July 1917; "Aus der Reichshauptstadt: Ein gutes Beispiel," *Tägliche Rundschau,* 5 July 1917.

144. BAL, 15.01, Rep. 77, Nr. 12478, 3 Sept. 1917, "Allgemeine Stimmung," AK XIV, AK XVIII; BLHA, PPB, Nr. 15821, p. 185, mood report, Faßhauer, 14 July 1917.

145. BLHA, PPB, Nr. 15821, p. 138, report, Hertzberg to Oppen, 28 June 1917.

146. Ibid., pp. 229–30, mood report, Schneider, 28 June 1917.

147. Ibid., pp. 233–34, mood report, Kurtz, 13 July 1917.

148. Cf. ibid., p. 306, mood report, Watplawctz, 12 Sept. 1917; pp. 151–52, mood report, Borchert, 27 June 1917.

149. In one instance a veteran bit a patrolman in the calf as interested women watched. See BLHA, PPB, Nr. 15821, pp. 279–80, mood report, Schneider, 22 July 1917.

150. Cf. "Gegen ungezogene Verkäufer," *Tägliche Rundschau,* 25 Sept. 1917.

151. "Aus der Reichshauptstadt: Ein gutes Beispiel," ibid., 5 July 1917.

152. Cf. BLHA, PPB, Nr. 15821, pp. 222–23, mood report, Schwarz, 5 July 1917.

153. Ibid. See also p. 157, memorandum, Oppen to police commissioners of Charlottenburg, Schöneberg, Lichtenberg, and Neukölln, 7 July 1917, anticipating new demonstrations and requesting careful reporting.

154. Ibid., Nr. 15822, p. 117, mood report, Dittmann, 19 Apr. 1918. Cf. p. 118, letter, Lindy to deputy commander of the Gardekorps, 22 Apr. 1918.

155. The relative indifference of this population was, in part, the reason that officials did not ultimately decide to reform the franchise for another year. Ute Daniel cites the view of some Social Democratic leaders that such women were simply too apolitical to be interested in the vote. Cf. Daniel, *Arbeiterfrauen,* 238.

156. Cf. BLHA, PPB, Nr. 15821, p. 187, report, Klonicki, 15 July 1917; p. 188, report, Dittmann, 16 July 1917. See Michaelis's own acerbic commentary in "Die Versorgung der Großstädte: Halbheiten und Schwierigkeiten," *Berliner Tageblatt,* 21 June 1917. OHL leaders had originally settled on Center Party leader Georg Graf von Hertling as chancellor, as a counterweight to the pro-peace position taken under Erzberger, but Hertling refused the position at that time.

157. See, e.g., Fritz Fischer, *Germany's Aims*, 401; Berghahn, *Modern Germany*, 55; Feldman, *Army, Industry, and Labor*, 366–67, 407–8. Feldman acknowledges consumers' admiration for Michaelis.

158. BLHA, PPB, Nr. 15821, pp. 225–27, mood report, Oppen, 21 July 1917, first draft. Oppen contrasts "the women" and "better circles." Cf. his excisions of other references to the prevailing "revolutionary mood" (pp. 135–36, mood report, Oppen, 18 June 1917).

159. Cited in "Gegen den Schleichhandel: Ein Aufruf des KEA," *Berliner Volkszeitung*, 22 Oct. 1917.

160. Cf. BLHA, PPB, Nr. 15821, p. 295, mood report, Seeger, 14 Sept. 1917, and p. 373, mood report, Faßhauer, 15 Oct. 1917; Nr. 15822, pp. 6, 8a, mood report, Klonicki, 15 Oct. 1917, and p. 47, mood report, Faßhauer, 8 Dec. 1917.

161. Cf. BLHA, PPB, Nr. 15821, p. 300, report, Faßhauer/Diercks, 14 Sept. 1917.

162. Ibid., Nr. 15821, pp. 303–4, report, Büchel/Schrott, 15 Sept. 1917; cf. earlier in the year, p. 185, mood report, Diercks/Faßhauer, 14 July 1917; BAL, 15.01, Nr. 12478, p. 21, 3 May 1917, concerning Danzig.

163. See, e.g., BLHA, PPB, Nr. 15821, pp. 371–72, mood report, Schneider, 15 Oct. 1917; p. 373, mood report, Faßhauer, 15 Oct. 1917; already in July, pp. 225–27, mood report, Oppen, 21 July 1917, first draft.

164. On the heated debate over the "fall crisis" and fear for its effect on the populace, cf. *Der Interfraktionelle Ausschuß*, 569–99. Michaelis was replaced by Georg von Hertling on 1 November. The Reichstag was directly behind forcing Michaelis out, but there is evidence of Ludendorff's own intrigues, possibly on the basis that the chancellor seemed too sincere in his concerns to respond to popular demands. Michaelis's replacement by Hertling, though the OHL's obvious choice, was hardly more appealing to the majority of Reichstag deputies. See ibid., Nr. 15954, p. 81, report, Schwarz, 19 Nov. 1917. Cf. Kitchen, *Silent Dictatorship*, 150.

165. On the original loss, see "Aus der Reichshauptstadt: Die Obstfahrten der Berliner nach Werder," *Berliner Lokal Anzeiger*, 27 June 1917; "Von Werder nach Berlin: Wo bleibt das Obst?," *Vossische Zeitung*, 29 June 1917; "Gegen Zurückhaltung von Obst und Gemüse," *Vorwärts*, 29 June 1917.

166. Cf. "Marmelade Statt Butter?," *Berliner Lokal Anzeiger*, 19 Oct. 1917.

167. Cf. ibid., Nr. 15822, p. 4, report, Diercks/Faßhauer, 13 Nov. 1917, and pp. 9–9a, mood report, Dittmann, 15 Nov. 1917; Nr. 15821, pp. 6, 8a, mood report, Klonicki, 15 Nov. 1917. Cf. *Grosse Sozialistische Oktoberrevolution und Deutschland*.

168. BLHA, PPB, Nr. 15822, pp. 1–3, mood report, Oppen, 19 Nov. 1917.

169. Ibid., Nr. 15803, pp. 109–11, notice of the chief of the General Staff, 15 Nov. 1917.

170. Ibid., Nr. 15822, p. 64, mood report, Faßhauer, 6 Feb. 1918. The case was similar to an incident one year earlier when promised jam for use as a butter substitute also failed to appear. Cf. articles in the *Berliner Volkszeitung* in November 1916, including "Wo ist die Marmelade? Ein Notruf."

171. "Neukölln: Zur Marmeladenverteilung," *Vorwärts*, 30 Nov. 1917; cf., too, BLHA, PPB, Nr. 15822, p. 63, mood report, Faßhauer, 18 Feb. 1918.

172. BANK, 24M 1/6, 24 Nov. 1917. Cf. ibid., memorandum, Neukölln Mayor Kaiser to Waldow, 25 Oct. 1917, and the active process drafting resolutions by the Kriegsnotstandskommission des Magistrats throughout November, particularly from Special Committee II.

173. "Kartoffel-Enthüllung," *Bremer Bürger Zeitung*, 10 Aug. 1917.

174. "Überzahlte Lebensmittel: Auswüchse in der Rüstungsindustrie," *Berliner Morgenpost,* 23 Nov. 1917. *Auswüchse* also suggests a tumor-like growth.

175. Cf. "Zu der Verhaftung von Gemeindeangestellten in Friedrichsfelde wegen angeblicher Butterverschiebungen," *Der Tag,* 2 Nov. 1917; "Ein Mißgriff?," *Deutsche Tageszeitung,* 2 Nov. 1917; "Die Lebensmittelschiebungen in Friedrichsfelde," *Tägliche Rundschau,* 3 Nov. 1917; GStAPK, Rep. 197A, Ih 5, p. 316, PSV to SVS, 11 Nov. 1917; BLHA, PPB, Nr. 15822, pp. 9–9a, report, Dittmann, 15 Nov. 1917.

176. BANK, 24M 1/6, Magistrat Neukölln to Waldow, "Anordnung von Maßnahmen zur gleichmäßigen Verteilung der vorhandenen Lebensmittel und zur Bekämpfung des Wuchers," 3 Dec. 1917. Cf. SAB, Neukölln Report.

177. "Zusammenbruch des Systems Waldow," *Vorwärts,* 16 Dec. 1917; "Ein Beitrag zu den Neuköllner Enthüllung: Es wird immer toller!," *Vorwärts,* 31 Dec. 1917. Cf. "System 'Waldow' oder System 'Müller-, Stegerwald, Scheidemann,'" *Deutsche Tageszeitung,* 17 Dec. 1917, which blamed the system and its deficiencies on the Social Democrats and hotly denied growers' lack of "love of country" and "Christianity." *Vorwärts* energetically responded with "Der agrarische Gegenangriff," 20 Dec. 1917. Compare the thick clippings file on the incident in BANK, 24M 1/6.

178. Cf. "Neukölln: Zur Marmeladenverteilung," *Vorwärts,* 30 Nov. 1917; "Die Neuköllner Denkschrift," *Wirtschaftliche Tagesberichte,* 18 Dec. 1917.

179. BAL, 15.01, Rep. 77, Nr. 12478, p. 396, 3 Dec. 1917.

180. See BLHA, PPB, Nr. 15822, p. 94, mood report, Seeger, 25 Feb. 1918.

181. Ibid., p. 175, mood report, Schrott/Büchel, 12 July 1918; cf. p. 179, mood report, Faßhauer, 18 June 1918, on the changing perspective.

182. Cf. BANK, 24M 1/6, copy of letter, Wilhelm II to Waldow, including pamphlet, 3 Dec. 1917.

183. Ibid., Magistrate Resolution, 3 Jan. 1918.

184. "Alles Mogelt," *Welt am Montag,* 24 Dec. 1917.

CHAPTER TEN

1. "Erst kommt das Fressen, dann kommt die Moral," originally, Friedrich Nietzsche; compare Bertolt Brecht, "Ballade über die Frage: Wovon lebt der Mensch?," from his musical *Drei Groschenoper.* Cf. C. Eifert, "Wann kommt 'das Fressen', wann 'die Moral'?," in Berliner Geschichtswerkstatt, *August 1914,* 103–14.

2. Cf. Arlette Farge, *Subversive Words;* Steven Kaplan, *Famine Plot;* Lefebvre, *Great Fear.*

3. Cf. "Preissturz im — Kettenhandel," *Berliner Tageblatt,* 29 Dec. 1917.

4. BLHA, PPB, Nr. 15822, p. 47, report, Faß, 8 Dec.1917; p. 71, report, Meier, 15 Jan. 1918.

5. Ibid., p. 97, mood report, Oppen, 25 Mar. 1918.

6. Cf. ibid., p. 72, report, Lamm, 15 Jan. 1918; p. 67, mood report, Oppen, 21 Jan. 1918; pp. 145–51, Oppen to Loebell, 6 Feb. 1918.

7. Cf. ibid., pp. 73–73a, report, Schneider, 15 Jan. 1918; p. 93, report, Görl, 15 Feb. 1918.

8. Ibid., pp. 89–90, report, Schrott/Büchel, 14 Feb. 1918.

9. Cf. ibid., p. 178, report, Diercks, 15 July 1918.

10. Ibid., p. 48, report, Seeger, 7 Dec. 1918.

11. On the important traffic in postcard images, see Kerbs, "Revolution in Bildern: Postkarten," in Hallen and Kerbs, *Revolution und Fotografie,* 217–29.

12. Cf. Carsten, *War against War,* 186–87; Chickering, *Imperial Germany and the Great War,* 103.

13. BLHA, PPB, Nr. 15822, pp. 9–9a, report, Dittmann, 15 Nov. 1917; p. 49, Görl, 20 Dec. 1917; p. 69, report, Faßhauer, 14 Jan. 1918; p. 99, report, Görl, 15 Mar. 1918; pp. 95–96, report, Schneider, 25 Feb. 1918; p. 94, report, Seeger, 25 Feb. 1918.

14. "Operation Michael," a last major drive in the West, was launched on 21 Mar. 1918. Deputy commanders outside Berlin reported a more positive reception—until the offensive failed in early April. Cf. BAL, 15.01, Nr. 12478, pp. 3–7, 3 Apr. 1918.

15. "Neues zur Neuköllner Denkschrift: Überschreitung der Höchstpreise erlaubt!," *Vorwärts,* 13 Jan. 1918; "Neukölln: Waldow auf dem Kriegspfad gegen Neukölln," ibid., 25 Jan. 1918; "Die Polizei im Neuköllner Rathaus," *Berliner Morgenpost,* 20 Apr. 1918. The last piece referred to imperial orders to confiscate the municipality's sensitive files in order to prevent further public embarrassment of the KEA. Cf. GStAPK, Rep. 197A, Ii ii, pp. 131–33. On popular response, see BLHA, PPB, Nr. 15822, pp. 73–73a, report, Schneider, 15 Jan. 1918; p. 69, report, Faß, 14 Jan. 1918; pp. 67–68, mood report, Oppen, 21 Jan. 1918.

16. *Dagens Nyhoter,* 2 Feb. 1918, translated into German, in BAL, 15.01, Nr. 13582, p. 32, 4 Feb. 1918. The file contains dozens of foreign press clippings focusing on the "patient hungry masses" in Germany and the government's desertion of its people.

17. *Morning Post,* 30 Jan. 1918, translated as "Streik in Kiel schon am 25.1," in BAL, 15.01, Nr. 13582, p. 36, 4 Feb. 1918.

18. "Wie bekomme ich Kohlen?," *Berliner Lokal Anzeiger,* 4 Nov. 1917. Cf. the 8 Nov. 1917 article of the same name.

19. "Aus dem Leserkreise," ibid., 17 Aug. 1918.

20. BLHA, PPB, Nr. 15822, p. 113, Oppen to SVS Groß-Berlin, 13 Feb. 1918; p. 114, SVS Groß-Berlin to Oppen, 15 Feb. 1918.

21. As with many of these rumors, circumstances bore these suspicions out. See ibid., pp. 95–96, report, Schneider, 15 Feb. 1918; p. 102, report, Faß, 14 Mar. 1918; p. 104, mood report, Schrott/Büchel, 13 Mar. 1918. This was all the more upsetting as Austria appeared such a weak military ally whose military failings were in part responsible for prevailing circumstances.

22. Ibid., pp. 51–52, report, Schneider, 10 Dec. 1917; p. 71, report, Meier, 15 Jan. 1918; p. 91, report, Faß, 15 Feb. 1918.

23. Ibid., p. 103, report, König, 15 Mar. 1918.

24. On ill-tempered communications within official hierarchies, cf. ibid., pp. 58–59, Oppen to Oberkommando, 17 Jan. 1918; pp. 60–61, Staatssekretär KEA to Oppen, 28 Jan. 1918, including marginalia, Faßhauer and Neumann; p. 62, report, Mahlow, 4 Feb. 1918; p. 65, Oppen to Staatssekretär KEA, 4 Feb. 1918; p. 63, report, Faßhauer, 18 Feb. 1918. Police referred as evidence of the state's failings to "Neukölln: Zur Marmeladenverteilung," *Vorwärts,* 30 Nov. 1917.

25. BLHA, PPB, Nr. 15822, p. 70, report, Seeger, 14 Jan. 1918; pp. 103, report, König, 15 Mar. 1918; p. 104, report, Schrott/Büchel, 13 Mar. 1918; pp. 73–73a, report, Schneider, 15 Jan. 1918; p. 94, report, Seeger, 25 Feb. 1918.

26. Ibid., p. 48, report, Seeger, 7 Dec. 1917; p. 69, Faßhauer, 14 Jan. 1918.

27. Ibid., p. 70, report, Seeger, 14 Jan. 1918; p. 74, Kieburz, 15 Jan. 1918.

28. Column by Gerlach, *Welt am Montag,* 28 Dec. 1917, quoting *Vorwärts,* in turn citing popular opinion.

29. BLHA, PPB, Nr. 15822, p. 102, report, Faßhauer, 14 Mar. 1918.

30. Ibid., p. 94, report, Seeger, 25 Feb. 1918; pp. 85–86, mood report, Oppen, 18 Feb. 1918.

31. "Neukölln wehrt sich: Die mangelhafte Versorgung mit Lebensmitteln," *Berliner Volkszeitung*, 28 Nov. 1917.

32. BLHA, PPB, Nr. 15821, pp. 229–30, mood report, Schneider, 28 June 1917; pp. 229–30, report, Schneider, 28 June 1917; Annemarie Lange, *Das Wilhelminische Berlin*, 735. Police and press anticipated self-help long before its arrival, as they had with unrest in the streets.

33. Compare Liepmann, *Krieg und Kriminalität*, 57, 156; Koppenfels, *Kriminalität der Frau*, 35. Anecdotally, see BLHA, PPB, Nr. 15822, p. 85, mood report, Oppen, 18 Feb. 1918; p. 100, report, Schneider, 15 Mar. 1918; pp. 97–98, mood report, Oppen, 25 Mar. 1918. Moreover, reports of the political police suggest that most incidents, particularly among women, were not prosecuted or recorded.

34. BLHA, PPB, Nr. 15822, p. 103, report, König, 15 Mar. 1918.

35. Ibid., p. 70, report, Seeger, 14 Jan. 1918. Cf. the hopelessness even among those who continued appeals to authorities, as in a petition "from a number of furious women," wives of functionaries, in GStAPK, 2.2.1, Rep. 197A, Ih 30, 30 Jan. 1918.

36. BLHA, PPB, Nr. 15822, p. 70, report, Seeger, 14 Jan. 1918; also p. 71, report, Meier, 15 Jan. 1918; pp. 89–90, report, Schrott/Büchel, 14 Feb. 1918; pp. 95–96, report, Schneider, 15 Feb. 1918.

37. From *Beiträge zur Geschichte der deutschen Gewerkschaftsbewegung*, p. 193, cited in Annemarie Lange, *Das Wilhelminische Berlin*, 750–51. Cf., on reception, A. Linke, *Als Sozialdemokrat an der Ostfront*, in 347–78; A. Holitscher, *Mein Leben*, in Glatzer and Glatzer, *Berliner Leben, 1914–1918*, 467.

38. BLHA, PPB, Nr. 15822, pp. 95–96, report, Schneider, 25 Feb. 1918.

39. Feldman, "War Economy and Controlled Economy"; Bessel, *Germany after the First World War*.

40. BLHA, PPB, Nr. 15822, pp. 69, report, Faßhauer, 14 Jan. 1918.

41. Cf. files of "defamatory writings," ibid., pp. 225–28, letter, "A.W.," 15 Aug. 1918, passed on by Schwarz, 21 Aug. 1918; pp. 229, report, Büchel, Aug. 1918. Most of the letters in the *Schmähschriften* file mention the prospective fate of Germans under foreign occupation.

42. Cf. ibid., p. 50, report, Faßhauer, 10 Dec. 1917.

43. Cf. BAL, 15.01, Nr. 2398/11, pp. 102–4, 15 Jan. 1918; BLHA, PPB, Nr. 15822, pp. 97–98, 25 Mar. 1918. Women had for some time demonstrated disinterest in the never ending public/private ventures in "collecting" for the war effort, from metals to human hair.

44. BAL, 15.01, Nr. 2398/11, pp. 102–4, 15 Jan. 1918.

45. BLHA, PPB, Nr. 15822, report, Schneider, 15 Jan. 1918; cf. pp. 89–90, report, Schrott/Büchel, 14 Feb. 1918; pp. 100–101, report, Schneider, 15 Mar. 1915.

46. Cf. ibid., p. 171, report, Schwarz, 17 Oct. 1918. Cf. police records of these "reading evenings," ibid., Nr. 15853, throughout this period.

47. Ibid., Nr. 15822, pp. 103–4, report, König, 15 Mar. 1918.

48. Cf. the original promise, "Sitzung des Ernährungsbeirats: Mehr Kartoffeln für Schwerarbeiter und Massenspeisung," *Vorwärts*, 24 Dec. 1917.

49. See BLHA, PPB, Nr. 15840, p. 96, notice, Kessel, Berge, 29 Jan. 1918; p. 128, Oppen's response, 29 Jan. 1918.

50. See "Streikleitung," *Vorwärts*, 29 Jan. 1918; BLHA, PPB, Nr. 15822, p. 96, notice, Kessel, 29 Jan. 1918.

51. Official sources agree on 185,000, with press sources slightly higher. See GStAPK, 2.2.1, Nr. 15095, pp. 6–21, report, Drews to Wilhelm, 6 Feb. 1918; BLHA, PPB, Nr. 15840, pp. 153–

56, mood report, Schwarz, 5 Feb. 1918. Cf. Bailey, "Berlin Strike of 1918"; Morgan, *Socialist Left and the German Revolution,* 87–90.

52. BLHA, PPB, Nr. 15842, p. 162, report of injuries, n.d. [ca. 1 Feb. 1918].

53. M. Globig, in Glatzer and Glatzer, *Berliner Leben, 1914–1918,* 364. *Strolch* is normally used to address youths; in this context it may also have questioned the policemen's failure either to serve on the front or even to join the protest.

54. BLHA, PPB, Nr. 15840, pp. 145–51, report, Oppen to Loebell, 6 Feb. 1918.

55. Ibid., Nr. 15822, pp. 153–56, report, Schwarz, 5 Feb. 1918.

56. Cf. ibid., p. 93, mood report, Görl, 15 Feb. 1918; p. 91, mood report, Faßhauer, 15 Feb. 1918; p. 94, report, Seeger, 25 Feb. 1918; "Zwei Arten Streikender," *Simplicissimus,* 2 Apr. 1918.

57. BLHA, PPB, Nr. 15822, p. 85, mood report, Oppen, 18 Feb. 1918; pp. 89–90, mood report, Schrott/Büchel, 14 Feb. 1918; p. 72, mood report, Lamm, 15 Jan. 1918; pp. 73–73a, mood report, Schneider, 15 Jan. 1918. Oppen observed unhappiness over rising unemployment, particularly among women, a factor not historically a cause for strikes. Schrott and Büchel claimed that many felt forced to go along with the strike and opined that this represented the peak of the USPD's influence.

58. Ibid., pp. 153–56, report, Schwarz, 5 Feb. 1918; GStAPK, 2.2.1, Nr. 15095, pp. 6–21, report, Drews, 15 Feb. 1918.

59. BLHA, PPB, Nr. 15840, pp. 153–56, report, Schwarz, 5 Feb. 1918.

60. See, e.g., ibid., Nr. 15822, pp. 73–73a, mood report, Schneider, 15 Jan. 1918; Nr. 15821, p. 369, mood report, Stolle, 22 Oct. 1917.

61. Ibid., Nr. 15840, pp. 153–56, mood report, Schwarz, 5 Feb. 1918.

62. Ibid., Nr. 15822, p. 93, mood report, Görl, 15 Feb. 1918; p. 92, mood report, Klonicki, 15 Feb. 1918; p. 85, mood report, Oppen, 18 Feb. 1918.

63. Cf. BAL, 15.01, Rep. 77, Nr. 12255, p. 175.

64. BLHA, PPB, Nr. 15851, p. 313, mood report, Palm, 22 Feb. 1918.

65. Cf. ibid., Nr. 15822, pp. 103–4, report, König, 15 Mar. 1918. Police believed this worked both ways. Oppen wrote in May that while, at that point, women demonstrated signs of potential unrest, their influence on working men was for the moment "extremely limited." He concluded, "As a result, this time we have no notable agitation" (ibid., pp. 152–54, mood report, Oppen, 22 May 1918). Oppen struck the final section from the ultimate draft of the report, leaving the impression of imminent unrest.

66. Ibid., pp. 100–101, mood report, Schneider, 15 Mar. 1918. Schneider added that the populace now believed that the state had pandered to industrial interests, purposefully extending the war. Cf. ibid.; p. 99, mood report, Görl, 15 Mar. 1918.

67. Cf., among hundreds of examples of such tensions, ibid., Nr. 15822, p. 139, report, 7 June 1918; Nr. 15842, edict, Loebell, 5 July 1917, and pp. 38–40, report, Oppen to Loebell, 13 July 1918. Compare, too, the flurry of acrimonious correspondence in January and February on jam deliveries.

68. Cf. ibid., Nr. 15822, p. 183, mood report, Förß, 15 July 1918. The replacement, Paul von Hintze, was sworn in in early August.

69. Cf. ibid., p. 185, report, Münn, 17 June 1918; p. 177, report, Schrott, 18 June 1918; p. 179, report, Faßhauer, 18 June 1918; p. 175, report, Schrott/Büchel, 12 July 1918; p. 178, Diercks, 15 July 1918.

70. See also GStAPK, 2.2.2, Rep. 197A, Ih 5, Lebensmittelversorgung Groß-Berlins, filled with letters from "Berliner Hausfrauen" written in this period.

71. "Das zurückgesetzte Berlin: Groß-Berlins Ernährungsnöte," *Berliner Allgemeine Zeitung,* 11 June 1918.

72. Cf. BLHA, PPB, Nr. 15822, p. 178, report, Diercks, 15 July 1918; p. 175, report, Schrott/Büchel, 12 July 1918.

73. Ibid., p. 175, report, Schrott/Büchel, 12 July 1918.

74. Cf. Deist, *Militär, Staat,* 211–34; Scheidemann, *Making of the New Germany,* 2:151–52.

75. Compare "Freie Gestaltung unserer Ernährungssysteme," *Deutsche Tageszeitung,* 23 May 1918; "System 'Waldow' oder System 'Müller-, Stegerwald-, Scheidemann,'" *Deutsche Tageszeitung,* 17 Dec. 1917. Cf. Feldman, "War Economy and Controlled Economy."

76. Cf. the early September battle among the KEA, Hertling, Wermuth, the SPD, and the Free Trade Unions over the failures of the controlled economy, publicized, e.g., in "Lebensmitteldebatte in der Berliner Stadtverordnetenversammlung," *Norddeutsche Allgemeine Zeitung,* 13 Sept. 1918, and "Der Reichskanzler zur Lebensmittelversorgung," ibid., 19 Sept. 1918.

77. BLHA, PPB, Nr. 15822, p. 196, mood report, Oppen, 20 June 1918. Official flour allowances were cut on 16 June from 200 to 160 grams per day.

78. Cf. ibid., pp. 22, 131, Lebensmittelübersicht, March 1918.

79. Cf. "Berliner Zuschauer: Das Verfahren wegen Höchstpreisüberschreitungen gegen Neukölln eingestellt," *Neue Preußische Zeitung,* 20 July 1918 (front page article). Cf. GStAPK, 2.2.2, Rep. 197A, Ii ii, pp. 167–70, 11 July 1918.

80. Cf. BLHA, PPB, Nr. 15822, pp. 196–97, mood report, Oppen, 20 June 1918; p. 183, mood report, Förß, 15 July 1918; "Noch immer kein Obst: Wo bleiben die nach Berlin gelieferten Mengen?," *Berliner Allgemeine Zeitunge,* 18 July 1918; "Der Magistrat Berlin zur Obstversorgung," *Berliner Morgenpost,* 27 July 1918; "Die Paketschnüsselei vor dem Postschalter: Polizei und Postverwaltung," *Berliner Lokal Anzeiger,* 24 Aug. 1918.

81. BLHA, PPB, Nr. 15822, p. 38, mood report, Oppen, 13 July 1918; pp. 201–3, mood report, Stolle, 22 July 1918.

82. Ibid., p. 229, report, Büchel, 30 Aug. 1918.

83. Ibid., p. 179, mood report, Faßhauer, 18 June 1918; BAL, 15.01, Rep. 77, Reichskanzlei 2398/12, p. 26, report, Oppen, 19 Aug. 1918, and Nr. 12479, pp. 1–2, 3 Aug. 1918; BLHA, PPB, Nr. 15822, p. 178, report, Diercks, 15 June 1918, and Nr. 15842, pp. 38–42, report, Oppen to Loebell, 13 July 1918.

84. Cf. BLHA, PPB, Nr. 15822, p. 175, report, Schrott/Büchel, 15 July 1918; p. 178, report, Diercks, 15 July 1918; BAL, 15.01, Nr. 12479, p. 18, monthly report, 3 July 1918, and pp. 1–2, 3 Aug. 1918.

85. BAL, 15.01, Nr. 12479, pp. 1–2, 3 Aug. 1918.

86. Ibid., p. 18, 3 July 1918, and p. 29, 3 Aug. 1918.

87. BLHA, PPB, Nr. 15822, pp. 201–3, mood report, Stolle, 22 July 1918.

88. Ibid., Nr. 15842, p. 109, mood report, Palm, 20 Aug. 1918.

89. "Zur Warnung!," *Münchener Post,* 10 Aug. 1918; "Zur Ernährungslage: Münchener Frauenabordnungen im Ministerium des Innern und im Rathaus," *Vorwärts,* 10 Aug. 1918; BAL, 15.01, Nr. 12476/1, Treutler to Hertling, Bavaria, 12 Aug. 1918.

90. BAL, 15.01, Rep. 77, Reichskanzlei, Nr. 2398/1, p. 26, report, Oppen, 19 Aug. 1918.

91. Cläre Casper-Denfert, "Steh auf," cited in Glatzer and Glatzer, *Berliner Leben, 1914–1918,* 380–81. Cf. *Das Große Beispiel,* 28–30; Dornemann, *Alle Tage ihres Lebens,* 74. On police engagement in a postal food delivery scam, cf. "Die Paketschnüsselei vor dem Postschalter: Polizei und Postverwaltung," *Berliner Lokal Anzeiger,* 24 Aug. 1918.

92. Cf. BAL, 15.01, Nr. 12476/1, p. 321, Treutler to Hertling, 12 Aug. 1918.

93. Cf. BLHA, PPB, Nr. 15842, pp. 109–10, report, Palm, 20 Aug. 1918; BAL, 15.01, Rep. 77, Nr. 12476/1, report, on Ruhrgebiet, 12 Sept. 1918, and Nr. 12479, pp. 13, 18, 3 Sept. 1918.

94. Cf. BLHA, PPB, Nr. 15842, pp. 145–46, Sergeant Lang, Düsseldorf, to Interior Ministry, 29 Sept. 1918.

95. Cf. the front-page article "Die kommenden Teuerungszulagen für die höheren Beamten," *Tägliche Rundschau,* 28 Aug. 1918; "Die neuen Kriegsteuerungszulagen: Erklärungen des Finanzministers," *Berliner Tageblatt,* 25 Aug. 1918; "Die Sonderbelieferung der Rüstungsarbeiter: Drohende Verteuerung der Lebenshaltung," *Vorwärts,* 29 Aug. 1918.

96. Cf. BAL, 15.01, Rep. 77, Nr. 12476/1, p. 320, Dr. Nieder to Dr. Francke, 10 Aug. 1918, and Nr. 12479, p. 13, 3 Sept. 1918.

97. BLHA, PPB, Nr. 15822, p. 230, report, Dittmann, 9 Sept. 1918.

98. "Der Reichskanzler zur Lebensmittelversorgung," *Norddeutsche Allgemeine Zeitung,* 19 Sept. 1918.

99. Cf. "Lebensmitteldebatte in der Berliner Stadtverordnetenversammlung," *Norddeutsche Allgemeine Zeitung,* 13 Sept. 1918.

100. Manifesto der kommunistischen Partei Deutschlands, in GStAPK, 2.2.1, Nr. 15266, pp. 74–75, 13 Sept. 1918.

101. Cf. Drabkin, *Die Novemberrevolution,* 76.

102. Ludendorff to deputy commanders, 1 Oct. 1918, cited in Berghahn, *Modern Germany,* 59. Compare the same expression in the *Deutsche Tageszeitung* after the January unrest, cited in Ay, *Entstehung,* 84.

103. BAL, 15.01, Rep. 77, Nr. 12479, pp. 3–10, 3 Oct. 1918.

104. Cf. BLHA, PPB, Nr. 15842, pp. 186–87, report, Borchert/Bunde/Rhein/Wodtke, 17 Oct. 1918; "Eine Demonstration Unter den Linden," *Vorwärts,* 17 Oct. 1918; cf. also "Friedensdemonstration in Berlin: Die Polizei bearbeitet Frauen mit dem Säbel," *Leipziger Volkszeitung,* 17 Oct. 1918. Materna and Schreckenbach claim there were 5,000 to 6,000 participants in the demonstration; see *Dokumente,* 293 n. They also assert clear aims concerning peace, revolution, and the release of Karl Liebknecht, though this clarity applied perhaps more to the leaders' aims than to those of the greater crowd.

105. GStAPK, 2.2.1, Nr. 15765, pp. 10–18, report, Oppen to Kaiser Wilhelm, 29 Oct. 1918. Oppen took the opportunity to express his own view of the responsibility of Jews for the prevailing circumstances.

106. BLHA, PPB, Nr. 15842, pp. 178–79, report, Oppen to Loebell, 17 Oct. 1918. Compare frequent reference to politically organized protesting women as the derogatory *Weiber,* e.g., ibid., Nr. 15822, pp. 225–28, letter, "A.W.," 15 Aug. 1918.

107. Cf. ibid., Nr. 15842, p. 173, report, Schwarz, 17 Oct. 1918.

108. Cf. GStAPK, 2.2.1, Rep. 77, Tit. 332r, Nr. 126, pp. 183–84, report, Oppen.

109. "Die Angst vor der Stimmung," *Deutsche Tageszeitung,* 26 Oct. 1918.

110. GStAPK, 2.2.2, Rep. 197A, Ih 5, Lebensmittelversorgung Groß-Berlins, p. 55, Lebensmittelverband to PVS, 26 Oct. 1915.

111. BLHA, PPB, Nr. 15842, p. 76, unsigned private letter to police commission, 13 Aug. 1918.

112. GStAPK, 2.2.1, Nr. 15765, pp. 10–16, report, Oppen to Kaiser Wilhelm, 29 Oct. 1918.

113. Cf. BAPK, Nr. 1578, Weltkrieg I, Krieg in der Heimat; Hallen and Kerbs, *Revolution und Fotografie;* Glatzer and Glatzer, *Berliner Leben, 1914–1918,* 429–569; Annemarie Lange, *Das Wilhelminische Berlin,* 787–97; Berliner Geschichtswerkstatt, *August 1914; Das Große Beispiel; 1918: Erinnerungen.* On flu and revolution, see *Vorwärts und nicht Vergessen,* 247–48.

114. See Hermann Duncker, in *Vorwärts und nicht Vergessen,* 52; among dozens of pamphlets, see *Frauen kämpft für den Frieden; Alle Macht den Räten!* USPD leaders may have believed the masses of women in the streets who were not formally organized would be harder to attract or control.

115. Cf. also in Altona, Erna Holm, "Alle bewaffneten nach vorn!," in *Vorwärts und nicht Vergessen,* 248.

116. *Das Große Beispiel,* 31.

117. *1918: Erinnerungen,* 293; *Das Große Beispiel.*

118. Cf. *1918: Erinnerungen,* 290.

119. Cf. sailor Franz Beiersdorf, in *Unter der roten Fahne,* 293.

120. Cf. Richard Müller, *Geschichte der Deutschen Revolution,* 2:10.

121. Kaiser's note of abdication, reprinted in Annemarie Lange, *Das Wilhelminische Berlin,* facing 753.

122. On the November revolution, cf. among others, Ryder, *German Revolution of 1918;* Eberhard Kolb, *Die Arbeiterräte;* Lucas, *Frankfurt unter der Herrschaft;* Oertzen, *Betriebsräte in der Revolution;* Tobin, "Revolution in Düsseldorf"; Rürup, "Demokratische Revolution und 'Dritter Weg.'"

CONCLUSION

1. Delbrück, *Wirtschaftliche Mobilmachung,* 139.

2. On the Weimar social compact, cf. Peukert, *Weimar Republic,* 130–32.

3. On demobilization, see Bessel, *Germany after the First World War;* Rouette, *Sozialpolitik.*

4. Cf. Winter and Robert, conclusion to *Capital Cities at War,* 532–36.

5. Cf. BAL, 31.01 R43, I/1255, telegram to Berlin, 11 Sept. 1919, regarding military intervention in food smuggling and speculation, pp. 139–40, and pp. 223–24 for correspondence on the Versailles Treaty and its relation to food commerce and distribution.

6. Cf. Feldman, *Great Disorder;* Martin Geyer, *Verkehrte Welt;* on Berlin, Andrea Lefevre, "Lebensmittelunruhen in Berlin 1920–1923," in Gailus and Volkmann, *Kampf um das tägliche Brot,* 346–60.

7. See, e.g., BAL, 31.01 R43, I/1253, p. 15, letter from officials of Mallmitz to Kopfsch, member of the Preussische Landesversammlung, regarding the response of the local population to prevailing food conditions, 4 Dec. 1919, and p. 26, telegram, Verein Elberfelder Handelsvertreter to Reichsmininsterpräsident, 14 July 1919, which reiterates the idea of unbearable pressures. Cf. Lüdtke, "'Ihr könnt nun wissen,'" in Lüdtke, *Eigen-Sinn,* 210–20.

8. Cf. Bumm, *Deutschlands Gesundheitsverhältnisse; Das Gesundheitswesen des preußischen Staates;* "Hungerblockade und Volksgesundheit."

9. BAL, 31.01 R43, I/1253, p. 23, letter, E. Wurm, 13 Jan. 1919; cf. p. 268, report, Schmidt to Landwirtschaftsministerium, 12 Sept. 1919.

10. See ibid., e.g., pp. 1–3, memo, State Secretary of the KEA to all soldiers' and sailors' councils, "Die Aufrechterhaltung der Volksernährung," November 1918, and p. 22, letter,

Reichsregierung to Imperial Committee for German Agriculture, 4 Jan. 1919, assuring the latter of their arrangements with the councils. The councils were likewise uncomfortably dependent on the Berlin government for national-level measures putatively confronting regional inequities.

11. Ibid., I/1254, p. 7, Antrag RAKI, May 1919.

12. See ibid., I/1253, pp. 110–11, 1 Apr. 1919, guidelines, REM to Rhenish grocers. Authorities attempted to render the roles of these organizations more "positive," setting them up virtually as wholesalers in this transcendent market system.

13. Ibid., I/1254, p. 7, May 1919. This passage was heavily underlined by officials.

14. It remained in place until 1920. Cf. Feldman, *Great Disorder*, on debates around the postwar forced economy. All of the European powers grappled with this to some degree. Particularly in Britain and France, heavy state intervention was cause for concern.

15. See, e.g., BAL, 15.01, Nr. 13545, n.p., Förderung der öffentlichen Moral, n.d. [January 1923].

16. See Imperial Food Minister Schmidt's ominous plea to President Ebert, BAL, 31.01 R43, I/1253, p. 202, 5 June 1919, and p. 203, Ebert's response. Cf. Harsch, *German Social Democracy,* including reproduction of SPD, Communist, and National Socialist posters playing on the theme of bread and politics.

17. Cf. Wurm, *Übergangswirtschaft;* Calwer, "Zerfall der deutschen Volkswirtschaft"; Stegerwald, *Wege der Volkswohlfahrt.*

18. Cf. BAL, 31.01 R43, I/1253, p. 128, R. Schmidt to F. Ebert, 16 Apr. 1919, regarding the equalization of food distribution between countryside and city, with particular concern to guarantee the needs of the big cities, I/2692, p. 252, report, A. Wermuth, n.d. [ca. 1 June 1919].

19. Cf. ibid., I/1253, p. 140, letter from officials of Mallmitz to Kopfsch, member of the Preussische Landesversammlung. Compare Seier, "Berlin und die deutsche Nation"; Tenfelde, "Stadt und Land," 37–57; Brandt and Rürup, *Volksbewegung,* 12.

20. See e.g. BAL, 31.01 R43, I/1253, p. 4, Nov. 1919, notice advising farmers of their responsibility to ensure the people's nutrition.

21. See ibid., p. 123, 15 Apr. 1919, and I/2692, p. 277, unsigned letter, Bund der Landwirte to Reichskanzler Scheidemann, 14 June 1919.

22. Ibid., I/1253, p. 79, Chamber of Commerce Graudenz, 28 Feb. 1919.

23. See ibid., p. 65, notice, Wurm to Freund, Neuhaus, Busch, Mügel, 15 Feb. 1919; the notice also indicated the War Profiteering Office would operate at a higher administrative level than before and that council members would participate on its board.

24. Cf. E. Ritter, *Reichskommissar für Überwachung.*

25. See BAL, 31.01 R43, I/2688, Polizei, Überwachung, p. 23, 2 Sept. 1921, memorandum, interior minister to Collective Regierungespräsidenten and Oberpräsidenten, 12 Mar. 1919. Cf. p. 13, 24 Feb. 1920; BAL, 15.01, Nr. 13348, Politische Lage Pr. Br., n.p., comment on *Deutsche Allgemeine Zeitung* of 18 Sept. 1920, n.d. [ca. 20 Sept. 1920].

26. See e.g. BAL, 31.01 R43, I/1253, p. 5, recommendation of the Deutscher Verein für Volksernährung to the Volksbeauftragten, 29 Nov. 1918. Cf. accounts of the Deutsche Wachgesellschaft, which fought smuggling, in BAL, 15.01, Nr. 13348, Politische Lage Pr. Br., n.d. [ca. July 1920].

27. See BAL, 31.01 R43, I/1253, regular letters from localities warning of further unrest and a return to self help.

28. Robert Weismann ironically describes this process as *hintenherum*. Cf. E. Ritter, *Reichs-kommissar für Überwachung*, ix. Compare Liang, *Berlin Police Force in the Weimar Republic*; Leßmann, *Die Preußische Schutzpolizei*. The new police patrol quickly readopted the hated *Pickelhaube*, symbol of Prussian military power.

29. Cf. *1918: Erinnerungen*, 312–22; *Das Große Beispiel*, 38–40.

30. Chap. 1, sec. 1, art. 1, of the Weimar constitution, reprinted in Kaes, Jay, and Dimendberg, *Weimar Republic Sourcebook*, 46.

31. The vast literature on the development of the welfare state, including in Germany, has been remarkably silent on the war. For an overview of German *Sozialpolitik* until the First World War, cf. Tennstedt, *Sozialgeschichte der Sozialpolitik*; Sachße and Tennstedt, *Geschichte der Armenfürsorge*; Sachße, "Wohlfahrtsstaat in historischer und vergleichender Perspecktive"; Gerhard A. Ritter, *Social Welfare*; Steinmetz, *Regulating the Social*; Lüdtke, *"Sicherheit" und "Wohlfahrt."* On the German welfare state in Weimar, see Crew, *Germans on Welfare*; Abelshauser, *Weimarer Republik als Wohlfahrtsstaat*; Hong, *Welfare, Modernity, and the Weimar State*; Preller's still important *Sozialpolitik*. Among recent comparative work, see Koven and Michel, *Mothers of a New World*; Gerhard A. Ritter, *Social Welfare*; Mommsen, *Emergence of the Welfare State*; Bock and Thane, *Maternity*; Pedersen, *Family, Dependence, and the Origins of the Welfare State*. Few traverse the war period; Gerhard A. Ritter, "Entstehung des Sozialstaates," does so, emphasizing patterns of continuity from Wilhelmine to Weimar welfare policy. But cf. new work by Eghigian, *Making Security Social* and Hong, "Contradictions of Modernization." Compare, too, Führer, *Arbeitslosigkeit*; Hausen, "German Nation's Obligations."

32. Rural as well as urban women looked sanguinely on state intervention after the war. See Bridenthal, "Rural Women." See also Rouette, *Sozialpolitik*. Russians demanded a return to free-market food distribution in civil-war St. Petersburg, on the basis of perceived state incompetence in that nation. See McAuley, "Bread without the Bourgeoisie."

33. On the contradictory promises of the Weimar social compact, cf. Führer, "Für das Wirtschaftsleben"; Crew, *Germans on Welfare*; Geyer, "Teuerungsprotest"; Feldman, *Great Disorder*, 555, 609; Rudloff, "Unwillkommene Fürsorge."

34. Cf. Eberhard Kolb, *Weimar Republic*; Bessel, *Germany after the First World War*.

35. Cf. Preller, *Sozialpolitik*; Peukert, *Weimar Republic*, 129–46; Doris Marquardt, *Sozialpolitik und Sozialfürsorge*; Führer, "Für das Wirtschaftsleben"; Crew, *Germans on Welfare*.

36. Cf. on the American case, Nelson, "Origins of the Two-Channel Welfare State." This issue is problematized in Koven and Michel, *Mothers of a New World*; Pedersen, *Family, Dependence, and the Origins of the Welfare State*.

37. On the "citizen consumer," see Davis, "Food Scarcity"; Lizabeth Cohen, "New Deal State"; Auslander, *Taste and Power*. This is not to suggest that it was inherently better that women were valued as workers rather than as mothers. Compare Koven and Michel, "Womanly Duties," 1077. On the necessity of revolution to liberate hungry civilians, cf. Friedrich Ebert's opening speech of the national assembly, 6 Feb. 1919, recorded in Heilfron, *Deutsche Nationalversammlung*, 214.

38. The concept also bore a longer-term, right-wing genealogy. Cf. Chickering, *We Men Who Feel Most German*, 38. On popular sovereignty in Weimar, cf. Caldwell, *Popular Sovereignty*.

39. Cf. Lindenberger and Lüdtke, *Physische Gewalt*; Kurz, *"Blutmai"*; Fritzsche, *Rehearsals for Fascism*; McElligott, "Das 'Abruzzenviertel'"; Rosenhaft, *Beating the Fascists?*; Weisbrod, "Gewalt in der Politik"; Martin Geyer, *Verkehrte Welt*. Compare Healy, "Divided Home."

40. BAL, 15.01, Nr. 13348, flyers posted in Berlin, 6 Nov. 1920.

41. Cf. D. Peukert, "Genesis of the 'Final Solution'"; Fritzsche, *Germans into Nazis;* Bartov, *Murder in Our Midst;* Feldman, *Great Disorder.*

42. Cf. "Neue Ausschreitungen: Sturm auf die Rathäuser in Neukölln und Pankow," *Deutsche Allgemeine Zeitung,* 29 Nov. 1921; BAL, 15.01, Nr. 13348, commentary on the article, n.d. [ca. 30 Nov. 1921]. By this time Social Democrats no longer led the ruling coalition.

43. BAL, 31.01 R43, I/2692, Sicherheitspolizei, pp. 4–5, memorandum, Oberpräsident Berlin, 3 June 1920.

44. See Social Democratic propaganda, e.g., BAL, 15.01, Nr. 13348, p. 2, reprinted in *Tägliche Rundschau,* 10 Feb. 1919; p. 32, propaganda leaflet, "Sozialisierung und Bürgertum"; p. 34, leaflet, "Wer hilft den Beamten?," n.d.

45. See, for example, the links between newly developed popular sovereignty, "nationalist feeling," and the Versailles Treaty, BAL, 15.01, Nr. 13529, Reichsministerium des Innern, the Nationalist Question, esp. pp. 7–10, 9 Mar. 1923, Reichstag Report. See also ibid., p. 13, 21 Mar. 1923, private letter to Reichsministerium linking nationalism, sacrifice, and "the most bitter *Not*" during the Ruhr occupation, and pp. 15–16, private letter to Reichsministerium, which names "hunger as the greatest enemy of passive resistance." Many seemed to think that girls and women could now demonstrate this nationalist sentiment. See ibid., p. 14, 21 Mar. 1923, "Aufruf an die deutsche Jugend," claiming "the fatherland is in danger" and that German girls as well as boys must dedicate themselves to protecting the nation—though as "fellow fighters" (*Mitkämpferinnen*) in this "army."

46. Compare Tiger and Hollaender, "Wenn der alte Motor wieder tackt," i.e., the song "Raus mit den Männern aus dem Reichstag," which completes the phrase "und rein in die Dinger mit der Frau."

47. Cf. L. Finckh, "Der Geist von Berlin," *Schwäbischer Merkur,* 10 Jan. 1919, reprinted in Kaes et al., *Weimar Republic Sourcebook,* 414–45. Compare Führer, "Für das Wirtschaftsleben."

48. See BAL, 15.01, 13348, pp. 85–91, anti-Semitic leaflets and manifestos.

49. Cf., e.g., Blessing, "Konsumentenprotest und Arbeitskampf"; Robert, "Drink and the Labour Movement"; Lindenberger, *Straßenpolitik.* Cf. Glaeßner, *Arbeiterbewegung;* Hasselmann, *Geschichte der deutschen Konsumgenossenschaften;* Nonn, *Verbraucherprotest;* before unification, see R. Reith, "Lohn- und Kostkonflikte," in Gailus and Volkmann, *Kampf um das tägliche Brot,* 85–106.

50. Cf. "Demonstrationen im Lustgarten," *Deutsche Allgemeine Zeitung.* Compare BAL, 15.01, Nr. 13348, reports on the strike of Berlin gasworkers, 12 Nov. 1921; Geyer, "Teuerungsprotest."

51. BAL, 31.01 R43, I/1253, pp. 51–54. Cf. pp. 63–64, Graevenitz, Reichsgetreidestelle, to the Reichsregierung and Nationale Versammlung in Weimar, 8 Feb. 1919, and pp. 105–8, letters and petitions of sugar factories, Mar., Apr. 1919.

52. Ibid., I/1255, p. 86, report to Scheidemann on conditions for postal workers, 25 Aug. 1919. The report also refers to the threat to the moral strength that postal workers had maintained to date under duress, but which now stood threatened. Cf. BAL, 15.01, Nr. 13582, p. 40, 1 Feb. 1919.

53. BAL, 31.01 R43, I/1254, p. 7, May 1919.

54. See, e.g., ibid., p. 13, "Grundlagen für die Preisbemessung der landwirtschaftlichen Erzeugnisse, im Jahr 1919," Denkschrift of the REM.

BIBLIOGRAPHY

ARCHIVAL SOURCES

Archiv des Freien Demokratischen Gewerkschaftsbundes, Berlin
  Nachlässe Hermann und Käte Duncker
Archiv des Diakonischen Werkes, Berlin
  CA 734
Bezirksarchiv Neukölln, Berlin-Neukölln
  24L 4/5
  35L 4/11
  24M 1/6
Bildarchiv Preußischer Kulturbesitz, Berlin
  1573b Frauenarbeit in der deutschen Rüstungsindustrie während des 1. Weltkrieges
  1578 Weltkrieg—Krieg in der Heimat
Brandenburgisches Landeshauptarchiv, Potsdam
  Provinz Brandenburg
    Repositur 1A
    Repositur 2A
    Repositur 30, Berlin C
      Titel 35, 94, 95 Polizeipräsidium Berlin
      Titel 133
Bundesarchiv, Berlin-Lichterfelde
  01.01 Reichstag
  07.01 Reichskanzlei
  15.01 Reichsministerium des Innern
  15.07 Reichskommissar für Überwachung der Öffentlichen Ordnung
  31.01 R43 Akten betreffend Volksernaehrung
  36.01 Reichsministerium für Ernährung und Landwirtschaft
  39.01 Arbeitsministerium
  Reichslandsbund Pressearchiv
  Reichswirtschaftsamt (from 1918) Nr. 18771
Evangelisches Zentralarchiv, Berlin
  Rep. 7, 14, 51
Geheimes Staatsarchiv Preußischer Kulturbesitz, Berlin-Dahlem
  2.2.1 Geheimes Zivilkabinett
  Rep. 72
  Rep. 77 Ministerium des Innern
  Rep. 84a

Rep. 87b

Rep. 191

Rep. 197A Preußischer Staatskommissar für Volksernährung

Rep. 221

Institut für Marxismus-Leninismus, Zentrales Parteiarchiv der Sozialistischen Einheitspartei
Deutschlands, Berlin-Lichterfelde

V DF V/5ü, v/7ü, v/13ü, v/16ü, v/8, v/23, v/28, v/4, viii/132ü

V SUF 182, v/11ü

Landesarchiv Berlin, Berlin

Collection Helene-Lange-Archiv

Allgemeiner Deutscher Frauenverein

Files 4-20, 4-21, 18-76

Nachlässe

Gertrud Bäumer

Alice Bensheimer

Alice Salomon

Anna von Gierke

Deutscher Städtetag

Rep. 142/2

Stadtarchiv Berlin, Berlin

Neukölln Report

Rep. 03

Rep. 13 Magistrat für Berlin, Abt. Brotversorgung

Ullstein Bilderdienst, Berlin

War File KM 12, 481, 3267

2153205516 Unruhen 1919

2153207202 Lebensmittelknappheit

PRIMARY SOURCES

1918: Erinnerungen von Veteranen der deutschen Gewerkschaftsbewegung an die Novemberrevolution (1914–1920). Berlin: Verlag Tribüne, 1958.

"Abhandlung des Preussischen Ministeriums des Innern über 'Ernährung und Teuerung,'"
Spring 1916.

Abraham, Hermann. *Drei Kriegsjahre*. Berlin: Wirtschaftliches Wochenblatt, 1917.

Aereboe, F. *Der Einfluss des Krieges auf die Landwirtschaftliche Produktion in Deutschland*. Stuttgart:
Deutsche Verlags-Anstalt, 1927.

Alle Macht den Räten! Ein Wort an die Frauen und Männer des werktätigen Volkes. Stuttgart: Verlag
KPD, 1919.

Altmann-Gottheimer, Elisabeth. *Die Entwicklung der Frauenarbeit in der Metallindustrie*. Jena:
G. Fischer, 1916.

Anthony, Katherine. *Feminism in Germany and Scandinavia*. New York: Hold, 1915.

Arnoldt, Fritz. *Die Kartoffelversorgung im Kriege*. Beiträge zur Kriegswirtschaft, no. 2. Berlin:
Hobbing, 1916.

Baader, Ottilie. *Ein Steiniger Weg*. Berlin: Dietz, 1979.

Bach, F. W. *Untersuchungen über die Lebensmittelrationierung im Kriege*. Munich: Parcus, 1921.

Ballod, Carl. "Deutsche Volksernährung im Kriege." *Preußische Jahrbücher* 157 (1914): 101–17.

———. "Die Volksernährung in Krieg und Frieden." *Schmollers Jahrbuch* 39, no. 1 (1915): 77–112.

Batocki, H. C. von. *Warenpreis und Geldwert im Kriege.* Königsberg: n.p., 1919.

Bauer, Max. *Der Große Krieg in Feld und Heimat: Erinnerungen und Betrachtungen.* Tübingen: Osiander, 1921.

Bäumer, Gertrud. *Die deutsche Frau in der sozialen Kriegsfürsorge.* Gotha: Perthes, 1916.

———. "Frauendienst in der Volksernährung." *Die Frau,* February 1915, 291–94.

———. *Heimatchronik.* Berlin: F. A. Herbig, 1930.

———. *Der Krieg und die Frau.* Stuttgart: Deutsche Verlags-Anstalt, 1914.

———. "Der Patriotismus im Wirtschaftsleben." *Die Frau,* March 1915, 326–32.

———. "Phantasien und Tatsachen in der Frage des weiblichen Dienstjahres." *Die Frau,* March 1916, 321–29.

———. "Die Regelung des Nahrungsmittelverbrauchs." *Die Frau,* February 1916, 215–24.

Baumgarten, Otto, ed. *Geistige und sittliche Wirkungen des Krieges in Deutschland.* Stuttgart: Deutsche Verlags-Anstalt, 1927.

Bebel, August. *Women under Socialism.* New York: New York Labor News, 1904.

Beck, Christian, ed. *Die Frau und der Kriegsgefangene.* Nuremberg: Döllinger, 1919.

Beiträge zur Geschichte der deutschen Gewerkschaftsbewegung 1, no. 2 (1918).

Berlepsch, H.-J. von. *"Neuer Kurs" im Kaiserreich: Die Arbeiterpolitik des Freiherrn von Berlepsch 1890 bis 1896.* Bonn: Neue Gesellschaft, 1987.

Berlin, 1917–1918. Berlin: Bezirksleitung der SED Gross-Berlin, 1957.

Bethmann Hollweg, Theobald von. *Betrachtungen zum Weltkriege.* Essen: Reimar Hobbing, 1989.

Birkenfeld, Günther. *A Room in Berlin: A Novel of Slum Life in Post-War Berlin.* London: Constable, 1930.

Blos, Anna. *Kommunale Frauenarbeit im Krieg.* Berlin: Verlag für Kommunale Wissenschaft, 1917.

Blücher von Wahlstatt, Evelyn. *An English Wife in Berlin.* New York: Dutton, 1920.

Braun, Adolf. *Die Arbeiterinnen und die Gewerkschaften.* Berlin: Vorwärts, 1913.

Braun, F. E. von. *Kann Deutschland durch Hunger besiegt Werden? Eine Kriegsbetrachtung.* Munich: C. Gerber, 1914.

Buerstner, Fritz. *Die Kaffee-Ersatzmittel vor und während der Kriegszeit.* Beiträge zur Kriegswirtschaft, no. 43. Berlin: Hobbing, 1918.

Braun, Lily. *Die Frauen und der Krieg.* Leipzig: Hirzel, 1915.

Bumm, F., ed. *Deutschlands Gesundheitsverhältnisse unter dem Einfluss des Weltkrieges.* Vols. 1–2. Stuttgart: Deutsche Verlags-Anstalt, 1928.

Calwer, Richard. *Die Brotgetreide und Kartoffelversorgung Deutschlands.* Berlin: Calwer, 1915.

———. *Die Ernährung der Städtischen Bevölkerung.* Berlin: Calwer, 1916.

———. *Verstaatlichung der Produktionsmittel?* Berlin: Calwer 1919.

———. *Der Zerfall der deutschen Volkswirtschaft.* Berlin: Calwer, 1920.

Caro, L. *Der Wucher: Eine socialpolitische Studie.* Leipzig: Carl Reissner, 1893.

Cauer, M. *Leben und Werk.* Gotha: Verlag F. A. Perthes, 1925.

Cooper, Ethel. *Behind the Lines: One Woman's War.* London: Jill Norman and Hobhouse, 1982.

David, Eduard. *Das Kriegstagebuch des Reichstagsabgeordneten E. David, 1914 bis 1918.* Düsseldorf: Droste, 1966.

Dawson, William H. *Bismarck and State Socialism: An Exposition of the Social and Economic Legislation of Germany since 1870.* New York: Howard Fertig, 1973.

Delbrück, Clemens von. *Die Wirtschaftliche Mobilmachung in Deutschland, 1914.* Munich: Verlag für Kulturpolitik, 1924.

Deutscher Maschinenbau 1837–1937 im Spiegel des Werkes Borsig. Berlin: n.p., 1939.

Deutscher Metallarbeiter Verband. *Die Frauenarbeit in der Metallindustrie während des Krieges.* Stuttgart: Schlicke, 1917.

Döblin, Alfred. *November 1918: Eine Deutsche Revolution.* Munich: DTV, 1978.

Doty, M. Z. *Short Rations: An American Woman in Germany.* New York: Century, 1915.

Duden deutsches Universalwörterbuch. 2d ed. Mannheim: Dudenverlag, 1989.

Eisenmenger, Anna. *Blockade: The Diary of an Austrian Middle-Class Woman, 1914–1924.* London: Constable, 1932.

Elsas, F. *Die Nährmittelverteilung im Kriege.* Berlin: Verlag der Beiträge zur Kriegswirtschaft, 1918.

Eltzbacher, Paul, ed. *Die Deutsche Volksernährung und der Englische Aushungerungsplan.* Brunswick: Vieweg, 1914.

Eltzbacher, Paul, et al. *Ernährung in der Kriegszeit: Ein Ratgeber für Behörden, Geistliche, Ärtze, Lehrer, usw.* Brunswick: Vieweg, 1914.

Engelhardt, Elisabeth. *Die Zentralisation der Städtischen Haushaltungen.* Munich: Parcus, 1916, 1917.

Die Ernährung im Wirtschaftsjahr 1917/18. [Berlin]: Aufklärungsstelleder KEA, 1918.

Erzberger, Matthias. *Erlebnisse im Weltkrieg.* Stuttgart: Deutsche Verlags-Anstalt, 1920.

———. *Schädigung der Deutschen Volkskraft durch die feindliche Blockade.* Berlin: Reichsdruckerei, 1918.

Ewald, M. *Die pflanzlichen und tierischen Öle und Fette, ausschliesslich der Molkereiprodukte, in Frieden und Krieg.* Beiträge zur Kriegswirtschaft, no. 33. Berlin: Hobbing, 1918.

Falck, Carl. *Die Bekämpfung des Kettenhandels."* Beiträge zur Kriegswirtschaft, no. 3. Berlin: Hobbing, 1916.

Fischer-Eckert, Li. *Die wirtschaftliche und soziale Lage der Frauen in dem modernen Industrieort Hamborn im Rheinland.* Hagen: Stracke, 1913.

Frauen kämpft für den Frieden. Berlin: Internationaler Arbeiterverlag, n.d. [1918].

Freud, Sigmund. *Group Psychology and the Analysis of the Ego.* New York: Bantam, 1965.

Die Front Gegen den Hunger. *Ernährungskrieg 1939/43.* Berlin: C. V. Engelhard, 1944.

Fuchs, C. *Die Deutsche Volkswirtschaft im Kriege.* Tübingen: Akademische Reden, 1915.

Gerlach, Hellmut von. *Die Große Zeit der Lüge.* Bremen: Donat, 1994.

Geschäfts- und Reviereinteilung des Polizeipräsidiums Berlin. Berlin: Verlag der Stadt Berlin, 1922.

Das Gesundheitswesen des preußischen Staates. Berlin: R. Schoetz, 1923.

Gläser, Ernst. *Class of 1902.* New York: Viking, 1929.

Gottstein, A. "Volksspeisung, Schulkinderspeisung, Notstandsspeisung, Massenspeisung." Berlin: n.p., 1917.

Gradnauer, Georg, and Robert Schmidt. *Die Deutsche Volkswirtschaft.* Berlin: Vorwärts, 1921.

Graf, Oskar Maria. *Wir sind Gefangene: ein Bekenntnis.* Munich: dtv, 1986.

Groener, Wilhelm. *Lebenserinnerungen.* Göttingen: Vandenhoeck und Ruprecht, 1957.

Das Große Beispiel: Lichtenburg auf den Spuren des roten Oktobers (1914–1922). Berlin: SED, 1967.

Grotjahn, Alfred. *Erlebtes und Erstrebtes: Erinnerungen eines Sozialistischen Arztes.* Berlin: Herbig, 1932.

Haenisch, Konrad. *Wo steht der Hauptfeind? Aus Aufsätzen der "Internationalen Korrespondenz."* Berlin-Karlshorst: Internationalen Korrespondenz, 1915.

Hanna, Gertrud. *Die Arbeiterinnen und der Krieg.* Berlin: Verlag der internationalen Korrespondenz, 1916.

Harnack, Agnes von. *Der Krieg und die Frauen.* Berlin: n.p., 1915.

Heilfron, Eduard. *Die deutsche Nationalversammlung, 1919/20.* Berlin: n.p., 1920.

Helfferich, Karl. *Der Weltkrieg vom Eingreifen Amerikas bis zum Zusammenbruch.* Berlin: Ullstein, 1919.

Hesse, Albert. *Freie Wirtschaft und Zwangswirtschaft im Kriege.* Beiträge zur Kriegswirtschaft, no. 39. Berlin: Hobbing, 1918.

Heuss, T. *Kriegssozialismus.* Stuttgart: Deutsche Verlags-Anstalt, 1915.

Heyl, Hedwig. *Drei Monate Volksspeisung.* Berlin: n.p., 1916.

Hirsch, Julius, and Carl Falck. *Der Kettenhandel als Kriegserscheinung.* Berlin: n.p., 1916.

———. *Der Kettenhandel in Wirtschaftlicher Darstellung.* Beiträge zur Kriegswirtschaft, no. 3. Berlin: Hobbing, 1916.

Hirsch, P. *Die Versorgung der Kriegsteilnehmer, ihrer Familien und Hinterbliebenen.* Berlin: Singer, 1915.

Hirschfeld, Magnus. *The Sexual History of the World War.* New York: Panurge, 1934.

Hoffmann, Margarete. "Das Gesetz betreffend die Unterstützung von Familien in den Dienst eingetretener Mannschaften vom 28.2.1888–4.8.1914 und seine Anwendung." Ph.D. diss., Kaiser Wilhelm Universität, Berlin, 1918.

In Einer Droschke Zweiter Klasse: Geschichten aus Berlin um die Jahrhundertwende. Berlin: Neues Leben, 1986.

Die innere Front. Berlin: A. Jandorf, 1917.

Institut für soziale Arbeit, Munich, ed. *Die weibliche Dienstpflicht.* Munich: O. Gmelin, 1916.

Jünger, Ernst. *Storm of Steel.* London: Chatto and Windus, 1929.

Kaeber, Ernst. *Beiträge zur Berliner Geschichte.* Berlin: Trowisssch und Sohn, 1921.

———. *Berlin im Weltkriege: Fünf Jahre Städtischer Kriegsarbeit.* Berlin: de Gruyter, 1964.

Die Kartoffel in der Kriegswirtschaft. Beiträge zur Kriegswirtschaft, no. 1. Berlin: Hobbing, 1916.

Kessler, Harry. *In the Twenties: The Diaries of Harry Kessler.* New York: Holt, Rinehart: 1971.

Klaus, Albert. *Die Hungernden: Ein Arbeitslosenroman.* Berlin: Verlag Der Bücherkreis, 1932.

Kolb, Annette. *Briefe einer Deutsch-Französin.* Berlin: Erich Reiss, 1916.

Köppe, H. *Kriegswirtschaft und Sozialismus.* Marburg: Elwert, 1915.

Koppenfels, S. *Die Kriminalität der Frau im Kriege.* Leipzig: Wiegandt, 1926.

Krüger, Hans. *Die Massenspeisung.* Beiträge zur Kriegswirtschaft, no. 14. Berlin: Hobbing, 1917.

Lange, Helene. *Das "Weibliche Dienstjahr."* Berlin: Moeser, 1913.

Lautenbach, Wilhelm. *Die Kartoffeltrocknung im Kriege.* Beiträge zur Kriegswirtschaft, no. 54/55. Berlin: Hobbing, 1919.

Le Bon, Gustav. *The Crowd.* London: Unwin, 1910.

———. *The Psychology of the Great War.* London: Unwin, 1916.

Leidigkeit, Hans. "Die Fabrikarbeit Verheirateter Frauen." Ph.D. diss., Universität Greifswald, 1919.

Lenz, Siegfried. *Lebensmittel-Zulagen.* Beiträge zur Kriegswirtschaft, no. 26/27. Berlin: Hobbing, 1917.

Lenze, Philipp. "Die Kartoffelversorgung der Stadt Berlin." Ph.D. diss., Universität Würzburg, 1921.

Levy-Rathenau, Josephine. "Die Eingliederung der weiblichen Hinterbliebenen in das Wirtschaftsleben." *Die Frau*, February 1916, 272–76.

Leyser, Erich. "Gross-Berliner Wohnungspolitik im Kriege." In *Grossstadt und Kleinhaus*, edited by K. F. von Siemens, F. Thielicke, and Erich Leyser, 5–30. Berlin: Verlag der Bauwelt, 1917.

Liepmann, Moritz. *Krieg und Kriminalität in Deutschland*. Stuttgart: Deutsche Verlags-Anstalt, 1930.

Lindemann, Hugo. *Die Deutsche Stadtgemeinde im Kriege*. Tübingen: Mohr, 1917.

Lindenberg, Paul. *Berlin in Wort und Bild*. Leipzig: Zentralantiquariat der Deutschen Demokratischen Republik, 1985.

Lion, Hilde. *Zur Soziologie der Frauenbewegung: Die sozialistische und katholische Frauenbewegung*. Berlin: Herbig, 1926.

Lippman, Leo. *Mein Leben und Meine Amtliche Tätigkeit: Erinnerungen und ein Beitrag zur Finanzgeschichte*. Hamburg: Hans Christians, 1964.

Lockhart, R. H. Bruce. *Guns or Butter*. Boston: Little, Brown, 1938.

Loewenfeld-Russ, Hans. *Im Kampf gegen den Hunger: Aus den Erinnerungen des Staatssekretärs für Volksernährung, 1918–1920*. Munich: Oldenbourg, 1986.

Lorenz, Charlotte. *Die gewerbliche Frauenarbeit während des Krieges*. Stuttgart: Deutsche Verlags-Anstalt, 1928.

Ludendorff, Erich von. *My War Memories, 1914–1918*. London: Hutchinson, 1919.

———, ed. *Urkunden der obersten Heeresleitung*. Berlin: Mittler und Sohn, 1922.

Lüders, Marie-Elisabeth. *Das unbekannte Heer: Frauen kämpfen für Deutschland*. Berlin: E. S. Mittler, 1936.

Lüdtke, Alf, ed. *"Mein Arbeitstag—mein Wochenende": Arbeiterinnen berichten von ihrem Alltag 1928*. Hamburg: Ergebnisse, 1991.

Luther, Hans. *Im Dienst des Städtetags*. Stuttgart: Kohlhammer, 1959.

———. "Das Problem der Massenspeisung." In *Praktische Durchführung von Massenspeisungen: Zentralstelle für Volkswohlfahrt. Außerordentliche Tagung der Zentralstelle für Volkswohlfahrt in Gemeinschaft mit dem Zentralverein für das Wohl der arbeitenden Klassen*, 3–10. Berlin: Heymann, 1916.

Magistrat Berlin, ed. *Die Versorgung Berlins mit Mehl und Brot im Erntejahr 1914–15*. Berlin: Verlag der Stadt Berlin, 1915.

Maier, Reinhold. *Feldpostbriefe aus dem Ersten Weltkrieg, 1914–1918*. Stuttgart: Kohlhammer, 1966.

Manz, Hermann. *Die Ersatzlebensmittel in der Friedens- und Kriegsgesetzgebung*. Beiträge zur Kriegswirtschaft, no. 56–58. Berlin: Hobbing, 1918.

Materna, Ingo, and Hans-Jürgen Schreckenbach, eds. *Dokumente aus Geheimen Archiven: Berichte des Berliner Polizeipräsidenten zur Stimmung und Lage der Bevölkerung in Berlin, 1914–1918*. Weimar: Böhlaus Nachfolger, 1987.

Meerwarth, Rudolf, Adolf Guenther, and Waldemar Zimmermann, eds. *Die Einwirkung des Krieges auf Bevölkerungsbewegung, Einkommen, und Lebenshaltung in Deutschland*. Stuttgart: Deutsche Verlags-Anstalt, 1932.

Mendelssohn-Bartholdy, F. *The War and German Society*. New Haven: Yale University Press, 1937.

Menz, August. *Rechte und Pflichten der Preussischen Kriminalpolizei im Kampf gegen das Verbrechen*. Berlin: Emil Ebering, 1917.

Merton, Robert. *Erinnernswertes aus meinem Leben*. Frankfurt am Main: Fritz Knapp, 1955.

Meyers Lexikon. Leipzig: Bibliographisches Institut, 1926.

Michaelis, Georg. *Für Staat und Volk: Eine Lebensgeschichte.* Berlin: Furche, 1921.

Mierisch. *Kamerad Schwester, 1914–1918.* Leipzig: Koehler & Amelang, 1934.

Mihaly, Jo. *. . . da gibt's ein Wiedersehn! Kriegstagebuch eines Mädchens, 1914–1918.* Freiburg: F. H. Kerle, 1982.

Moll, Albert. *Polizei und Sitte.* Berlin: Gersbach, 1926.

Moltke, Graf von. "Noch ein Wort über Krieg und Volksernährung." *Preußische Jahrbücher* 155 (1914): 473–87.

Moltke, Helmuth. *Erinnerungen, Briefe, Dokumente, 1877–1916.* Stuttgart: Kommender Tag, 1922.

Monatsberiche des Städtischen Amtes der Stadt Berlin. Berlin: Verlag der Stadt Berlin, 1914–18.

Moszeik, C., ed. *Aus der Gedankenwelt einer Arbeiterfrau von Ihr Selbst Erzählt.* Berlin-Lichterfelde: E. Runge, 1909.

Müller, Richard. *Geschichte der Deutschen Revolution.* Vol. 2, *Die Novemberrevolution.* Berlin: Olle und Wolter, 1973.

Naumann, Friedrich, and Gertrud Bäumer. *Kriegs- und Heimatchronik.* Berlin: Reimer, 1916.

Nicolai, W. *Nachrichtendienst, Presse, und Volksstimmung im Weltkrieg.* Berlin: E. S. Mittler, 1920.

Pick, Rudolf. "Die Entwicklung des Systems der Brot- und Fleischkarte in Berlin." Ph.D. diss., Universität Greifswald, 1919.

Polte, Heinrich. *Die Lebensmittelnot und Ihre Abwehr durch Selbsthilfe.* Berlin: Lebenskunst-Heilkunst, 1917.

Polzer, Wilhelm. *Handbuch für den praktischen Kriminaldienst.* Munich: Schweitzer, 1922.

Praktische Durchführung von Massenspeisungen: Zentralstelle für Volkswohlfahrt. Außerordentliche Tagung der Zentralstelle für Volkswohlfahrt in Gemeinschaft mit dem Zentralverein für das Wohl der arbeitenden Klassen. Berlin: Heymann, 1916.

Die Preisbildung im Kriege. Beiträge zur Kriegswirtschaft, no. 2. Berlin: Hobbing, 1916.

Rageot, Gaston. *La Française et la Guerre.* No. 11. Paris: Petite Bibliotheque de la Guerre, 1918.

Rathenau, Walther. *Walther Rathenau, Industrialist, Banker, Intellectual, Politician: Notes and Diaries, 1907–1922.* Edited by Hartmut Pogge von Strandmann. Oxford: Clarendon, 1985.

Reichardt, Dr. *Das Gemüse in der Kriegswirtschaft.* Beiträge zur Kriegswirtschaft, no. 41/42. Berlin: Hobbing, 1918.

———. *Die Kriegsmaßnahmen zur Regelung des Verkerhrs mit Obst.* Beiträge zur Kriegswirtschaft, no. 28. Berlin: Hobbing, 1917.

Reichs-Gesetzblatt. Berlin: Büro des Bundeskanzlers, 1914–18.

Retzlaw, Karl. *Spartakus Aufstieg und Niedergang: Erinnerungen eines Parteiarbeiters.* Frankfurt am Main: Neue Kritik, 1985.

Reichs-Gesetzblatt. Berlin: Büro des Bundeskanzlers, 1914–18.

Der richtige Berliner in Worten und Redensarten. Berlin: H. S. Herrmann, 1882.

Roesle, E. E. "Die Geburts- und Sterblichkeitsverhältnisse." In *Deutschlands Gesundheitsverhältnisse unter dem Einfluss des Weltkrieges,* edited by F. Bumm, 1 : 3–62. Stuttgart: Deutsche Verlags-Anstalt, 1928.

Rubmann, Max, ed. *Hunger! Wirkungen Moderner Kriegsmethoden.* Berlin: Reimer, 1919.

Rubner, Max. *Deutschlands Volksernährung im Kriege.* Leipzig: Verlag "Naturwissenschaften," 1916.

———. "Das Ernährungswesen im allgemeinen." In *Deutschlands Gesundheitsverhältnisse unter dem Einfluss des Weltkrieges,* edited by F. Bumm, 2 : 1–42. Stuttgart: Deutsche Verlags-Anstalt, 1928.

————. *The Starving of Germany*. Berlin: L. Schumacher, 1919.

————. *Die Volksernährung im Kriege*. Jena: n.p., 1915.

Ruge, L. *Deutschlands Milch- und Speisefettversorgung im Krieg*. Beiträge zur Kriegswirtschaft, no. 47/48. Berlin: Hobbing, 1918.

Rüsser, Paul. *Die Fabrikpflegerin*. Berlin-Dahlem: Burckhardthaus, 1918.

Scheidemann, Philipp. *The Making of the New Germany*. 2 vols. New York: Libraries Press, 1970.

Schinkäthe, Robert. "Die Entwicklung der Unterstützenden und Producktiven Erwerbslosenfürsorge in Berlin." Ph.D. diss., Universität Würzburg, 1923.

Schmeling, M. von. *Sechs Jahre Pionierarbeit unter Fabrikarbeiterinnen*. Berlin: Druckerei des Sonntagsblattes, 1916.

Schreiner, George. *The Iron Ration*. New York: Harper, 1918.

Schulthess' Europäischer Geschichtskalender, 1918. Munich: Beck, 1919.

Schulze, Adolph. *Aus dem Notizbuch eines Schutzmannes: Bilder aus dem Leben der Reichshauptstadt*. Leipzig: Carl Reissner, 1887.

Sichler, Richard, and Joachim Tibertius. *Die Arbeiterfrage, eine Kernfrage des Weltkrieges. Ein Beitrag zur Erklärung des Kriegsausgangs*. Berlin: Deutsche Verlag-Aktiengesellschaft, 1920.

Simon, R. *Das Kriegs-Ernährungsproblem*. Berlin: n.p., 1916.

Skalweit, August. *Branntweinwirtschaft und Volksernährung*. Beiträge zur Kriegswirtschaft, no. 30. Berlin: Hobbing, 1918.

————. *Die Deutsche Kriegsernährungswirtschaft*. Stuttgart: Deutsche Verlags-Anstalt, 1927.

Skalweit, August, and Walter Klaas. *Das Schwein in der Kriegsernährungswirtschaft*. Beiträge zur Kriegswirtschaft, no. 20/21. Berlin: Hobbing, 1917.

Skiebe, Karl. "Die Milchversorgung der Grossstädte in Deutschland: Ein Stück vom Wiederaufbau unter besonderer Berücksichtigung Berlins." Ph.D. diss., Kaiser Wilhelm Universität, Berlin, 1921.

Sombart, Werner. *Händler und Helden: Patriotische Besinnungen*. Munich: Duncker and Humblot, 1915.

Sorel, George. *Reflections on Violence*. New York: Collier, 1961.

Spont, Henri. *La Femme et la Guerre*. Paris: Perrin, 1916.

Stadthagen, Hans. *Die Ersatzlebensmittel in der Kriegswirtschaft*. Beiträge zur Kriegswirtschaft, no. 58/59. Berlin: Hobbing, 1919.

Statistik der Stadt Berlin. Berlin: P. Stankiewicz, 1919.

Stegemann-Runk, A. *Die Hauswirtschaft im Kriege*. Beiträge zur Kriegswirtschaft, no. 25. Berlin: Hobbing, 1917.

Stegerwald, A. *Adam Stegerwald: Leben, Werk, Erbe*. Edited by H. Neugebauer. Würzburg: Bentheim, 1995.

————. *Wege der Volkswohlfahrt*. Berlin: Vereinigung wissenschaftlicher Verleger, 1920.

————. *Zur Schwer- und Schwerstarbeiterversorgung mit Zusatzlebensmitteln*. Beiträge zur Kriegswirtschaft, no. 26–27. Berlin: Hobbing, 1917.

Stein, Phillip. *Der Besuch der Massenspeisung*. Berlin: n.p., 1916.

————. *Kriegshilfsmaßnahmen deutscher Städte*. Berlin: n.p., 1917.

Stenographischer Bericht über die Öffentlichen Sitzungen der Stadtverordnetenversammlung der Stadt Berlin. Berlin: Verlag der Stadt Berlin, 1914–18.

Tannenbaum, Eugen, ed. *Kriegsbriefe Deutscher und Österreichischer Juden*. Berlin: Neuer Verlag, 1915.

Thiess, Karl, Kurt Wiedenfeld, and Adolf von Batocki. *Die Preisbildung im Kriege.* Beiträge zur Kriegswirtschaft, no. 1. Berlin: Hobbing, 1916.

Thimme, H. *Weltkrieg ohne Waffen: Die Propaganda der Westmächte gegen Deutschland, ihre Wirkung und ihre Abwehr.* Stuttgart: Cotta, 1932.

Thomas, Theodor. *Die Massenspeisung in Wort und Bild: Ein Beitrag zur Entwicklung der Frankfurter Kriegsküchen.* Frankfurt am Main: Zentral-Küchenkommission, 1916.

Thönnessen, Werner. *The Emancipation of Women: The Rise and Decline of the Women's Movement in German Social Democracy.* Frankfurt am Main: Pluto Press, 1969.

Tiger, Theobald, and Friedrich Hollaender. "Wenn der alte Motor wieder tackt." In *Bei uns um die Gedächtniskirche rum: Friedrich Hollaender und das Kabarett der zwanziger Jahre.* Berlin: edel, 1996. Compact disk.

Tresckow, Hans von. *Von Fürsten und Anderen Sterblichen: Erinnerungen eines Kriminalkommissars.* Berlin: F. Fontane, 1922.

Tyszka, Carl von. *Der Konsument in der Kriegswirtschaft.* Tübingen: Mohr, 1916.

———. *Konsument und Produzent.* Tübingen: Mohr, 1916.

———. *Teuerung und Krieg.* Berlin: n.p., 1916.

———. "Die Veränderungen in der Lebenshaltung städtischer Familien im Kriege." *Archiv für Sozialwissenschaft und Sozialpolitik* 43 (1916–17): 841–76.

Umbreit, Paul. *Der Krieg und die Arbeitsverhältnisse: Die Deutschen Gewerkschaften im Kriege.* Stuttgart: Deutsche Verlags-Anstalt, 1928.

Unter der roten Fahne: Erinnerungen alter Genossen. Berlin: Verlag der SED, 1958.

Voigt, Andreas. *Kriegssozialismus und Friedenssozialismus: Eine Beurteilung der gegenwärtigen Kriegs-Wirtschaftspolitik.* Leipzig: Deichert, 1916.

Volksernährung im Kriege: Vorträge. Berlin: Reimar Hobbing, 1915.

Vorwärts und nicht Vergessen: Erlebnisberichte aktiver Teilnehmer der Novemberrevolution 1918–1919. Berlin: Verlag der SED, 1957.

War Food Office. *Hauptergebnisse der Volkszählung im Deutschen Reich am 5.12.1917.* Berlin: n.p., 1918.

Weiss, Bernhard. *Polizei und Politik.* Berlin: Gersbach & Sohn, 1928.

Wellmann, Wilhelm. *Meine Mutter: Lebensgeschichte einer Zieglerfrau und Tagelöhnerin in Lippe.* Essen: Klartext, 1991.

Wermuth, Adolf. *Ein Beamtenleben.* Berlin: A. Scherl, 1922.

Wiedfeldt, Otto. *Die Bewirtschaftung von Korn, Mehl und Brot im Deutschen Reiche, ihre Entstehung und ihre Grundzüge.* Beiträge zur Kriegswirtschaft, no. 50–53. Berlin: Hobbing, 1919.

Wiernik, Lucian. *Die Arbeiterernährung in der Kriegsorganisation der Industrie.* Beiträge zur Kriegswirtschaft, no. 26/27. Berlin: Hobbing, 1917.

Winnig, August. *Neuorientierung.* Berlin: Singer, 1915.

———. *Vom Proletariat zum Arbeitertum.* Hamburg: Hanseatische Verlags-Anstalt, 1930.

Wittig, Richard. *Die 64. Kriegs-Volksküche zu Dresden-N.* Dresden: n.p., 1919.

Wohltmann, F. *Unsere Volksernährung und die Deutsche Hausfrau.* Berlin: Paul Parey, 1915.

Wolff, Theodor. *Tagebücher, 1914–1919.* 2 vols. Boppard am Rhein: Harald Boldt Verlag, 1984.

Wunderlich, Frieda. *Fabrikpflege: Ein Beitrag zur Betriebspolitik.* Berlin: n.p., 1926.

Würfel, Gotthard. *Der Sieg der Deutschen Volksgesundheit im Weltkriege.* Stuttgart: Deutsche Verlags-Anstalt, 1916.

Wurm, Emanuel. *Richtlinien für ein Gemeindeprogramm.* Berlin: Freiheit, 1919.

————. *Die Teuerung, ihre Ursachen und Bekämpfung: Ein Überblick über die Lebensmittelversorgung seit Kriegsbeginn insbesondere in Gross-Berlin*. Berlin: Verlag des Verbands Sozialdemokratischer Wahlvereine Berlins, 1915.

————. *Die Übergangswirtschaft und die Arbeiter*. Berlin: A. Cohen, 1918.

————. *Die Volksernährung*. Berlin: Singer, 1915.

Zentrale für Private Fürsorge. *Die Wohlfahrtseinrichtungen von Gross-Berlin*. Berlin: Julius Springer, 1910.

Zepler, Wally. "Beruf und Weibliche Psyche." In *Sozialismus und Frauenfrage*, edited by W. Zepler. Berlin: Cassirer, 1919.

————. *Die Frauen und der Krieg*. Berlin: Cassirer, 1916.

Zietz, Luise. *Die Frauen und die Reichstagswahlen*. Magdeburg: Parteileitung der U.S.P.D., 1920.

————. *Komm zu Uns! Ein Weckruf an die Junge Arbeiterin*. Berlin: Singer, 1913.

————. *Die Sozialdemokratischen Frauen und der Krieg*. Stuttgart: Dietz, 1915.

————. *Willst Du arm und unfrei bleiben? Ein Aufruf an die Frauen des werktätigen Volkes*. Berlin: Freiheit, 1919.

————. *Zur Frage der Frauenerwerbsarbeit während des Krieges und nachher*. Berlin: Vorwärts, 1916.

Zimmermann, W. "Unser Täglich Brot." *Soziale Praxis* 24 (October 1914): 432–65.

————. "Die Veränderungen der Einkommens- und Lebensverhältnisse der Deutschen Arbeiter durch den Krieg." In *Die Einwirkung des Krieges auf Bevölkerungsbewegung, Einkommen, und Lebenshaltung in Deutschland*, edited by Rudolf Meerwarth, Adolf Guenther, and Waldemar Zimmermann, 281–474. Stuttgart: Deutsche Verlags-Anstalt, 1932.

Zodtke-Heyde, Else. *Ausbildung von Leiterinnen für Massenspeisung*. Berlin: Leonhard Simien, 1917.

NEWSPAPERS

Berliner Lokal Anzeiger
Berliner Tageblatt
Der Deutsche Kurier
Ulk
Vorwärts
Vossische Zeitung

SECONDARY SOURCES

Abelove, Henry. "Colonialism and Philosophy: Berkeley to Thoreau." Unpublished manuscript.

Abelshauser, Werner. *Die Weimarer Republik als Wohlfahrtsstaat*. Wiesbaden: Steiner, 1987.

Abrams, L. *Workers' Culture in Imperial Germany*. London: Routledge, 1992.

Allen, A. T. *Feminism and Motherhood in Germany, 1800–1914*. New Brunswick, N.J.: Rutgers University Press, 1991.

Allen, Keith. "Sharing Scarcity: Bread Rationing and the First World War in Berlin, 1914–1923." *Journal of Social History* 32, no. 2 (1998): 371–96.

Amdur, K. A. *Syndicalist Legacy: Trade Unions and Politics in Two French Cities in the Era of World War I*. Urbana: University of Illinois Press, 1986.

Anderson, Karen. *Wartime Women: Sex Roles, Family Relations, and the Status of Women during World War II*. Westport, Conn.: Greenwood Press, 1981.

Angress, Werner T. "Das Deutsche Militär und die Juden im ersten Weltkrieg."
    Militärgeschichtliche Mitteilungen 19 (1976): 77–146.

Appadurai, Arjun. "How to Make a National Cuisine: Cookbooks in Contemporary India."
    Comparative Study of Society and History 12 (1988): 3–24.

Appelbaum, Peter. *Popular Culture, Educational Discourse, and Mathematics.* Albany: State
    University of New York Press, 1995.

Applewhite, Harriet, and Darline Levy, eds. *Women and Politics in the Age of Democratic Revolution.*
    Ann Arbor: University of Michigan Press, 1990.

Armeson, Robert. *Total Warfare and Compulsory Labor: A Study of the Military-Industrial Complex
    in Germany during World War I.* The Hague: M. Nijhoff, 1964.

Assion, Peter, ed. *Transformationen der Arbeiterkultur.* Marburg: Jonas Verlag, 1986.

Audoin-Rouzeau. *Men at War: National Sentiment and Trench Journalism in France during the First
    World War.* Providence, R.I.: Berg, 1992.

Auslander, Leora. *Taste and Power: Furnishing Modern France.* Berkeley: University of California
    Press, 1996.

Ay, Karl-Ludwig. *Die Entstehung einer Revolution: Die Volksstimmung in Bayern während des Ersten
    Weltkrieges.* Berlin: Duncker and Humblot, 1968.

Baier, Frank, and Detlef Puls. *Arbeiterlieder aus dem Ruhrgebiet: Texte und Noten mit
    Begleitakkorden.* Frankfurt am Main: Fischer, 1981.

Bailey, S. "The Berlin Strike of 1918." *Central European History* 13, no. 2 (June 1980): 158–74.

Bajohr, Stefan. *Die Hälfte der Fabrik: Geschichte der Frauenarbeit in Deutschland, 1914–1945.*
    Marburg: Verlag Arbeiterbewegung und Gesellschaftswissenschaft, 1984.

Barnett, L. Margaret. *British Food Policy during the First World War.* London: Allen and Unwin,
    1985.

Barrows, Susanna. *Distorting Mirrors: Visions of the Crowd in Late Nineteenth-Century France.* New
    Haven: Yale University Press, 1981.

Bartel, W. "Der Januarstreik 1918 in Berlin." In *Revolutionäre Ereignisse und Probleme in
    Deutschland während der Periode der Grossen Sozialistischen Oktoberrevolution 1917/1918,* edited by
    A. Schreiner, 141–83. Berlin: Akademie-Verlag, 1957.

Bartov, Omer. *Murder in Our Midst: The Holocaust, Industrial Killing, and Representation.* New
    York: Oxford University Press, 1996.

Becker, Annette. *La guerre et la foi: De la mort à la mémoire, 1914–1930.* Paris: A. Colin, 1994.

Becker, Jean-Jacques. *The Great War and the French People.* Leamington Spa: Berg, 1985.

Beier, Rosemarie. *Frauenarbeit und Frauenalltag im Deutschen Kaiserreich: Heimarbeiterinnen in der
    Berliner Bekleidungsindustrie, 1880–1914.* Frankfurt am Main: Campus, 1983.

Bell, Archibald. *A History of the Blockade of Germany and the Countries Associated with Her in the
    Great War, Austria-Hungary, Bulgaria, and Turkey, 1914–1918.* London: H. M. Stationery
    Office, 1937.

Bell, Rudolph. *Holy Anorexia.* Chicago: University of Chicago Press, 1985.

Bergmann, Anna. "Frauen, Männer, Sexualität, und Geburtenkontrolle: Zur
    'Gebärstreikdebatte' der SPD 1913." In *Frauen Suchen Ihre Geschichte: Historische Studien zum
    19. und 20. Jahrhundert,* edited by Karin Hausen, 83–111. Munich: Beck, 1987.

———. *Die Verhütete Sexualität: Die Anfänge der moderern Geburtenkontrolle.* Hamburg: Rasch
    und Röhring, 1992.

Bergmann, Klaus. *Agrarromantik und Großstadtfeindschaft.* Meisenheim/G: Hain, 1970.

Berghahn, Volker. *Germany and the Approach of War in 1914.* New York: St. Martin's Press, 1993.

————. *Imperial Germany*. New York: Berghahn, 1994.

————. *Modern Germany: Society, Economy, and Politics in the Twentieth Century*. Cambridge: Cambridge University Press, 1982.

Berghahn, Volker, and Martin Kitchen, eds. *Germany in the Age of Total War*. London: Croom Helm, 1981.

Berkin, Carol R., and Clara M. Lovett, eds. *Women, War, and Revolution*. New York: Holmes and Meier, 1980.

Berliner Geschichtswerkstatt, e.V., ed. *August 1914: Ein Volk Zieht in den Krieg*. Berlin: Nishen, 1989.

————. *Die Rote Insel*. Berlin: Nishen, 1987.

Bertrand, Charles L., ed. *Situations révolutionaires en Europe, 1917–1922*. Montreal: Centre Interuniversitaire d'Etudes Européenes, 1977.

Bessel, Richard. *Germany after the First World War*. Oxford: Oxford University Press, 1994.

————. "The Great War in German Memory: The Soldiers of the First World War, Demobilization, and Weimar Political Culture." *German History* 6, no. 1 (1988): 20–34.

————. "Eine nicht allzu große Beunruhigung des Arbeitsmarktes: Frauenarbeit und Demobilmachung in Deutschland nach dem Ersten Weltkrieg." *Geschichte und Gesellschaft* 9 (1983): 211–29.

Bieber, Hans-Joachim. *Gewerkschaften in Krieg und Revolution: Arbeiterbewegung, Industrie, Staat, und Militär in Deutschland, 1914–1920*. Hamburg: Christians, 1981.

Blackbourn, David. *Marpingen: Apparitions of the Virgin Mary in Bismarckian Germany*. New York: Oxford University Press, 1993.

————. "The *Mittelstand* in German Society and Politics, 1871–1914." *Social History* 2 (1977): 409–33.

Blessing, Werner K. "Konsumentenprotest und Arbeitskampf: Vom Bierkrawall zum Bierboykott." In *Streik: Zur Geschichte des Arbeitskampfes in Deutschland während der Industrialisierung*, edited by Klaus Tenfelde and Heinrich Volkmann, 109–23. Munich: Beck, 1981.

Bock, Gisela, and Pat Thane, eds. *Maternity and Gender Policies: Women and the Rise of the European Welfare States, 1880s–1950s*. New York: Routledge, 1991.

Boehlich, Walter. *Der Berliner Antisemitismusstreit*. Frankfurt am Main: Insel-Verlag, 1965.

Bohstedt, John. *Riots and Community Politics in England and Wales, 1790–1810*. Cambridge, Mass.: Harvard University Press, 1983.

Böker, Alexander R. "German Food Planning, 1914–1918." Ph.D. diss., Harvard University, 1943.

Boll, Friedhelm. *Massenbewegungen in Niedersachsen, 1906–1920: Eine sozialgeschichtliche Untersuchung zu den unterschiedlichen Entwicklungstypen Braunschweig und Hannover*. Bonn: Neue Gesellschaft, 1981.

————. "Spontaneität der Basis und politische Funktion des Streiks, 1914 bis 1918: Das Beispiel Braunschweig." *Archiv für Sozialgeschichte* 17 (1977): 337–66.

————, ed. *Arbeiterkulturen zwischen Alltag und Politik*. Vienna: Europa-Verlag, 1986.

Bollenbeck, G. "Zur Bedeutung der Ernährung in den Arbeiterlebenserinnerungen." *SoWi* 14, no. 2 (1985): 110–17.

Bonzon, Thierry, and Belinda J. Davis. "Feeding the Cities." In *Capital Cities at War: Paris, London, and Berlin, 1914–1919*, edited by Jay M. Winter and Jean-Louis Robert, 305–41. Cambridge: Cambridge University Press, 1997.

Boswell, J. S., and B. R. Johns. "Patriots or Profiteers? British Businessmen and the First World War." *Journal of European Economic History* 11, no. 2 (1982): 423–46.

Bourdieu, Pierre. *Distinction: A Social Critique of the Judgement of Taste.* Cambridge, Mass.: Harvard University Press, 1984.

Bourke, Joanna. *Dismembering the Male: Men's Bodies, Britain, and the Great War.* Chicago: University of Chicago Press, 1996.

Bouton, Cynthia. *The Flour War: Gender, Class, and Community in Late Ancien Régime France.* University Park: Pennsylvania State University Press, 1993.

Boyd, Catherine E. "'Nationaler Frauendienst': German Middle-Class Women in Service of the Fatherland, 1914–1918." Ph.D. diss., University of Georgia, 1980.

Brandt, Peter, and Reinhard Rürup. *Volksbewegung und demokratische Neuordnung in Baden 1918/19.* Sigmaringen: Jan Thorbecke, 1991.

Braybon, Gail. *Women Workers in the First World War: The British Experience.* London: Croom Helm, 1981.

Breckman, Warren. "Disciplining Consumption: The Debate about Luxury in Wilhelmine Germany, 1890–1914." *Journal of Social History* 24, no. 3 (1991): 485–506.

Brewer, John, ed. *The Police, Public Order, and the State.* Basingstoke: Macmillan, 1988.

Bridenthal, Renate. "Organized Rural Women and the Conservative Mobilization of the German Countryside in the Weimar Republic." In *Between Reform, Reaction, and Resistance,* edited by Larry E. Jones and James N. Retallack, 375–406. Providence, R.I.: Berg, 1993.

Bridenthal, Renate, and Claudia Koonz. "Beyond 'Kinder, Küche, Kirche': Weimar Women in Politics and Work." In *When Biology Became Destiny: Women in Weimar and Nazi Germany,* edited by Renate Bridenthal, 33–65. New York: Monthly Review Press, 1984.

Brubaker, Rogers. *Citizenship and Nationhood in France and Germany.* Cambridge, Mass.: Harvard University Press, 1992.

Bruch, Rüdiger vom, ed. *Weder Kommunismus noch Kapitalismus: Bürgerliche Sozialreform in Deutschland vom Vormärz bis zur Ära Adenauer.* Munich: Beck, 1985.

Brunn, Gerhard, and Jürgen Reulecke. *Metropolis Berlin: Berlin als Deutsche Hauptstadt im Vergleich Europäischer Städte.* Bonn: Bouvier Verlag, 1992.

Bruntz, George G. *Allied Propaganda and the Collapse of the German Empire in 1918.* Stanford, Calif.: Hoover, 1938.

Bry, Gerhard. *Wages in Germany, 1871–1945.* Princeton: Princeton University Press, 1960.

Burchardt, Lothar. "Die Auswirkungen der Kriegswirtschaft auf die deutsche Zivilbevölkerung im Ersten und Zweiten Weltkrieg." *Militärgeschichtliche Mitteilungen* 1 (1974): 65–97.

———. *Friedenswirtschaft und Kriegsvorsorge.* Boppard am Rhein: Boldt, 1968.

———. "The Impact of the War Economy on the Civilian Population of Germany during the First and the Second World Wars." In *The German Military in the Age of Total War,* edited by Wilhelm Deist, 111–36. Leamington Spa: Berg, 1985.

Burk, Kathleen. *War and the State: The Transformation of the British Government, 1914–1919.* London: Allen and Unwin, 1982.

Burleigh, Michael. *Germany Turns Eastwards: A Study of Ostforschung in the Third Reich.* Cambridge: Cambridge University Press, 1988.

Burnett, John. "Food Adulteration in Britain in the Nineteenth Century and the Origin of Food Legislation." In *Ernährung und Ernährungslehre,* edited by Edith Heischkel-Artelt, 117–30. Göttingen: Vandenhoeck und Ruprecht, 1976.

Butler, Judith P. *Gender Trouble: Feminism and the Subversion of Identity*. New York: Routledge, 1990.

Butler, Judith, and Joan Scott, eds. *Feminists Theorize the Political*. New York: Routledge, 1992.

Cadogan, Mary, and Patricia Craig. *Women and Children First*. London: Gollancz, 1978.

Caldwell, Peter. *Popular Sovereignty and the Crisis of German Constitutional Law*. Durham, N.C.: Duke University Press, 1997.

Camaroff, Jean, and John Camaroff. "Goodly Beasts, Beastly Goods: Cattle and Commodities in a South African Context." *American Ethnologist* 17, no. 2 (1990): 195–216.

Canetti, Elias. *Crowds and Power*. New York: Farrar Straus and Giroux, 1973.

Canning, Kathleen. *Languages of Labor and Gender: Female Factory Work in Germany, 1850–1914*. Ithaca: Cornell University Press, 1996.

Caplan, Jane. "The Imaginary Universality of Particular Interests: The 'Tradition' of the Civil Service in German History." *Social History* 4, no. 2 (1979): 299–317.

Carsten, Francis L. *Revolution in Central Europe, 1918–1919*. Berkeley: University of California Press, 1972.

———. *War against War: British and German Radical Movements in the First World War*. London: Batsford, 1982.

Carter, Erica. *How German Is She? Postwar West German Reconstruction and the Consuming Woman*. Ann Arbor: University of Michigan Press, 1997.

Cecil, Hugh, and Peter Liddle. *Facing Armageddon: The First World War Experienced*. London: Cooper, 1996.

Certeau, Michel de. *The Practice of Everyday Life*. Berkeley: University of California Press, 1988.

Chambers, Frank. *The War behind the War, 1914–1918: A History of the Political and Civilian Fronts*. New York: Harcourt, Brace, 1939.

Chevalier, Louis. *Laboring Classes and Dangerous Classes in Paris during the First Half of the Nineteenth Century*. Princeton: Princeton University Press, 1973.

Chickering, Roger. "'Casting Their Gaze More Broadly': Women's Patriotic Activism in Imperial Germany." *Past and Present* 118 (1988): 156–85.

———. *Imperial Germany and the Great War, 1914–1918*. Cambridge: Cambridge University Press, 1998.

———. *We Men Who Feel Most German*. Boston: Allen and Unwin, 1984.

Cobb, Richard. *The People and the Police: French Popular Protest, 1789–1820*. Oxford: Oxford University Press, 1970.

Coetzee, F., and M. Shevin-Coetzee, eds. *Authority, Identity, and the Social History of the Great War*. Providence, R.I.: Berg, 1995.

Cohen, Deborah. "The War Come Home: Disabled Veterans in Great Britain and Germany, 1914–1939." Ph.D. diss., University of California, Berkeley, 1996.

Cohen, Lizabeth. "The New Deal State and the Making of Citizen Consumers." In *Getting and Spending: European and American Consumer Societies in the Twentieth Century*, edited by Susan Strasser, Charles McGovern, and Matthias Judt, 111–26. Cambridge: Cambridge University Press, 1998.

Conze, Werner, and Dieter Groh. *Die Arbeiterbewegung in der nationalen Bewegung*. Stuttgart: Klett, 1966.

Conze, Werner, and Ulrich Engelhardt, eds. *Arbeiterexistenz im 19. Jahrhundert: Lebensstandard und Lebensgestaltung Deutscher Arbeiter und Handwerker*. Stuttgart: Klett-Cotta, 1981.

Creutz, Martin. *Die Pressepolitik der kaiserlichen Regierung während des Ersten Weltkriegs: Die*

Exekutive, die Journalisten, und der Teufelskreis der Berichterstattung. Frankfurt am Main: P. Lang, 1996.

Crew, David. "Bedürfnisse und Bedürftigkeit: Wohlfahrtsbürokratie und Wohlfahrtsempfänger in der Weimarer Republik, 1919–1933." *SoWi* 18, no. 1 (1989): 217–45.

———. *Germans on Welfare from Weimar to Hitler.* Oxford: Oxford University Press, 1998.

———. *Town in the Ruhr: A Social History of Bochum, 1860–1914.* New York: Columbia University Press, 1979.

———. "'Wohlfahrtsbrot ist bitteres Brot': The Elderly, the Disabled, and the Local Welfare Authorities in the Weimar Republic, 1924–1933." *Archiv für Sozialgeschichte* 30 (1990): 217–46.

Cullen, Michael S. *Der Reichstag: Die Geschichte eines Monumentes.* Stuttgart: Parkland, 1995.

Dallas, Gloden. *The Unknown Army.* London: Verso, 1985.

Dammer, Susanne. *Mütterlichkeit und Frauendienstpflicht: Versuche der Vergesellschaftung "weiblicher Fähigkeiten" durch eine Dientsverpflichtung (Deutschland 1890–1918).* Weinheim: Deutscher Studien, 1988.

Daniel, Ute. *Arbeiterfrauen in der Kriegsgesellschaft.* Göttingen: Vandenhoeck und Ruprecht, 1989.

———. "The Politics of Rationing versus the Politics of Subsistence: Working-Class Women in Germany, 1914–1918." In *From Bernstein to Brandt,* edited by Roger Fletcher, 89–95. London: E. Arnold, 1987.

———. *The War from Within: German Working-Class Women in the First World War.* New York: Berg, 1997.

Daniel, Ute, and Wolfram Siemann, eds. *Propaganda, Meinungskampf, Verführung, und politische Sinnstiftung, 1789–1989.* Frankfurt am Main: Fischer, 1994.

Darnton, Robert. "The Police Inspector Sorts His Files." In *The Great Cat Massacre and Other Episodes in French Cultural History,* 145–90. New York: Basic Books, 1984.

Dasey, Robyn. "Women's Work and the Family: Women Garment Workers in Berlin and Hamburg before the First World War." In *The German Family: Essays on the Social History of the Family in Nineteenth- and Twentieth-Century Germany,* edited by Richard J. Evans and W. R. Lee, 221–53. London: Croom Helm, 1981.

Daum, Andreas. *Wissenschaftspopularisierung im 19. Jahrhundert: Bürgerliche Kultur, naturwissenschaftliche Bildung und die Deutsche Öffentlichkeit, 1848–1914.* Munich: R. Oldenbourg, 1998.

Davin, Anna. "Imperialism and Motherhood." *History Workshop Journal* 7 (Spring 1978): 9–65.

Davis, Belinda J. "L'Etat *Contre* la Société? Nourrir la Cité." *Guerres Mondiales et Conflits Contemporains,* July 1996, 47–62.

———. "Food Scarcity and the Empowerment of the Female Consumer in World War I Germany." In *The Sex of Things: Gender and Consumption in Historical Perspective,* edited by Victoria de Grazia, with Ellen Furlough, 287–310. Berkeley: University of California Press, 1996.

———. "Gendered Images of the Nation in Wilhelmine Germany." Manuscript.

———. "Geschlecht und Konsum: Rolle und Bild der Komsumentin in den Verbraucherprotesten des ersten Weltkrieges." *Archiv für Sozialgeschichte* 38 (1998): 119–39.

———. "Reconsidering Habermas, Politics, and Gender: The Case of Wilhelmine Germany." In *Society, Culture, and the State in Germany, 1870–1930,* edited by Geoff Eley, 397–426. Ann Arbor: University of Michigan Press, 1996.

Dehne, Harald. "Dem Alltag ein Stück Näher?" In *Alltagsgeschichte: Zur Rekonstruktion historischer Erfahrungen und Lebensweisen,* edited by Alf Lüdtke, 137–68. Frankfurt am Main: Campus, 1984.

Deist, Wilhelm. *Militär, Staat, und Gesellschaft: Studien zur Preußisch-Deutschen Militärgeschichte.* Munich: R. Oldenbourg, 1991.

———, ed. *Militär- und Innenpolitik im Weltkrieg, 1914–1918.* 2 vols. Düsseldorf: Droste, 1970.

Denham, Scott. *Visions of War: Ideologies and Images of War in German Literature before and after the Great War.* Berne: P. Lang, 1992.

Dewey, Peter E. "Nutrition and Living Standards in Wartime Britain." In *The Upheaval of War: Family, Work, and Welfare in Europe, 1914–1918,* edited by Richard Wall and Jay M. Winter, 197–220. Cambridge: Cambridge University Press, 1988.

Dickinson, Edward R. *The Politics of German Child Welfare from the Empire to the Federal Republic.* Cambridge, Mass.: Harvard University Press, 1996.

Dieckmann, W. *Die Behördenorganisation in der Deutschen Kriegswirtschaft, 1914–1918.* Hamburg: Hanseatische Verlags-Anstalt, 1937.

Dietrich, Richard. "Berlins Weg zu Industrie- und Handelsstaat." In *Berlin: Neun Kapitel seiner Geschichte,* edited by R. Dietrich, 159–98. Berlin: de Gruyter, 1960.

Domansky, Elisabeth. "Der Erste Weltkrieg." In *Die Bürgerliche Gesellschaft,* edited by Lutz Niethammer, 285–319. Frankfurt am Main: Fischer, 1990.

———. "Militarization and Reproduction in World War I Germany." In *Society, Culture, and the State in Germany, 1870–1930,* edited by Geoff Eley, 427–64. Ann Arbor: University of Michigan Press, 1996.

Dornemann, Luise. *Alle Tage ihres Lebens: Frauengestalten aus zwei Jahrhunderten.* Berlin: Dietz, 1988.

Downs, Laura L. *Manufacturing Inequality: Gender Division in the French and British Metalworking Industries, 1914–1939.* Ithaca: Cornell University Press, 1995.

Drabkin, J. S. *Die Novemberrevolution 1918 in Deutschland.* Berlin: Deutscher Verlag der Wissenschaften, 1968.

Drèze, Jean, and Amartya Sen. *Hunger and Public Action.* New York: Oxford University Press, 1989.

Drèze, Jean, Amartya Sen, and Athar Hussain, eds. *The Political Economy of Hunger: Selected Essays.* Oxford: Clarendon, 1995.

Dülffer, Jost, and Karl Holl, eds. *Bereit zum Krieg: Kriegsmentalität im wilhelminischen Deutschland, 1890–1914.* Göttingen: Vandenhoeck und Ruprecht, 1986.

Eghigian, Gregory. *Making Security Social: Disability, Insurance, and the Birth of the Social Entitlement State in Germany.* Ann Arbor: University of Michigan Press, in press.

Ehlert, Hans G. *Die Wirtschaftliche Zentralbehörde des deutschen Reiches 1914 bis 1919: Das Problem der "Gemeinschaft" in Krieg und Frieden.* Wiesbaden: F. Steiner, 1982.

Eifert, Christiane. "Die Berliner 'Heimatfront' im Kriege." Master's thesis, Technische Universität Berlin, 1983.

———. "Frauenarbeit im Krieg: Die Berliner 'Heimatfront' 1914 bis 1918." *Internationale Wissenschaftliche Korrespondenz* 21, no. 3 (1985): 281–95.

Eifert, Christiane, and Susanne Rouette, eds. *Unter Allen Umständen: Frauengeschichte(n) in Berlin.* Berlin: Rotation, 1986.

Eley, Geoff. *From Unification to Nazism: Reinterpreting the German Past.* London: Allen and Unwin, 1986.

——. *Reshaping the German Right: Radical Nationalism and Politics after Bismarck.* Ann Arbor: University of Michigan Press, 1991.

——. "Re-thinking the Political: Social History and Political Culture in Eighteenth- and Nineteenth-Century Britain." *Archiv für Sozialgeschichte* 21 (1981): 427–57.

Elias, Norbert. *The Civilizing Process.* New York: Urizen Books, 1978.

Engel, Barbara A. "Not by Bread Alone: Subsistence Riots in Russia during World War I." *Journal of Modern History* 69, no. 4 (1997): 696–721.

Enloe, Cynthia. *Does Khaki Become You?* London: Pluto, 1983.

Erbe, Michael. "Berlin im Kaiserreich." In *Geschichte Berlins: Von der Frühgeschichte bis zur Gegenwart,* edited by Wolfgang Ribbe, 2:691–793. Munich: Beck, 1988.

Evans, Richard. *Proletarians and Politics: Socialism, Protest, and the Working Class in Germany before the First World War.* New York: Harvester Wheatsheaf, 1990.

——, ed. *Kneipengespräche im Kaiserreich: Stimmungsberichte der Hamburger politischen Polizei, 1892–1914.* Reinbek: Rowohlt, 1989.

Fairbairn, Brett. *Democracy in the Undemocratic State: The German Reichstag Elections of 1898 and 1903.* Toronto: University of Toronto Press, 1997.

Fait, Barbara. "Arbeiterfrauen und -familien im System sozialer Sicherheit." *Jahrbuch für Wirtschaftsgeschichte* (1997): 171–207.

Farge, Arlette. *Subversive Words: Public Opinion in Eighteenth-Century France.* University Park: Pennsylvania State University Press, 1995.

Farquharson, John. *The Western Allies and the Politics of Food.* Leamington Spa: Berg, 1985.

Farrar, Marjorie M. "Preclusive Purchase: Political and Economic Warfare in France during the First World War." *Economic History Review* 26, no. 1 (1973): 117–33.

Faust, Manfred. *Sozialer Burgfrieden im ersten Weltkrieg: Sozialistische und christliche Arbeiterbewegung in Köln.* Essen: Klartext, 1992.

Feldman, Gerald. *Army, Industry, and Labor in Germany, 1914–1918.* 1966. Reprint, Providence, R.I.: Berg, 1992.

——. "Economic and Social Problems of the German Demobilization, 1918–19." *Journal of Modern History* 47, no. 1 (1975): 1–23.

——. *The Great Disorder: Politics, Economics, and Society in the German Inflation, 1914–1923.* New York: Oxford University Press, 1993.

——. "Streiks in Deutschland, 1914–1933: Probleme und Forschungsaufgaben." In *Streik: Zur Geschichte des Arbeitskampfes in Deutschland während der Industrialisierung,* edited by Klaus Tenfelde and Heinrich Volkmann, 271–86. Munich: Beck, 1981.

——. "War Economy and Controlled Economy: The Discrediting of 'Socialism' in Germany during World War I." In *Confrontation and Cooperation: Germany and the United States in the Era of World War I, 1900–1924,* edited by H.-J. Schroeder, 229–52. Providence, R.I.: Berg, 1993.

——, ed. *Vom Weltkrieg zur Weltwirtschaftskrise: Studien zur Deutschen Wirtschafts- und Sozialgeschichte, 1914–1932.* Göttingen: Vandenhoeck und Ruprecht, 1984.

Feldman, Gerald, and Heinrich Winkler, eds. *Organisierter Kapitalismus.* Göttingen: Vandenhoeck und Ruprecht, 1974.

Feldman, Gerald, Eberhard Kolb, and Reinhard Rürup. "Die Massenbewegungen der

Arbeiterschaft in Deutschland am Ende des Ersten Weltkrieges." *Politische Vierteljahrschrift* 13 (1972): 84–105.

Feldman, Gerald, Carl-Ludwig Holtfrerich, Gerhard A. Ritter, and Peter-Christian Witt, eds. *The Adaption to Inflation.* Berlin: de Gruyter, 1986.

———. *The Experience of Inflation: International and Comparative Studies.* Berlin: de Gruyter, 1984.

Ferguson, Niall. *Paper and Iron: Hamburg Business and German Politics in the Era of Inflation, 1897– 1927.* Cambridge: Cambridge University Press, 1995.

———. *The Pity of War.* London: Penguin Press, 1998.

Fischer, Fritz. *Germany's Aims in the First World War.* New York: Norton, 1967.

———. *War of Illusions: Germany Policies from 1911 to 1914.* New York: Norton, 1975.

Fischer, Heinz-Dietrich, ed. *Pressekonzentration und Zensurpraxis im Ersten Weltkrieg: Texte und Quellen.* Berlin: V. Siess, 1973.

Flemming, Jens. *Landwirtschaftliche Interessen und Demokratie.* Bonn: Neue Gesellschaft, 1978.

Flemming, Jens, Klaus Saul, and Peter-Christian Witt, eds. *Familienleben im Schatten der Krise: Dokumente und Analysen zur Sozialgeschichte der Weimarer Republik.* Düsseldorf: Droste, 1988.

Forster, Robert, and Orest Ranum, eds. *Food and Drink in History: Selections from the Annales.* Baltimore: Johns Hopkins University Press, 1979.

Fout, John. "The Woman's Role in the German Working-Class Family in the 1890s from the Perspectives of Women's Autobiographies." In *German Women in the Nineteenth Century,* edited by John Fout, 295–319. New York: Holmes and Meier, 1984.

Fraser, Nancy. "Women, Welfare, and the Politics of Needs Interpretation." In *Unruly Practices: Power, Discourse, and Gender in Contemporary Social Theory,* 144–60. Minneapolis: University of Minnesota Press, 1989.

Frevert, Ute. *"Mann und Weib, und Weib und Mann": Geschlechter-Differenzen in der Moderne.* Munich: Beck, 1995.

Fricke, Dieter. *Bismarcks Prätorianer: Die Berliner politische Polizei im Kampf gegen die Deutsche Arbeiterbewegung, 1871–1898.* Berlin: Rütten und Loening, 1962.

Fridenson, Patrick. "The Impact of the War on French Workers." In *The Upheaval of War: Family, Work, and Welfare in Europe, 1914–1918,* edited by Richard Wall and Jay M. Winter, 235–48. Cambridge: Cambridge University Press, 1988.

———, ed. *The French Home Front.* Providence, R.I.: Berg, 1992.

Friedemann, Peter, and Paul Munch, eds. *Öffentliche Festkultur: Politische Feste in Deutschland von der Aufklärung bis zum Ersten Weltkrieg.* Reinbek: Rowohlt, 1988.

Fritzsche, Peter. *Germans into Nazis.* Cambridge, Mass.: Harvard University Press, 1998.

———. *Reading Berlin 1900.* Cambridge, Mass.: Harvard University Press, 1996.

———. *Rehearsals for Fascism: Populism and Political Mobilization in Weimar Germany.* Oxford: Oxford University Press, 1990.

Führer, Karl Christian. *Arbeits losigkeit und die Entstehung der Arbeitslosenversicherung in Deutschland, 1902–1927.* Berlin: Colloquium, 1990.

———. "Für das Wirtschaftsleben 'mehr oder weniger wertlose Personen.'" *Archiv für Sozialgeschichte* 30 (1990): 145–80.

———. *Mieter, Hausbesitzer, Staat, und Wohnungsmarkt: Wohnungsmangel und Wohnungszwangswirtschaft in Deutschland, 1914–1960.* Stuttgart: Franz Steiner, 1995.

Fuller, John G. *Troop Morale and Popular Culture in the British and Dominion Armies, 1914–1918.* Oxford: Clarendon, 1990.

Funk, Albrecht. *Polizei und Rechtsstaat: Die Entwicklung des staatlichen Gewaltmonopols in Preussen, 1848–1918.* Frankfurt am Main: Campus, 1986.

Furlough, Ellen. *Consumer Cooperation in France: The Politics of Consumption, 1834–1930.* Ithaca: Cornell University Press, 1991.

Fussell, Paul. *The Great War and Modern Memory.* Oxford: Oxford University Press, 1975.

Gailus, Manfred. *Straße und Brot.* Göttingen: Vandenhoeck und Ruprecht, 1990.

———, ed. *Pöbelexzesse und Volkstumulte in Berlin.* Berlin: Europäische Perspektiven, 1984.

Gailus, Manfred, and Thomas Lindenberger. "Zwanzig Jahre 'moralische Ökonomie': Ein sozialhistorisches Konzept ist volljährig geworden." *Archiv für Sozialgeschichte* 20 (1994): 469–77.

Gailus, Manfred, and Heinrich Volkmann, eds. *Der Kampf um das tägliche Brot: Nahrungsmangel, Versorgungspolitik, und Protest, 1770–1990.* Opladen: Westdeutscher, 1994.

Geary, Dick. "Radicalism and the Worker: Metalworkers and Revolution, 1914–1923." In *Society and Politics in Wilhelmine Germany,* edited by Richard Evans, 267–86. London: Croom Helm, 1978.

Geisel, Elke. *Im Scheunenviertel: Bilder, Texte, und Dokumente.* Berlin: Severin und Seidler, 1981.

Geiss, Imanuel. *Das Deutsche Reich und der Erste Weltkrieg.* Munich: Beck, 1985.

Gerhard, Ute. "Den Sozialstaat neu denken? Voraussetzungen und Preis des Sozialstaatskompromisses." *Vorgänge* 26 (1987): 29–55.

Gersdorff, Ursula von. "Frauenarbeit und Frauenemanzipation im Ersten Weltkrieg." *Francia* 2 (1974): 502–23.

———. *Frauen im Kriegsdienst, 1914–1945.* Stuttgart: Deutsche Verlags-Anstalt, 1969.

Gershonkron, Alexander. *Bread and Democracy in Germany.* Berkeley: University of California Press, 1943.

Geyer, Martin. "Formen der Radikalisierung in der Münchener Revolution, 1918–19." In *Revolutionäres Potential in Europa am Ende des Ersten Weltkrieges,* Bohlaus Zeitgeschichtliche Bibliothek no. 16, edited by H. Konrad and K. M. Schmidlechner, 63–87. Vienna: Bohlau, 1991.

———. "Teuerungsprotest, Konsumentenpolitik, und soziale Gerechtigkeit während der Inflation: München, 1920–1923." *Archiv für Sozialgeschichte* 30 (1990): 181–215.

———. "Recht, Gerechtigkeit, und Gesetze." *Zeitschrift für Neuere Rechtsgeschichte* 16 (1994): 349–72.

———. *Verkehrte Welt: Revolution, Inflation und Moderne: München, 1914–1924.* Göttingen: Vandenhoeck und Ruprecht, 1998.

Geyer, Michael. "The Stigma of Violence: Nationalism and War in Twentieth-Century Germany." *German Studies Review* 15 (1992): 75–110.

———. "Ein Vorbote des Wohlfahrtsstaates: Die Kriegsopferversorgung in Frankreich, Deutschland, und Grossbritannien nach dem ersten Weltkrieg." *Geschichte und Gesellschaft* 9 (1983): 230–77.

Glaeßner, Gert-Joachim. *Arbeiterbewegung und Genossenschaft: Entstehung und Entwicklung der Konsumgenossenschaften in Deutschland am Beispiel Berlins.* Göttingen: Vandenhoeck und Ruprecht, 1989.

Glaeßner, Gert-Joachim, Detlef Lehnert, and Klaus Sühl, eds. *Studien zur Arbeiterbewegung und Arbeiterkultur in Berlin.* Berlin: Colloquium, 1989.

Glatzer, Dieter, and Ruth Glatzer. *Berliner Leben, 1900–1914: Eine Historische Reportage aus Erinnerungen und Berichten.* Vols. 1–2. Berlin: Rütten und Loening, 1986.

————. *Berliner Leben, 1914–1918: Eine Historische Reportage aus Erinnerungen und Berichten.*
Berlin: Akademie, 1983.

Goody, Jack. *Cooking, Cuisine, and Class.* Cambridge: Cambridge University Press, 1982.

Greenwald, Maurine. *Women, War, and Work: The Impact of World War I on Women Workers in the United States.* Westport, Conn.: Greenwood Press, 1980.

Gregory, Adrian. *The Silence of Memory.* Oxford: Berg, 1997.

Grimm, Ingrid. *Berliner Geschichten.* Munich: Heyne Verlag, 1986.

Groh, Dieter. "The 'Unpatriotic Socialists' and the State." *Journal of Contemporary History* 1, no. 4 (1966): 151–77.

Gronefeld, Gerhard. *Frauen in Berlin, 1945–1947.* Kreuzberg, Berlin: Dirk Nishen Verlag, 1984.

Die Grosse Sozialistische Oktoberrevolution und Deutschland. Berlin: Dietz, 1967.

Grossmann, Atina. *Reforming Sex: The German Movement for Birth Control and Abortion Reform, 1920–1950.* New York: Oxford University Press, 1995.

Grzywatz, Berthold. *Arbeit und Bevölkerung im Berlin der Weimarer Zeit.* Berlin: Colloquium, 1988.

Gutmann, Amy, ed. *Democracy and the Welfare State.* Princeton: Princeton University Press, 1988.

Gutsche, Willibald. "Bethmann Hollweg und die Politik der Neuorientierung." *Zeitschrift für Geschichte* 13, no. 2 (1965): 270–98.

Gutt, Barbara. *Frauen in Berlin: Mit Kopf und Herz und Hand und Fuß.* Berlin: arani-Verlag, 1991.

Habermas, Jürgen. *Strukturwandel der Öffentlichkeit: Untersuchungen zu einer Kategorie der bürgerlichen Gesellschaft.* Frankfurt am Main: Suhrkamp, 1990.

Hagemann, Karen. *Frauenalltag und Männerpolitik: Alltagsleben und gesellschaftliches Handeln von Arbeiterfrauen in der Weimarer Republik.* Bonn: Dietz, 1990.

————. "'Heran, heran, zu Sieg oder Tod.'" In *Männergeschichte, Geschlechtergeschichte: Männlichkeit im Wandel der Moderne,* edited by Thomas Kühne, 51–68. Frankfurt am Main: Campus, 1996.

————. "Men's Demonstrations and Women's Protests." *Gender and History* 5, no. 1 (1993): 101–19.

Hagen, William. *Germans, Poles, and Jews: The Nationality Conflict in the Prussian East, 1772–1914.* Chicago: University of Chicago Press, 1980.

Hahn, Walter, ed. *Der Ernährungskrieg: Grundsätzliches und Geschichtliches.* Hamburg: Hanseatische Verlags-Anstalt, 1939.

Hall, Stuart, et al., eds. *Policing the Crisis: Mugging, the State, and Law and Order.* London: Macmillan, 1978.

Hallen, Andreas, and Dieter Kerbs, eds. *Revolution und Fotografie: Berlin, 1918/19.* Berlin: Nishen, 1989.

Hallgarten, G. W. F. *Imperialismus vor 1914: Die soziologischen Grundlagen der Aussenpolitik europäischer Grossmächte vor dem Ersten Weltkrieg.* Munich: Beck, 1963.

Hammerle, Christa, ed. *Kindheit im Ersten Weltkrieg.* Vienna: Böhlau, 1993.

Hardach, Gerd. *The First World War, 1914–1918.* Berkeley: University of California Press, 1977.

Harsch, Donna. *German Social Democracy and the Rise of Nazism.* Chapel Hill: University of North Carolina Press, 1993.

Hartewig, Karin. *Das unberechenbare Jahrzehnt: Bergarbeiter und ihre Familien im Ruhrgebiet, 1914–1924.* Munich: Beck, 1993.

Harvey, Elizabeth. *Youth and the Welfare State in Weimar Germany.* Oxford: Clarendon, 1994.

Hasselmann, Erwin. *Geschichte der Deutschen Konsumgenossenschaften.* Frankfurt am Main: Knapp, 1971.

Hatry, Gilbert. "Shop Stewards at Renault." In *The French Home Front,* edited by Patrick Fridenson, 219–40. Providence, R.I.: Berg, 1992.

Hausen, Karin. "The German Nation's Obligations to the Heroes' Widows of World War I." In *Behind the Lines: Gender and the Two World Wars,* edited by Margaret Higonnet, Jane Jenson, Sonya Michel, and Margaret Weitz, 126–40. New Haven: Yale University Press, 1987.

———. "Öffentlichkeit und Privatheit: Gesellschaftspolitische Konstruktionen und die Geschichte der Geschlechterbeziehungen." In *FrauenGeschichte/Geschlechtergeschichte,* edited by Karin Hausen and Heide Wunder, 81–88. Frankfurt am Main: Campus, 1992.

Haxthausen, Charles, and Heidrun Suhr. *Berlin Culture and Metropolis.* Minneapolis: University of Minnesota Press, 1990.

Healy, Maureen. "Divided Home: Total War and Everyday Life in World War I Vienna." Ph.D diss., University of Chicago, 1999.

Hegemann, Werner. *Das Steinerne Berlin: Geschichte der Grössten Mietskasersnenstadt der Welt.* Brunswick: Vieweg, 1976.

Heineman, Elizabeth D. *What Difference Does a Husband Make? Women and Marital Status in Nazi and Postwar Germany.* Berkeley: University of California Press, 1999.

Hepelmann, Hildegard, ed. *Beiträge zur Geschichte der Frauenarbeit im Weltkrieg.* Münster: Coppenrath, 1938.

Hering, Sabine. *Die Kriegsgewinnlerinnen: Praxis und Ideologie der Deutschen Frauenbewegung im ersten Weltkrieg.* Pfaffenweiler: Centaurus, 1990.

Higonnet, Margaret, Jane Jenson, Sonya Michel, and Margaret Weitz, eds. *Behind the Lines: Gender and the Two World Wars.* New Haven: Yale University Press, 1987.

Hinton, James. "Militant Housewives: The British Housewives' League and the Attlee Government." *History Workshop Journal* 38 (1994): 128–55.

Hirschfeld, Gerhard, and Gerd Krumeich, eds. *Keiner fühlt sich hier mehr als Mensch: Erlebnis und Wirkung des Ersten Weltkriegs.* Essen: Klartext, 1993.

Hirschmann, Nancy J., and Christine Di Stefano, eds. *Revisioning the Political: Feminist Reconstructions of Traditional Concepts in Western Political Theory.* Boulder, Co.: Westview Press.

Hoheisel, Susanne, and Andreas Hoheisel. "Die Tätigkeit der Berliner politischen Polizei von 1878 bis 1914." Diplom-Arbeit, Humboldt-Universität, Berlin, 1980.

Holtfrerich, Carl-Ludwig. *Die Deutsche Inflation, 1914–1924.* Berlin: de Gruyter, 1980.

Homburg, Heidrun. *Rationalisierung und Industriearbeit.* Berlin: Haude und Spener, 1991.

Honey, Maurine. *Creating Rosie the Riveter: Class, Gender, and Propaganda during World War II.* Amherst: University of Massachusetts Press, 1984.

Hong, Young-Sun. "The Contradictions of Modernization in the German Welfare State: Gender and the Politics of Welfare Reform in First World War Germany." *Social History* 17, no. 2 (1992): 251–70.

———. *Welfare, Modernity, and the Weimar State, 1919–1933.* Princeton, N.J.: Princeton University Press, 1998.

Horn, Daniel. *The German Naval Mutinies of World War I.* New Brunswick, N.J.: Rutgers University Press, 1969.

Horne, John. "L'Impot du Sang: Republican Rhetoric and Industrial Welfare in France, 1914–1918." *Social History* 14, no. 2 (1989): 20–23.

———. *Labour at War: France and Britain, 1914–1918.* New York: Oxford University Press, 1991.

———, ed. *State, Society, and Mobilization in Europe during the First World War.* Cambridge: Cambridge University Press, 1997.

Horne, John, and Alan Kramer. "German 'Atrocities' and Franco-German Opinion, 1914: The Evidence of German Soldiers' Diaries." *Journal of Modern History* 66, no. 11 (1994): 1–33.

Howard, N. P. "The Social and Political Consequences of the Allied Food Blockade of Germany, 1918–19." *German History* 11, no. 2 (1993): 161–88.

Hufton, Olwen H. *The Poor of Eighteenth-Century France, 1750–1789.* Oxford: Clarendon, 1974.

Hughes, Michael. "Private Equity, Social Equity." *Central European History* 16, no. 1 (March 1983): 76–94.

"Hunger." *Beiträge zur historischen Sozialkunde* 2 (1985). Special issue.

"Hunger and History: The Impact of Changing Food Production and Consumption Patterns on Society." *Journal of Interdisciplinary History* 14, no. 2 (1983). Special issue.

"Hunger, Ernährung, und Politik." *SoWi* 14, no. 2 (1985). Special issue.

Hunt, James C. "Peasants, Grain Tariffs, and Meat Quotas: Imperial German Protectionism Reexamined." *Central European History* 7, no. 4 (December 1974): 311–31.

Der Interfraktionelle Ausschuß, 1917/18. Quellen zur Geschichte des Parlamentarismus und der politischen Parteien. Düsseldorf, Droste, 1970.

Jarausch, Konrad Hugo. *The Enigmatic Chancellor: Bethmann Hollweg and the Hubris of Imperial Germany.* New Haven: Yale University Press, 1973.

Jessen, Ralph. *Polizei im Industrierevier: Modernisierung und Herrschaftspraxis im westfälischen Ruhrgebiet, 1848–1914.* Göttingen: Vandenhoeck und Ruprecht, 1991.

John, Michael. *Politics and the Law in the Late Nineteenth Century.* Oxford: Oxford University Press, 1989.

Jones, Jennifer. "*Coquettes* and *Grisettes:* Women Buying and Selling in Ancien Régime Paris." In *The Sex of Things: Gender and Consumption in Historical Perspective,* edited by Victoria de Grazia, with Ellen Furlough, 25–53. Berkeley: University of California Press, 1996.

Joris, Elisabeth, and Heidi Witzig. *Brave Frauen, aufmüpfige Weiber: Wie sich die Industrialisierung auf Alltag und Lebenszusammenhänge von Frauen auswirkte (1820–1940).* Zurich: Chronos, 1992.

Kaelble, Hartmut. *Industrielle Interessenpolitik in der Wilhelminischen Gesellschaft.* Berlin: de Gruyter, 1967.

Kaes, Anton, Martin Jay, and Edward Dimendberg. *The Weimar Republic Sourcebook.* Berkeley: University of California Press, 1994.

Kaplan, Steven. *Bread, Politics, and Political Economy in the Reign of Louis XV.* 2 vols. The Hague: Nijhoff, 1976.

———. *The Famine Plot: Persuasion in Eighteenth-Century France.* Philadelphia: American Philosophical Society, 1982.

Kaplan, Temma. *Red City, Blue Period: Social Movements in Picasso's Barcelona.* Berkeley: University of California Press, 1992.

Kehr, Eckart. *Der Primat der Innenpolitik: Gesammelte Aufsätze zur Preußisch-Deutschen Sozialgeschichte im 19. und 20. Jahrhundert.* Berlin: de Gruyter, 1965.

Kent, Susan Kingsley. *Making Peace: The Reconstruction of Gender in Interwar Britain.* Princeton: Princeton University Press, 1993.

Kickbusch, P., and B. Riedmüller, eds. *Die Armen Frauen: Frauen und Sozialpolitik.* Frankfurt am Main: Suhrkamp, 1984.

Kiessig, Inge, ed. *Berliner Sagen.* Berlin: Berliner-Information, 1984.

Kitchen, Martin. *The Silent Dictatorship: The Politics of the German High Command under Hindenburg and Ludendorff, 1916–1918.* London: Croom Helm, 1976.

Klein, Fritz, et al. *Deutschland im Ersten Weltkrieg.* Berlin: Akademie-Verlag, 1968–69.

Kluge, Ulrich. *Die Deutsche Revolution, 1918/1919: Staat, Politik, und Gesellschaft zwischen Krieg und Kapp-Putsch.* Frankfurt am Main: Suhrkamp, 1985.

Knoch, Peter, ed. *Kriegsalltag: Die Rekonstruktion des Kriegsalltags als Aufgabe der historischen Forschung und der Friedenserziehung.* Stuttgart: J. B. Metzler, 1989.

Kocka, Jürgen. *Facing Total War: German Society, 1914–1918.* Leamington Spa: Berg 1984.

Kolb, Eberhard. *Die Arbeiterräte in der Deutschen Innenpolitik, 1918–1919.* Düsseldorf: Droste, 1962.

———. *The Weimar Republic.* New York: Routledge, 1992.

Koselleck, Reinhardt, and Michael Jeismann, eds. *Der politische Totenkult: Kriegerdenkmäler in der Moderne.* Munich: Fink, 1994.

Kosyk, Kurt. *Deutsche Pressepolitik im Ersten Weltkrieg.* Düsseldorf: Droste, 1968.

Koven, Seth, and Sonya Michel, eds. *Mothers of a New World.* New York: Routledge, 1993.

———. "Womanly Duties: Maternalist Politics and the Origins of the Welfare States in France, Germany, Great Britain, and the United States, 1880–1920." *American Historical Review* 96, no. 2 (1990): 1076–1108.

Krabbe, Wolfgang. "Munizipalsozialismus und Interventionsstaat." *Geschichte in Wissenschaft und Unterricht* 5 (1979): 132–61.

Krause, Hartfried. *USPD: Zur Geschichte der Unabhängigen Sozialdemokratischen Partei Deutschlands.* Frankfurt am Main: 1975.

Krell, Gerträude. *Das Bild der Frau in der Arbeitswissenschaft.* Frankfurt am Main: Campus, 1984.

Kruger-Lorenzen, Kurt. *Deutsche Redensarten und was dahinter Steckt.* Wiesbaden: VMA-Verlag, 1978.

Kuczynski, Jürgen. *Die Geschichte der Lage der Arbeiter in Deutschland unter dem Kapitalismus.* Vol. 13. Berlin: Akademie-Verlag, 1960.

Kühne, Thomas. *Wahlkultur Kultur und Politik.* Frankfurt am Main: Suhrkamp, 1984.

———, ed. *Männergeschichte, Geschlechtergeschichte: Männlichkeit im Wandel der Moderne.* Frankfurt am Main: Campus, 1996.

Kundrus, Birthe. *Kriegerfrauen, Familienpolitik, und Geschlechterverhältnisse im Ersten und Zweiten Weltkrieg.* Hamburg: Christians, 1995.

Kurz, Thomas. *"Blutmai": Sozialdemokraten und Kommunisten im Brennpunkt der Berliner Ereignisse von 1929.* Berlin: Dietz, 1988.

Küster, Rogers. *Alte Armut und neues Bürgertum: Öffentliche und private Fürsorge in Münster von der Ära Fürstenberg bis zum Ersten Weltkrieg (1756–1914).* Münster: Aschendorff, 1995.

Ladd, Brian. *Urban Planning and Civic Order in Germany, 1860–1914.* Cambridge, Mass.: Harvard University Press, 1990.

Lange, Annemarie. *Das Wilhelminische Berlin.* Berlin: Dietz, 1967.

Langewiesche, Dieter, and Klaus Schönhoven. "Arbeiterbibliotheken und Arbeiterlektüre im Wilhelminischen Deutschland." *Archiv für Sozialgeschichte* 16 (1976): 134–204.

———, eds. *Arbeiter in Deutschland: Studien zur Lebensweise der Arbeiterschaft im Zeitalter der Industrialisierung.* Paderborn: Schöningh, 1981.

Lee, Joe. "German Administrators and Agriculture during the First World War." In *War and Economic Development,* edited by Jay M. Winter. Cambridge: Cambridge University Press, 1975.

Leed, Eric. *No Man's Land: Combat and Identity in World War I.* Cambridge: Cambridge University Press, 1979.

Lees, Andrew. "Berlin and Modern Urbanity in German Discourse, 1845–1945." *Journal of Urban History* 17, no. 2 (1991): 153–78.

———. *Cities Perceived: Urban Society in European and American Thought, 1820–1940.* New York: Columbia University Press, 1985.

Lefebvre, George. *The Great Fear of 1789.* New York: Pantheon, 1973.

Lehnert, Detlef. "Das 'rote' Berlin: Hauptstadt der deutschen Arbeiterbewegung." In *Studien zur Arbeiterbewegung und Arbeiterkultur in Berlin,* edited by Gert-Joachim Glaeßner, Detlef Lehnert, and Klaus Sühl, 1–36. Berlin: Colloquium, 1989.

Leßmann, Peter. *Die Preußische Schutzpolizei in der Weimarer Republik.* Düsseldorf: Droste, 1989.

Liang, H.-H. *The Berlin Police Force in the Weimar Republic.* Berkeley: University of California, 1970.

Lidtke, Vernon L. *The Alternative Culture: Socialist Labor in Imperial Germany.* Oxford: Oxford University Press, 1985.

Lih, Lars. *Bread and Authority in Russia, 1914–1921.* Berkeley: University of California Press, 1990.

Lindenberger, Thomas. "Die Fleischrevolte am Wedding: Lebensmittelversorgung und Politik in Berlin am Vorabend des Ersten Weltkriegs." In *Der Kampf um das tägliche Brot: Nahrungsmangel, Versorgungspolitik, und Protest, 1770–1990,* edited by Manfred Gailus and Heinrich Volkmann, 282–304. Opladen: Westdeutscher, 1994.

———. *Straßenpolitik: Zur Sozialgeschichte der öffentlichen Ordnung in Berlin, 1900 bis 1914.* Berlin: Dietz, 1995.

Lindenberger, Thomas, and Alf Lüdtke, eds. *Physische Gewalt: Studien zur Geschichte der Neuzeit.* Frankfurt am Main: Suhrkamp, 1995.

Lipp, Anne. "Friedenssehnsucht und Durchhaltebereitschaft: Wahrnehmungen und Erfahrungen Deutscher Soldaten im Ersten Weltkrieg." *Archive für Sozialgeschichte* 36 (1996): 279–92.

Lipp, Carola, ed. *Schimpfende Weiber und patriotische Jungfrauen im Vormärz und in der Revolution 1848/49.* Baden-Baden: Elster, 1986.

Lipp, Wolfgang, ed. *Industriegesellschaft und Regionalkultur: Untersuchungen für Europa.* Cologne: C. Heymanns, 1984.

Loehlin, Jennifer. "Consumers and the State: British and German Food Policy during the First World War." Master's thesis, University of Texas, 1987.

Lucas, Erhard. *Frankfurt unter der Herrschaft des Arbeiter- und Soldatenrats 1918/19.* Frankfurt: Verlag Neue Kritik, 1969.

———. *Zwei Formen von Radikalismus in der Deutschen Arbeiterbewegung.* Frankfurt am Main: Roter Stern, 1976.

Lüdtke, Alf. "Cash, Coffee-Breaks, Horseplay: Eigensinn and Politics among Factory Workers in Germany circa 1900." In *Confrontation, Class Consciousness, and the Labor Process: Studies in Proletarian Class Formation,* edited by Michael Hanagan and Charles Stephenson, 65–95. New York: Greenwood, 1986.

———. *Eigen-Sinn: Fabrikalltag, Arbeitererfahrungen, und Politik vom Kaiserreich bis in den Faschismus.* Hamburg: Ergebnisse, 1993.

———. "The Historiography of Everyday Life: The Personal and the Political." In *Culture, Ideology, and Politics,* edited by Raphael Samuel and Gareth Stedman Jones, 38–54. London: Routledge and Kegan Paul, 1983.

———. "Hunger, Essens-'Genuss' und Politik bei Fabrikarbeitern und Arbeiterfrauen:

Beispiele aus dem rheinisch-westfälischen Industriegebiet, 1910–1940." *SoWi* 14, no. 2 (1985): 118–25.

———. "Hunger in der grossen Depression." *Archiv für Sozialgeschichte* 27 (1987): 145–76.

———. *Police and State in Prussia, 1815–1850.* Oxford: Oxford University Press, 1989.

———. "Polymorphous Synchrony: German Industrial Workers and the Politics of Everyday Life." *International Review of Social History* 38 (1993): 39–84.

———, ed. *"Sicherheit" und "Wohlfahrt": Polizei, Gesellschaft, und Herrschaft im 19. und 20. Jahrhundert.* Frankfurt am Main: Suhrkamp, 1992.

McAuley, Mary. "Bread without the Bourgeoisie." In *Party, State, and Society in the Russian Civil War,* edited by Diane Koenker, William Rosenberg, and Ronald G. Suny, 158–79. Bloomington: Indiana University Press, 1989.

McElligott, Anthony. "Das 'Abruzzenviertel': Arbeiter in Altona, 1918–1932." In *Arbeiter in Hamburg,* edited by Arno Herzig, Dieter Langewiesche, and Arnold Sywottek, 493–507. Hamburg: Verlag Erziehung und Wissenschaft, 1983.

———. *Contested City: Municipal Politics and the Rise of Nazism in Altona, 1917–1937.* Ann Arbor: University of Michigan Press, 1998.

McKibbin, David. *War and Revolution in Leipzig, 1914–1918: Socialist Politics and Urban Evolution in a German City.* Lanham, Md.: University Press of America, 1998.

Mai, Günther, ed. *Arbeiterschaft in Deutschland, 1914–1918. Studien zu Arbeitskampf und Arbeitsmarkt im ersten Weltkriege.* Düsseldorf: Droste, 1985.

———. *Kriegswirtschaft und Arbeiterbewegung in Württemburg, 1914–1918.* Stuttgart: Klett-Cotta, 1983.

Maier, Charles. *Recasting Bourgeois Europe: Stabilization in France, Germany, and Italy in the Decade after World War I.* Princeton: Princeton University Press, 1988.

Maier, Reinhold. *Feldpostbriefen: Aus dem Ersten Weltkrieg, 1914–1918.* Stuttgart: Kohlhammer, 1966.

Marquardt, Doris. *Sozialpolitik und Sozialfürsorge der Stadt Hannover in der Weimarer Republik.* Hanover: Hahn, 1994.

Marquis, H. G. "Words as Weapons: Propaganda in Britain and Germany during the First World War." *Journal of Contemporary History* 12 (1978): 467–98.

Materna, Ingo. "Das Erste Echo des Roten Oktober in Berlin." *Berliner Geschichte* 3 (1982): 54–79.

Materna, Ingo, Lorenz Demps, et al., eds. *Geschichte Berlins von den Anfängen bis 1945.* Berlin: Dietz, 1987.

Mathews, William C. "The German Social Democrats and the Inflation: Food, Foreign Trade, and the Politics of Stabilization, 1914–1920." Ph.D. diss., University of California, Riverside, 1982.

Mattern, Daniel. "Creating the Modern Metropolis: The Debate over Greater Berlin, 1890–1920." Ph.D. diss., University of North Carolina, 1991.

Medick, Hans. "'Hungerkrisen' in der historischen Forschung." *SoWi* 14, no. 2 (1985): 95–102.

———. *Weben und Überleben in Laichingen, 1650–1900: Lokalgeschichte als allgemeine Geschichte.* Göttingen: Vandenhoeck und Ruprecht, 1996.

Melling, Joseph. *Rent Strikes: People's Struggle for Housing in West Scotland, 1890–1916.* Edinburgh: Polygon, 1983.

Merkel, Ina. *Wunderwirtschaft: DDR-Konsumkultur in den 60er Jahren.* Cologne: Böhlau, 1996.

Meyer-Renschhausen, Elisabeth. "Geschichte der Gefühle," in *Unter allen Umständen,* edited by Christiane Eifert and Susanne Rouette, 99–121. Berlin: Rotation, 1986.

———. "Radical, Weil Sie Konservativ Sind?" In *Die Ungeschriebene Geschichte: Historische Frauenforschung,* edited by Wiener Historikerinnen, 20–36. Vienna: Wiener Frauenverlag, 1989.

———. "Von der Schwarzen zur weißen Küche: Versuche zum ambivalenten Zusammenhang von Leiblichkeit, Weiblichkeit und der Mahlzeit." Habilitationsschrift, Freie Universität, Berlin, 1995.

Michalka, Wolfgang, ed. *Der Erste Weltkrieg: Wirkung, Wahrnehmung, Analyse.* Munich: Piper, 1994.

Miller, Judith A. *Mastering the Market: The State and the Grain Trade in Northern France, 1700–1860.* Cambridge: Cambridge University Press, 1999.

Miller, Susanne. *Burgfrieden und Klassenkampf: Die Deutsche Sozialdemokratie im Ersten Weltkrieg.* Düsseldorf: Droste, 1974.

Mintz, Sidney. *Sweetness and Power: The Place of Sugar in Modern History.* New York: Viking, 1985.

———. *Tasting Food, Tasting Freedom.* Boston: Beacon, 1996.

Mock, Wolfgang. "'Manipulation von Oben' oder Selbstorganisierung an der Basis?" *Historische Zeitschrift* 232 (1981): 358–75.

Moeller, Robert G. "Dimensions of Social Conflict in the Great War: A View from the Countryside." *Central European History* 14, no. 2 (June 1981): 142–68.

———. *German Peasants and Agrarian Politics, 1914–1924: The Rhineland and Westphalia.* Chapel Hill: University of North Carolina Press, 1986.

———. *Protecting Motherhood: Women and the Family in the Politics of Postwar West Germany.* Berkeley: University of California Press, 1993.

Mommsen, Wolfgang. "The German Revolution, 1918–1920." In *Social Change and Political Development in Weimar Germany,* edited by Richard Bessel and E. J. Feuchtwanger, 21–36. London: Croom Helm, 1981.

———. "Die Regierung Bethmann Hollweg und die öffentliche Meinung, 1914–1917." *Vierteljahrschrift für Zeitgeschichte* 17 (1969): 117–55.

———, ed. *The Emergence of the Welfare State in Britain and Germany, 1850–1950.* London: Croom Helm, 1981.

———. *Das Zeitalter des Imperialismus.* Frankfurt am Main: Fischer, 1983.

Mommsen, Wolfgang, and Elisabeth Müller-Lückner, eds. *Kultur und Krieg: Die Rolle der Intellektuellen, Künstler, und Schriftsteller im Ersten Weltkrieg.* Munich: Oldenbourg, 1996.

Moore, Barrington. *Injustice: The Social Bases of Obedience and Revolt.* New York: Pantheon, 1978.

Mooser, Josef. *Arbeiterleben in Deutschland, 1900–1970: Klassenlagen, Kultur, und Politik.* Frankfurt am Main: Suhrkamp, 1984.

Morgan, David. *The Socialist Left and the German Revolution: A History of the German Independent Social Democratic Party, 1917–1922.* Ithaca: Cornell University Press, 1975.

Mosse, George. *Fallen Soldiers: Reshaping the Memory of the World Wars.* Oxford: Oxford University Press, 1990.

Mosse, Werner E., ed. *Deutsches Judentum in Krieg und Revolution, 1916–1923.* Tübingen: Mohr, 1971.

Mouffe, Chantal, ed. *Dimensions of Radical Democracy: Pluralism and Citizenship.* Verso, 1992.

Mühlberg, Detlev, et al. *Arbeiterleben um 1900.* Berlin: Dietz, 1985.

Müller, Dirk. *Gewerkschaftliche Versammlungsdemokratie und Arbeiterdelegierte vor 1918.* Berlin: Colloquium, 1985.

Neef, Anneliese. *Mühsal ein Leben Lang: Zur Situation der Arbeiterfrauen um 1900.* Berlin: Dietz, 1988.

Nelson, Barbara J. "Origins of the Two-Channel Welfare State: Workmen's Compensation and Mothers' Aid." In *Women, the State, and Welfare,* edited by Linda Gordon, 123–51. Madison: University of Wisconsin Press, 1990.

Nicolai, Britta. *Die Lebensmittelversorgung in Flensburg, 1914–1918.* Flensburg: Schriften der Gesellschaft für Flensburger Stadtgeschichte, 1988.

Niehuss, Merith. *Arbeiterschaft in Krieg und Inflation: Soziale Schichtung und Lage der Arbeiter in Augsburg und Linz, 1910 bis 1925.* Berlin: de Gruyter, 1985.

Nolan, Mary. "Economic Crisis, State Policy, and Working-Class Formation in Germany, 1870–1900." In *Working-Class Formation,* edited by Ira Katznelson and Aristide R. Zolberg, 352–96. Princeton: Princeton University Press, 1986.

———. *Social Democracy and Society: Working-Class Radicalism in Düsseldorf, 1890–1920.* Cambridge: Cambridge University Press, 1981.

———. *Visions of Modernity.* New York: Oxford University Press, 1994.

Nonn, Christoph. *Verbraucherprotest und Parteiensystem im Wilhelminischen Deutschland.* Düsseldorf: Droste, 1996.

Oertzen, Peter von. *Betriebsräte in der Revolution.* Düsseldorf: Droste, 1963.

Offer, Avner. *The First World War: An Agrarian Interpretation.* Oxford: Clarendon, 1989.

Orthmann, Rosemary. *Out of Necessity: Women Working in Berlin at the Height of Industrialization, 1874–1913.* New York: Garland, 1991.

Ottenjahn, Helmut, and Karl-Heinz Ziessow, eds. *Die Kartoffel: Geschichte und Zukunft einer Kulturpflanze.* Cloppenburg: Museumdorf Cloppenburg, 1992.

Ozouf, Mona. *Festivals and the French Revolution.* Cambridge, Mass.: Harvard University Press, 1991.

Pateman, Carole. *The Disorder of Women: Democracy, Feminism, and Political Theory.* Stanford: Stanford University Press, 1989.

Patemann, Reinhard. *Der Kampf um die Preußische Wahlreform im Ersten Weltkrieg.* Düsseldorf: Droste, 1964.

Pecheux, Michel. *Language, Semantics, and Ideology: Stating the Obvious.* London: Macmillan, 1982.

Pedersen, Susan. *Family, Dependence, and the Origins of the Welfare State.* Cambridge: Cambridge University Press, 1993.

———. "Gender, Welfare, and Citizenship in Britain during the Great War." *American Historical Review* 96, no. 2 (1991): 983–1006.

Pence, Katharine. "Relieving the Life of the Working Woman, or Does Socialism Liberate Women from Shopping?" Unpublished manuscript.

Pennington, J. A. T., and E. N. Church. *Food Values.* New York: Harper and Row, 1985.

Perrot, Michelle. *Workers on Strike: France, 1871–1890.* New Haven: Yale University Press, 1987.

Peukert, Detlev J. K. "The Genesis of the 'Final Solution' from the Spirit of Science." In *Reevaluating the Third Reich,* edited by Thomas Childers and Jane Caplan, 234–52. New York: Holmes and Meier, 1993.

———. *Grenzen der Sozialdisziplinierung: Aufstieg und Krise der Deutschen Jugendfürsorge von 1878 bis 1932.* Cologne: Bund-Verlag, 1986.

————. *Jugend zwischen Krieg und Krise: Lebenswelten von Arbeiterjungen in der Weimarer Republik.* Cologne: Bund-Verlag, 1987.

————. *The Weimar Republic.* New York: Hill and Wang, 1990.

Piven, Frances Fox. "Women and the State: Ideology, Power, and the Welfare State." In *Gender and the Life Course,* edited by A. S. Rossi, 265–87. New York: Aldine, 1985.

Planert, Ute. "Antifeminismus im Kaiserreich: Indikator einer Gesellschaft in Bewegung." *Archiv für Sozialgeschichte* 38 (1998): 93–118.

Preller, Ludwig. *Sozialpolitik in der Weimarer Republik.* Düsseldorf: Droste, 1978.

Preteceille, Edward. *Capitalism, Consumption, and Needs.* Oxford: Blackwell, 1985.

Prinz, Michael. *Brot und Dividende.* Göttingen: Vandenhoeck und Ruprecht, 1996.

Procacci, Giovanna. "Popular Protest and Labour Conflict in Italy, 1915–1918." *Social History* 14, no. 1 (1989): 31–58.

Proctor, Robert. *Racial Hygiene: Medicine under the Nazis.* Cambridge, Mass.: Harvard University Press, 1988.

Puhle, Hans-Jürgen. *Agrarische Interessen und Preussischer Konservatismus im Wilhelminischen Reich, 1893–1914.* Hanover: Verlag für Literatur und Zeitgeschehen, 1967.

Pulzer, Peter G. J. *The Rise of Political Anti-Semitism in Germany and Austria.* London: Halban, 1988.

Quataert, Jean. "Demographic and Social Change." In *Imperial Germany: An Historical Companion,* edited by Roger Chickering, 97–130. Westport, Conn.: Greenwood Press, 1996.

————. "German Patriotic Women's Work in War and Peacetime." In *On the Road to Total War: The American Civil War and the German Wars of Unification, 1861–1871,* edited by Stig Förster and Jörg Nagler, 449–77. New York: Cambridge University Press, 1997.

————. "The Politics of Rural Industrialization: Class, Gender, and Collective Action in the Saxon Oberlausitz of the Late Nineteenth Century." *Central European History* 20, no. 2 (June 1987): 91–124.

Rappaport, Roy. *Pigs for the Ancestors: A Ritual in the Ecology of a New Guinea People.* New Haven: Yale University Press, 1984.

Rath, Claus-Dieter. *Reste der Tafelrunde: Das Abenteuer der Eßkultur.* Reinbek: Rowohlt, 1984.

Rauh, Manfred. *Die Parlamentarisierung des Deutschen Reiches.* Düsseldorf: Droste, 1977.

Reagin, Nancy R. "Comparing Apples and Oranges: Housewives and the Politics of Consumption in Interwar Germany." In *Getting and Spending: European and American Consumer Societies in the Twentieth Century,* edited by Susan Strasser, Charles McGovern, and Matthias Judt, 241–62. Cambridge: Cambridge University Press, 1998.

————. *A German Women's Movement: Class and Gender in Hanover.* Chapel Hill: University of North Carolina Press, 1995.

Reidegeld, Eckart. *Staatliche Sozialpolitik in Deutschland: Historische Entwicklung und theoretische Analyse von den Ursprüngen bis 1918.* Opladen: Westdeutscher Verlag, 1996.

Retallack, James. *Notables of the Right.* Boston: Unwin Hyman, 1988.

Reulecke, Jürgen. "Der Erste Weltkrieg und die Arbeiterbewegung im Rheinisch-Westfälischen Industriegebiet." In *Arbeiterbewegung an Rhein und Ruhr: Beiträge zur Geschichte der Arbeiterbewegung in Rheinland-Westfalz,* edited by Jürgen Reulecke, 205–39. Wuppertal: Hammer, 1974.

Riley, Denise. *War in the Nursery: Theories of the Child and Mother.* London: Virago, 1983.

Ritter, E., ed. *Reichskommissar für Überwachung der öffentlichen Ordnung und Nachrichtensammelstelle im Reichsministerium des Innern.* Münster: Saur, 1979.

Ritter, Gerhard A. *Die Deutsche Parteien.* Göttingen: Vandenhoeck und Ruprecht, 1985.

———. "Entstehung des Sozialstaates in vergleichender Perspektive." *Historische Zeitschrift* 243 (1986): 1–90.

———. *Social Welfare in Germany and Britain: Origins and Development.* New York: Berg, 1986.

———. *Der Sozialstaat: Entstehung und Entwicklung in internationalem Vergleich.* Munich: R. Oldenbourg, 1991.

———, ed. *Arbeiterkultur.* Hanstein: Verlag Athenäum, 1979.

Ritter, Gerhard A., and Klaus Tenfelde, eds. *Arbeiter im Deutschen Kaiserreich.* Bonn: Dietz, 1992.

Robert, James. "Drink and the Labour Movement: The *Schnaps* Boycott of 1909." In *The German Working Class,* edited by Richard Evans, 80–107. London: Croom Helm, 1982.

Roberts, Elizabeth A. M. "'Women's Strategies,' 1890–1940." In *Labour and Love: Women's Experience of Home and Family, 1850–1940,* edited by Jane Lewis, 223–48. New York: Blackwell, 1986.

Roberts, Mary Louise. *Civilization without Sexes: Reconstructing Gender in Postwar France, 1917–1927.* Chicago: University of Chicago Press, 1994.

Roerkohl, Anne. *Hungerblockade und Heimatfront: Die kommunale Lebensmittelversorgung in Westfalen während des Ersten Weltkrieges.* Stuttgart: Franz Steiner 1991.

Roper, Katherine. *German Encounters with Modernity: Novels of Imperial Berlin.* Atlantic Highlands, N.J.: Humanities, 1991.

Rosenhaft, Eve. *Beating the Fascists? The German Communists and Political Violence, 1929–1933.* Cambridge: Cambridge University Press, 1983.

———. "Women, Gender, and the Limits of Political History in the Age of 'Mass' Politics." In *Elections, Mass Politics, and Social Change in Modern Germany: New Perspectives,* edited by Larry Eugene Jones and James Retallack, 149–73. Cambridge: Cambridge University Press, 1992.

Rosenhaft, Eve, and W. R. Lee. "State and Society in Modern Germany: Beamtenstaat, Klassenstaat, Wohlfahrtsstaat." In *The State and Social Change in Germany, 1880–1960,* edited by W. R. Lee and Eve Rosenhaft, 1–33. New York: St. Martin's, 1990.

Roshwald, Aviel, and Richard Stites. *European Culture in the Great War: The Arts, Entertainment, and Propaganda, 1914–1918.* Cambridge: Cambridge University Press, 1999.

Ross, Ellen. "'Fierce Questions and Taunts': Married Life in Working-Class London, 1870–1914." *Feminist Studies* 8 (1982): 575–602.

———. *Love and Toil: Motherhood in Outcast London, 1870–1918.* New York: Oxford University Press, 1993.

———. "Survival Networks: Women's Neighborhood Sharing in London before World War I." *History Workshop Journal* 15 (Spring 1983): 4–27.

Roth, Guenther. *The Social Democrats in Imperial Germany.* Totowa, N.J.: Bedminster Press, 1963.

Rouette, Susanne. *Sozialpolitik als Geschlechterpolitik: Die Regulierung der Frauenarbeit nach dem ersten Weltkrieg.* Frankfurt am Main: Campus, 1993.

Rudé, George. *The Face of the Crowd: Studies in Revolution, Ideology, and Popular Protest: Selected Essays of George Rudé.* New York: Harvester 1988.

Rudloff, Wilfried. "Unwillkommene Fürsorge." *Westfälische Forschungen* 43 (1993): 163–90.

Rupp, Leila. *Mobilizing Women for War: Germany and American Propaganda, 1939–1945.* Princeton: Princeton University Press, 1978.

Rürup, Reinhard. "Demokratische Revolution und 'Dritter Weg.'" *Geschichte und Gesellschaft* 9 (1983): 278–303.

———. "'Der Geist von 1914' in Deutschland: Kriegsbegeisterung und Ideologisierung des Kriegs im ersten Weltkrieg." In *Ansichten vom Krieg: Vergleichende Studien zum Ersten Weltkrieg in Literatur und Gesellschaft,* edited by Bernd Hüppauf, 208–47. Königstein: Forum Academicum, 1984.

———. "'Parvenu Polis' and 'Human Workshop': Reflections of the History of the City of Berlin." *German History* 6, no. 3 (1988): 233–49.

———, ed. *Jüdische Geschichte in Berlin.* Berlin: Hentrich, 1995.

Ryan, Mary P. "The Power of Women's Networks." In *Sex and Class in Women's History,* edited by Judith Newton, Mary Ryan, and Judith Walkowitz, 167–86. London: Routledge and Kegan Paul, 1983.

Ryder, A. J. *The German Revolution of 1918.* Cambridge: Cambridge University Press, 1967.

Sachse, Carola. *Betriebliche Sozialpolitik als Familienpolitik in der Weimarer Republik und im Nationalsozialismus: Mit einer Fallstudie über die Firma Siemens, Berlin.* Hamburg: Forschungsberichte des Hamburger Instituts für Sozialforschung, 1987.

Sachße, Christoph. *Mütterlichkeit als Beruf.* Frankfurt am Main: Suhrkamp, 1986.

———. "Der Wohlfahrtsstaat in historischer und vergleichender Perspektive." *Geschichte und Gesellschaft* 16 (1990): 479–90.

Sachße, Christoph, and Florian Tennstedt, eds. *Geschichte der Armenfürsorge in Deutschland.* Vol. 2. Stuttgart: Kohlhammer, 1980.

———. *Soziale Sicherheit und Soziale Disziplinierung: Beiträge zu einer historischen Theorie der Sozialpolitik.* Frankfurt am Main: Suhrkamp, 1986.

Saldern, Adelheid von. *Häuserleben.* Bonn: Dietz, 1995.

———. *Politik—Stadt—Kultur: Aufsätze zur Gesellschaftsgeschichte des 20. Jahrhunderts.* Hamburg: Ergebnisse, 1999.

Samuel, Raphael, ed. *Patriotism: The Making and Unmaking of the British National Identity.* 3 vols. London: Routledge, 1987.

Saul, Klaus. *Staat, Industrie, Arbeiterbewegung im Kaiserreich.* Düsseldorf: Droste, 1974.

———. "Der Staat und die 'Mächte des Umsturzes.'" *Archiv für Sozialgeschichte* 12 (1972): 293–350.

Schäfer, Hans-Dieter, ed. *Berlin im Zweiten Weltkrieg: Der Untergang der Reichshauptstadt in Augenzeugenberichten.* Munich: Piper, 1988.

Schäfer, Hermann. *Regionale Wirtschaftspolitik in der Kriegszeit: Staat, Industrie, und Verbände während des Ersten Weltkrieges in Baden.* Stuttgart: Klett-Cotta, 1983.

Schäffer, Werner. *Krieg gegen Frauen und Kinder: Englands Hungerblockade gegen Deutschland, 1914– 1920.* Berlin: Deutsche Informationsstelle, 1940.

Schaffner, Martin. *Brot, Brie und was Dazugehört.* Zurich: Chronos, 1992.

Scheck, Manfred. *Zwischen Weltkrieg und Revolution: Zur Geschichte der Arbeiterbewegung in Württemburg, 1914–1920.* Cologne: Bohlau, 1981.

Schiffers, Reinhard. *Der Hauptausschuß des Deutschen Reichstags, 1915–1918.* Düsseldorf: Droste, 1979.

Schivelbusch, Wolfgang. *Tastes of Paradise: A Social History of Spices, Stimulants, and Intoxicants.* New York: Pantheon, 1992.

Schlegel-Matthies, Kirsten. *"Im Haus und am Herd": Der Wandel des Hausfrauenbildes und der Hausarbeit, 1880–1930.* Stuttgart: Franz Steiner, 1995.

Schmauderer, Eberhard. "Die Beziehungen zwischen Lebensmittelwissenschaft, Lebensmittelrecht, und Lebensmittelversorgung im 19. Jh., problematisch betrachtet." In

Ernährung und Ernährungslehre, edited by Edith Heischkel-Artelt, 131–97. Göttingen: Vandenhoeck und Ruprecht, 1976.

Schneeringer, Julia. *Mobilizing Women for Politics: Gender and Propaganda in Weimar Germany, 1918–1932.* Chapel Hill: University of North Carolina Press, forthcoming.

Scholz, Robert. "Die Auswirkungen der Inflation auf das Sozial- und Wohlfahrtswesen der neuen Stadtgemeinde Berlin." In *Konsequenzen der Inflation,* edited by G. Feldman et al., 45–75. Berlin: Colloquium, 1989.

———. "Ein Unruhiges Jahrzehnt." In *Pöbelexzesse und Volkstumulte in Berlin,* edited by Martin Gailus, 79–124. Berlin: Europäische Perspektiven, 1984.

Schönhoven, Klaus, ed. *Die Gewerkschaften in Weltkrieg und Revolution, 1914–1919.* Cologne: Bund-Verlag, 1985.

Schorske, Carl. *German Social Democracy, 1905–1917.* Cambridge, Mass.: Harvard University Press, 1983.

Schumacher, M. *Land und Politik.* Düsseldorf: Droste, 1978.

Schwarz, Klaus-Dieter. *Weltkrieg und Revolution in Nürnberg: Ein Beitrag zur Geschichte der Deutschen Arbeiterbewegung.* Stuttgart: Klett, 1971.

Scott, James C. *Weapons of the Weak: Everyday Forms of Peasant Resistance.* New Haven: Yale University Press, 1985.

Scott, Joan. *Gender and the Politics of History.* New York: Columbia University Press, 1988.

Segalen, Martine. "'Sein Teil Haben'. Geschwisterbeziehungen in einem Egalitären Vererbungssystem." In *Emotionen und Materielle Interessen,* edited by Hans Medick and David Sabean, 81–98. Göttingen: Vandenhoeck und Ruprecht, 1984.

Seidel, Anneliese. *Frauenarbeit im Ersten Weltkrieg als Problem der staatlichen Sozialpolitik: Dargestellt, am Beispiel Bayerns.* Frankfurt am Main: Fischer, 1979.

Seier, Hellmut. "Berlin und die deutsche Nation: Die Hauptstadt und ihr Modernisierungspotential im Bewußtsein der Deutschen." *Berlin in Geschichte und Gegenwart: Jahrbuch des Landesarchivs Berlin* (1989): 33–52.

Sen, Amartya. *Poverty and Famines: An Essay on Entitlement and Deprivation.* Oxford: Clarendon, 1981.

Sewell, William H., Jr. "Ideologies and Social Revolutions." *Journal of Modern History* 57, no. 1 (1985): 57–85.

———. *Work and Revolution in France: The Language of Labor from the Old Regime to 1848.* Cambridge: Cambridge University Press, 1980.

Shevin Coetzee, Marilyn. *The German Army League: Popular Nationalism in Wilhelmine Germany.* Oxford: Oxford University Press, 1990.

Siney, Marion. *The Allied Blockade of Germany, 1914–1916.* Ann Arbor: University of Michigan Press, 1957.

Smith, Bonnie G. *The Gender of History: Men, Women, and Historical Practice.* Cambridge, Mass.: Harvard University Press, 1998.

Smith, Woodruff D. *The German Colonial Empire.* Chapel Hill: University of North Carolina Press, 1978.

———. *The Ideological Origins of Nazi Imperialism.* New York: Oxford University Press, 1989.

Spalding, Keith. *An Historical Dictionary of German Figurative Usage.* Oxford: Blackwell, 1952.

Spencer, Elaine Glovka. *Police and the Social Order in German Cities: The Düsseldorf District, 1848–1914.* DeKalb: Northern Illinois University Press, 1992.

Spree, Reinhard. *Health and Social Class in Imperial Germany: A Social History of Mortality, Morbidity, and Inequality.* New York: St. Martin's, 1988.

Stegmann, Dirk. "Die Deutsche Inlandspropandanda, 1917/1817: Zum innenpolitischen Machtkampf zwischen OHL und ziviler Reichsleitung in der Endphase des Kaiserreichs." *Militärgeschichtliche Mitteilungen* 12 (1972): 75–116.

———. *Die Erben Bismarcks: Parteien und Verbände in der Spätphase des Wilhelminischen Deutschlands: Sammlungspolitik, 1897–1918.* Cologne: Kiepenhauer und Witsch, 1970.

Stein, Hartwig. *"Inseln im Häusermeer": Eine Kulturgeschichte des deutschen Kleingartenwesens bis zum Ende des Zweiten Weltkriegs.* Forthcoming.

Steinmetz, George. *Regulating the Social: The Welfare State and Local Politics in Imperial Germany.* Princeton: Princeton University Press, 1993.

Stern, Fritz. *Bethmann Hollweg und der Krieg: Die Grenzen der Verantwortung.* Tübingen: Mohr, 1968.

Stöckel, Sigrid. "Die Bekämpfung der Säuglingssterblichkeit im Kaiserreich und in der Weimarer Republik." Ph.D. diss., Freie Universität, Berlin, 1992.

Stoehr, Irene. "Housework and Motherhood: Debates and Policies in the Women's Movements in Imperial Germany and the Weimar Republic." In *Maternity and Gender Policies: Women and the Rise of the European Welfare States, 1880s–1950s,* edited by Gisela Bock and Pat Thane, 213–32. New York: Routledge, 1991.

———. "Organisierte Mütterlichkeit." In *Frauen Suchen Ihre Geschichte: Historische Studien zum 19. und 20. Jahrhundert,* edited by Karin Hausen, 221–49. Munich: Beck, 1987.

Struve, Walter. *Elites against Democracy: Leadership Ideals in Bourgeois Political Thought in Germany, 1890–1933.* Princeton: Princeton University Press, 1973.

Stürmer, Michael. *Regierung und Reichstag im Bismarckreich.* Düsseldorf: Droste, 1974.

Summers, Anne. *Angels and Citizens: British Women as Military Nurses, 1854–1914.* New York: Routledge and Kegan Paul, 1988.

Suval, Stanley. *Electoral Politics in Wilhelmine Germany.* Chapel Hill: University of North Carolina Press, 1985.

Tenfelde, Klaus. "La Riscoperta dell''Autodifesa Collettiva': Protesta Sociale in Germania durante l'Inflazione del 1923." *Annali dell'Istituto Storico Italo-Germanico* 11 (1983): 379–422.

———. "Stadt und Land in Krisenzeiten: München und das Münchener Umland zwischen Revolution und Inflation, 1918–1923." In *Soziale Räume in der Urbanisierung: Studien zur Geschichte Münchens im Vergleich, 1850–1933,* edited by Wolfgang Hardtwig und Klaus Tenfelde, 37–58. Munich: Oldenbourg, 1990.

Tennstedt, Florian. *Sozialgeschichte der Sozialpolitik in Deutschland.* Göttingen: Vandenhoeck und Ruprecht, 1981.

Teuteberg, Hans Jürgen. "Wie Ernähren sich Arbeiter im Kaiserreich?" In *Arbeiterexistenz im 19. Jahrhundert: Lebensstandard und Lebensgestaltung Deutscher Arbeiter und Handwerker,* edited by Werner Conze und Ulrich Engelhardt, 57–73. Stuttgart: Klett-Cotta, 1981.

———. "Die Nahrung der Sozialen Unterschichten im Späten 19. Jahrhundert." In *Ernährung und Ernährungslehre,* edited by Edith Heischkel-Artelt, 205–81. Göttingen: Vandenhoeck und Ruprecht, 1976.

———, ed. *Stadtwachstum, Industrialisierung, sozialer Wandel: Beiträge zur Erforschung der Urbanisierung im 19. und 20. Jahrhundert.* Berlin: Duncker and Humblot, 1986.

Teuteberg, Hans Jürgen, and Günther Wiegelmann. *Unsere tägliche Kost: Geschichte und Regionale Prägung.* Münster: Coppenrath, 1986.

————, eds. *Der Wandel der Nahrungsgewohnheiten unter dem Einfluß der Industrialisierung.*
Göttingen: Vandenhoeck und Ruprecht, 1972.

Thébaud, Françoise. *La Femme au Temps de la Guerre de '14.* Paris: Stock, 1987.

Theweleit, Klaus. *Male Fantasies.* Minneapolis: University of Minnesota Press, 1988.

Thom, Deborah. *Nice Girls and Rude Girls: Women Workers in World War I.* New York: Tauris, 1998.

Thompson, E. P. "The Moral Economy Revisited." In *Customs in Common,* 259–351. New York: New Press, 1993.

Tilly, Louise. "Paths of Proletarianization: Organization of Production, Sexual Division of Labour, and Women's Collective Action." *Signs* 7, no. 2 (1981): 400–417.

Titmuss, Richard. *War and Social Policy: Essays on the Welfare State.* Boston: Beacon, 1969.

Tobin, Elizabeth. "Revolution and Alienation." In *Towards the Holocaust: The Social and Economic Collapse of the Weimar Republic,* edited by M. Dobkowski and I. Walliman, 155–76. Westport, Conn.: Greenwood, 1983.

————. "The Revolution in Düsseldorf, 1918–1919." Ph.D. diss., Princeton University, 1984.

————. "War and the Working Class: The Case of Düsseldorf, 1914–1918." *Central European History* 13, nos. 3/4 (September/December 1985): 257–98.

Tramwitz, Angelika. "Vom Umgang mit Helden: Kriegs(vor)schriften und Benimmregeln für deutsche Frauen im Ersten Weltkrieg." In *Kriegsalltag: Die Rekonstruktion des Kriegsalltags als Aufgabe der historischen Forschung und der Friedenserziehung,* edited by Peter Knoch, 84–113. Stuttgart: J. B. Metzler, 1989.

Trepp, Anna-Charlott. *Sanfte Männlichkeit und selbständige Weiblichkeit.* Göttingen: Vandenhoeck und Ruprecht, 1996.

Triebel, Armin. "Consumption in Wartime Germany." In *The Upheaval of War: Family, Work, and Welfare in Europe, 1914–1918,* edited by Richard Wall and Jay M. Winter, 159–96. Cambridge: Cambridge University Press, 1988.

————. *Zwei Klassen und die Vielfalt des Konsums: Haushaltsbudgetierung bei abhängig Erwerbstätigen in Deutschland im ersten Drittel des 20. Jahrhunderts.* Berlin: Max-Planck-Institut für Bildungsforschung, 1991.

Ullmann, H.-P. *Der Bund der Industriellen.* Göttingen: Vandenhoeck und Ruprecht, 1976.

Ullrich, Volker. *Die Hamburger Arbeiterbewegung vom Vorabend des Ersten Weltkrieges bis zur Revolution 1918/19.* Hamburg: Ludke, 1976.

————. *Kriegsalltag: Hamburg im Ersten Weltkrieg.* Cologne: Prometh, 1982.

Ulrich, Bernd. "Feldpostbriefe des Ersten Weltkrieges: Möglichkeit und Grenzen einer alltagsgeschichtlichen Quelle." *Militärgeschichtliche Mitteilungen* 53 (1994): 73–84.

Ulrich, Bernd, and Benjamin Ziemann, eds. *Frontalltag im Ersten Weltkrieg: Wahn und Wirklichkeit: Quellen und Dokumente.* Frankfurt am Main: Fischer, 1994.

————. *Krieg im Frieden: Die umkämpfte Erinnerung an den Ersten Weltkrieg: Quellen und Dokumente.* Frankfurt am Main: Fischer, 1997.

Ungern-Sternberg, Jürgen von, and Wolfgang von Ungern-Sternberg. *Der Aufruf an die Kulturwelt.* Stuttgart: Klett-Cotta, 1996.

Usborne, Cornelie. "Pregnancy Is a Woman's Active Service." In *The Upheaval of War: Family, Work, and Welfare in Europe, 1914–1918,* edited by Richard Wall and Jay M. Winter, 289–416. Cambridge: Cambridge University Press, 1988.

Verhey, Jeff. "The 'Spirit of 1914': The Myth of Enthusiasm and the Rhetoric of Unity in World War I Germany." Ph.D. diss., University of California, Berkeley, 1991.

Vincent, C. Paul. *The Politics of Hunger.* Athens: Ohio University Press, 1985.

Vobruba, G. "Arbeiten und Essen." In *Politik der Armut und die Spaltung des Sozialstaates,* edited by Stephan Leibfried and Florian Tennstedt, 41–63. Frankfurt am Main: Suhrkamp, 1985.

Vondung, Klaus. *Die Apokalypse in Deutschland.* Munich: dtv, 1988.

Waites, Bernard. *A Class Society at War.* Leamington Spa: Berg, 1987.

Wall, Richard, and Jay M. Winter, eds. *The Upheaval of War: Family, Work, and Welfare in Europe, 1914–1918.* Cambridge: Cambridge University Press, 1988.

Warneken, Bernd Jürgen, ed. *Massenmedium Strasse: Zur Kulturgeschichte der Demonstration.* Frankfurt am Main: Campus, 1991.

Weber-Kellermann, Ingeborg. *Die Deutsche Familie: Versuch einer Sozialgeschichte.* Frankfurt am Main: Suhrkamp, 1989.

Wehler, Hans-Ulrich. *The German Empire.* Dover, N.H.: Berg, 1984.

Weisbrod, Bernd. "Gewalt in der Politik." *Geschichte in Wissenschaft und Unterricht* 43 (1992): 391–404.

Weitz, Eric. *Creating German Communism, 1890–1990.* Princeton: Princeton University Press, 1997.

Wertheimer, Jack. *Unwelcome Strangers: East European Jews in Imperial Germany.* Oxford: Oxford University Press, 1997.

Wette, Wolfram, ed. *Der Krieg des kleinen Mannes: Eine Militärgeschichte von unten.* Munich: Piper, 1992.

Wheeler, Robert F. "German Women and the Communist International: The Case of the Independent Social Democrats." *Central European History* 8, no. 2 (June 1975): 113–39.

Wheldon, Robert Whalen. *Bitter Wounds: German Victims of the Great War, 1914–1939.* Ithaca: Cornell University Press, 1984.

Wierlacher, Alois, Gerhard Neumann, and Hans Jürgen Teuteberg, eds. *Kulturthema Essen: Ansichten und Problemfelder.* Berlin: Akademie-Verlag, 1993.

Wildt, Michael. *Am Beginn der "Konsumgesellschaft": Mangelerfahrung, Lebenshaltung, Wohlstandshoffnung.* Hamburg: Ergebnisse, 1994.

Winkler, Heinrich A. *Mittelstand, Demokratie, und Nationalsozialismus: Die politische Entwicklung von Handwerk und Kleinhandel in der Weimarer Republik.* Cologne: Kiepenhauer und Witsch, 1972.

———. *Von der Revolution zur Stabilisierung: Arbeiter und Arbeiterbewegung in der Weimarer Republik, 1918–1924.* Berlin: Dietz, 1984.

Winnecken, Andreas. *Ein Fall von Antisemitismus: Zur Geschichte und Pathogenese der Deutschen Jugendbewegung vor dem Ersten Weltkrieg.* Cologne: Verlag Wissenschaft und Politik, 1991.

Winter, Jay M. *The Great War and the British People.* Cambridge: Cambridge University Press, 1985.

———. *Sites of Memory, Sites of Mourning: The Great War in European Cultural History.* New York: Cambridge University Press, 1998.

Winter, Jay M., and Joshua Cole. "Fluctuations in Infant Mortality Rates in Berlin during and after the First World War." *European Journal of Population* 9 (1993): 329–58.

Winter, Jay M., and Jean-Louis Robert, eds. *Capital Cities at War: Paris, London, and Berlin, 1914–1919.* Cambridge: Cambridge University Press, 1997.

Wirz, Albert. *Die Moral auf dem Teller: Dargestellt an Leben und Werk von Max Bircher-Benner und John Harvey Kellogg.* Zurich: Chronos, 1993.

Witt, Peter Christian. *Die Finanzpolitik des Deutschen Reiches von 1903 bis 1913.* Lübeck: Matthiesen, 1970.

Wolff, Raymond. "Zwischen formaler Gleichberechtigung, Zionismus, und Antisemitismus, 1871–1918." In *Juden in Berlin, 1671–1945: Ein Lesebuch,* 127–64. Berlin: Nicolai, 1988.

Woollacott, Angela. *On Her Their Lives Depend: Munitions Workers in the Great War.* Berkeley: University of California Press, 1994.

Woyke, James. *Birth Control in Germany, 1871–1933.* London: Routledge, 1988.

Yaney, George L. *The World of the Manager: Food Administration in Berlin during World War I.* New York: Peter Lang, 1994.

Young, Iris Marion. "The Ideal of Community and the Politics of Difference." In *Feminism/Postmodernism,* edited by Linda J. Nicholson, 300–323. London: Routledge, 1990.

Zechlin, Egmont. *Die Deutsche Politik und die Juden im Ersten Weltkrieg.* Göttingen: Vandenhoeck und Ruprecht, 1969.

Ziemann, Benjamin. *Front und Heimat: Ländliche Kriegserfahrungen im südlichen Bayern, 1914–1923.* Essen: Klartext, 1997.

Zunkel, Friedrich. *Industrie und Staatssozialismus: Der Kampf um die Wirtschaftsordnung, 1914–1918.* Düsseldorf: Droste 1974.

INDEX

War psychosis, 149
Wars of Unification, 33
War-weariness, 96, 185, 224
Weimar Republic, 4, 7, 238
Welfare/charitable organizations, 138, 139, 145, 158
Welfare state/social politics, 3, 45–47, 176, 241; entitlements, 74, 241. *See also* Social insurance
Wengels, Margarete, 231
Wermuth, Adolf, 18, 61, 105, 130, 139–44, 149, 152, 157, 200
Westarp, Kuno Graf von, 135
Weyer, 111
Wheat, 25, 29, 31, 37, 112
Wiernik, Lucien, 145, 188
Wild, Adolf, 170
Wilhelm II, Kaiser, 2, 13, 83, 92, 107, 119, 129, 198, 213, 217, 225, 227, 231–35
Willingness to sacrifice (*Opferwilligkeit*), 34, 74, 106, 132
Wilson, Woodrow: Fourteen Points, 232

Wimmer, Franz, 118
Wolff, Theodor, 67, 134, 139, 211
Women and femininity: negative images of, 34, 39–43, 57–58, 81. *See also* Mothers of many children; Munition workers: wives of; Soldiers' wives
Women of lesser (little) means, 2, 3, 4, 48, 56–64, 159–60
Women's Bureau (Frauenreferat), 173
Women's world, 43, 44
Wurm, Emanuel, 66, 131, 233
Wurm, Mathilde, 233
Württemburg, 132

Youth, 82–83, 85, 99–100; radical Social Democratic, 201, 234

Zabern, 94
Zille, Heinrich, 182
Zimmerwald, 98
Zodtke-Heyde, Else, 142